The WORLD OF BIRDS

The WORLD OF BIRDS

James Fisher and
Roger Tory Peterson

DOUBLEDAY & COMPANY, INC., GARDEN CITY, NEW YORK

BIRD PAINTINGS BY ROGER TORY PETERSON

Designed by PATRICIA COYLE NICHOLSON
and PETER CONSTABLE POPE

Library of Congress Catalog Card Number: 64–17398

Made and printed in Great Britain by Purnell and Sons Limited
Paulton (Somerset) and London

Contents

Introduction

Each of us has enjoyed a life in which, for close on half a century, his major preoccupation has been with birds. The most beautiful, the most observable animals of the world have occupied our daily lives, have filled our dreams, dominated our reading, directed our conversation.

For the last twelve years we have watched birds together in eleven countries, disputed them in our homes, pursued them, or their literature, or their skins, in a dozen libraries or museums and scores of zoos. For the last five we have been planning and researching this book; Roger Tory Peterson (RTP) has painted the pictures (other than maps) mostly in his studio in New England, and the text was put into the first draft by James Fisher (JF) mostly at his desk in England.

Of the modern books on the birds of the world two outstanding examples have been made by men whom we are proud to claim as friends and respected colleagues. They are *Living Birds of the World* by E. Thomas Gilliard (1958) and *Birds of the World* by Oliver L. Austin Jr., illustrated by Arthur Singer (1961). Both these fine works have presented the avifauna of our planet, family by family. We have approached the subject in a different way, though we have figured at least one member of nearly every family, past and present.

In 1962, according to our own researches, 8,580 good, full species of birds were known to be alive on earth. Our aim has been to analyze this galaxy, the end-product of 140 million years of evolution: and to present birds as animals, in an illustrated introduction to their general natural history, from important approaches that have inspired ornithologists through the years.

The first part of this book considers some of these approaches, in the hope that ornithology's many-sidedness can be appreciated, and that our beloved science can be understood as a branch of biology in its widest sense that happens to be blessed with gorgeous material.

Just how varied this material is must be known to all without turning the page where RTP has painted (key on p. 13) 23 birds from all over the world, from 23 of the 154 families now living.

The second part gets down to the techniques, tools and tasks of international bird watching; and in it we include a full classification and mapping of the class of birds down to families (and in some cases beyond), with a census of the acceptable genera and species in each – those fossil, those recently extinct and those living. The book closes with an essay on birds in their relation to men.

James Fisher and Roger Tory Peterson

CHAPTER I

The Variety of Birds

Distribution of bird variety

There is no square mile of the surface of our planet, wet or dry, that has not been crossed by the shadow of a bird – except perhaps some of the Antarctic Continent.

Though at least four species of birds have been seen at or near the North Pole, only one (a skua) has visited the South Pole. But two petrels breed on mountains jutting through the ice-cap, miles inland on the frozen continent; and some penguin colonies are out of sight of its shore. Altogether, sixteen species, all sea birds, nest on the Antarctic Continent or on islands within sight of it. If we bring in the antarctic and subantarctic islands, we cannot raise our list to much over 50.

All the areas with a poor avifauna (1 on the map) are polar or oceanic; land birds are lacking or few. Thus going east across the Pacific's scattered archipelagos we find a progressive diminution in the number of native land birds, from about 127 in the Solomons, 77 in New Caledonia, 54 in Fiji, 33 in Samoa, 17 in the Society Is.,

11 in the Marquesas, 4 on distant Henderson I. to none on Easter I., most isolated of all (though a pigeon, tinamou and an icterid have been introduced there). Such birds as inhabit the poor areas are, however, specialized and often very successful, with enormous populations. The antarctic Wilson's storm petrel may be the world's most numerous sea bird. Some polar and subpolar auk and penguin islands have over a million birds in a single rookery.

Areas which have an impoverished (2) or low (3) avifauna include important archipelagos which have been more or less difficult for birds to colonize because of their remoteness, and most of the deserts, both hot and cold. Large areas of the northern world within the tree line – the taiga zone in Eurasia, the conifer zone in Canada and Alaska – have lists of under 250 species.

Medium-sized avifaunas of under 500 species (4) are found mainly in temperate savannah countries; also in some semidesert tropics and in the central East Indies. These are the faunas most of us know best. Typical lists are Tasmania 255, New Zealand 256, Serbia 288, Hong Kong 289, Portugal 315, Alberta 317, Macedonia 319, Finland 327, Norway 333, Greece 339, Afghanistan 341, Maine 350, Ussuriland 353, Iraq 354, Ceylon 379,

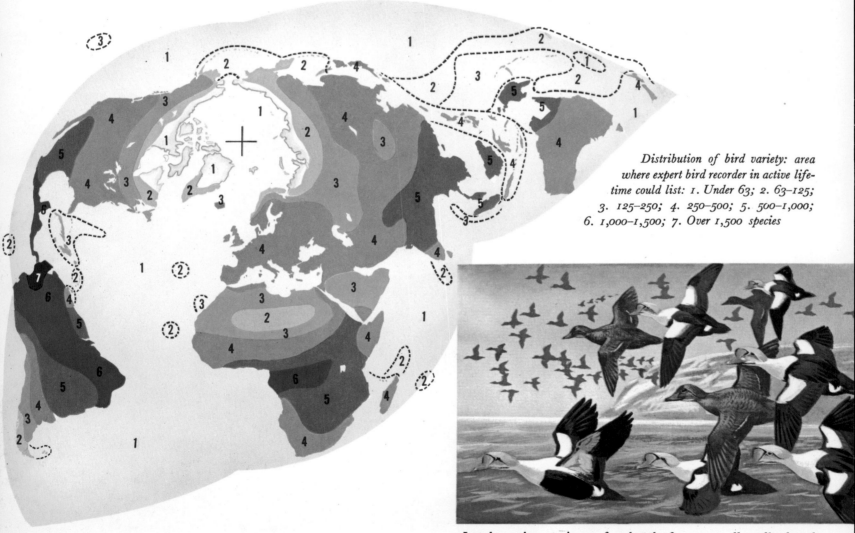

Distribution of bird variety: area where expert bird recorder in active lifetime could list: 1. Under 63; 2. 63–125; 3. 125–250; 4. 250–500; 5. 500–1,000; 6. 1,000–1,500; 7. Over 1,500 species

In polar regions species are few, but the few are usually well adapted and abundant. Great flocks of king eiders arrive in May in high arctic North Greenland, where in some districts they are commonest water birds

Racket-tailed hummingbird, Perú

Cape pigeon, Antarctic

Long-crested hornbill, S.E. Asia

Collared forest falcon, C. & S. America

Standard-wing nightjar, Africa

Ross's gull, Arctic

Long-tailed broadbill, S.E. Asia

Azure tit, Eurasia

Painted redstart, N. & C. America

Queen Victoria crowned pigeon, New Guinea

Crimson-winged parakeet, Australasia

African wood ibis

Chestnut-eared aracari, S. America

Great bird of paradise, New Guinea

Red-crested cardinal, S. America

Crowned crane, Africa

Golden cock-of-the-rock, S. America

Bluethroat, Eurasia

Lady Amherst pheasant, S.E. Asia

White-faced ibis Americas

Key to the birds figured on pages 10 and 11

Pondicherry vulture, Asia

Wood duck, N. America

Lapwing, Eurasia

Israel nearly 400, Japan 425, Western Australia 436, Great Britain and Ireland – and the Philippines, about 450, Senegal and Sierra Leone 485, Eastern Nigeria 488.

Large avifaunas of under 1,000 species (5) are found in the oriental tropics (e.g. Borneo 554, Malaya 575, Burma 953), New Guinea (650) and neighboring tropical Australia, the tropical savannahs and forest-edge of Africa (e.g. Eritrea 551, Ghana 627, Cameroons 670, N. Rhodesia 674, Sudan 871, Africa s. of Angola and the Zambesi 875), N. and C. America (Texas 545, México 967) and S. America (Surinam 567).

Really huge bird lists (6) are few. The only country in Africa with a bird list of over a thousand is the basin of the River Congo, the most densely forested part of equatorial Africa: what was the Belgian Congo and Ruanda Urundi combined have 1,040. But for Central America from southern México to Panamá about 1,190 species are listed, for Venezuela 1,282, for Ecuador 1,357, for Brazil about 1,440, mostly contributed by the great Amazon belt and other tropical forest zones. In tropical forests species swarm – though few have the vast populations typical of some of the temperate and many of the polar species – and (p. 64) belong to three communities at different levels.

The only country with a bird list over 1,500 (7) is Colombia. In 1963 its recorded species totaled over 1,700, twice as many birds as those of continental U.S.A. and Canada combined (775). It is the heartland of ornithological variety on our planet.

Tropics support much bird variety. First met by us one day in C. México; l. to r., above: mountain trogon, masked tityra, emerald toucanet, red-legged honeycreeper; below: rufescent tinamou, white-fronted dove

Winter in temperate eastern U.S. Three black-capped chickadees; two slate-colored juncos; two blue jays; cardinal and white-breasted nuthatch at feeder; cowbird flying; hairy woodpecker on post; white-throated sparrow on ground

13

Long-tailed
skua

Racing pigeon

Red-tailed
tropic bird

Broad-winged
hawk

Great
horned owl

Laysan albatross

Ruffed
grouse

House ma

White
ibis

Greenland
white-fronted
goose

Corncra

Wings and flight

Within their limits of speed and height, birds are more efficient aircraft than man has yet been able to design. Boundary layer control, which reduces drag by drawing air through the wing from top to bottom, was probably solved by Archaeopteryx. Human engineers are still only at the experimental stage with this principle.

Some techniques, notably dynamic soaring, are known to man in theory only. Yet albatrosses and the larger petrels have been masters of the ocean for millions of years by exploiting the fact that in a windy sea there is (owing to friction) a steep descending gradient of wind speed downwards to the surface of the sea.

This layer-cake of wind at different velocities enables big long-winged gliding sea birds to glide in a complex way in any direction within a segment of much more than 180 degrees. They tack and zigzag if their objective is in the wind's eye; and use their engines mainly for maneuver.

Figured on these pages are some typical examples of wing adaptation. The Laysan albatross has a wing of the highest aspect ratio – span high in proportion to its fore-aft wing breadth, or chord – which gives the greatest lift for its dynamic style of flight. A bird which needs to accelerate fast, such as a ruffed grouse, has a low aspect ratio.

The wing-loading of birds (weight per square foot of wing area) varies from about a tenth of a pound to $2\frac{1}{2}$ pounds. The most agile flyers, which range from frigate birds, tropic birds and the long-tailed skua to some fly-catchers, wood swallows and hummers tend to have low wing-loadings and rather high aspect ratios: the red-tailed tropic bird is perhaps the biggest bird that has been seen to fly momentarily backwards when checking in maneuver. Birds of prey like the broad-winged hawk, which are long-distance migrants, make much ground by soaring, taking advantage of rising columns of air, and tend to have a lowish aspect ratio and low or medium wing-loading. A typical broad general-purpose wing is that of the white ibis which makes longish regular flights and also soars. Owls, like the great horned owl, have a rather similar wing formula with feather adaptations for silent flight.

Some birds with fairly high wing loadings are capable of long migratory journeys; thus the white-fronted goose

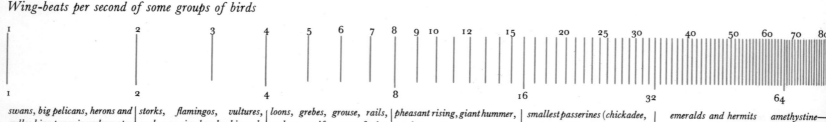

Wing-beats per second of some groups of birds

swans, big pelicans, herons and gulls; king penguin under water | storks, flamingos, vultures, eagles, soaring hawks, big owls | loons, grebes, grouse, rails, cuckoos, swifts, some finches | pheasant rising, giant hummer, mockers, sparrows, weavers | smallest passerines (chickadee, etc.); middle-sized hummers | emeralds and hermits amethystine→ ruby-throated h.

14

Peregrine

own-throated ne-tailed swift

Pectoral sandpiper

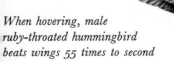

When hovering, male ruby-throated hummingbird beats wings 55 times to second

crosses about 2,000 Atlantic miles from Greenland to Ireland, and the weak-looking corncrake reaches Iceland from Europe. Birds that use their wings under water, like auks, diving petrels and some ducks and cormorants, have high wing loadings which enable them to 'fly' in the denser medium. Other underwater birds like loons and grebes swim with their feet.

Many observations have been made on the speeds of birds, by timing them over measured distances, pacing them from cars and aircraft, tracking them by radar or rangefinder. Half the world's birds probably never exceed 40 m.p.h. High speeds are not easy to measure; and speeds of over 60 are proved without reasonable doubt for only the loon, some birds of prey, waterfowl, the racing pigeon and swifts. The brown-throated spine-tailed swift of Asia has been alleged to reach 200 m.p.h.; but the measurement was unreliable, and most ornithologists would put the maximum speed of the swift family around 68. The fastest birds admitted without reservation in the critical list of Colonel Richard Meinertzhagen are lammergeier 79.5, loon 90, racing pigeon 94.3. The highest recorded speeds in this list, which rejects higher records as pure fancy, are stop-watch and airspeed indicator observations of peregrines at 165–180, in stoops. Birds were the fastest animals until aircraft reached 195 m.p.h. in 1920.

Fast birds put pronounced sweep-back on their wings; this reduces drag and gives stability. Most waders, exemplified here by the pectoral sandpiper, migrate at between 50 and 62. The swallow family can reach 46 (house martin); this is fast for a small bird, though faster are horned lark 54, European starling 55 and – surprisingly – ruby-throated hummingbird up to 60.

Peruvian diving petrel (l.) and black guillemot swim with full wing; velvet (white-winged) scoter with half-folded wing, alula (p. 16) projecting

Anatomy

The central framework of a bird is a column of from about 37 to over 60 articulating vertebrae, the 'backbone', culminating in a strong light skull to which its jaws are attached. Few skull-bones are more than plates and struts. A bird's huge orbits leave only a very thin partition between its eyes; its brain is restricted to the broadened back of its skull.

The vertebrae of the neck vary in number from 16 to 25. Below them comes a box, the thorax, based on 4 to 6 back vertebrae and connected by ribs to a breastbone or sternum, keeled in flying birds. To the front part of this bone is firmly attached a pair of coracoids. These bones are braced together across the front by the paired clavicles or collar bones (which in most birds fuse below to form a wishbone): and to their upper ends are attached the scapulae or shoulder blades, which run back along the ribs and back vertebrae. These three pairs are the pectoral girdle, bound to the thorax by strong ligaments.

The upper arm-bone's head articulates with the coracoid-scapula joint. This bone, the humerus, is a very strong rod, to the outer end of which are joined the fore-arm bones – radius and ulna. To them are joined several wrist bones, thumb and second and third fingers.

To these hand bones the great primary flight (and steering) feathers are strongly attached. The thumb carries a group of three feathers, the alula, which acts as an aeronautical slot. The secondary flight feathers originate from the ulna, the lower and thicker fore-arm bone. Sometimes tertiary flight feathers are attached to the humerus. No normal flying bird has less than nine primaries; secondaries vary in number and can reach 32 on albatrosses. The primitive Andean condor probably has more flight feathers than any other bird, with 11 primaries, 25 secondaries and 13 tertiaries.

The only truly flying vertebrates besides birds are the extinct pterosaurs and the living bats. The first depended on a skin flap from little finger to feet; the second depends on the same sort of patagium over all fingers to feet. With the evolution of feathers, birds kept their legs free for efficient locomotion and shock absorbing.

The pelvic or hip girdle of a bird depends on the fusion of 10 to 23 vertebrae; the top two may contribute ribs to the thorax. These vertebrae – the synsacrum – fuse with three pairs of bones (ilium, ischium, pubis) to form a powerful ring, to which is articulated by ball and socket joint the femur or thigh-bone. Below the knee, often hidden in the feathers, the upper long bone usually visible is the true shin or tibiotarsus, equivalent to the tibia and fibula of reptiles; and the lower is the tarsometatarsus or 'tarsus', a fusion equivalent to part of the

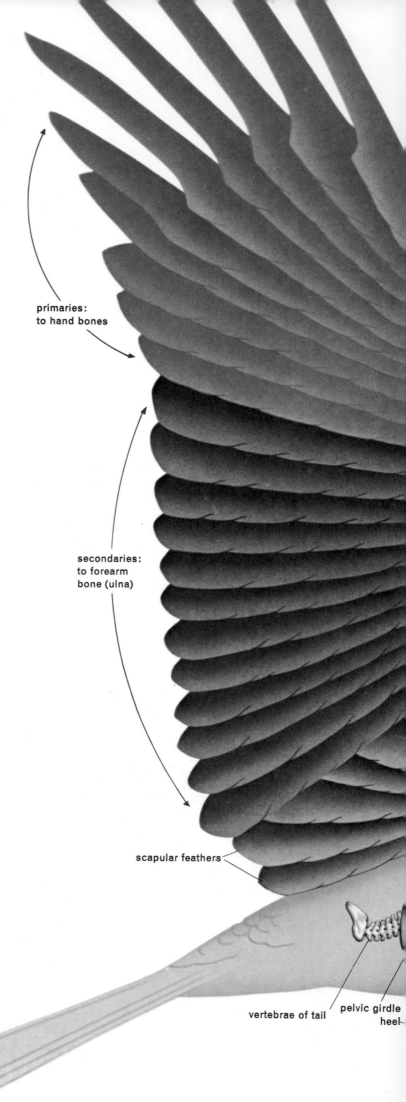

primaries:
to hand bones

secondaries:
to forearm
bone (ulna)

scapular feathers

vertebrae of tail

pelvic girdle
heel

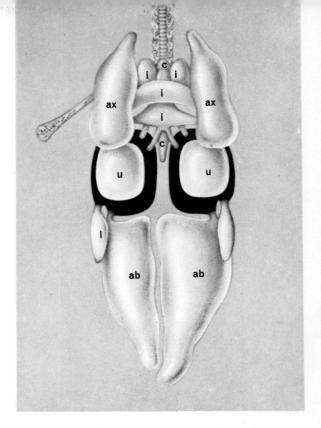

Typical flight feather with enlarged details of its vane

rachis

vane

calamus

barb

posterior, anterior barbules

Below: bone structure and wing system of the three vertebrate classes that have attained true flight

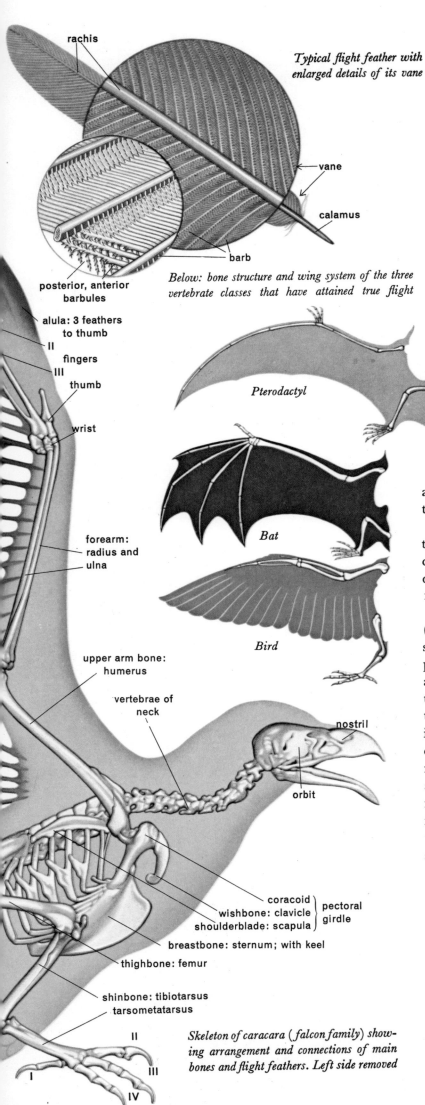

Pterodactyl

Bat

Bird

alula: 3 feathers to thumb

II

fingers

III

thumb

wrist

forearm: radius and ulna

upper arm bone: humerus

vertebrae of neck

nostril

orbit

coracoid
wishbone: clavicle } pectoral girdle
shoulderblade: scapula

breastbone: sternum; with keel

thighbone: femur

shinbone: tibiotarsus
tarsometatarsus

II

III

I

IV

Skeleton of caracara (falcon family) showing arrangement and connections of main bones and flight feathers. Left side removed

Air sacs of fowl, from front. c: *cervical;* i: *interclavicular;* ax: *axillary;* u: *upper thoracic;* l: *lower thoracic;* ab: *abdominal. Lungs shown black*

ankle and upper ends of three toes. Birds have no fifth toe; and their first or big toes usually turn backwards.

Lowermost in the backbone are 4 to 9 free caudal or tail vertebrae and a final fusion of 4 to 7 vestigial vertebrae called the pygostyle, in which are firmly inserted the quills of the tail feathers, the rectrices. Usually there are 12 of these, but their number may vary from 6 to 20.

A typical feather consists of a main stem whose quill (calamus) is hollow and top part or rachis solid. From both sides of the rachis stretches the vane, which is composed of parallel barbs angled toward the feather tip. To these barbs are attached barbules; and those barbules which point toward the feather tip have hooks along the middle of their undersides which catch on to their opposite numbers, interlock and make the vane firm and elastic. Ordinary contour, or body-covering, feathers tend to have downy, non-interlocking barbs on the inner part of the rachis, and below them grow downy plumules and hair-like filoplumes, special feathers whose function is to give insulation. At least once, often twice and sometimes thrice a year every feather is molted and replaced. A selection of fine feathers is on page 19.

Nearly all the larger bones of birds are pneumatic – hollow, with very little marrow. This is an adaptation for lightness; and the hollow bones also communicate with internal air sacs. Injected with plastic, these reveal vast size and complexity. When a bird breathes in, air passes through its lungs into the sacs; when it breathes out, the sac air passes through the lungs once more. Oxygenation of the blood can take place at both stages, much faster than in an animal without air sacs.

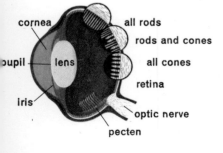

Breast and wing of the extinct Bourbon crested starling, displaying the intricate network of the muscles and pulley-tendons used in flight

Bird anatomy; Australian aboriginal version

Perhaps the two greatest bits of precision engineering in a bird's anatomy are its engine and its eye. By engine we mean the wing muscles which stem from its breastbone and produce all the movements of steered flight. The array often weighs more than a fifth of the whole bird, and involves a complicated pulley system, in which several muscle tendons work over or through bone notches which can turn their pull through over a right angle.

Birds have the most highly evolved eyes in the animal kingdom. The eyes of many owls are larger than those of men. In basic structure bird eyes resemble those of other vertebrates; but in modifications they are refined. The retina, the sensitive back of the inner chamber, is so much more elaborately bestowed with the light-sensitive rod and cone cells than that of other vertebrates that a special avian organ has developed, the pecten. This is an auxiliary blood-tank which boosts the retina's nourishment. Some bird retinas have two specially sensitive areas which assist side as well as forward vision, the foveae. Nocturnal birds like owls have only rods, which are most sensitive to light and are the only cells that work when it is nearly dark. The cones need more light for results, but give sharper resolution and can distinguish colors. A few diurnal birds have only cones; most birds have both. Some birds have colored oily droplets in their cones which filter blue light, cut down dazzle and give better vision.

In general plan and relative size the bird brain equals or approaches a lowly mammal brain. But its cerebellum, which coordinates movement, is larger, as is its optic lobe. Its cerebrum is smaller, with the central part concerned with instinctive (unlearned) activities relatively larger, and the outer cortex, concerned with learned activities, rather small. Its olfactory lobe is small: birds have little sense of taste and few much sense of smell.

Birds swallow morsels whole, after lacing them with saliva, down a gullet which in many broadens into a large storage bag in the throat – the crop. As soon as the gullet has passed behind the heart into the thorax it becomes a large bag, the stomach, of which the upper end is provided with acid cells for digestion and the lower part is usually a muscular gizzard, where rough or hard food is crushed.

After the stomach the food tube is continued as a loop – the duodenum. This is fed by ducts from the pancreas (a gland) with secretions that change starch to sugar and break down proteins and fats. Ducts also run to the duodenum from the liver, a huge storage organ which hoards sugar and keeps the blood constitution constant. Most material emptied into the duodenum from the liver is waste, but some of it helps digestion.

Now comes the small intestine, which can be very long, with many loops, in plant-eating birds. Here the main absorption of the digested food takes place. Waste products, dead bacteria and unabsorbable food are finally discharged into the wide short rectum which leads to the cloaca. The cloaca is the final passage, and leads to the only opening in the lower part of the bird's body. It receives the waste-ducts from the kidneys and the ducts from the reproductive organs. In birds the male organs or testes are held internally and lie over the kidneys, and the ovary is a single one which lies between the kidneys.

A bird's heart and blood system is more reptile-style than mammal-style, but highly efficient. One fortieth the weight of a high-altitude hummingbird is heart. Few birds have a temperature of less than 100°F., and some rate 114°F. Birds are the nervous athletes of the animal world, with a high metabolic rate.

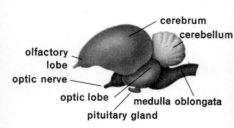

cornea
all rods
rods and cones
pupil — lens
all cones
retina
iris
optic nerve
pecten

cerebrum
cerebellum
olfactory lobe
optic nerve
optic lobe
medulla oblongata
pituitary gland

Above: a vertical cross-section of eye; below: brain from left. Both are colored for distinction

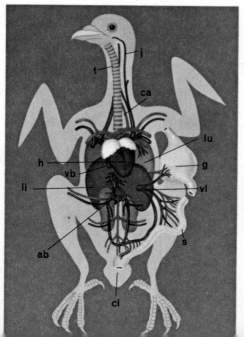

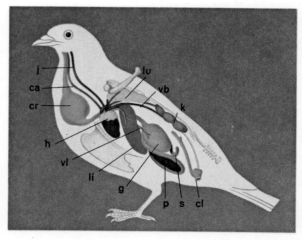

Blood and digestive systems of the pigeon, simplified. ab: *main artery of body;* ca: *carotid artery;* cl: *cloaca;* cr: *crop;* g: *gizzard;* h: *heart;* j: *jugular vein;* k: *kidney;* li: *liver;* lu: *lung;* p: *pancreas;* s: *small intestine;* t: *trachea (windpipe);* vb: *main vein of body;* vl: *of liver*

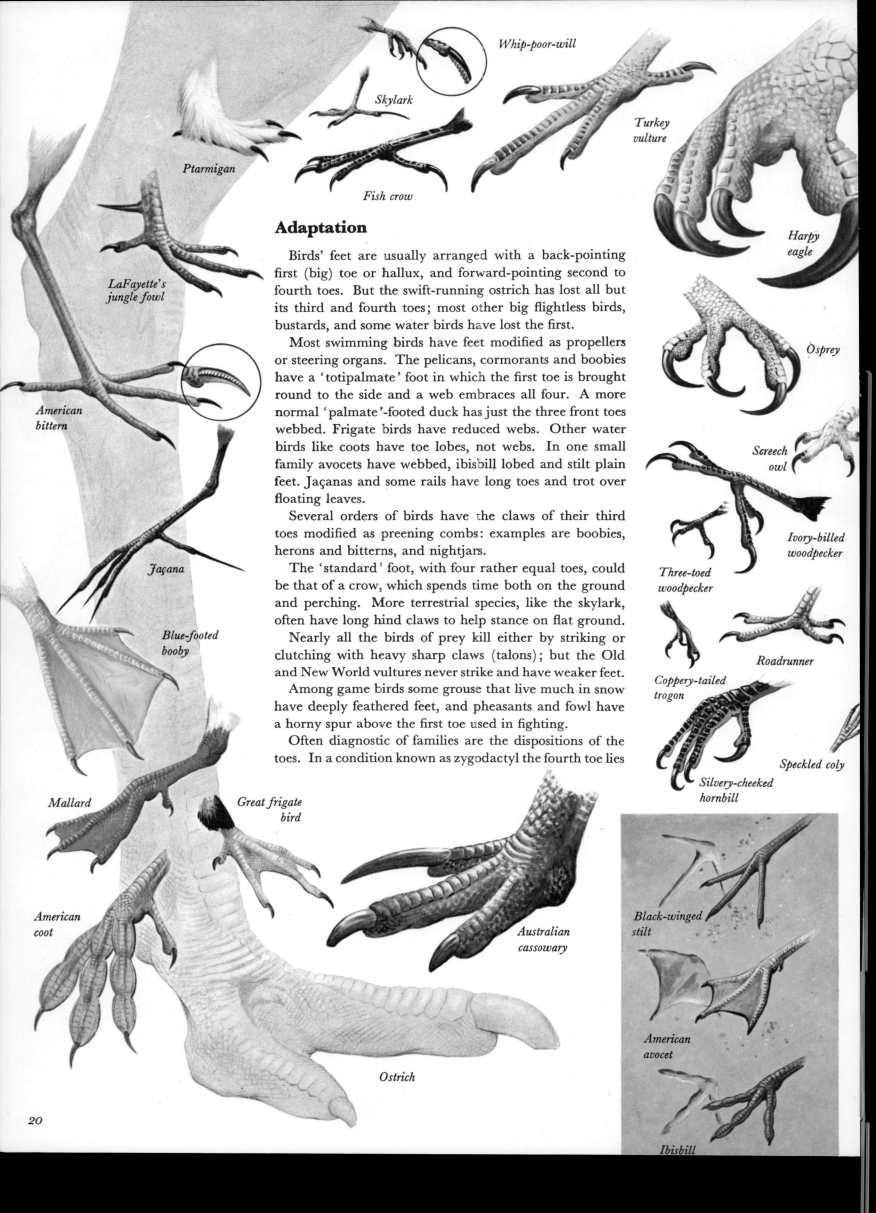

Adaptation

Birds' feet are usually arranged with a back-pointing first (big) toe or hallux, and forward-pointing second to fourth toes. But the swift-running ostrich has lost all but its third and fourth toes; most other big flightless birds, bustards, and some water birds have lost the first.

Most swimming birds have feet modified as propellers or steering organs. The pelicans, cormorants and boobies have a 'totipalmate' foot in which the first toe is brought round to the side and a web embraces all four. A more normal 'palmate'-footed duck has just the three front toes webbed. Frigate birds have reduced webs. Other water birds like coots have toe lobes, not webs. In one small family avocets have webbed, ibisbill lobed and stilt plain feet. Jaçanas and some rails have long toes and trot over floating leaves.

Several orders of birds have the claws of their third toes modified as preening combs: examples are boobies, herons and bitterns, and nightjars.

The 'standard' foot, with four rather equal toes, could be that of a crow, which spends time both on the ground and perching. More terrestrial species, like the skylark, often have long hind claws to help stance on flat ground.

Nearly all the birds of prey kill either by striking or clutching with heavy sharp claws (talons); but the Old and New World vultures never strike and have weaker feet.

Among game birds some grouse that live much in snow have deeply feathered feet, and pheasants and fowl have a horny spur above the first toe used in fighting.

Often diagnostic of families are the dispositions of the toes. In a condition known as zygodactyl the fourth toe lies

Whip-poor-will

Skylark

Fish crow

Turkey vulture

Ptarmigan

Harpy eagle

LaFayette's jungle fowl

Osprey

American bittern

Screech owl

Ivory-billed woodpecker

Three-toed woodpecker

Jaçana

Roadrunner

Blue-footed booby

Coppery-tailed trogon

Speckled coly

Silvery-cheeked hornbill

Mallard

Great frigate bird

Black-winged stilt

American coot

Australian cassowary

American avocet

Ostrich

Ibisbill

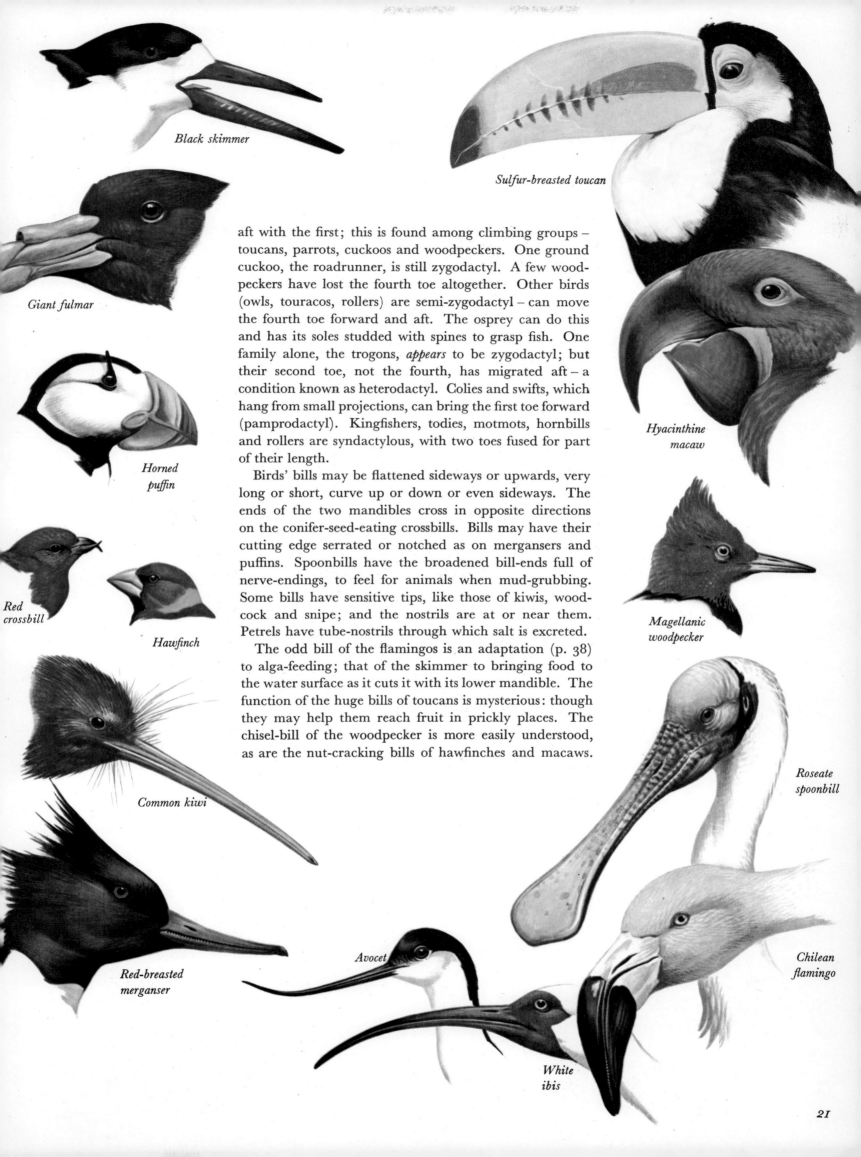

Black skimmer

Sulfur-breasted toucan

Giant fulmar

Horned
puffin

Red
crossbill

Hawfinch

Hyacinthine
macaw

Common kiwi

Magellanic
woodpecker

Red-breasted
merganser

Avocet

White
ibis

Roseate
spoonbill

Chilean
flamingo

aft with the first; this is found among climbing groups – toucans, parrots, cuckoos and woodpeckers. One ground cuckoo, the roadrunner, is still zygodactyl. A few woodpeckers have lost the fourth toe altogether. Other birds (owls, touracos, rollers) are semi-zygodactyl – can move the fourth toe forward and aft. The osprey can do this and has its soles studded with spines to grasp fish. One family alone, the trogons, *appears* to be zygodactyl; but their second toe, not the fourth, has migrated aft – a condition known as heterodactyl. Colies and swifts, which hang from small projections, can bring the first toe forward (pamprodactyl). Kingfishers, todies, motmots, hornbills and rollers are syndactylous, with two toes fused for part of their length.

Birds' bills may be flattened sideways or upwards, very long or short, curve up or down or even sideways. The ends of the two mandibles cross in opposite directions on the conifer-seed-eating crossbills. Bills may have their cutting edge serrated or notched as on mergansers and puffins. Spoonbills have the broadened bill-ends full of nerve-endings, to feel for animals when mud-grubbing. Some bills have sensitive tips, like those of kiwis, woodcock and snipe; and the nostrils are at or near them. Petrels have tube-nostrils through which salt is excreted.

The odd bill of the flamingos is an adaptation (p. 38) to alga-feeding; that of the skimmer to bringing food to the water surface as it cuts it with its lower mandible. The function of the huge bills of toucans is mysterious: though they may help them reach fruit in prickly places. The chisel-bill of the woodpecker is more easily understood, as are the nut-cracking bills of hawfinches and macaws.

Black korhaan, l., has conspicuous plumage, is distasteful; highly edible Rüppell's korhaan has protective countershading

Cock ptarmigan molts white winter plumage after hen, deflects enemy from her at incubation time

Colors and adornments

Every stage designer's trick to convey terror, companionship, love, alarm, meal-time, to conceal, lead away, astray or on, has been incorporated, millions of years ago, in the avian make-up. Birds signal with their plumage, bodies, movements and voices.

A cryptic (Greek, hiding) resemblance to the environment is found almost throughout the bird class. Nightjars, woodcock, snipe, grouse and pheasants incubating their eggs have disruptive or outline-breaking patterns which, though not so contrasting as those of a ringed plover, blend wonderfully with their environment. Tropical forest birds of almost clashing coloration can disappear from sight among the shadows, or even when sitting on open leafless branches in front of a background of foliage. On the forest floor the pittas have such gorgeous plumage that they are known as jewel thrushes; yet their rich contrasts can be concealing. In self-colored open country many birds have underparts light-colored in contrast to their mantles and use the concealing device of counter-shading.

Some birds have few enemies because they are distasteful to eat, or peculiarly aggressive, or both. In Africa the black korhaan, a bustard, has a contrasting pattern that draws attention to it, is distinctly distasteful to humans and almost certainly so to animals of prey. The contrasting plumage of many kingfishers and some honey-eaters and the shiny black plumage of the aggressive drongos may be a warning of distastefulness. Some birds with warning coloration even have a few mimics among gentler species of other families which are spared by enemies because of their resemblance to the models.

Some birds use adornments and voice to produce bluff or false warnings. Some kingfishers and owls have false eyes at the back of their heads. Many birds have displays which confuse enemies, and involve snake imitations and the flashing of strange patterns of bars and eye-like spots.

A few birds have developed special methods of alluring prey. In the Americas the eastern kingbird and the royal flycatcher have been said to attract insects within reach with their flower-like crests. The Australasian frogmouths can open their huge gapes to disclose a colored inner mouth surface which may possibly also act as an insect-trap.

Much of the high coloration of birds has an aggressive function, or a courtship function, or both. The great train of the male quetzal is a badge of territorial ownership, and a courtship organ besides. The spread train of the peacock is used primarily in courtship; other game birds like grouse reach their full glory in territorial aggression. Among the most extraordinary display organs of all are the courtship dresses of pheasants and ducks, though some passerines (like umbrella birds) run them close. The late molt of cock willow grouse and ptarmigan makes them conspicuous in spring and deflects predation from the hens, which incubate alone and are then more valuable biologically.

Concealing coloration; l. to r., disruptive pattern of incubating red-necked nightjar; back of sand lark matches desert, underparts grade lighter toward belly to cancel shadow; ringed plover, conspicuous on plain ground, melts on a pebble beach like the Cheshire cat in Alice

False eyes on back of American pigmy owl's head prevent birds' mob-attacks in daylight

Above, male quetzal, finest of trogons; pair of eclectus parrots, male in front; displaying peacock: below, umbrella bird in display; black-backed pitta; mandarin drake in courtship posture

All plumage and adornment, of course, enables birds to recognize each other. Male and female may be equally bright or dull; those of about half the birds of the world are outwardly indistinguishable, except from their behavior. In most of the rest males outshine females, though a few females outshine males. In some cases, like eclectus parrots, each has a special rich plumage of its own. On some cryptic birds the badge of identity is shown only at take-off, when the flock is in danger, or in display.

At rest countershaded willet is inconspicuous; on take-off not. In flight white identity patches flash on wings and tail

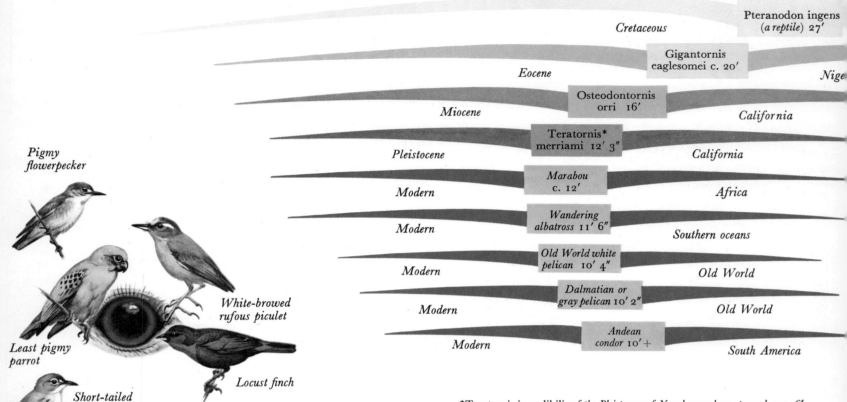

Cretaceous	Pteranodon ingens (a reptile) 27'	
Eocene	Gigantornis eaglesomei c. 20'	Nige
Miocene	Osteodontornis orri 16'	California
Pleistocene	Teratornis* merriami 12' 3"	California
Modern	Marabou c. 12'	Africa
Modern	Wandering albatross 11' 6"	Southern oceans
Modern	Old World white pelican 10' 4"	Old World
Modern	Dalmatian or gray pelican 10' 2"	Old World
Modern	Andean condor 10' +	South America

Pigmy
flowerpecker

*White-browed
rufous piculet*

*Least pigmy
parrot*

*Short-tailed
pigmy tyrant*

Locust finch

*Pigmy
tit*

*Some of world's
smallest birds
(half size)
compared with
ostrich's eye*

*Teratornis incredibilis *of the Pleistocene of Nevada may have spanned over 16'*

Size

The smallest living bird is the bee hummingbird of Cuba. Healthy adults weigh one eighteenth of an ounce, which means that with a little wrapping a dozen could be sent through the post for threepence, or four cents.

If we could persuade a hundred thousand of them (which must be more than there are in the world) to sit still on a balance they would just weigh as much as a large ostrich.

The bee hummingbird is only 2¼ inches from beak-tip to tail-tip, with a wingspan under 4 inches. All the members of the hummingbird family are small: the largest weighs well under an ounce. Nearly all suck nectar from flowers. They eat about half their own weight daily, mostly sugar; and some species go torpid at night to save energy. A bird less than two inches long would probably need more fuel than it had time to get, even in the tropics, where food is abundant. Most of the smallest birds live in the tropics; those in the illustration are each from a different family.

The high limit to the size of flying birds is linked with the mechanics of flight. All the biggest are water-landers, dwellers in open plains or soarers.

Larger flying animals than any living have been found as fossils. Only a few thousand years ago *Teratornis*, a great soaring bird of prey, lived in California and probably weighed over 50 pounds. A gigantic bird was recently found in Miocene deposits in California (about 20 M. years old) and named *Osteodontornis*. In an order between the pelicans and the storks it had a 16-foot wingspan and must have been very heavy. All we know of *Gigantornis* is a fossil breastbone from rock of Eocene age (between 34 and 58 M. years) in Nigeria. It was probably an albatross, and if so had long narrow wings of span as much as 20 feet – nearly twice that of the largest living albatross.

The largest flying animal ever known to have lived was not a bird but a reptile, a pterosaur. Flying reptiles flourished in the Jurassic and Cretaceous periods, for over 100 M. years, with skin-wings stretching from vastly elongated little fingers to their ankles. Greatest of them was *Pteranodon*, which soared over the waves of a sea that covered what is now Kansas. Its fossils are found in chalk deposits 80 or 90 M. years old. *Pteranodon's* wingspan reached 27 feet; it probably weighed around 66 pounds, of which 17 pounds were skin.

The biggest birds are (or were) flightless. The heaviest lived in the recent past. *Aepyornis*, the elephant bird of Madagascar, stood 9–10 feet high and probably weighed about 965 pounds. The New Zealand moas (*Dinornis*) stood taller (to 13), weighed less (about 520). The African

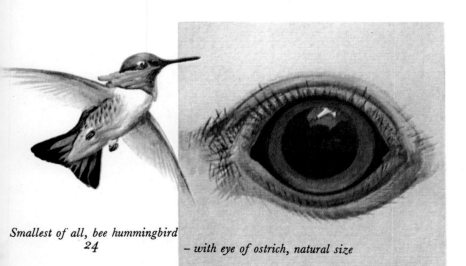

Smallest of all, bee hummingbird

– with eye of ostrich, natural size

24

ostrich can stand 9 and weigh 345; compare this with the Australian emu (5, 88) and cassowary (5, 74) and the South American rhea (4½, 44).

Diatryma, a curious bird between cranes and waders, from the Lower Eocene of Wyoming (over 50 M. years ago) stood nearly 7 feet. The living emperor penguin stands 3¾ and weighs up to 94 pounds; but the fossil penguin *Anthropornis* from the Lower Miocene of the Antarctic (about 24 M.) stood about 5 and may have weighed about 240.

HEAVIEST LIVING FLYING BIRDS
– all the reliable record weights we could find of 22 pounds (10 kilograms) or more

Mute swan (male)	50·6
Great bustard (male)	46·2
Trumpeter swan (male)	38
Manchurian crane (male)	33
Kori (giant) bustard	30
(Dalmatian) gray pelican	28·6
Old World black vulture (female)	27·5
Wandering albatross (male)	26·75
Griffon vulture (male)	26·4
Royal albatross	26·25
Old World white pelican (male)	24·2
(Wild) turkey (male)	23·8
California condor (male)	23
Andean condor (male)	22·7
Pink-backed pelican (male)	22·4
Asian white crane	22
Stanley bustard (Denham's race, male)	22
Arabian bustard (male)	22

1. Anthropornis nordenskjöldi
2. *Emperor penguin*
3. Diatryma steini
4. *Common rhea*
5. Dinornis maximus
6. *Emu*
7. *Australian cassowary*
8. *Ostrich*
9. Aepyornis maximus

Restorations of three extinct New Zealand flightless birds. Left, giant flightless wood-hen; r., Cnemiornis, a goose

One of 15 living penguins, gentoo breeds on subantarctic and antarctic isles

Great moa, Dinornis maximus

Great auk, flightless Atlantic sea bird

Common kiwi

Flightless cormorant, Galápagos Is.

Falkland flightless steamer duck

Titicaca grebe, also flightless

Flightless race of brown teal, Auckland I.

Rufous scrub bird, Australia

New Zealand huia was also very weak flyer

Kakapo, flightless N.Z. parrot

Weka, flightl N.Z. rail

Zapata rail, very weak flyer

CHAPTER II

How Birds Live

Flightless birds

The flightless birds are probably all descended from birds that once flew – even the great elephant birds and moas and the living 'ratites' – ostrich, emu, cassowaries, kiwis and rheas – and the penguins.

All these families lost flight many millions of years ago. Most ratites occupy the same niche as grazing mammals. The kiwis are nocturnal worm-eaters, with (for birds) an acute sense of smell, which evolved in New Zealand where there are no native mammals. The penguins are also very specialized, with their wings completely adapted to flying under water.

Nearly all the rest live, or lived, on islands. Most peculiar is the fruit-eating family of the dodo (p. 56) and solitaires, derived from pigeon-like ancestors that colonized the Mascarene Islands millions of years ago.

The flightless grebe of Lake Titicaca may be a degenerate cousin of the bright-cheeked grebe of the Andes. A cormorant in the Galápagos Islands has reduced wings and is flightless; and the extinct spectacled cormorant of the Bering Sea was nearly so. The extinct great auk of the North Atlantic had a wing about the size of that of a razorbill, which is half its length. The three South American steamer ducks all have the same size wings, but the two flightless species are twice the weight of the other. Among the ducks, also, two outlying island races of the brown teal of New Zealand have lost flight.

In New Zealand the kakapo cannot truly fly, though it uses its wings to help it hop. The extinct Stephen Island wren (p. 56) was never seen to fly; it belonged to a small New Zealand family. Four queer relict families are almost

Rockhopper, also of sub-antarctic and antarctic isles

L. to r.: yellow-eyed penguin (N.Z.), king (subantarctic and antarctic is.), blue (Australia, N.Z.), jackass (S. Afr.), and chinstrap (antarctic is.)

if not entirely flightless: the roatelos of Madagascar which have normal wings but rudimentary collarbones; the kagu of New Caledonia; Australia's scrub birds; and the wattled crows of New Zealand which include the extinct huia.

Sixteen of the rails show every stage of flightlessness. All are island birds and half have become recently extinct. In New Zealand the takahé (p. 57) has practically no keel on its breastbone and a reduced wing; the weka a scarcely reduced wing with which it just cannot fly. Cuba's Zapata rail has a normal wing but is a very weak flyer.

Forty-six living and 16 recently extinct birds are or were flightless. Most have become so on small islands, where competition and predators are less exacting (until man arrives). On small isolated islands flightlessness has one obvious advantage: birds that do not fly cannot get gale-blown away from home; birds that do, can.

Game birds and the like

Certain flying birds are very fleet of foot. The American tinamous have a style of running under cover, keeping vocal touch and escaping from danger by short flights with noisy acceleration, shared by many members of the six true game bird families: the Australian megapodes (p. 85); the American guans and curassows; the grouse; the quails, partridges and pheasants; the African guinea-fowl; and the American turkeys. Some of these live in open country and make prolonged flights; a few migrate.

Four other families have a superficial resemblance to game birds. The bustard quails and plains wanderer of the Old World look like true quails. In S. America the trumpeters run fast, fly poorly. The bustards of Old World plains run very fast indeed, and can fly strongly.

L. to r.: martinetta, a swift-running tinamou, Argentina; Senegal bustard, Africa s. of the Sahara; vulturine guineafowl, dry tropical E. Africa; satyr tragopan, a pheasant, Himalayas; capercaillie, biggest grouse, northern Europe and Asia; mountain quail, U.S. West, n. Lower California

Large birds, l. to r.: James's and Chilean flamingos, Andes and S. America; African saddlebill; scarlet ibis, S. America; Old World little egret

Water birds

Over 600 living birds, belonging to 27 families, are adapted to life in the wetlands.

The loons and many of the grebes, which pursue fish under the water, and two of the three phalaropes become sea birds in the winter. Some of the ducks are sea birds. But the vast majority of long-legged marsh birds, waders and wildfowl are paddlers or swimmers in lakes, rivers, streams and marshes, or on shores and estuaries.

Flamingos (p. 38) and the limpkin (p. 38) are very specialized. Most herons are stalkers of the shallows that catch fish or frogs with darts of lance-like bills. Storks have many differing animal diets. Ibises are fishers and shrimpers and, with their long downcurved bills, worm-probers; in the same family spoonbills (p. 21) are mud-sifters. The rather short-billed cranes are omnivorous.

With the exception of the coots, which swim in the open, the large rail family is more often heard than seen.

At night marshes the world over resound with eerie groans, barks, gobblings, gabblings and shrieks as these undercover birds seek water animals and plants.

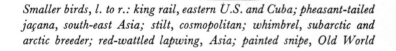

Smaller birds, l. to r.: king rail, eastern U.S. and Cuba; pheasant-tailed jaçana, south-east Asia; stilt, cosmopolitan; whimbrel, subarctic and arctic breeder; red-wattled lapwing, Asia; painted snipe, Old World

The shy finfoots can run fast, swim well, and dive for fish or amphibians; the rare kagu (p. 60) is a night bird of the forests of New Caledonia; the handsome sun bittern hunts small animals in forest streams of tropical America.

Oystercatchers, with their chisel beaks, deftly knock limpets off the rocks and specialize in eating shore molluscs. Plovers and turnstones have short beaks and pick their food; curlew, whimbrel, godwits, snipe and sand-

Black-throated loon, northern world; and black-necked grebe, northern world and Africa

Wilson's phalarope breeds in highland north, winters in southern South America

Nine Anatids from eight tribes. Swimming: in back row, l. to r., red-crested pochard, Europe and Asia; shelduck, Europe and Asia; black-necked swan, southern South America; in front, ruddy duck, N. America and West Indies; African pigmy goose. On land: goosander, northern world; Baikal teal, breeds eastern Siberia; red-billed whistling duck, Texas, C. and S. America; pair of red-breasted geese, arctic Siberian nesters

pipers probe; painted snipe probe also; the long-legged stilts wade in water above the leg-joint and pick animals from or near the surface, and their avocet cousins sweep the water-surface with their upcurved bills or duck for crustaceans and worms. Phalaropes spin while swimming to stir up animals from below. The unique crab plover specializes in large crustaceans. The jaçanas hunt insects, snails and seeds across the water lily pads of tropical pools.

The swans, geese and ducks belong to a family with just over a gross of surviving members, since four of the 150 modern Anatids have become extinct. A recent classification would divide them into eleven groups.

The strange magpie goose of the Australian swamps may be the most primitive. The 6 swans, 15 true geese and the coscoroba are mainly grazers. The 8 whistling ducks are goose-like, mainly vegetarian and dive well. The unique freckled duck of Australia is a plant-eater. Long-legged and often highly colored are the 8 sheld-geese (grazers) and 6 shelducks (omnivorous). The 3 steamer ducks of S. America mainly eat marine molluscs.

The 13 perching ducks, which include the pigmy geese

and the gay wood and mandarin ducks, often nest in tree-holes and are mainly vegetarian. Also mainly plant-eating are dabbling ducks, a tribe of 42 living species – mallard, teal, shovelers and allies. The 15 pochards are a related tribe which feed under water, partly on animals.

In the true diving duck tribe of 18 species are the eiders and scoters, mollusc-eating sea ducks; the goldeneyes and their kin, and the saw-billed mergansers which eat mainly fish. Typical of the odd tribe of 9 stifftails is the ruddy duck of the Americas, which dives and swims under water, yet eats mostly plants.

Common oystercatchers: the European race of a cosmopolitan, specialized wader

Sun grebe, from central South America, one of the three peculiar finfoots

Tufted puffin

Atlantic puffin **Sea birds**

Magellan penguin

About 260 species, or 3 per cent of the birds of the world, are adapted to life at sea. Many of them feed only in salt water, and drink only salt water, and the fully oceanic sea birds can feed as far from land as any animal can get.

Some large albatrosses probably spend the first nine years of their lives without resting on the land at all. Sea birds on the whole tend to have long periods of adolescence before they can breed – time to learn to solve the problems of navigating the trackless ocean. Most breed slowly and live long – though just how long we can so far only guess.

Flying below the horizon in the big picture are (left to right) the snow petrel, which nests nearer the South Pole than any other bird; Leach's petrel of the northern seas; the great shearwater which nests in some millions only

on the remote South Atlantic archipelago of Tristan da Cunha, and is common off Newfoundland hunting capelin in our northern summer; and the red-tailed tropic bird.

Above the horizon (l. to r.) fly a northern gannet, largest sea bird of the North Atlantic; the black-browed albatross, whose dynamic soaring in the southern oceans is helped by rough weather; the sooty tern, a common sea bird of the tropics; the great skua, a 'bipolar' bird found in both subarctic and antarctic; a flock of herring gulls, a successful northern species; and (in front of cliff) the brown pelican of the Americas.

On the cliff (top down) are some handsome blue-eyed shags of the southern seas; the magnificent frigate bird of the tropics, the most agile flyer of all sea birds; the rare red-legged kittiwake, an ocean-going gull; with a darker mantle the western gull, also from the North Pacific; and the red-footed booby, a tropical relative of the gannets.

Inca tern

Red-thighed falconet

Montagu's harrier

Bateleur

Caracara

Long-crested hawk eagle

Fish eagle

Gyrfalcon

Red-tailed hawk

Swallow-tailed kite

Birds of prey: and owls

About 280 of the world's birds belong to the Falconi-formes, or day-flying birds of prey; the day raptors.

Most raptors kill prey by striking or clutching, hold it in their sharply clawed feet (talons) and tear it with their powerful hooked bills or swallow it whole.

The big broad-winged raptors, the condors, vultures, eagles and buzzards, all soar hundreds of miles a day with but little use of power. The largest are carrion-feeders, with naked heads and rather weak talons; these often patrol at a great height, watching not only the ground but their searching neighbors; when one descends on a find, others follow.

Eagles can dive fast and in one blow of their powerful talons clutch, kill and carry off an animal almost their own weight. Big falcons can strike bird prey in power-dives at speeds close to those of light aircraft. The goshawks are the most agile pursuit-craft of all; the gabar goshawk of Africa easily overtakes weaver-birds through dense thorny thickets.

The Cathartidae, or New World vultures, include the condors and the turkey vulture, and are quite unrelated to the Old World vultures such as the Egyptian and lappet-eared which belong to the Accipitridae. Also in the Accipitridae are kites; eagles and buzzards – of which the red-tailed hawk is an example; harriers; harrier-eagles like the bateleur. The Falconidae include, besides the true sharp-winged falcons, the broad-winged caracaras and the tiny insect-hawking falconets, not much bigger than sparrows. The snake-catching secretary bird of the African veldt and the fish-catching osprey each has a family all to itself.

The order of owls is a gross of species strong. These raptors of dusk, night and dawn are related in no way to the day raptors. They kill with powerful talons; but nearly all overtake their prey by stealth; soft-feathered and silent in flight. Their eyesight is adapted for night vision; their huge ears (*not* marked by feather tufts) are asymmetrical and arranged for scanning the range and direction of sounds.

Gabar goshawk (black phase)

Barn owl

Spectacled owl

Long-eared owl

Short-eared owl

Osprey stooping on fish

Secretary bird

Turkey vulture

Egyptian vulture

Lappet-eared vulture

Pretty fruit pigeon, Papua: chestnut-eared aracari, S. America: orange-wattled bird of paradise, Papua: yellow-breasted fig bird, Australia

Fruit- and seed-eaters

Over the forests flocks of bright birds call in loud voices, swing through the air in long flights, across broad brown tropical rivers, turn in wide sweeps with yet louder voices, and suddenly drop and disappear in the tree canopy.

In the shades their violent patterns of violet, purple, blue, green, yellow, orange, red, white and black seem to vanish entirely. Down on the forest floor, 150 feet below, we can hear them only, shouting still. Then the shouts and hoots and shrieks die down, and all we listen to is the rustle of wings and leaves, and an occasional rushing noise as a dropped or loosened fruit tears down to earth through the layers of foliage.

The nomads of the forests are of many kinds, belonging to about thirty bird families. Each bird in the picture is a member of a different one. All roam in flocks,

Nutcracker and cone of Swiss pine; by habit this crow buries pine seeds for winter store

moving the year round in bands (sometimes of several species mixed) in search of fruit in season. When a crop of fruit on a clump of trees is exhausted they move to another crop; as one kind of fruit falls out of season they find another kind.

The success of fruit-eaters depends on certainty of supply; their bright colors are not just happy inventions of nature: they have a purpose, as has their raucous language. Clumps of fruit are sharable treasures, and often miles apart; so the fruit-eaters have it that the discovery of one becomes the prize of all. This they do by working in groups, and with the aid of vivid patterns and violent voices that enable them to recognize their own (and probably other) kinds at a distance in the open.

Under the canopy, however, their strongly contrasting plumage actually makes them blend with the shadows of the foliage and sunflecks so that they are very hard to find when they are quiet. Thus when they have discovered their food and are busy with it, or when they are nesting (often in holes in trees) they are safeguarded from some of their enemies.

Common waxbill

Blue-black grosbeak

Lapland bunting

Cuban trogon : crimson-backed tanager, C. & S. America : common touraco, Africa : blossom-headed parakeet, S. Asia : double-toothed barbet, Africa

Among the great order of the Passerines there are many fruit-eaters. There are even flower-eaters, though no bird has (as far as we know) become specialized for eating flowers only. Specialist seed-eaters, however, are rather common.

Some members of the crow family specialize not only in seed-eating but in seed-storing. The Old World jay, for instance, eats many things; but acorns – the big seeds of the oak – are its favorite food. It manages to eat acorns all the year round by burying them in the ground in chosen caches around its woodland beat.

Nutcrackers, too, are great storers of the seeds of conifers and other trees. The nutcracker of the forests of Europe and Asia figured in the picture hides pine seeds or nuts in all kinds of slits – for instance in the bark of trees and between stones; and tame birds in houses will put food between books or cushions, in the bowls of pipes or even in envelopes!

An eater of moderate-sized seeds needs a sharp-edged strong beak for splitting its food's hard jacket; a beak like that of a finch, in fact. This is one of the reasons why the classification of the finch-like birds is so difficult. When in the course of evolution members of different groups of

birds, only very distantly related to each other, have taken to seed-eating they have ended up looking very much alike in their general anatomy – and particularly in the structure of their bills.

The finch-beak turns up in over two dozen groups of Passerine birds belonging to well over a dozen families. Five of the six seed-eaters figured on this page belong to five different subfamilies of four different families. The sixth, a grassquit, *may* belong to the same subfamily as the blue-black grosbeak; but some authorities would put it with the buntings and others with the true finches. The evolutionary convergence (see p. 47) of these birds is sometimes close enough to confuse the experts.

Long-tailed tit and bullfinch eat apple buds. House sparrow tears crocus

European goldfinch

-eaters all

Red-billed quelea

Yellow-faced grassquit

These eat mainly fruit; but readily take animals when available: red-fronted barbet, E. Africa, ants, termites; king bird of paradise, Papua, eggs, young birds; crimson finch, an Australian waxbill, termites; cedar waxwing, N. America, insects

These eat mainly fruit or seeds, but in breeding season eat insects and feed them to young: snow bunting, northern world; dunnock, Eurasia; rose-throated becard, C. America

Omnivores

To find out what birds eat we must watch birds; collect the food they bring to young; examine stomach contents; analyze the remains of food in feces and in the pellets of undigested stuff that many species regurgitate.

Each wild species has what we can call a 'food-spectrum', with wide bands in it which represent favorite foods, and narrow bands which represent less frequent or available choices. No two closely related species that live in the same place seem to have the same food-spectrum, except in times of the occasional superabundance of some special food. On the other hand, related species in different areas may have very similar spectra, like the American robin and the European blackbird. Though each bird has its characteristic food pattern, this pattern may change very much with the seasons – especially at the time of feeding

young – and from area to area within the species' range.

No birds have food-spectra more complicated than the omnivores; those which eat varied food, both animal and plant. Many animal-eaters switch to wild fruits in season. Nuthatches and creepers eat beechmast and seeds in the autumn. The carnivorous yellow-billed cuckoo of America eats elderberries, mulberries and grapes in season; in tropical Asia some insect-eating cuckoo shrikes and babblers eat fruit when berries fall and guavas and figs are ripe; in Australia two insectivorous silvereyes are quite important orchard pests when the figs, grapes and soft fruits are ready for market. Both American and Old World warblers may take ripe fruit.

Many plant-eating birds switch specially to insects when they are rearing young, thus giving their offspring a high protein diet during growth. Others readily take animals whenever they swarm. Ants and other

Acorn woodpecker, w. North America, finds or makes holes to wedge acorns, seek insects; sucks sap from holes already made by sapsuckers

Suspected bird pests have been investigated by measuring percentage of different foods in their stomachs by volume. In Britain skylark (mid.) eats 46% animal food, mostly insects, 54% vegetable, mostly weed seeds. Food of starling (l.) is much the same in Britain (51% animal; 49% vegetable) as in U.S. (57% animal; 43% vegetable); over half its plants are wild fruits. In England much grain was grown in World War II; rook (r.) ate 18% animal; 82% vegetable, most animal (54%) in June, least (4%) in January–February

Normally these eat insects. But in fall myrtle warbler (l.), N. America, eats bayberries; golden oriole (below), Old World, eats fruit. Narina trogon, Africa, may take berries

These eat nearly everything. Spotted bower bird (l.), Australia, has wide tastes, may be garden pest: gray jay, N. America, will rob camps, store biscuits in holes. Scarlet-rumped tanager, C. America, eats bananas, berries, spiders, mice and eggs

insects are snapped up by vegetarians ranging from barbets to blue grouse, from waxbills to waxwings.

Some birds like the gray jay have diets so mixed that they seem to eat anything they can get. But most with wide tastes still show a food-spectrum specially their own, even though it changes strongly from month to month. When the food of the mocking bird is measured through a whole year, it bulks about half animal, half plant on average, as does that of the skylark and common starling. But in May the mocker's food is about 85 per cent animal, in December January about 87 per cent plant. The others' diets vary as much, though not in the same way.

A bird which, through the year, eats mainly animal matter (82 per cent by bulk) is the common or black-billed magpie in America. Its plant food varies from hardly any in May to more than half from November to January. Conversely, the rook in war-time England averaged the same percentage (82) of *plant* matter.

An interesting and variable food-spectrum is shown by the great spotted woodpecker of Europe. In Finland its northern race is largely an eater of pine and spruce seeds in winter; only in summer does it have ants and the grubs of wood-boring insects as its main food. The British race, however, has larvae the year around, and acorns as a minor band in its pattern. Some (not all) great spotted woodpeckers make rings of holes round trees to get sap. In North America this is a speciality of the sapsuckers, and, at second hand, of the acorn woodpecker which sucks from sapsucker holes. The acorn woodpecker bores holes itself, of course, and indeed may riddle trees with hundreds of them in which it stores acorns and some other largish nuts. The nut band is over half, the insect band under a quarter of this bird's yearly food-spectrum.

In Europe start of great tits' breeding season depends closely on spring climate, so young are fed in nest hole during peak caterpillar fortnight

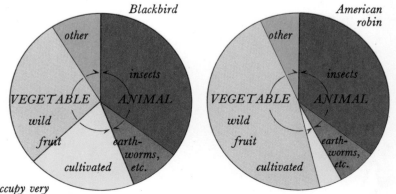

Blackbird

American robin

other

VEGETABLE

wild fruit

cultivated

insects

ANIMAL

earth-worms, etc.

European blackbird and American robin occupy very similar niches. Volume of food types is almost same, though blackbird eats more cultivated fruit than other thrush

Birds that catch insects on the wing. Flying (l. to r.): nighthawk, N. America; vermilion flycatcher, U.S. to Argentina; swift, Eurasia, Africa; great racket-tailed drongo, Asia; white-fronted bee eater and rufous-chested swallow, Africa. Perching: Cuban tody; pied flycatcher, Eurasia

Insect-eaters

By 1960 the zoologists had described almost exactly a million full species of animals, of which no less than 700,000 were insects. Some expert taxonomists, or classifiers, have guessed that the insects so far named are roughly only a third of those that remain to be named!

Only a handful of insects are marine: but the class absolutely dominates the planet's land surface in variety and numbers. It makes the solid base of the pyramid of life on land, being the most important prey of the animal-eating animals, including the birds.

Of the 154 living bird families, no less than 128 have insect-eating members. Of these 34 eat insects mainly, and another ten eat insects and insect-like animals wholly.

It is no surprise, then, that we find nearly 20 bird families that hunt insects on the wing. The true nightjars, such as the nighthawk, can hover or sharply jink as they hunt at twilight or night. Fastest of all insect-interceptors are the narrow-winged swifts and their allies, many of which may log a thousand miles in a normal feeding day.

Nightjars and swallows seldom, and swifts and wood swallows never, use perches to make sallies from: but the rest of the flying insect-eaters do. The strange potoos of tropical America dart from favorite posts, on which they sit almost invisible, to snap up passing prey in their enormous mouths; the owlet nightjars, an Australasian family, have mouths nearly as big. These dusk birds have concealing coloration; but day feeders tend to be very brightly colored. The brilliant todies (a small family restricted to the West Indies) and the almost

Gleaners of insects from leaves. N. America: hooded warbler (top l.), yellow-throated vireo (r.), scarlet tanager. Europe: wood warbler (c.)

Ground feeders: seven examples ranging from northern moors to tropical forest floors. Pied wagtail, Eurasia; fox sparrow, Canada; Japanese robin

equally colorful motmots of tropical America have strict territories and hunting perches. In the Old World the handsome rollers often carry live prey to their perches for killing and eating; and many of the lovely bee eaters do the same. So do the slender, shining jacamars, long-billed dragonfly specialists of tropical America. The related but less highly colored and broader-billed puffbirds from the same area dive on flying prey from their watching-posts and sometimes take beetles on the ground.

Over a sixth of the passerine birds are air-catchers; the swallows and wood swallows are most aerial of all. A huge family of 364 species, the tyrant flycatchers of the Americas, has an unrelated counterpart in the rest of the world – the 398 Old World flycatchers, monarchs and whistlers. These are perch-darters, as are the aggressive drongos of the tropical Old World.

Every autumn the gardens around our houses in England and New England resound with the sharp communication-notes of mixed flocks of insect-gleaning birds, working their way through the trees in search of insects and spiders under leaves and bark. The species are nearly all different, but most have a counterpart; in place of those figured here in Connecticut (in brackets) the Northamptonshire birds are: great spotted woodpecker (downy); great tit or blue tit – occasionally coal or marsh tit (black-capped chickadee); common nuthatch (white-breasted); tree creeper (brown creeper, close species); goldcrest (golden-crowned kinglet); blackcap – an Old World warbler (myrtle warbler – different family of American wood warblers). England has no very good counterpart to the Carolina wren; though insect-hunting lower down, usually in the undergrowth, its common (and only) wren is just the same species as the North American winter wren.

About two-fifths of all the passerine species of birds are insect or small animal hunters among trees and bush or on the ground. Some of the ground-feeders are specialists: thus on the forest-floor of tropical America whole groups of birds, of several different families, follow the big army ants and eat them and other insects they stir up: ant thrushes, ant pipits, ant tanagers belong to such gangs, as do some of the manakins and wood warblers.

Roger Peterson's studio in autumn. Mixed flocks include (top down) golden-crowned kinglet, myrtle warbler, black-capped chickadee, downy woodpecker, Carolina wren, white-breasted nuthatch, brown creeper

Fairy pitta, E. Asia, Australia

S. America: black-faced ant thrush; red-crowned ant tanager; chestnut-belted ant pipit

*Typical associates of Ankole cattle in Africa:
shoulder, piapiacs; neck, red-billed oxpeckers;
horn, carmine bee eater; flying, wire-tailed
swallow; below, cattle egrets, yellow wagtail*

*In African lakes lesser flamingo feeds at sur-
face, greater at bottom. Tongues pump water
full of plankton through filters in bills*

Some specialists

The army ant followers are not the only specialists that
rely on other animals to disturb food for them. Where-
ever cattle range they have bird associates, for instance.

The oxpeckers that spend so much time on native cattle
in Africa search their hosts for ticks. The rest of the
African cattle club watch for the insects that the animals
kick up as they graze, or seek beetle larvae in their dung:
the noisy piapiac (a crow) and the carmine bee eater are
members; present often are swallows, the yellow wagtail,
the cattle egret, and sometimes plovers. In other parts of
the world are other tick-birds, such as the fire-crowned
tyrant and the smooth-billed ani in S. America; and other
snatchers of disturbed insects, like the common starling,
the N. American cowbird, the European jackdaw, the
Asiatic king crow and a New Zealand parrot, the kea.

The five living flamingos are specialists of quite another
kind, for all live on the minute plant and animal life
that swarms in the water and bottom mud of warm fresh
water and salty lakes. Most of this food they take by
pumping the water or mud over filter-plates in their bills.

In some parts of the tropics giant water snails are
abundant. Two storks, the open-bills of Asia and Africa,
have a ridged gap in their bills which is a device to grip
and crush the snails or take them to a hard place where
they can be broken with the bill-tip. In the Americas,
the quite unrelated limpkin also has a bill-gap for the
same purpose; and at least three species of kites are giant
snail specialists, with fine hooks on their beaks.

Other snail specialists use tools. The stagemaker bower
bird of Australia uses stones to break large land snails.
The song thrush of Europe and Asia and the ruddy
kingfisher of the Philippines both smash land snails on
favorite stone anvils. The kingfisher family are not all
fishers – one species in New Guinea digs earthworms –
but the typical members are among the few land birds
that dive for fish. The members of the dipper family hunt
animals on the beds of clear streams, walking below the
surface by bending their bodies at an angle to the flow.

*In Old World brooks common kingfisher hunts by
diving, dipper by walking under water*

*As greater flamingo moves forward,
water, sucked over filter-plates,
is expelled at nick of gape*

Nectar birds: l. to r., above, Mexican cacique; ruby topaz, helmet-crest, S. American hummers; beautiful sunbird, E. Africa; below, bananaquit, C., S. America; scarlet honeyeater, Australia; iiwi, Hawaiian Is.; rainbow lorikeet, Australasia

Lorikeets crush blossoms, lap nectar with fringed tongue (inset)

Flowering plants did not appear until the insects already dominated the land. As they evolved, they produced honey-making organs which attracted insects: moving from flower to flower to suck sugar, the insects pollinated them. Vast numbers of flowers evolved with insect-luring colored petals and individual smells, and vast numbers of insects evolved with long sucking tongues.

About a fifth of the world's birds are now also involved in flower pollination. Red scentless flowers have evolved in the tropics very largely with honey-sucking birds – for birds see colors better than insects at the red end of the spectrum and have hardly any sense of smell.

The hummingbirds of the Americas do all their honey-sucking on the wing. They have long tubular tongues. The pretty Chilean fire-crown has been seen feeding at the red fuchsias of Tierra del Fuego in a snow-storm; the rufous hummer regularly summers in Alaska. Many suck flowers with long corolla-tubes; for instance, the sword-billed hummer of the Andes is the only bird whose (5-inch) bill is longer than the rest of it.

Several of the other nectar-bird families have tubed tongues, though the Hawaiian honeycreepers have trough-like ones with a fringed tip. Most important are the honeyeaters, sunbirds and flowerpeckers of the Old World; and a group of New World birds generally classed as the honeycreeper family, which includes the bananaquit and the flower piercers. Many other families, too, have a few members which are on the way to nectar specialization; for instance among the American icterids the oro-péndolas and caciques suck tree nectar.

A large tribe of parrots, the honey parrots or brush-tongued lorikeets, have become rather crude nectar-feeders, for they grasp flowers with their beaks and specialized tongues, crush them and lick up the honey with the fringes on their tongues' ends.

Florida, C. and S. America limpkin, l., above, and everglade kite giant snail Pomacea. *Kite's bill-hook pierces, paralyzes prey*

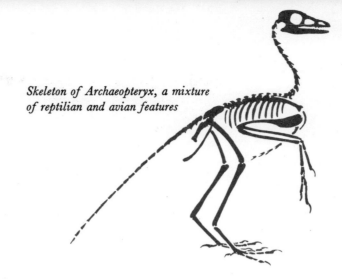

Skeleton of Archaeopteryx, a mixture of reptilian and avian features

CHAPTER III

Birds of the Past

The bird ancestor

The bedrock of part of Bavaria is a fine slate, formed from mud-silt rapidly deposited at the bottom of a fresh-water lake in late Jurassic times, about 140 million years ago. It is called Solnhofen limestone.

A slate-splitter, in 1861, found a fossil feather on a slab – with its impression on the counter-slab; and later in the same year the incomplete skeleton of a feathered animal was found in a Solnhofen quarry at Langenaltheim. It came into the possession of the district medical officer, Dr. Karl Häberlein, who sold it next year (with a fine collection of other fossils) to the British Museum in London, for enough to give his daughter a good dowry. It was named *Archaeopteryx lithographica* – 'the ancient winged creature of the stone for drawing' – in the year in which it was found.

In 1877 a second specimen turned up in another Solnhofen quarry at Blumenberg, about ten miles away. Some researchers have thought it to belong to a species different from the London specimen: but it does not, and neither does the third, found at Langenaltheim in 1956, only 275 yards away from the site of the first specimen and in a bed of almost exactly the same age. The second Archaeopteryx seems to have been an immature one. All three specimens are so excellent that a very close reconstruction can be made from them.

Archaeopteryx is so far the oldest known bird – about 10 million years older than the next oldest certain fossil bird – the goose- or flamingo-like *Gallornis straeleni*, described in 1931 from Lower Cretaceous beds in France. The species seems to have survived unchanged for quite a time in the cycad forests of the late Jurassic period; and it may indeed have been one of the very earliest of birds, as we can judge from the large array of purely reptilian features it shares with no other known bird.

Among the reptilian features of Archaeopteryx, which are found in no other bird, are the long tail of twenty vertebrae; an uncomplicated backbone with no fusions of its vertebrae; three fingers with claws; no fusions of certain bones in the hand; simple ribs; and a simple brain with a small cerebellum (the part that co-ordinates muscular activities).

No reptile, however, has been found with feathers; and the structure of those of Archaeopteryx is identical with those of modern birds. The fossil's wing, with primary flight feathers (8) attached to hand and wrist, secondaries attached to forearm, and covert feathers, is just like many a modern bird's wing. Only in birds do the collar-bones join to form a wishbone, and those of Archaeopteryx so join; and some bones in the fossil's hip are arranged like those of birds only.

Archaeopteryx, then, was a bird; and a bird of forests, judging by the position of the 'big' toe opposite the other three – an adaptation to perching. But it had no hollow bones – an adaptation for lightness already present in the reptilian flying pterosaurs. Its powers of flight must have been limited. It had no keel on its breastbone, so could not have had very powerful flying muscles. With its small cerebellum it could not have been much of an acrobat. It was basically a powered glider, probably capable of rising flight from branch to branch, or from rock to rock, but quite unable to dodge or indeed to change direction quickly when in the air. It had teeth; but some later fossil birds also had teeth.

What sort of reptiles was this crow-sized early bird descended from? Long-tailed lizard-like scaly reptiles of about the same size lived in the previous Triassic period. They are known as Thecodonts, and surely ran with their tails used as balancers. Land-forms of these developed into two-legged runners with smallish arms; but (the theory is) tree-forms developed their arms equally as climbing and hanging organs. With their strong legs and balancing tails the tree-forms leaped from branch to branch; with their strong arms they climbed, caught and steadied themselves. Gradually their arms developed enlarged scales at the trailing edge, at first simple flaps, later flaps with joining hooks to enable them to work together when fanned out. The feather, in fact, is descended from a Thecodont reptile's scale, and evolved as an adaptation to increase its arm area, grip air and steady it in long leaps.

Fine feathers make fine birds; and it is certain that with the first feathers came the first birds.

Parascaniornis
Upper Cretaceous

Enaliornis
Lower Cretaceous

Elopteryx
Upper Cretaceous

Gallornis
Lower Cretaceous

Sea birds fossilized miles to sea in the mid
Upper Cretaceous Niobrara chalk of western Kansa
l. Ichthyornis victor; *on r. rock* Hesperornis reg
alis; *swimming l.* Baptornis advenus, *r.* Hespero
nis gracilis; *beyond, another* Ichthyornis speci

Cretaceous

A rough calculation by Professor Pierce Brodkorb suggests that rather over 1½ million bird species have existed at one time or another in the 140 million years or more since the first. James Fisher's own belief is that the number is rather under half a million.

The evolution of birds was slow in their early years, and from the whole of the mild, long Cretaceous period, from about 135 to 70 million years ago, under thirty species are known. The Cretaceous can be split into lower and upper subperiods of about 35 and 30 million years. Gallornis (p. 41) is the only bird so far known from the lower part of the Lower Cretaceous; and only two species are known from its upper part. These belong to the genus Enaliornis, and constitute a primitive family, known only from England, which is possibly ancestral to the loons.

All the species described from the Upper Cretaceous, apart from a couple of pigeon-sized mysteries (known from shoulder-bones only) from Wyoming, are water birds. Most of them come from the famous Niobrara chalk of Kansas which was then a seabed, hundreds of miles from land. Over this sea the dominant flyers were huge reptiles like Pteranodon (p. 24) which were the largest animals ever known to have flown; not till the end of the Cretaceous did these pterosaurs become extinct.

All the Niobrara birds were described by the American palaeontologist Marsh between 1872 and 1880. One of them is Baptornis, in a family near the grebes. Three of them are the biggish flightless swimming sea birds of the Hesperornis genus, which includes the only birds since Archaeopteryx proved to have retained true teeth. The Hesperornithids looked rather like loons, but were probably closer to grebes, on the same stem as Baptornis; their wings were very much reduced and they swam with their very powerful legs and feet. The rest comprise six flying sea birds of the genus Ichthyornis and one which has been called Apatornis: they represent two families in an order of birds which looked rather like terns but seems to have been closer to the loons.

Without the Niobrara birds the Upper Cretaceous record is rather scanty. From a slightly later deposit in Alabama comes the recently discovered Plegadornis, in a family ancestral to the ibises. Later still are another Hesperornithid (Coniornis) from Montana, and Parascaniornis from Sweden, in a family ancestral to the flamingos. In the uppermost Cretaceous rocks a second Baptornithid (Neogaeornis) has been found in Chile; Elopteryx from Rumania is in a family probably ancestral to cormorants; Lonchodytes and Torotix from Wyoming are new finds on the loon and flamingo stems.

Paleocene and Eocene

Seventy million years ago great changes took place on the earth's surface. The Atlantic and Indian Oceans were formed, and much of the chalky sea-bottom of Cretaceous times was raised up to form land. Large parts of Europe and North America were tropical. The great reptiles died out and the mammals and birds became dominant.

The Eocene period (in the old sense) lasted until forty million years ago. Its first ten million years, now usually separated as the Paleocene period, have produced, so far, only fifteen bird fossils: but they include the first belonging to modern families. From New Jersey marl come true cormorants, rails and sandpipers. From the Upper Paleocene of France comes the first true loon, and from France and England Gastornis and Remiornis. Gastornis and its allies continued into strict Eocene times; as large as ostriches, and flightless, they are (with the Diatrymids) placed in an order near the bustards and waders.

In the twenty million years of the strict Eocene the birds really began to radiate all over the world, and many modern families evolved. In the Lower Eocene we find in the London clay the first tropic bird, heron, hawk and true gull, as well as Odontopteryx, a big sea bird with tooth-like growths on its jaws, that has been placed near the pelican order. The flightless Diatrymids (p. 25) flourished in both Europe and North America. In North America, also, were the first grouse; Geranoides, in a primitive crane-like family; Presbyornis, in a wader family; and the first auks. Bone fragments from New Zealand indicate that penguins were already on the scene.

Middle Eocene rocks give us the first known snake bird, in Sumatra; the first Cathartid vulture, in Germany, showing that the family, now restricted to the New World, may have originated in the Old; many true cranes in Europe and America including one of the modern genus *Grus*; also from Germany the first bustard, painted snipe and hornbill; from Wyoming what may be an earliest motmot.

Nearly half the known Eocene birds come from its upper third. England shows the first ibis; the earliest Agnopterus in a primitive flamingo family; the earliest true flamingo. Beds in France show a gooselike waterfowl, an early harrier, the first members of the pheasant family, curlew (p. 68), kingfisher and advanced passerines – three starlings and what may be an ancestor of the long-tailed tit. Other Upper Eocene fossils are long-legged Neocathartes from Wyoming, sole member of a superfamily close to the Cathartids; and Eogrus from Inner Mongolia, first of a primitive crane family.

Other families that first show in the Eocene are albatrosses (Gigantornis, p. 24) and, from Wyoming, a primitive passerine which was, perhaps, a tapaculo.

Wasatch, Lower Green River and Colton faunas *Lower Eocene Wyoming and Utah are (l.-r.)* Para- rus prentici, *earliest true crane;* Palaeorallus oxelli, *an early rail; flying,* Coltonia recurvi- stra, *earliest stilt; huge flightless* Diatryma eini; Protostrix mimica, *earliest owl;* Gallinul- des wyomingensis, *forerunner of chachalacas*

Palaeotis, *Middle Eocene→*

Neocathartes *Upper Eocene*

Palaeotringa, *Paleocene*

Eocathartes *Middle Eocene*

43

Some Eocene–Oligocene birds of Quercy, France (downwards): Cypselavus, *true swift;* Archaeotrogon, *trogon;* Propelargus, *big stork;* Plesiocathartes, New World *vulture;* Geranopterus, *roller;* Amphiserpentarius, *secretary bird;* sand grouse of modern genus Pterocles

Oligocene

The Oligocene period lasted from about 40 to about 25 million years ago, a warm dry time of mountain building, with an increase in grassland and a decrease of forests.

Just over a hundred fossil birds are known from the Oligocene. From the very end of the Eocene to the early Oligocene phosphorite deposits were laid down in Quercy in south-central France: and these have so far provided a fauna of nearly 50 species, among them the earliest known storks, secretary bird, kite, hoatzin-like birds, partridges, plover, sand grouse, cuckoo, owl, swift, trogons and roller, as well as a rail-like and a swift-like family.

Elsewhere, in the Lower Oligocene, we find the earliest gannet, guan and seriema-like bird; and in South America the first falcon and limpkin and three of the families of the flightless Phororhacoids, like giant big-headed seriemas.

As the Oligocene went on, new birds appeared; in the Middle Oligocene the earliest *Buteo* hawks, the earliest petrel and lapwing; in the Upper Oligocene an extinct family – Palaeospiza, between larks and swallows.

Down: Palaeoborus, Old World *vulture;* Dendrochen, *tree duck;* Strix* dakota, *owl;* Megapaloelodus, *pre-flamingo;* Ortalis* pollicaris, *chachalaca;* Anas* integra, *between wigeon and teal;* Tympanuchus* stirtoni, *a prairie chicken. Asterisks, modern genera*

Miocene

During the Miocene, from 25 to 11 million years ago, the Alps and Himalayas were built; and it was warm.

About 250 Miocene birds are now known, 37 per cent belonging to modern genera. Families first known from the Lower Miocene are pelicans; Palaelodids, near flamingos; Paranyroca, duck-like; plover-like Rhegminornis; oystercatchers, thick-knees, pigeons, parrots and wagtails: from the Middle Miocene Pelagornis, close to gannets; Palaeoscinis, like dipper or wren; and crows: from the Upper Miocene storm petrels.

Pliocene

From 11 to 2 million years ago mountain building died down, and the planet's surface stabilized. The Pliocene was cooler than the Miocene, warmer than the present; its temperate zone extended far toward the poles.

We show an early Pliocene fauna here from Florida, which then enjoyed a desert rocky coast like that of modern Perú. The species were first described by our colleague Professor Pierce Brodkorb. More than 120 fossil birds are Pliocene, and no less than 71 per cent of them belong to modern genera. Indeed, about 14 Pliocene species still live – the oldest probably the sandhill crane, known from early Pliocene deposits in Nebraska.

Brodkorb's Bone Valley birds include (downwards): Australca, probably direct ancestor of great auk; Wetmore's cormorant; guano booby; Elmore's gull, perhaps ancestor of ring-billed gull; Bone Valley goldeneye; Florida flamingo; a species of godwit. These forms are now extinct

Bone Valley phosphates show that in the Lower Pliocene Florida's coast had limestone cliffs and big sea bird colonies producing rich guano deposits

Pleistocene

Something unusual happened to our planet about two million years ago: it went into an Ice Age.

Geologists have been able to trace about a dozen glaciations during the Pleistocene Period, at irregular intervals, during which ice caps expanded from the polar regions. Four were severe; and the last one ended around ten thousand years ago.

The Ice Ages had a profound effect on plants and animals, reducing the number of their species. Bird species probably survived an average of a million and a half years at the end of the Pliocene, before they died out. By the end of the Pleistocene their life expectation was only about 40 thousand years, and the teratorn family (the largest flying birds of prey) and the Phororhacoid superfamily (the last of the flightless birds of prey) had become extinct. The vast elephant birds, tall moas and squat dodos followed them in historical times.

Nevertheless there was still a rich avifauna in some areas at the end of the Pleistocene. In California the great fossil fauna at Rancho la Brea had an amazing community of giant mammals; and many of the fraction of its birds that has now become extinct were giants too.

Inset left: Titanis walleri, late Pleistocene bird lately discovered in Florida by Brodkorb; first evidence of Phororhacoid superfamily outside S. America, and of Phororhacid family after Middle Pliocene

Extinct animals trapped in Pleistocene asphalt of Rancho la Brea 14 or 15 thousand years ago include (downwards): imperial mammoth; great condor; Brea caracara; asphalt stork; Brea turkey; Brea blackbird

Teratorn descends on remains of superbison, is trapped in Brea tarpit

CHAPTER IV

Birds on the Tree of Life

Evolution

There is no fossil fauna in the world so great as that of the asphalt tarpits of Rancho la Brea. For years at the time of the last glaciation (which did not cover that part of California) thousands of animals got trapped, embedded and fossilized in bubbling pitch pools. One of the pits has been carbon-dated at 14,500 years.

The Brea fauna lived in a warm climate rather drier than the California coast of today, among plains of grass and chaparral with thickets of live oak, cypress and pine. Some of its extinct animals were very big: huge ground sloths, a giant short-faced bear, a mastodon, two vast mammoths, a tall supercamel, a superbison over 7 feet at the hump, the dire wolf and several great cats. Most of its small mammals and birds still live today. Among the birds, too, were giants; the ancestor of the California condor, a huge teratorn, the tall (4 ft. 5 in.) asphalt stork. Over 120 birds are known from the late Pleistocene of California, and most of the 22 extinct species among them are represented by many, many bones from which complete skeletons have been reconstructed.

As we will see, there are many ways in which the evolution and relationships of birds can be studied and deduced. The basic study is, of course, anatomy; from the arrangement of organs, the patterns of feathers, the insertions of muscles, the modifications of bones,

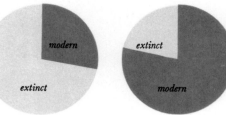

27% Blancan	78% Illinoian	85% Late Wisconsin
Idaho, Kansas, Arizona	Florida	Florida, California
about 2,000,000 years	184,000 years	14-25,000 years

Above: red areas show the percentage of modern bird species found in 3 Pleistocene faunas. The approximate ages of these faunas are indicated

anatomists can uncover similarities and differences which enable them to erect families, to gather families in appropriate superfamilies, suborders and orders. Fossil bones show the taxonomists, who strive for a classification based on true evolutionary relationships, the branches of the family tree that are buried in the past. About 9,517 described bird species can be recognized (p. 241): of these 854 (9%) are known only as fossils. Of the 200 bird families known by 1962 a fifth are fossil only.

Since the first fossil bird was named in 1838, the list of them has grown at a rather steady rate. But bird fossil work in Africa, Asia and even Europe has been lately neglected: a pity, since fossils are strong tools for reconstructing the true family tree. Tentative though the chart on the following pages is, it could not have been attempted without the work of the paleontologists.

Much remains to be solved by some new comparison in the dissecting room or by a lucky fossil find. The relationship of the birds of prey is a case in point. We can guess that the most primitive living day-flying birds of prey are the Cathartids – the so-called New World

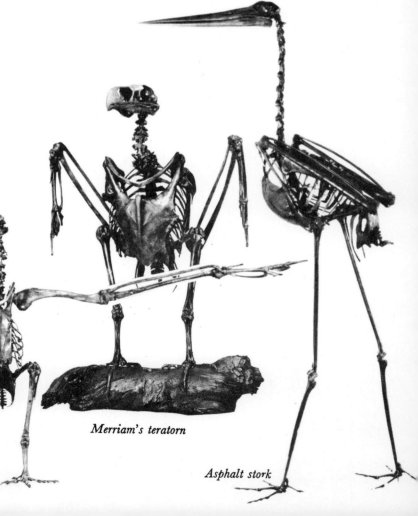

Great condor

Brea turkey

Brea caracara

Merriam's teratorn

Asphalt stork

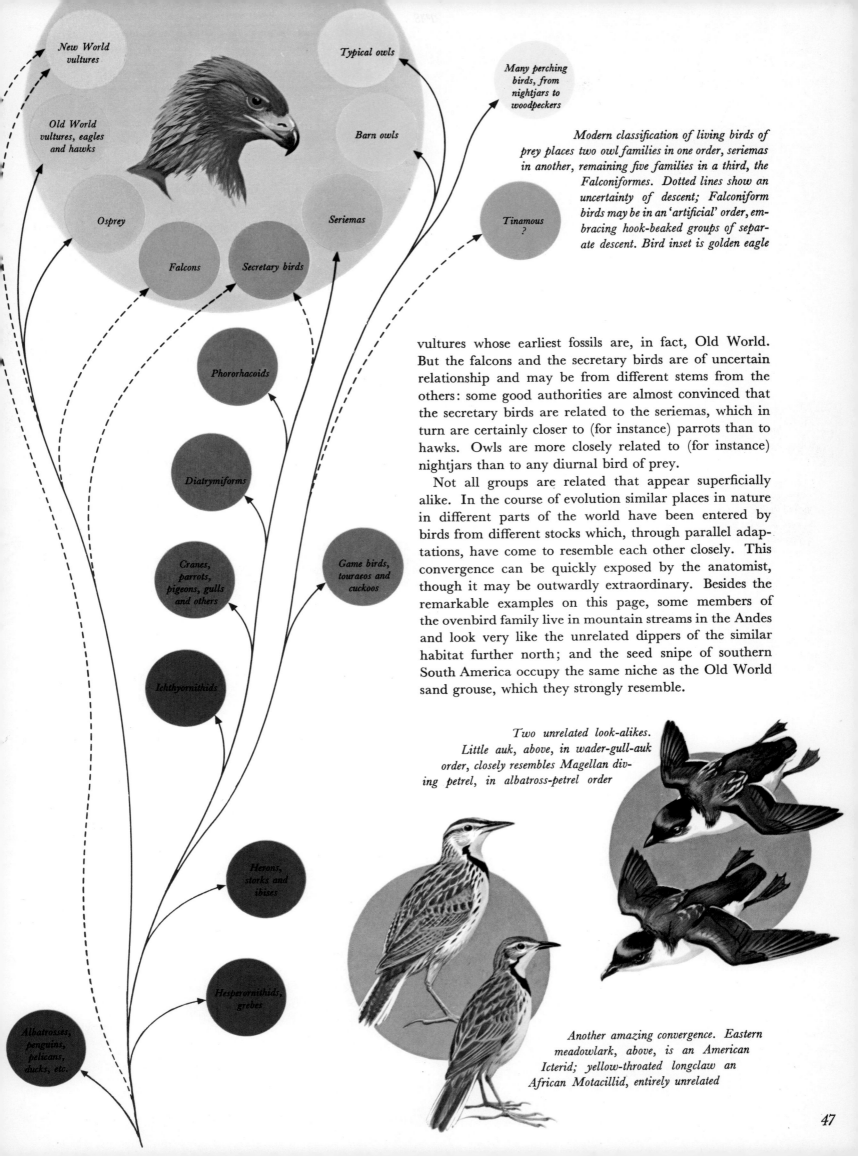

New World vultures

Old World vultures, eagles and hawks

Osprey

Falcons

Secretary birds

Typical owls

Barn owls

Seriemas

Many perching birds, from nightjars to woodpeckers

Tinamous ?

Modern classification of living birds of prey places two owl families in one order, seriemas in another, remaining five families in a third, the Falconiformes. Dotted lines show an uncertainty of descent; Falconiform birds may be in an 'artificial' order, embracing hook-beaked groups of separate descent. Bird inset is golden eagle

Phororhacoids

Diatrymiforms

Cranes, parrots, pigeons, gulls and others

Game birds, touraeos and cuckoos

Ichthyornithids

Herons, storks and ibises

Hesperornithids, grebes

Albatrosses, penguins, pelicans, ducks, etc.

vultures whose earliest fossils are, in fact, Old World. But the falcons and the secretary birds are of uncertain relationship and may be from different stems from the others: some good authorities are almost convinced that the secretary birds are related to the seriemas, which in turn are certainly closer to (for instance) parrots than to hawks. Owls are more closely related to (for instance) nightjars than to any diurnal bird of prey.

Not all groups are related that appear superficially alike. In the course of evolution similar places in nature in different parts of the world have been entered by birds from different stocks which, through parallel adaptations, have come to resemble each other closely. This convergence can be quickly exposed by the anatomist, though it may be outwardly extraordinary. Besides the remarkable examples on this page, some members of the ovenbird family live in mountain streams in the Andes and look very like the unrelated dippers of the similar habitat further north; and the seed snipe of southern South America occupy the same niche as the Old World sand grouse, which they strongly resemble.

Two unrelated look-alikes. Little auk, above, in wader-gull-auk order, closely resembles Magellan diving petrel, in albatross-petrel order

Another amazing convergence. Eastern meadowlark, above, is an American Icterid; yellow-throated longclaw an African Motacillid, entirely unrelated

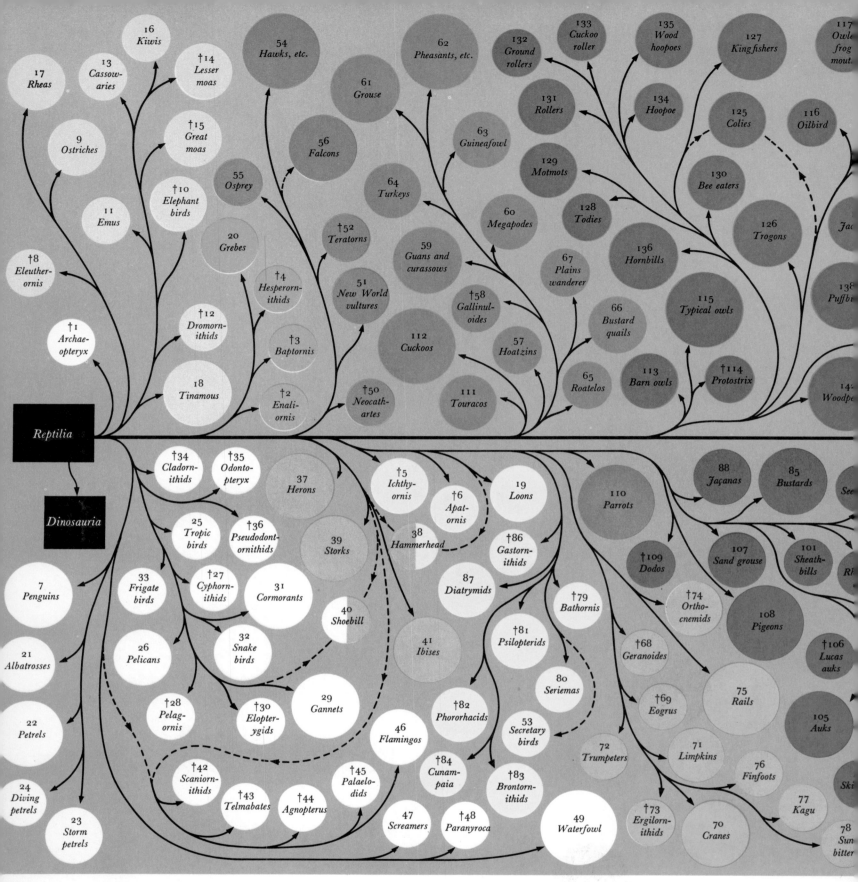

The family tree

The diagram on these pages is a very tentative sketch of what the family tree of the birds may be like.

In our regiment of birds (Chapter VIII, pp. 144–241) we have numbered every family, fossil (†) and living, from 1 to 199; and have given a, b, etc., 'numbers' to the subfamilies of the two largest families – the Muscicapidae which has nearly 1,400 species, including the thrushes and Old World warblers and flycatchers, and the Emberizidae which has well over 500, including the buntings and American sparrows, cardinals and tanagers. Here we plot these families and subfamilies in circles corresponding to their present size, represented as flowers or fruits upon a tree of life intended to show what is now suspected of their true relationship and descent. The colors of the circles have been selected simply as an aid to picking out the branches of the tree.

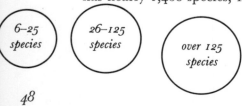

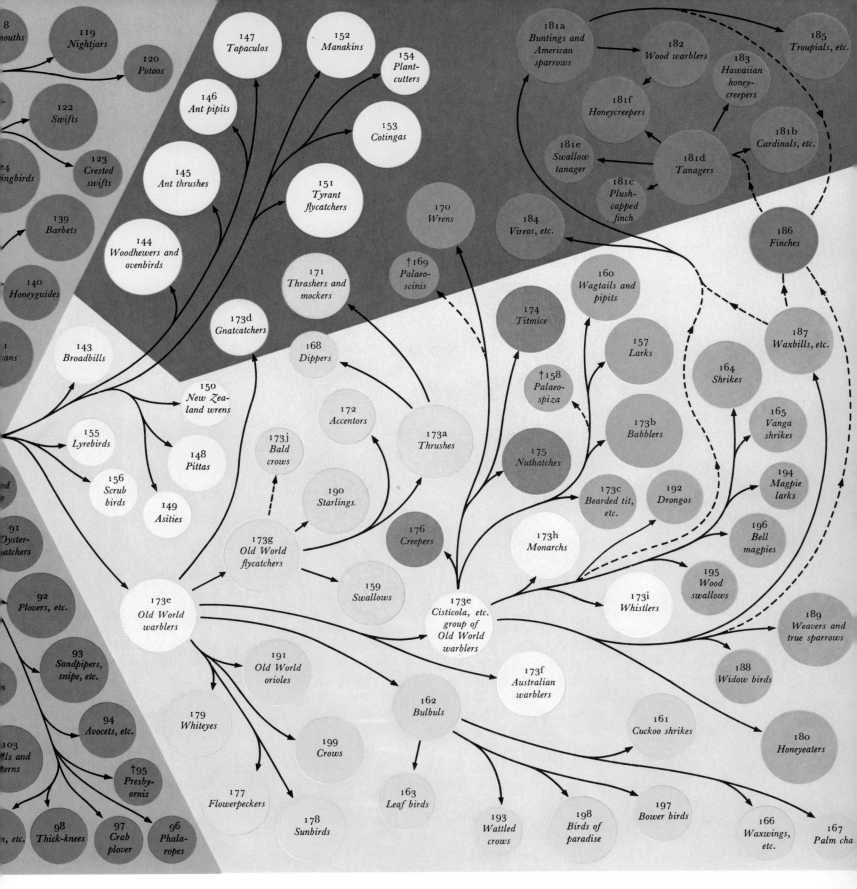

Among the giant order of the Passeriformes we have placed on light gray and brown the families or subfamilies which have probably undergone their main evolution in the Old and New Worlds respectively.

In compiling this diagram we have taken much advice and have read hundreds of papers on fossil and living anatomy, on physiology and behavior. The final judgment is ours, and it may look foolish already or quite soon; for new work is published every year. For instance, since this diagram was made, new work finds †2 (and a new fossil family) near 19, †8 near †86 and †87, and two new fossil families close to †41 and †42. The branches that are dotted, some shown as alternatives, represent relationships that are quite uncertain. Every part is based on the ideas of one or more workers whom we respect: but we doubt whether any would agree with all of it.

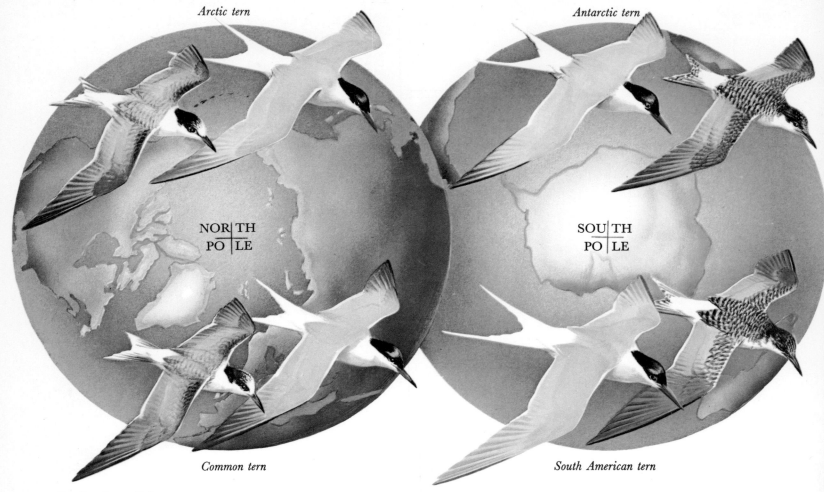

Arctic tern

Antarctic tern

NORTH POLE

SOUTH POLE

Common tern

South American tern

Relationship

The hunt for relationship clues is a never-ending pursuit. The examples here are chosen from a host of researches devoted to the solution of knotty points by methods other than pure anatomy.

A novel biochemical investigation depends upon the apparent fact that no two species of birds have the same molecular protein structure. Proteins when compared show degrees of difference which may indicate distance of relationship. Thus Professor Charles Sibley has shown that on egg-white proteins Old and New World vultures and eagles are close, but not close to falcons (see p. 47); that penguins are near petrels, the gulls, plovers and auks all close, the Pelecaniform order has well-related families.

On Sibley's results it seems that the flamingos have proteins similar to those of storks and herons and unlike those of ducks and geese. But the question remains vexed, for in behavior flamingos resemble geese in many ways: and their parasites are far closer to those of anatids than storks. Flamingos, Miss Theresa Clay finds, share three feather louse genera with anatids (not found on any other

order), only one with storks and herons (found also on four other orders); storks and ducks share only one.

Within the family much can be understood about evolution by watching behavior. For instance, Dr. and Mrs. Nicholas Collias have shown a graded evolution of nest constructions in the weaver bird family from simple cups to the huge colonial nests of the South African sociable weaver and to the delicate spheres and latticed snake-proof funnels of the tree-nesting malimbes.

Another good example is the case of the wood thrush. This is the type species of a genus, *Hylocichla*, which for years has been used to embrace the other spotted thrushes of North America – hermit, Swainson's, gray-cheeked, veery. Certainly the wood thrush *looks* more like these than the American robin. But the American robin's big genus, *Turdus*, also includes many spotted thrushes in other parts of the world. Dr. William C. Dilger has found that in most display behavior traits the wood thrush has a *Turdus* style, the other spotted thrushes not. Based on Dr. Dilger's own fine drawings, hostile postures of medium intensity are shown here. The wood thrush's

American robin   Wood thrush   Hermit thrush   Veery

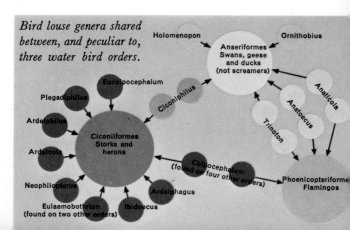

Bird louse genera shared between, and peculiar to, three water bird orders.

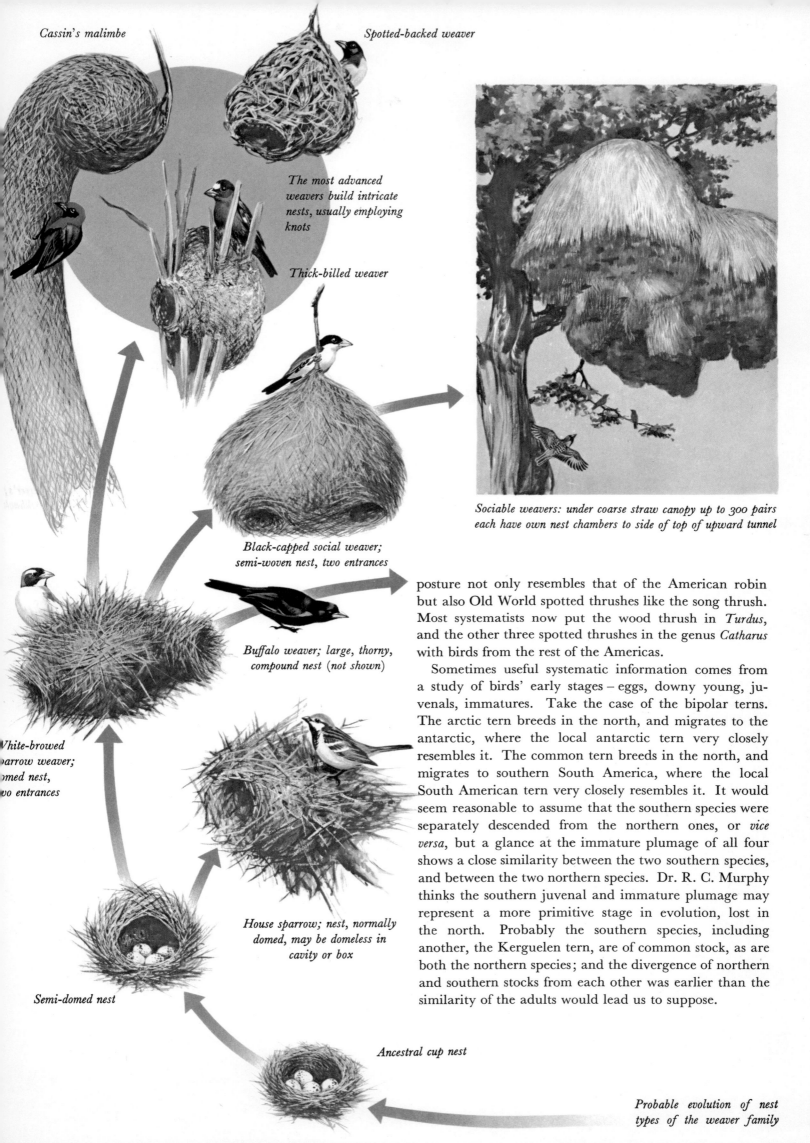

Cassin's malimbe

Spotted-backed weaver

The most advanced
weavers build intricate
nests, usually employing
knots

Thick-billed weaver

Sociable weavers: under coarse straw canopy up to 300 pairs
each have own nest chambers to side of top of upward tunnel

Black-capped social weaver;
semi-woven nest, two entrances

Buffalo weaver; large, thorny,
compound nest (not shown)

White-browed
sparrow weaver;
domed nest,
two entrances

House sparrow; nest, normally
domed, may be domeless in
cavity or box

Semi-domed nest

Ancestral cup nest

Probable evolution of nest
types of the weaver family

posture not only resembles that of the American robin
but also Old World spotted thrushes like the song thrush.
Most systematists now put the wood thrush in *Turdus*,
and the other three spotted thrushes in the genus *Catharus*
with birds from the rest of the Americas.

Sometimes useful systematic information comes from
a study of birds' early stages – eggs, downy young, juvenals, immatures. Take the case of the bipolar terns.
The arctic tern breeds in the north, and migrates to the
antarctic, where the local antarctic tern very closely
resembles it. The common tern breeds in the north, and
migrates to southern South America, where the local
South American tern very closely resembles it. It would
seem reasonable to assume that the southern species were
separately descended from the northern ones, or *vice
versa*, but a glance at the immature plumage of all four
shows a close similarity between the two southern species,
and between the two northern species. Dr. R. C. Murphy
thinks the southern juvenal and immature plumage may
represent a more primitive stage in evolution, lost in
the north. Probably the southern species, including
another, the Kerguelen tern, are of common stock, as are
both the northern species; and the divergence of northern
and southern stocks from each other was earlier than the
similarity of the adults would lead us to suppose.

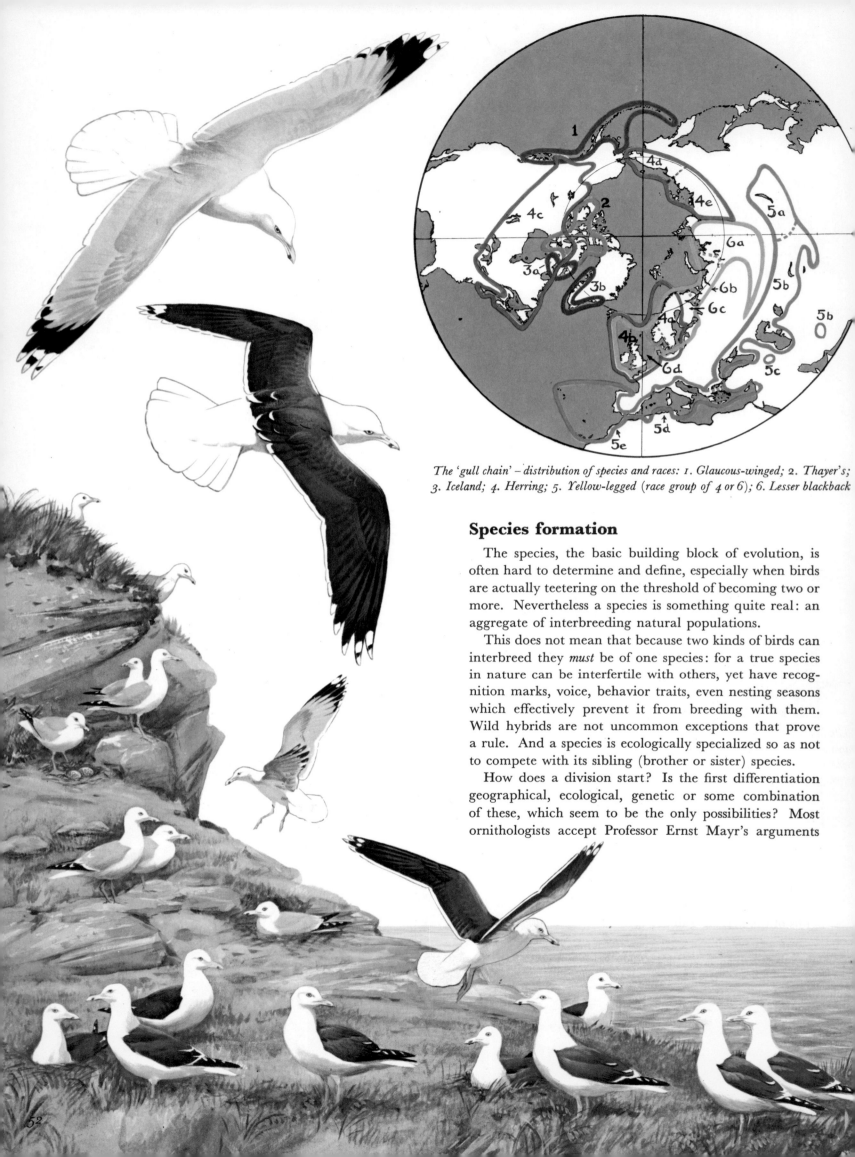

The 'gull chain' – distribution of species and races: 1. Glaucous-winged; 2. Thayer's; 3. Iceland; 4. Herring; 5. Yellow-legged (race group of 4 or 6); 6. Lesser blackback

Species formation

The species, the basic building block of evolution, is often hard to determine and define, especially when birds are actually teetering on the threshold of becoming two or more. Nevertheless a species is something quite real: an aggregate of interbreeding natural populations.

This does not mean that because two kinds of birds can interbreed they *must* be of one species: for a true species in nature can be interfertile with others, yet have recognition marks, voice, behavior traits, even nesting seasons which effectively prevent it from breeding with them. Wild hybrids are not uncommon exceptions that prove a rule. And a species is ecologically specialized so as not to compete with its sibling (brother or sister) species.

How does a division start? Is the first differentiation geographical, ecological, genetic or some combination of these, which seem to be the only possibilities? Most ornithologists accept Professor Ernst Mayr's arguments

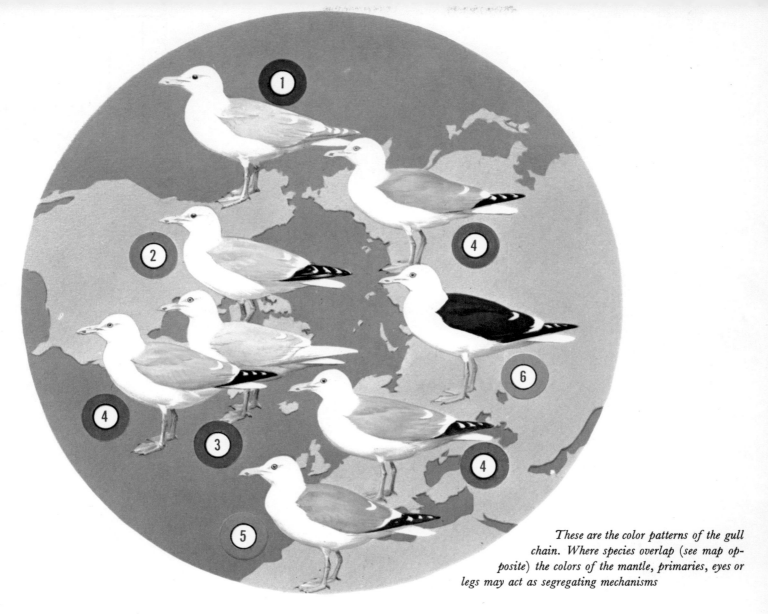

These are the color patterns of the gull chain. Where species overlap (see map opposite) the colors of the mantle, primaries, eyes or legs may act as segregating mechanisms

for a purely geographical origin of species. Bird species, in fact, are descended from subspecies or geographical races; and all have gone through a period in which they have been, as a race, isolated. In this isolation they have evolved separately in different environments, and after some success have often overlapped their sibling's ranges, and thus encountered a natural testing-time. The test is whether reproductively and ecologically the siblings are different enough. The mechanisms which can ensure reproductive and ecological isolation come into play. If they work, the differentiating traits will be improved by natural selection and the siblings will stabilize as two good species, breeding with their own kind, eating different foods and behaving in other separate ways. If they do not, there will be a period of much hybridization and variation until a single species stabilizes again.

Nature provides us with tests under our very eyes. The gulls of the herring gull group were probably represented by one species at the end of the Ice Ages, 10 to 15 thousand years ago. Since then five full sibling species have evolved, some so new and close to the threshold that several expeditions have gone to find out whether the isolation mechanisms were working: they are. The maps on this page incorporate the latest key work in the Canadian Arctic.

What evidently has happened is that the herring gull ancestor spread both west and east from the Bering Sea. In both directions the birds colonized new areas fast, and in various zones stabilized as races. Some of the successful races spread again. Overlap ensued: the most spectacular is that of the herring gull, which spread east across the Atlantic from North America with its light mantle, and the dark mantled lesser blackback, which spread west in Europe from Siberia. End-members of the same race chain, the two in n.-w. Europe behave as (and are) different species, with good color and food differences, slightly different size, different voice, nesting preferences and migratory habits. Hybrids are very rare.

The only outstanding difficulty is whether to regard the yellow-legged, light mantled birds of the Mediterranean and southern Russia as a race chain of herring gulls or of lesser blackbacks. They have by some been put in *Larus fuscus*, though they do not have black backs.

The other overlaps have taken much more sorting out, and indeed Thayer's gull has been restored to a full species as recently as 1961, when it was finally proved that it, a race of the Iceland gull and a race of the herring gull were sympatric; that is, shared a (small) breeding range in which they behaved as full species.

Welsh island of Skomer lies in overlap area of herring gull and lesser blackback. Nest sites differ ecologically: former favors rocky cliff edge, latter flat plateau

The scientific names of the species and races of the *Larus* chain on these pages are 1. *Larus glaucescens*; 2. *L. thayeri*; 3. *L. glaucoides*, races a. *kumlieni*, b. *glaucoides*; 4. *L. argentatus*, *argentatus* race group, a. *omissus*, b. *argentatus*, c. *smithsonianus*, d. *vegae*, e. *birulai*; 5. *L. argentatus* (or *L. fuscus*), *cachinnans* race group, a. *mongolicus*, b. *cachinnans*, c. *armenicus*, d. *michahelles*, e. *atlantis*; 6. *L. fuscus*, races a. *heuglini*, b. *antelius*, c. *fuscus*, d. *graellsii*

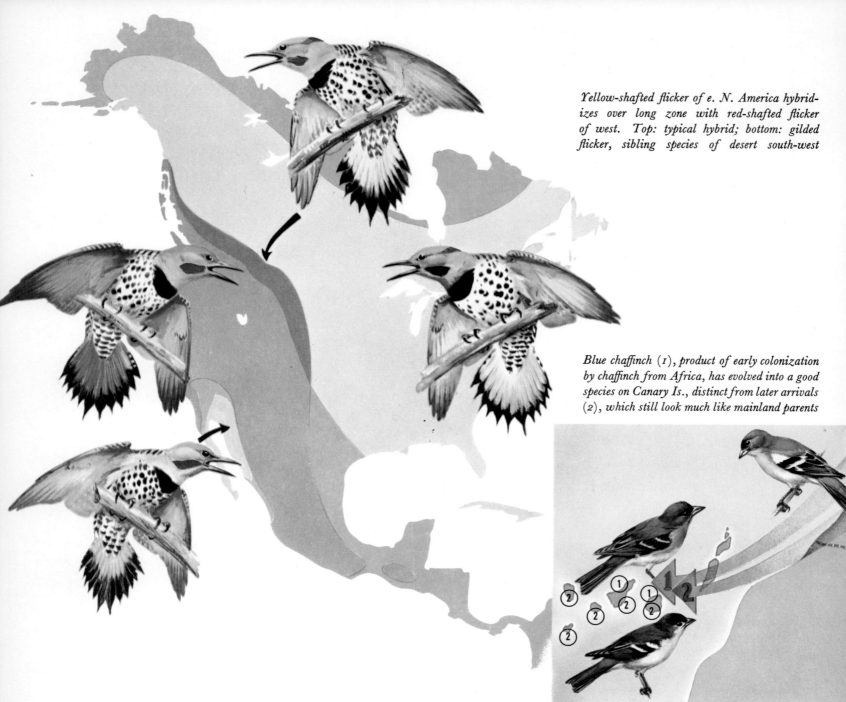

Most standard books regard the yellow-shafted flicker of northern and eastern North America, and the red-shafted flicker of the west, as different species. Certainly the red-shafted flicker with its red wing- and tail-linings, brown crown and red (not black) cheek flash looks *very* different from the eastern bird: though the differences may depend only on a few hereditary characters.

There is reason, nevertheless, to regard these flickers as very well marked races. Clearly they must have evolved their separate ways in isolation; and equally clearly spread and met later. Now on a broad front their overlap zone runs for nearly two thousand miles along the edge of the Great Plains. Within it they hybridize: a typical hybrid looks like a yellow-shaft with a red cheek-flash. The hybrid zone has been of the same general extent for a couple of human generations; it is fairly stable, and though it is big the hereditary units (or genes) that control the recognition characters of the two species do not seem often to penetrate beyond it.

Here then is a case where the formation of species is not quite complete. We have caught it in the act. Interestingly, in the south-west the boundaries between the red-shaft and a very close sibling species, the gilded flicker, are stable. The gilded, to look at, is nearly a red-shaft with yellow-shaft linings; occasionally it has a red-lined form but this is not certain evidence of hybridization. It must be regarded as a good species.

In Europe there is a broad hybrid zone between the hooded and carrion crows, now generally regarded as races, not species, and others among tits, nuthatches and buntings: and such zones have been also found in Asia and Australasia. Many are rather mysteriously stable.

Many fairly remote islands, and some isolated mountains, have earned their bird fauna not by gradual but by sudden colonization, often as a consequence of winds and storms. A small population arrives by chance that can

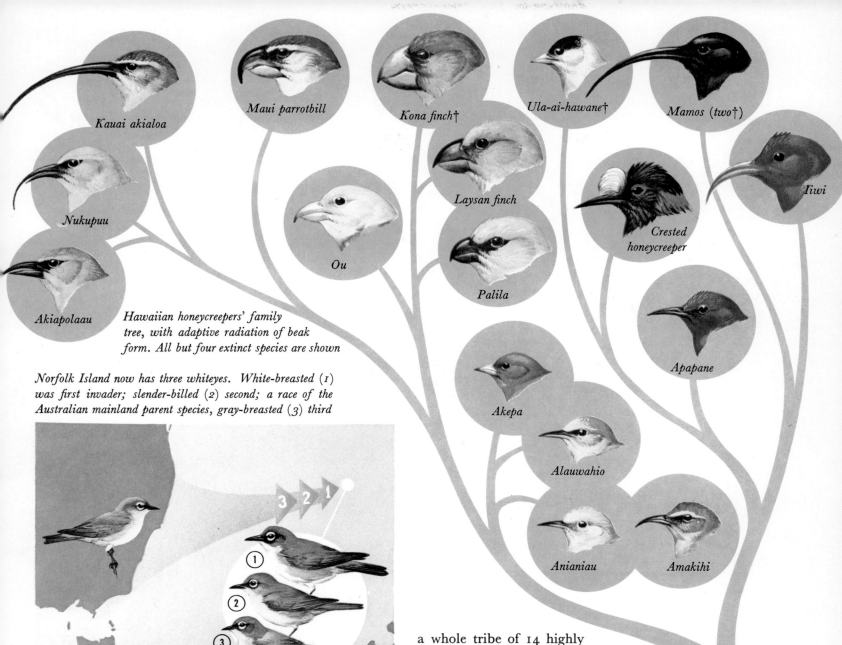

Kauai akialoa

Maui parrotbill

Kona finch†

Ula-ai-hawane†

Mamos (two†)

Nukupuu

Ou

Laysan finch

Crested honeycreeper

Iiwi

Akiapolaau

Palila

Apapane

Hawaiian honeycreepers' family tree, with adaptive radiation of beak form. All but four extinct species are shown

Akepa

Alauwahio

Anianiau

Amakihi

Norfolk Island now has three whiteyes. White-breasted (1) was first invader; slender-billed (2) second; a race of the Australian mainland parent species, gray-breasted (3) third

fit into an unoccupied niche. In isolation it may quite quickly evolve into a form unlike that of its parent species: and if the parent species survives, a second invasion from it after a time may settle down with the first, and both will behave like (and indeed will be) good, separate species. Sibling pairs from double invasions are found in many places, including the Samoan, Hawaiian, Galápagos and Canary Islands; quite large islands such as Luzon in the Philippines, Celebes, Ceylon and Tasmania; mountains like Borneo's Kina Balu and several in Africa. Norfolk Island even has a sibling trio.

The island colonists we have discussed and figured here show evolution at species level. Now island invasion may lead to higher evolution: for a whole, remote archipelago can be early colonized by an original stock which has time to evolve further and radiate into more niches than one or two. In the Galápagos and Cocos Islands

a whole tribe of 14 highly differentiated species may be descended from a single bunting-like ancestor: Darwin, who first studied them, realized something of the sort years before he published his *Origin of Species*. The best example is in the Hawaiian Archipelago. At an unknown time these remote islands were colonized across thousands of miles of sea, by bunting-, tanager-, honeycreeper-, or finch-like American birds. The invaders gave rise to a whole special family, the Drepanididae, of which eight are now extinct and 14 survive. Apart from many introduced birds, their most important competitors are thrushes, warblers and honey-eaters that have colonized Hawaii from the west.

The Hawaiian honeycreepers have had a remarkable adaptive radiation, forming species in at least a dozen major niches; though the most specialized have tended to be most prone to extinction. They have evolved into nectar-sipping, probing, seed-eating, nutcracking and even parrot-bill forms. One, the rare akiapolaau, has a strong straight lower mandible used for pecking wood; its curved upper mandible is used for digging; and it occupies a woodpecker niche.

Extinct birds

1. *Laysan rail, extinct (†)*
   Midway I. 1944

2. *Carolina parakeet,*
   † in captivity 1914

3. *Leguat's starling,*
   † Rodriguez I. c. 1832

4. *Passenger pigeon,*
   † in captivity 1914

5. *Cuban red macaw, † c. 1885*

6. *Seychelles Island owl,*
   believed † 1906, returned
   from the dead 1959

7. *Hawaii oo, † c. 1934*

8. *Mamo, † Hawaii 1898*

9. *Crested Choiseul pigeon,*
   † Choiseul 1904

10. *Huia, † North Island,*
    New Zealand c. 1907

11. *Tahitian sandpiper, † 1777*

12. *Dodo, † Mauritius c. 1681*

13. *Crested shelduck,*
    † Korea c. 1943

14. *Labrador duck, † Long*
    Island, New York 1875

15. *Great auk, † Eldey,*
    Iceland 1844

16. *Riu Kiu Island kingfisher,*
    † 1887

CHAPTER V

The Distribution of Birds

Extinct and rare birds

All but one of the birds pictured on this page are almost certainly as dead as the dodo. No dodo was seen on Mauritius by anybody after 1681; and since then 75 other full species of birds have in all probability died out.

Of our seventy-six dodos and others about thirteen were done in by human hunting for food. About eleven were extinguished by predation or possibly competition of cats, rats and other animals introduced into their living space. Another fourteen (or so) can be proved to have died out after the direct destruction, by draining, tree-felling, fire and agriculture, of their natural habitat.

Some of the others probably died out naturally; but others of these, even, may (as in Hawaii, where fourteen have become extinct) have been driven to rarity and extinction by the competition of better-adapted species introduced into their habitat from elsewhere.

The last bird provedly to become extinct was the Wake Island rail, which was undoubtedly wiped out by the Japanese garrison (probably for food) and has not been seen since 1945. The Laysan rail went in 1944.

Wild birds may have had an average expectation of survival as a species of about 40,000 years at the start of man's main civilizing mission around the world. Now it is only about 16,000 years.

One of the birds on the opposite page was long believed to be extinct but is not quite so: the Seychelles Island owl. Others thought gone have returned from the dead, most famous perhaps the flightless takahé rail of New Zealand, rediscovered in 1948. In Puerto Rico a nightjar known only from bones and an old skin was found again in 1961. Also rediscovered in 1961 was the noisy scrub bird of W. Australia, thought extinct since 1920.

Probably 12 of the 15 birds figured above have world populations under the 100 mark, as may about 22 others we could name. The rarest bird may be the ivory-billed woodpecker. Its race in the south-east U.S. may or may not survive; its Cuban race had but 12 or 13 in 1956. Over 80 rare birds are known from but one or a few specimens; their status is a mystery. More than 140 others all have a population of under 2,000.

To sum up, about 2 per cent of our planet's birds are very rare indeed. One per cent, or nearly so, may be naturally toward the end of life. One per cent, or rather more, may have man to thank for their parlous state. Conservationists seek to restore their fortunes, simply because, like Mount Everest, they are (still) *there*.

Nyctibiidae, potoos
Common potoo

Dulidae, palm chat

Todidae, todies
Puerto Rican tody

Steatorn⟨...⟩
oil bi⟨...⟩

Momotidae,
motmots
Turquoise-browed
motmot

Piqridae, manakins
Red-capped manakin

Galbulidae, j⟨...⟩
Great jacan⟨...⟩

Cotingidae, cotingas
Three-wattled bellbird

Cracidae, guans, etc.
Great curassow

Phytotomidae, plantcutters
Chilean plantcutter

Ramphastidae, toucans
Toco toucan

Great bird faunas: Neotropical

In 1858 the ornithologist P. L. Sclater classified the world's surface into zoogeographical regions, largely from the study of birds. Based on subsequent refinements, modern animal geographers now recognize six great zones of the earth, each of which contains a peculiar fauna or animal community – that is, one which differs markedly from the next. The present distribution of the great bird faunas is shown on page 62; through the age of birds their borders have moved quite a lot, and some still move (though slowly) in our own times.

The world's richest, strangest and most varied bird community is the Neotropical avifauna, which occupies the Americas from tropical México south, including the West Indies. About half the kinds of birds of the world breed in the community, or visit its zone in winter.

If we include five extinct families, no less than thirty of the 199 known families of birds are peculiarly Neotropical. Examples of all living ones are figured here. By 'peculiarly Neotropical' we mean families that do not normally range outside the present zone, though the guans, limpkin and cotingas just overlap the neighboring Holarctic (Nearctic) fauna. Besides all these, about a dozen other living families (like hummingbirds, tyrant flycatchers, icterids and the bunting-cardinal-tanager family) which have penetrated into the Holarctic and often beyond, must have had their place of origin, their theater of evolution, in the Neotropical.

The word 'Neotropical' was coined by Sclater, and though it strictly means 'New World tropical' embraces Tierra del Fuego and the Falkland Islands, and may

Opisthocomidae, hoatzin

Psophiidae, trumpeters
White-winged trumpeter

Aramidae, limpkin

Eurypygidae, sun bittern

Cariamidae, seriemas
Crested seriema

Anhimidae, screamers
Crested screamer

Rhinocryptidae, tapaculos
Gallito

Bucconidae, puffbirds
Swallow-winged puffbird

Rheidae, rheas
Darwin's rhea

Tinamidae, tinamous
Martinetta
tinamou

Furnariidae,
ovenbird subfamily
Hornero

even extend to distant Tristan da Cunha, whose land birds seem to be mostly of South American origin.

The blend zone between the Neotropical and Holarctic around the Rio Grande is but 200 miles wide: so on our first Méxican trip it took us half a day to move fully into the Neotropical region. In another world we both saw or heard our first wild parrots, potoos, cotingas, tinamous, guans, motmots, honeycreepers, woodcreepers, trogons and toucans. We both understood, for the first time, what it really meant to see a new fauna, how the word exotic (belonging to another country) has so much come to be used for animals and plants of unfamiliar and rich beauty; and why so many of the world's ornithologists have given the best years of their lives to work on the greatest galaxy of bird stars in the world.

Barred woodcreeper, Furnariidae, woodhewer subfamily.
Below, cinnamon-chested ant pipit, Conopophagidae;
r., white-bellied ant pitta, Formicariidae, ant thrushes

Thinocoridae, seed snipe
Small seed snipe

Other great bird faunas

Next in variety to the great Neotropical bird fauna,
the Ethiopian fauna occupies the south-west corner of
Arabia and Africa south of the Sahara. It is the theater
of evolution of many remarkable families; besides the
nine indigenous ones figured here, continental Africa
probably nourished the world's first bustards, pratincoles, sandgrouse, bee eaters and some other arid country
groups; probably also hornbills, bulbuls and weavers
and certainly honeyguides; maybe the first larks.

The island of Madagascar and its satellites has rightly
been considered to support a subfauna – for no less
than five of its living bird families are indigenous, and
in the quite recent past – in historic times – the great
elephant birds or Aepyornithids lived there and gave rise
to the legend of the Roc. On the curious neighboring
Mascarene islands the Raphids – the dodo and the two
solitaires – became extinct between 1681 and 1791.

The fauna of Australasia is nearly as rich as that of
the Ethiopian zone, with but one indigenous living family
fewer. New Zealand and its satellite islands, where the
two families of moas flourished until historical times, is

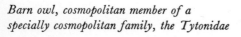

60

often regarded as supporting a subfauna, as also is the Antarctic and Subantarctic, probably the evolutionary home of the penguins, albatrosses and petrels, and of the peculiar sheathbill family. The honeyeaters, which have one outpost in South Africa, are clearly of Australasian origin, as are probably those world-wide colonists of the tropics, the parrots, and possibly the now cosmopolitan pigeons. Hawaii's natural avifauna is Australasian with some Holarctic elements and an indigenous family, the Hawaiian honeycreepers or Drepanididae, which is probably descended from birds from the Americas.

The Oriental fauna is rather less rich than that of Australasia. Probably owing to its central position in relation to two other great faunas it has but one indigenous family; but in it most if not all of the following families have evolved to colonize neighboring faunas: swallows, frogmouths, crested swifts, pittas, wood swallows, whiteyes and flowerpeckers.

The fauna upon which the majority of the world's ornithologists have learned their business is the least rich in the world: the Holarctic fauna, which occupies roughly the temperate and arctic northern world. It divides well,

at the Bering Sea and through the middle of Greenland, into a northern Old World (Palearctic) subfauna and a northern New World (Nearctic) subfauna. Of its five indigenous families the auks probably originated in the Bering Sea, the phalaropes, grouse and loons in North America, the accentors in Eurasia. Families of probable Holarctic origin that have spread into other faunas are many. The pheasants, cranes, owls, barn owls, Old World flycatchers, shrikes, true finches, tits, creepers, nuthatches and crows may have come from the Palearctic; the New World vultures, turkeys, waxwings and dippers from the Nearctic; the sandpipers, skuas and gulls from somewhere in the northern world.

We must reiterate that the present distribution of the world's great bird faunas, as depicted on the map on the following page, is different from what it was two million years ago, and very different from what it was at different times in the 140 million years of birds' life on earth. Throughout history not only the bird communities have shifted, but the lands themselves have changed; indeed the continents themselves, and the poles, have most probably drifted great distances. The evolutionary changes of the birds have taken place upon an earth crust that has also been evolving and changing. The modern student of the distribution of birds (or any other animals or plants) needs to know his geological geography – his physiography – as well as his ornithology.

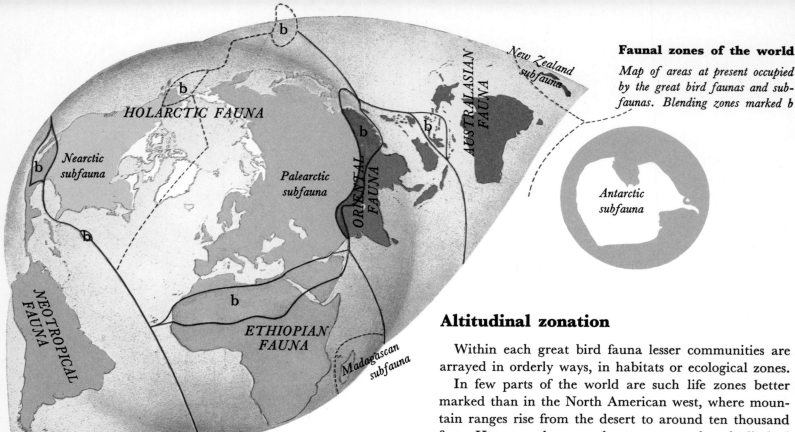

The faunal map

The blending zones in the map above are relatively small; outside them each great fauna has its own powerful individuality, its own special congregation of families and successful species.

The blending zones, indeed, are the exceptions that prove the rule that the distribution of birds over the world is always in a state of motion. Species and groups continually explore, or are driven by winds, beyond their boundaries, and often colonize. Elsewhere in this book (e.g. pp. 76–77) such colonizations are examined.

The blending zone between the Neotropical and Nearctic faunas is relatively small, and may be slowly moving north. Bermuda is shown in such a zone as it is primarily Nearctic with a small Neotropical element: Tristan da Cunha and Gough Island are apparently mainly Neotropical with an Ethiopian element.

West Alaska is mainly Nearctic with a Palearctic element. The broad blend-zones between the Palearctic and its Ethiopian and Oriental neighbors are mostly desert areas, with elements of the more tropical faunas in a minority.

East of Wallace's Line, between Bali and Lombok, Borneo and Celebes, a number of Oriental birds have pushed into the Australasian fauna. Hawaii (p. 61) is a blend-zone with natural elements from three faunas.

Altitudinal zonation

Within each great bird fauna lesser communities are arrayed in orderly ways, in habitats or ecological zones.

In few parts of the world are such life zones better marked than in the North American west, where mountain ranges rise from the desert to around ten thousand feet. Here together one day we motored and climbed from a subtropical Méxican environment to that of Hudson's Bay – 2,000 horizontal miles in one vertical mile.

Roger Peterson has painted some of the birds we saw in each zone that are typical of it, and prefer it so much to adjacent zones that they seldom stray.

We started in the Lower Austral zone of the desert of Arizona. Around 3,000 feet we found a land of mesquite and chaparral, cholla and other full desert plants, with willow and cottonwoods in the river channels.

The Upper Austral zone, around 5,000 feet, had sycamore groves; hot canyon slopes with live oaks; yuccas, agaves and semidesert plants, each with its typical birds.

Next, around 7,500 feet in the Transition zone, Arizona pine ousted the live oaks and brought in new birds. In the Canadian zone at 8,200 feet, the forest had become more fir than pine, with moist open flowery glades.

Over 9,000 feet we were in yet another zone, the Hudsonian, dominated by the Engelmann spruce; and if we had made our climb further north, in California, we would have found an Arctic-alpine zone above that.

Life zones in the mountains of Arizona, and some birds typical of each

Black-throated gray warbler

Lucy's warbler

White-winged dove

ARCTIC – ALPINE ZONE
Gray-crowned rosy finch

Clark's nutcracker

Above: further north high
Rocky Mountains bring
in yet other birds
and one more zone

HUDSONIAN ZONE
Golden-crowned kinglet

CANADIAN ZONE

Evening grosbeak   Red crossbill   Mexican chickadee

TRANSITION ZONE

Pigmy nuthatch   Western bluebird   Broad-tailed hummingbird   Coues's flycatcher   Red-faced warbler

UPPER AUSTRAL ZONE

Scott's oriole   Cassin's kingbird   Mexican jay   Acorn woodpecker   Virginia's warbler

LOWER AUSTRAL ZONE

w-breasted
chat

Black-chinned
hummingbird

Black phoebe

Cactus wren

Vermilion flycatcher

63

Tropical forest zonation

For his great study, *The Birds of the Belgian Congo*, Dr. James P. Chapin worked in the heartland of tropical Africa for many years, following the game paths worn by elephants and buffalo in one of the most luxuriant virgin forests in the world. In a smallish area as many as 70 different species of great tree could be found. Upon their trunks orchids, ferns, mosses, liverworts and the beardy *Usnea* lichen grew profusely at all levels.

Dr. Chapin found that the birds of the Ituri Forest occupied three levels. A distinctive community lived on or near the ground: a different one lived around mid-tree level, 'keeping low down enough to be in dense shade': and a third group inhabited the tops of the trees. In the rest of the Upper Congo Forest, and in other tropical forests – in South America and Asia – we find much the same thing; though of course the *members* of the three communities are quite different.

Typical tree-top birds are the green pigeons; one of four is just alighting on an upper branch in search of fruit. Below it the gray-chinned sunbird feeds not only on flower-nectar but on red fruit and insects. Perched highest, the giant plantain eater (a touraco) is another fruit-bird, while the red-bellied malimbe under it is an insect-eating weaver. On the wing, a blue-breasted king-fisher snaps up flying termites. Another insect-eater, the golden-crowned woodpecker, hacks for larvae; and a male emerald cuckoo perches with a caterpillar in its beak. A small parrot, the black-collared lovebird, looks around for ripe figs. Two rare swifts – Chapin's spine-tails – are hunting winged ants; and above all soars that great bird, the crowned hawk eagle, seeking monkeys.

Many of the mid-level birds hunt in the shade in mixed parties; and all those shown here are insect-eaters. From left to right we meet the gray-breasted paradise flycatcher, which usually moves rather nervously along about 30 feet from the ground: the abundant buff-spotted wood-pecker which lives on little black ants that build earthy nests in the trees: the shining drongo, member of a bold flycatching family that seldom leaves the 20- to 30-foot zone of the primeval forest: a pair of Jameson's antpeckers – these waxbills continually seek ants and other insects among the leaves and have never been seen on the ground: the common West African nicator, a bulbul that special-izes in grasshoppers, katydids and the like: and the crested malimbe, a weaver fond of beetles and cicadas.

On the forest floor of tropical America we have en-countered diverse ant birds (p. 37) which follow army ants. Their African counterparts follow driver ants in the same way to eat them, or the insects these ants flush or leave part eaten. Four of the birds here live this life: the bulbul on the left – the green-tailed bristle-bill; the fire-crested ant chat next to it, which is a thrush; the white-tailed ant thrush on the ground; and the partridge-like forest francolins. The blue-headed wood doves are looking for seeds or slugs, and the hovering waxbill (the chestnut-breasted negro finch) for caterpillars.

Zonation of birds in Ituri Forest (Congo). Inset: not found in Ituri, but on floor of other forests of Upper Congo, is Congo peacock (pair), only peacock known in Africa, described by Dr. Chapin in 1936

Swainson's hawk
S. America to U.S., Canada

Barn swallow
Argentina to Canada

Chimney swift
Perú to U.S., Canada

Common crane
N. Africa to n. Europe

Common cuckoo
S. Africa to Europe

*Some champion long-distance travelers from various parts
of the world as they appear in spring migration*

The migrants

In the arctic the winter makes life impossible for all but a few very hardy and specialized birds; but the short summer is a time of snow-melt, quick plant-growth and insect life: food is comparatively abundant.

In temperate countries there is always more food in summer and autumn than in winter and spring.

In many parts of the tropics there are wet and dry seasons, usually with a special abundance of food after the wet season.

This seasonal change in the abundance of food governs the life of birds. Nearly all fit their breeding season to the greatest supply of food. But many just cannot survive in their breeding place at the hardest time of year.

Quite a number of animals, it is true, solve the winter problem by hibernation, by going into a long sleep, with lowered temperature and breathing rate and thus little loss of energy during the period of food-shortage. However, only one bird (so far) is known to hibernate truly – the poor-will of the North American West. One hibernating in a hollow in a rock in the desert had a temperature of only 66°F., and the temperature of others has been recorded as low as 56°F. The normal temperature of an active bird is about 108°F.

The poor-will is quite exceptional. Birds normally solve the seasonal food-supply problem in quite a different way: by migration. Nearly half the birds of the world – over 4,000 species – are animals with two addresses, a summer home and a winter home.

To understand the extent to which birds migrate let us consider an arctic country, a temperate Old World country, and a mostly tropical New World country.

Of the 64 species of birds regularly found in Greenland no less than 36 leave the great island entirely for the winter. Most of the remaining 28 migrate to south Greenland or to the seas off its shore. Perhaps only ptarmigan, black guillemot, snowy owl, fieldfare and raven are true residents, wintering near their nesting-places.

About 240 species of birds are regular in Britain and Ireland. About 55 (23%) are summer visitors only, 27 (11%) winter visitors only, 20 (8%) migrants that breed further north and winter further south and are seen only on passage. Many others migrate within the countries.

About 950 species of birds have been found in México. Of these about 750 (79%) are resident; the other 200 (21%) are winter visitors or passage-migrants.

Even in the tropics, then, a big minority of the bird community is migrant. Elsewhere the migrant species easily outnumber those resident.

Over 60% of all the families of birds have migrant members, and each of the 23 bird species in the illustrations here comes from a different one, and is what Abel Chapman once called a "globe-spanner".

*Penguins disperse far after breeding. Rockhopper swims
thousands of miles from base in ocean tours*

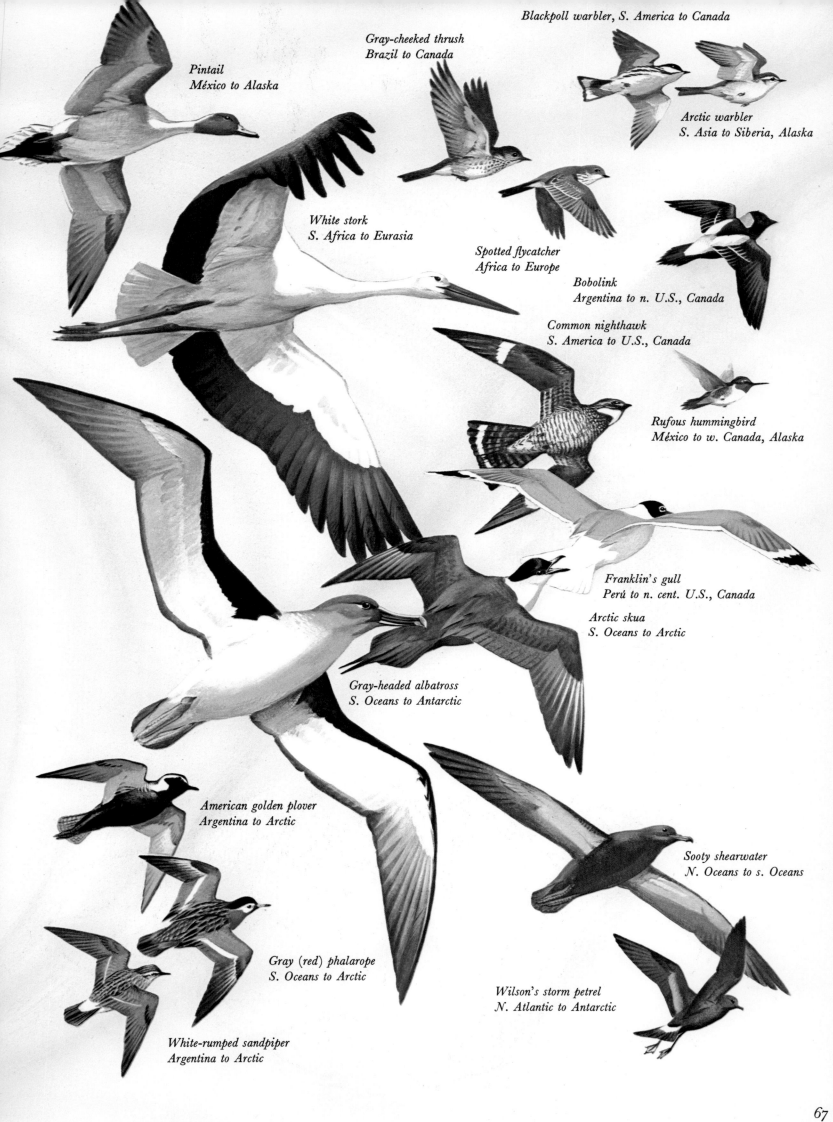

Pintail
México to Alaska

Gray-cheeked thrush
Brazil to Canada

Blackpoll warbler, S. America to Canada

Arctic warbler
S. Asia to Siberia, Alaska

White stork
S. Africa to Eurasia

Spotted flycatcher
Africa to Europe

Bobolink
Argentina to n. U.S., Canada

Common nighthawk
S. America to U.S., Canada

Rufous hummingbird
México to w. Canada, Alaska

Franklin's gull
Perú to n. cent. U.S., Canada

Arctic skua
S. Oceans to Arctic

Gray-headed albatross
S. Oceans to Antarctic

American golden plover
Argentina to Arctic

Sooty shearwater
N. Oceans to s. Oceans

Gray (red) phalarope
S. Oceans to Arctic

Wilson's storm petrel
N. Atlantic to Antarctic

White-rumped sandpiper
Argentina to Arctic

67

The habit of migration must be very old among the birds. Just how old we may, of course, never be able to judge; for it is not possible to tell whether an early fossil was a migrant just by looking at its skeleton.

We can, however, consider the relationships of the fossil. All the members of many modern genera of birds are very strongly migratory. We may safely assume that when these genera appeared for the first time they were then at least capable of long-distance movement.

Now fossils of modern genera first appear at the end of Eocene times. What may be a curlew, *Numenius*, is known from the Uppermost Eocene deposits of France, about 36 million years old. Birds from France at the threshold of Eocene and Oligocene (about 34 M.) include four modern genera, of which the eagle, *Aquila*, and sandgrouse, *Pterocles*, are good migrants.

Another good migrant, the buzzard genus *Buteo*, is first found in the Middle Oligocene of South Dakota (about 30 M.); and if we examine the swarm of modern genera in the Upper Oligocene of France (about 27 M.) we find many excellent migrants, such as shearwaters, geese, ducks, kites, waders, gulls, swifts, wagtails and Old World warblers.

Billions* of birds belonging to nearly half the world's species pour along the flyways of the world each fall, and rather fewer billions pour back each spring. Migration is often on a broad front, but more often by favored routes, along coasts, through mountain passes, along hill ridges where the prevailing winds give air-lift, over deserts where by day the hot air rises and saves the migrants' energy.

*We mean thousands of millions – not millions of millions, as the English mean by billions.

A small thrush, the wheatear, has three races. One nests in Morocco and Tunis; the most widespread nests from Alaska through Eurasia – and migrates (Alaskan birds included) to winter in Arabia and Africa.

The third race, the Greenland wheatear, is the largest, but only weighs around an ounce. It nests (red) in Greenland, Labrador and the eastern Canadian Arctic: and makes the longest regular ocean journey of any small bird; for it winters in south-west Europe and west Africa.

Probably the wheatear was once a bird only of the Old World, which spread into the two corners of the New World. The American birds have never lost their habit of migrating toward Africa in autumn.

From many ship observations it seems clear that in the fall the Greenland race normally makes a direct Atlantic crossing of 2,000 miles. Apart from prevailing winds, the birds depend only on their own power; before starting they store up fuel – much fat under skin and in liver. Against the winds, on the spring return, the Greenland wheatears 'island-hop' by Scotland – Faeroes – Iceland – Greenland

Some of the most important flyways of migrants across oceans and continents in September – northern fall, southern spring

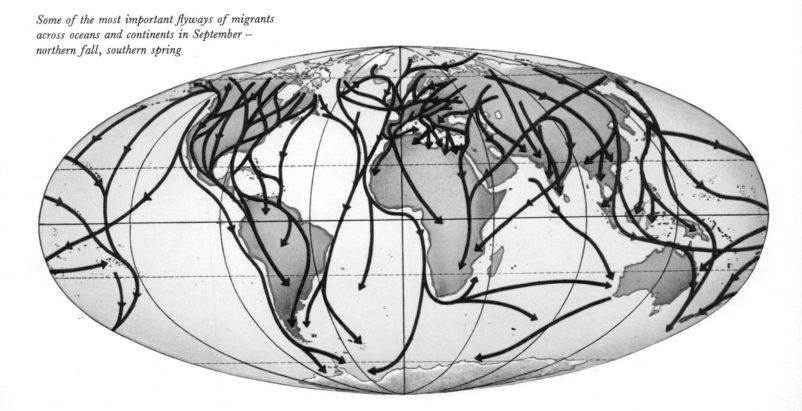

All this has been going on for tens or scores of millions of years. The cranes flew, and the swallows assembled in twittering bands long, long before there were any men to see them, let alone poets to sing of spring and fall, and ornithologists with binoculars and banding-stations to measure the great treks of the birds.

Great these treks are. Africa is a most hospitable winter home of migrants. Nearly a third of all the small birds that breed in Britain winter south of the Sahara desert. Nearly as many birds go to Africa from Central Asia as do from Europe. Some small land birds even go to Africa from the Far East; and the wheatear even reaches it from Alaska, 7,000 miles away.

Tiny birds like the arctic warbler and the yellow wagtail travel all the way from Alaska to tropical South-east Asia and back. Between North and South America, and Europe and South Africa, the barn swallow can fly at least 7,000 miles out, 7,000 back.

Greatest globe spanner in distance covered is the arctic tern. Breeders in the Arctic and N. Atlantic area winter at the edge of the frozen Antarctic Continent or on the shores of the Indian Ocean. One arctic tern was banded as a nestling in West Greenland on 8 July 1951. On 30 October of the same year it was picked up dead at Durban on the east coast of South Africa, having flown over eleven thousand miles in its first three months on the wing.

Another bird may travel further, though perhaps not regularly. A Manx shearwater from Wales has lately been found in S. Australia. This is the most distant recovery of any marked bird, about 12,000 miles by the nearest sea route.

Albatrosses make vast wandering journeys, though they usually keep within their own hemisphere. The Tristan great and the sooty shearwaters, which breed far down in the south, spend a non-breeding time slowly circling the North Atlantic five thousand miles and more from base in our northern summer; and the little Wilson's storm petrel does the same.

These last three birds are examples of southern hemisphere breeders that migrate to the north. They are sea birds. The main reason why so few land birds breed in the south and migrate north is simply space. If we exclude the Antarctic, where there are practically no land birds, there is five times as much land in the northern hemisphere as in the south; but just as big a share of the little birds of Patagonia moves north in winter as share of those in New England moves south. Only a few southern hemisphere land bird breeders are known to cross the equator to winter: but some of these birds travel at least a thousand miles.

Perhaps the most remarkable transocean passages by birds that do not normally swim are made in the Pacific. The regular ocean-hop between Alaska and the Hawaiian islands, flown by the western race of the American golden plover, exceeds 2,000 miles. The bristle-thighed curlew,

Atlantic flyways of the arctic tern, greatest of all migrants

which breeds only in Alaska, winters over Pacific Oceania from the Hawaiian Islands south and west. Some of the wandering tattlers from the American north-west have a similar winter range. The banded plover of New Zealand regularly crosses to Australia; and two New Zealand cuckoos, the shining and the long-tailed, regularly make the long ocean journey to New Caledonia, the Solomons and Polynesia.

Migration involves risks; yet it is worth the steady toll of bird lives lost by exhaustion and the perils of changed weather. It is the most remarkable adaptation that the most mobile of the world's animals have won. Millions of years of evolution by natural selection, on the basis of the muscled wing, have secured that no rock in the loneliest ocean, no oasis in the broadest desert, is unvisited by birds.

Typical day migrants of North America: 1. Chimney swift, winters to Perú; 2. Barn swallow, to Chile and Argentina, same species as Old World swallow; 3. American robin, to Guatemala; 4. American goldfinch, to México; 5. Blue jay, to southern United States; 6. Red-winged blackbird, to Costa Rica

Bird navigation

Over twenty years ago our friend R. M. Lockley sent two Manx shearwaters from their nesting burrows on Skokholm Island, in Wales, by air to Venice, where they were released at once. The Adriatic Sea is outside the range of the Welsh race of shearwater; the Alps intervened between the birds and home; yet one homed in 14 days. By sea the return journey was 3,700 miles; by land 930 only. Ten years later another Skokholm shearwater was released at Boston airport in Massachusetts – also outside its normal range. Its shortest Atlantic passage home was 3,200 miles; and it was back in its burrow in 12½ days.

Many other homing experiments have been made with results almost as spectacular. They prove that birds have

Each dot on chart shows 10 seconds of activity pointed to a bearing by a starling caged by Kramer at the time of westerly migration in Europe. L.: random movements in overcast; r.: directed movements with clear sky

wonderful homing ability, and must be prodigious navigators. All migrants are natural navigators. Most non-migrants are provable navigators, too.

Matthews in England, Kramer and Sauer in Germany, and many other experimenters in the last two decades, have shown us that while bird navigation is still mysterious, at least the mysteries are now probably limited.

Birds navigate by sight, with a built-in "chronometer" or innate time sense: and they use as guides by day the sun and by night the stars and doubtless the moon. That they can sense magnetic forces, or forces in their internal ears due to the earth's rotation, seems to have been effectively disproved. Birds do not learn the basic techniques of navigation. These are born with them; they are innate; though they are improved by experience.

The late Gustav Kramer and Geoffrey Matthews have positively established sun navigation among birds. Matthews has suggested that a bird can extrapolate the sun's movement, forward or back, to its highest point (the azimuth), and by time sense also get both latitude and longitude. With his ingenious planetarium experiments and other observations Sauer has gone far toward proving that birds are born with an innate knowledge of the constellations, and that the night-flying migrants use them normally, and naturally, and

North American night migrants: 1. Red-eyed vireo, winters to Perú; 2. Swainson's thrush, to Argentina; 3. White-crowned sparrow, to México, Cuba; 4. Black-throated green warbler, to Panamá, Greater Antilles; 5. Rose-breasted grosbeak, to Ecuador; 6. Great crested flycatcher, to Colombia

unconsciously in a style that Captain Cook could only attain with sextant and the newly invented chronometer.

Birds no doubt employ other techniques that experience may contribute more to than instinct. They learn the map of their neighborhood and, after they have lived a year or two, their flyways. They may exploit the set of sea-currents, use changes in temperature as guides, watch other birds of their own or other kinds, or other animals. What we can be quite certain of is that birds, without instruments, can often do better than humans with them. In overcast, though, when sun and stars are clouded out, the compass-less birds are much inferior to man. They stop migrating, if they can. Yet in complete darkness a very few birds *can* navigate.

In 1940 Donald R. Griffin and Robert Galambos made the first of their wonderful proofs that bats emit a succession of high-frequency clicks and can detect the echoes of these sounds from very small or moving objects with their ultra-sensitive ears. They find their

roost in the dark, and catch their insect prey by sonar.

By 1954 Griffin had proved that the oilbird – a relative of the nightjars that belongs to a family entirely of its own – also used sonar, at a considerably lower frequency than that of bats: indeed its chirps are well within the range of human hearing. Soon others had discovered sonar among other birds of dark caves – the edible-nest swiftlets of the Philippines and East Indies. Probably our typical swifts use sonar, possibly nightjars and nighthawks; though it is not yet proved.

Oscillograph records (adapted diagram) from tape recordings made by Griffin of oilbird flying out of cave. The 6 sonar clicks were uttered in a period of one fiftieth of a second

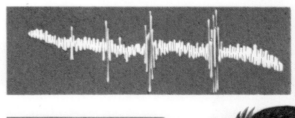

Studying night orientation in planetarium, observer in felt tent under cage watched bird's position as projector rotated artificial night sky. Solid line, sector visible to bird from right end of perch; broken line, from left. Adapted from Sauer

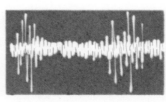

Population

It is half a century since J. H. Gurney realized that it was possible to count the world population of a bird. His bird was the northern gannet; and he believed that all the colonies of this bird were known, and that it was possible to count or estimate the number of nests at each. His own guess that about 55,000 gannets' nests were occupied in 1912 was probably not far short of the truth.

Since then quite a few birds have been world censused, usually by counting nests but sometimes by counting winter flocks. Aerial photography has been used on sea bird cliffs and the feeding grounds of grazing birds. And a principle, worked out by Dr. F. C. Lincoln in 1930, enables banders who catch and mark large numbers of some birds to arrive at estimates of total populations from the number of marked birds they recapture.

All the same, very few birds with large or even average populations have been censused. One of us organized,

during World War II, a census of the nests in every rookery in two-thirds of the area of England, Wales and Scotland. There were nearly a million nests, and to count and plot them about 400 volunteers thoroughly covered an average of 150 square miles each. The survey was spread over three years. To extend it throughout the rook's wide range in Europe and Asia would be a major, almost military operation.

It can thus be understood why the only birds with a population of over a million that have been fully censused are a few sea birds: it is usually much easier to find and estimate the numbers of a sea bird's nests than those of an equally numerous land bird. The most abundant bird that has been the subject of a really careful and repeated census is the northern gannet. There are now 29 colonies, and the total number of nests around 1959 was about 140,000. The Cape gannet of Africa, from a photographic survey, had about 225,000 nests in 1956, and the Australasian gannet about 23,000 in 1946–47.

Birds below are among over 40 whose world population has been recently estimated. Geese and crane have been counted in winter flocks, rest from nests occupied annually. Only one estimated living world population exceeds puffin's; arctic murre may number c. 42,000,000. Numbers of piquero and guanay, guano birds of Perú and Chile, fluctuate widely. Most royal albatrosses breed Campbell I., N. Z.; estimate includes adolescents, up to 8 years old

Atlantic puffin
15,000,000

Northern gannet
280,000

Tristan great shearwater
4–5,000,000

Sandhill crane
170,000

Piquero
4–?40,000,000

Guanay
5–30,000,000

Barnacle goose
30,000

Ross's goose
2–3,000

Royal albatross
19,000

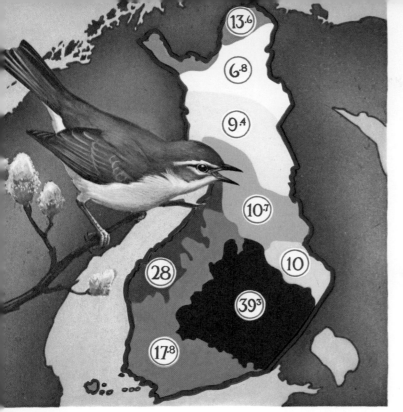

Density (pairs/sq.km.) of Finland's commonest bird, willow warbler

Starling, house sparrow: probably world's commonest wild birds after man-aided colonization

World's most numerous bird by far is fowl, domesticated 5,000 years

About 44 birds have had their population estimated with more or less certainty, 14 of them sea birds, and half of them rarities (p. 57) with numbers under 2,000. Some of the more exact censuses have been of birds with small numbers. One of the best was the census of Kirtland's warbler in 1949 and 1961. This bird nests only in 32 square miles of central Michigan and nowhere else in the world. A band of good field men found every singing male in the state in both seasons (432 and 502): the world population in the spring cannot be much over 1,000.

Early in the present century field workers in North America and England began to measure the density of spring breeding birds on sample areas of different kinds of land. What they did was plot all singing males, and find as many nests as they could, so as to arrive at figures for the number of territories of each species per unit area. This method has, through the years, been very much refined. Different habitats have been found to house very varying populations of land birds. Deserts, tundras, moors and certain kinds of conifer forest support less than one bird to the acre, most agricultural land between 2 and 4, most temperate deciduous or mixed woodland 4 or 5, gardens, orchards, parks and open suburbs anything between 6 and 20 (and in certain cases much more), tropical forests up to 20, some kinds of tropical grassland with bushy cover up to 40. More figures are cited on p. 112.

With suitable samples measured, and the national statistics on the total areas of each habitat to help them, ornithologists have been able to calculate the population of whole countries. Thus England, Wales and Scotland may have about 120 million breeding land birds in a normal May, Finland about 64 million: and rough figures for all but the most scattered species can be arrived at. Probably the commonest birds in the British area are starling and blackbird, around 10 million; robin and chaffinch around 7 million; the house sparrow runs them close. In Finland the commonest bird is the willow warbler, over 11 million, followed by the chaffinch, over 10 million. Two separate estimates for the present spring land bird population of the United States have been made around $5\frac{1}{2}$ and at 6 billion. When the passenger pigeon (p. 56) was in its heyday it was possibly half as much again.

The total bird population of the world, including sea birds, may be of the order of a hundred billion. By far the most abundant species now living is the domestic fowl, whose numbers may now approximate to the human population of the world, which is over 3 billion. Widely introduced by man into new countries, the common starling and house sparrow must be the most numerous wild species. One sea bird, Wilson's storm petrel, which breeds in the Antarctic and sub-Antarctic in formidable numbers, may be the next.

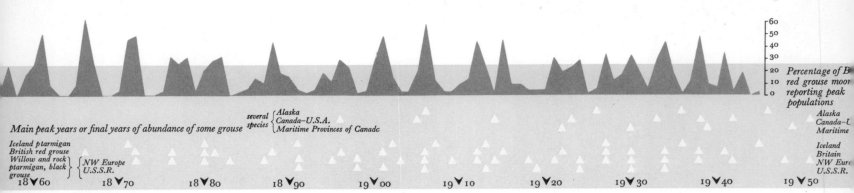

Main peak years or final years of abundance of some grouse | several species { Alaska, Canada–U.S.A., Maritime Provinces of Canada

Iceland ptarmigan
British red grouse
Willow and rock
ptarmigan, black } { NW Europe, U.S.S.R.
grouse

18▼60   18▼70   18▼80   18▼90   19▼00   19▼10   19▼20   19▼30   19▼40   19▼50

60
50
40
30
20
10
0
Percentage of British red grouse moors reporting peak populations

Alaska
Canada–U...
Maritime

Iceland
Britain
NW Euro...
U.S.S.R.

Numbers of most grouse fluctuate regularly; for quite a stretch of time cycle's period may average 4⅔ years in Old World, twice that in New

Changing numbers: cycles and irruptions

All animals vary in number: and some variations are remarkably, oddly regular. For instance, the voles, lemmings and mice of the northern world have a rather regular four-year cycle. In some years of abundance the little animals wander in droves, cross water, are followed by foxes and several kinds of weasels and by skuas, buzzards, harriers and owls. In a big rodent year there is plenty of food for them to rear extra young, so the animals of prey usually have peaks of number in the next year.

The snowy owl is a rarish winter visitor to the United States from the North American Arctic. But after most of the big rodent years – that is, about every fourth winter – the lovely white birds invade south in unusual numbers. In the winter of 1926/27 so many snowy owls were shot in New England that a Boston bird stuffer had to cable to Europe for 250 extra pairs of glass eyes. Fortunately, sportsmen do not shoot so many now.

In Norway the changes in the numbers of the willow ptarmigan often go for many years with the four-year rodent cycle. This may be a coincidence, for ptarmigan and grouse do not depend on, or indeed ever eat, rodents, though some of the animals that eat them also eat rodents, and part of what they eat is also eaten by rodents. Not all grouse cycles are of four years, though. The cycles of the British red grouse (a race of the willow ptarmigan which does not go white in winter) vary from 3 to 10 years, with an average of 5.3. Black game cycles seem to average about 4½ years. In North America the grouse cycle is about twice as long as that in the Old World, and for several species runs between 9 and 11 years.

Other population changes seem to be quite irregular. In 1863 and again in 1888 a strange bird arrived along the whole east coast of England and Scotland and spread west as far as Ireland and the Hebrides. In 1888 Pallas's sand grouse even nested in Denmark, England and Scotland. Since 1909 it has invaded western Europe now and then, but never so far west from its nearest regular home in the half-desert scrub of south-eastern European Russia.

In England we are finding that stocks of quite common birds like blue and great tits invade now and then from the Continent. Some of the more usual irruptive birds (as we call them) of the northern world are red and white-winged crossbills and the Bohemian waxwing. As we write this book, both of us have watched invasions of red-breasted nuthatches and boreal chickadees in North America. In England it has been a waxwing winter, and waxwing invasions have been getting more common lately. Among the finches a frequent invader in North America is the pine siskin, in Europe the brambling. Western Europe is irregularly visited in summer and autumn by the rosy starling which normally ranges no further than rocky plains in Hungary.

What makes bird numbers change? A partial answer is food-supply. Many of the irruptive birds are driven to travel by bad weather and the failure of a food-crop, or both. Many of the cycle birds are so because their food has cycles. One of the causes of the regular cycles may be the lag period between the abundance of food and the abundance of the eater. Lemmings go up: and in the *next* year snowy owls are common. The lemmings increase, push up the owls' numbers; the owls increase, push down the lemmings' numbers; the lemmings decrease, push down the owls' numbers; the owls decrease, push up the lemmings' numbers. Like a see-saw, the owl-lemming relationship may produce a rhythm. But this cannot be the whole story, for we must bring in weather-cycles and other natural rhythms.

Meteorologists have found weather-cycles of various kinds ranging from 41 months through 3⅔, 7½, 9⅔; 11·2 and 22·3 (these two linked with sunspots); 35, 45, 68, 90, 170 to 510 years – and some much longer periods. Our planet is full of cycles of change, which may support each other or cancel each other out, and some of which affect the birds.

Snowy owl and brown lemming

White-winged crossbill

Rosy starling

Bohemian waxwing

Red-breasted nuthatch

Willow ptarmigan

Pallas's sand grouse

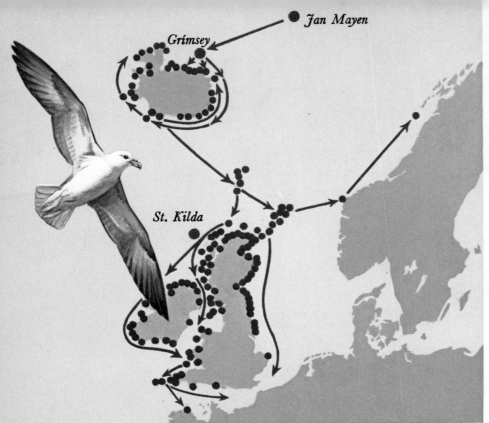

In 200 years fulmar established about 1000 colonies (dots: main groups), some over 2000 mi. from two old northern bases (red). St. Kilda doubtful source of spread

Fieldfare's wind-aided invasion of Greenland in Jan. 1937

Changing numbers: long-term trends

During the present century there has been a general improvement in the climate of late spring and early summer in Europe. New birds have settled as regular nesters in Iceland, the Faeroes, Britain and Scandinavia.

The most extraordinary spread over Europe was that of the collared dove. This bird from Asia had an outpost in the Balkans till about 1912. It reached Hungary in about 1928. It enlarged its range by 1200 miles in 20 years, now breeds in a broad belt with its north-west end in the Scottish Highlands, and is still increasing fast.

The collared dove has little fear of man and likes places where there is waste grain, including zoos. The climatic change may have aided its spread, but this must also have been helped by the dove's natural attachment to human settlements and the Europeans' liking for birds.

Even more spectacular has been the saga of the fulmar. The spread of this sea-bird from the arctic has taken place in the wrong direction to have had anything to do with the improving climate: and is probably due to man. Two hundred years ago the fulmars started founding new colonies when the arctic whaling was at its height. Whales were stripped of their blubber at ship's side in the Greenland ice. The fulmars, which go mad about blubber, found free meals throughout the breeding season from bases in Iceland. And just when the whaling began to peter out, another industry – trawling – took its place in the North Atlantic. To this day, thousands of fulmars attend trawlers for offal, liver, unwanted fish and squids. Although the fulmar breeds slowly, it has multiplied throughout its new range, nested first in the Faeroes in about 1816, in Shetland in 1878, and in the Hebrides

Cattle egret's recent invasion of New World from the Old

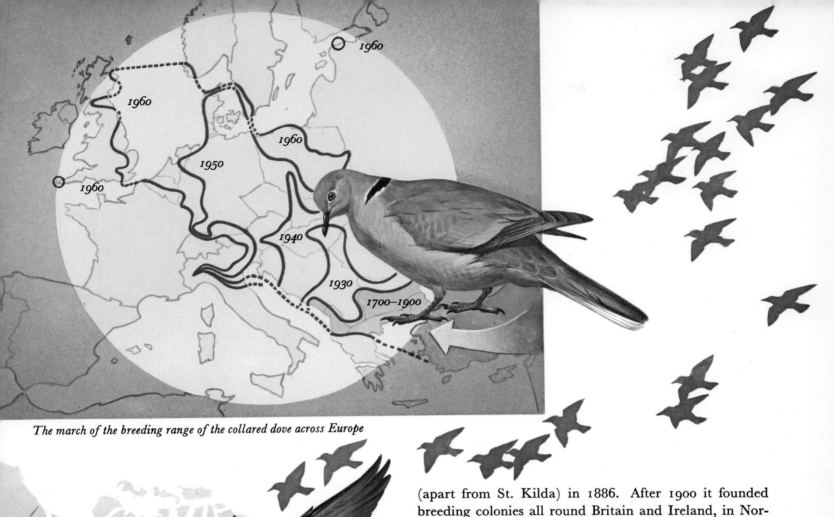

The march of the breeding range of the collared dove across Europe

March of the European starling's breeding range across North America from Central Park, New York City, where introduced in 1890

(apart from St. Kilda) in 1886. After 1900 it founded breeding colonies all round Britain and Ireland, in Norway and in Brittany. The spread may continue as long as trawlers make waste.

Great spreads have followed introductions by man. The natural range of the common starling was Europe and w. Asia: but it now covers as big an area of the planet again, having been introduced in four other continents. In N. America introduced birds started breeding in 1890–91. After a short pause they made a wildfire colonization of the entire U.S. and much of Canada and México.

Sometimes a bird has been brought to new range that suits it by nature, not man. A gale may have blown cattle egrets to South America from West Africa. They were first certainly seen in British Guiana in 1930, and in Florida in 1941 or 1942. By 1962 their New World range ran from north-east Perú to the Caribbean and Atlantic states of U.S.A., and Ontario in Canada, and wanderers had been found as far as the U.S. Mid-West and Newfoundland.

Everywhere throughout its New World spread the cattle egret has become an associate of cattle, previously introduced, of course, by man. But there have been windborne spreads of birds whose success has had no man's help. Most of the bird species peculiar to remote islands must be descended from wind-blown ancestors.

A fine example of wind-colonization is the conquest of Greenland by the fieldfare. The actual strong gale from the south-east, which drove a flock of colonists across the Atlantic, is known. The survivors eventually found the only part of Greenland that grows birchwoods to their taste – down in the south-west – and their descendants have lived there naturally until this day.

CHAPTER VI

Bird Society

Sociability

All successful and numerous birds appear to be in some way sociable, in their breeding life, their feeding life or their traveling life. Perhaps the least sociable birds are some eagles, hawks, falcons and owls.

All the true sea birds are sociable on their breeding grounds. Only at a few remote tropic islets are nesting birds crowded because the space is limited: and here the sea birds may even take turns and nest in 'shifts'. But most sea bird colonies are at places long favored by tradition, with unoccupied but suitable spaces between: the breeders gather because it is in their nature to gather.

On land some social breeders have enormous colonies. Rooks are the commonest large birds in Great Britain. Rookeries usually contain a few score nests, often over a hundred, and sometimes thousands. But rooks have a second level of social organization: the autumn roost, to which thousands of individuals adhere, usually from about ten miles' radius. Rookeries, with all their members, 'belong' to particular roosts: as populations grow, rookeries, and sometimes roosts, may 'burst' and bud off new satellites, probably colonized by young birds.

Within a social group of birds two forces or drives conflict. A social drive makes birds seek each other's company; an anti-crowding drive makes birds repel each other when they get too close for comfort. Gannets' nests on flat rock are spaced evenly just beyond beak range. Starlings in a roost (some roosts can house over a million) jostle until they get out of touch. Swallows gathering on a wire have their individual distance. Waders on passage pack tight on small sandbars where food is abundant, then bicker till each has won room to probe undisturbed. Some social birds have a very low anti-crowding drive. The passenger pigeon used to roost in huge solid masses. It may have been *too* sociable: when its great flocks were broken up by hunters its surviving groups quickly collapsed and it faded fast to extinction.

Social feeder: the marbled godwit, one of the largest waders of North America, probes the sands of California beaches in flocks as it passes north in spring

This is England, not New England; for no American crow nests in large rookeries like the Old World rook

Social traveler: blue goose calls shrilly as it passes in big V-skeins in fall from arctic to Louisiana

Social breeder: on Bonaventure Island in Québec the gannet has its largest colony in the New World. On broad flat ledges nesters sit just out of beak range of neighbors, occupy just over a square yard

The advantages of some kinds of sociability are easy to understand. Sociable flockers gain mutual protection from enemies, are able to find and share massed food-supplies evenly. The advantages of nesting sociability are less easy to prove. Large colonies tend to produce a higher proportion of young than small colonies; but many small colonies consist largely of inexperienced birds that are nesting for the first time: birds that have not bred do far more pioneering and colony founding than old ones, which tend to be true to the site where they have already nested. Sociable breeders certainly find mates more easily than those which are not, and are more highly stimulated to go through their yearly cycle.

Many birds travel in flocks: the geese which nest in the north pack on their nesting grounds when the adults are in flightless molt and the goslings are growing their first flight feathers. All become full winged at about the same time and soon migrate south, sometimes across great distances of sea. The traveling flocks often adopt a V form, and may be led by experienced birds. When they arrive on their winter grounds they spread out evenly over the grazing, moving steadily under 'pressure' from those at the back so that all get a fair sample; and within each moving group are lesser groups – the mated geese and ganders with their young of the year, showing that family ties still lie strong in the broader community.

Great frigate bird, courtship

Wallace's standard wing, aggression or courtship

Display

Every day of its life, a bird makes hundreds of signals, of many different sorts, in response to birds of its own or other kinds, to other animals, or to noises or light or other changes in its surroundings. It makes use of its colors, shapes and adornments to produce patterns of enthralling beauty.

In short, birds display: and by display can hide from enemies, surprise prey or competitors, give signals to flee, approach, scatter or band together, deflect or distract enemies from their young, mimic fiercer or more dangerous animals, recognize or find their own mates and families, court or intimidate or submit to their own kind, and make many other demands and statements. Birds talk as much with ritual movements of their bodies, with mime and dance, as with their voices.

Most wonderful of birds' displays are those of breeding time. Bright colors and fantastic adornments have been evolved for the sole function of courting mates or threatening sexual rivals.

On tropical islets the great frigate bird males attract the females to mate with them and start nest building by perching on a bush, opening their wings, rocking to and fro, inflating huge red throat-pouches to the size of toy balloons and trumpeting a loud greeting which one observer has written *trr trr trr kyu, kyukyu yu huhuhuhu*.

In courtship the little Adélie penguin has an ecstatic ritual in which the bird slowly upstretches head and bill, beats flippers in jerks, throws out its chest and makes a crescendo of drum-like noise whose climax ending has been written *Ku-ku-ku-ku-ku-kug-gu-gu-gu-gu-ga-aaaa*. Pairs bow deeply to each other in the early days of their mated life; and in the most typical mutual display face each other with up-pointed bills, eyes rolled down and back, crests raised and flippers at their sides, and sway with a raucous braying that can be heard half a mile away. Sometimes mutual display starts when a bird brings a stone to its mate at the nest-site.

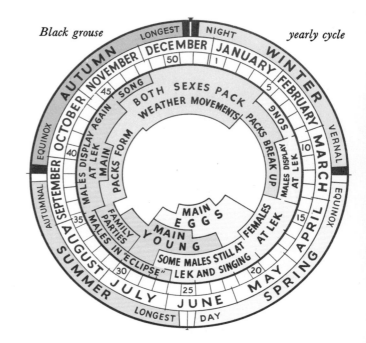

Black grouse ... *yearly cycle*

Adélie penguin, greeting

White stork, greeting

Blackcock at the 'lek'

Ruffs at the 'hill'

The greeting ceremonies of mated birds at their nests have been admired by writers back to the poets of ancient Rome. Petronius liked the stork with its 'bill rattling like castanets'. Sometimes, at the changeover, white storks bend their heads right back until their crowns nearly touch their backs and then bring them right forward and down, clappering their bills all the time.

Many birds have special display grounds. Male racket-tailed hummingbirds (figured on p. 10) assemble at certain spots and hover with their bodies vertical opposite each other, bobbing from side to side with clicking sounds, and curve their tails under themselves so as to frame their faces with the rackets at the end of them.

Male birds of paradise have meeting places where they spend much time bluffing their rivals with incredible postures, using all their colors and adornments, and eventually find mates. Wallace's standard wing has been described in its posturing as slowly raising and stretching as if it was in a fit. In another part of its display it back-somersaults from its perch and lands with closed wings.

One of the most beautiful waders has no two males alike. Ruffs in spring grow huge fans of feathers on head and nape which in full display rise to form circles of bright color around their heads. At the traditional 'hills', the males crouch facing each other, shivering with erected ruffs, and bluff each other. Seldom do they really fight. The females, the reeves, are not even always present at the hill; but come there to choose their mates.

The display grounds of black grouse are known as 'leks'. The cocks can be found at them most regularly in March and April. They stimulate each other by crowing and jumping: stand with spread tail, swollen head-combs, head and much-swollen neck thrust forward, and shake as they make a musical, bubbling *roo-koo* noise at rivals: and having thus carved out territories or 'courts' for themselves on the lek they court the grey hens there with a circling, crouching dance ritual.

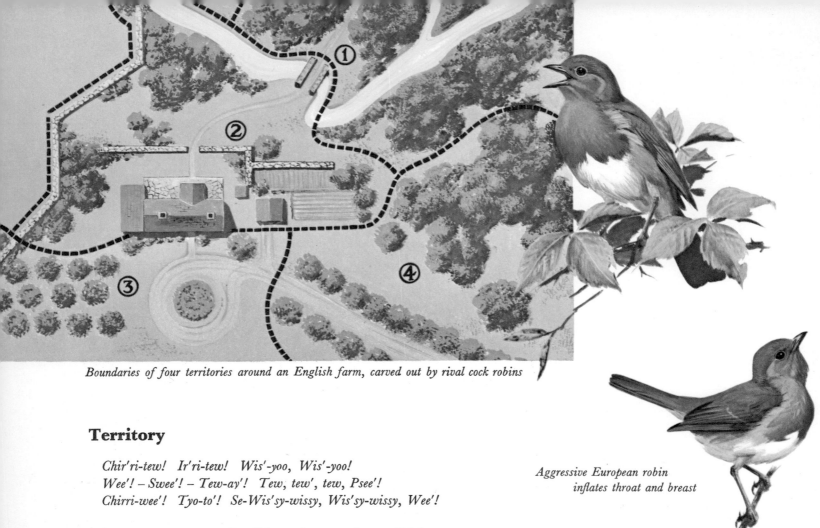

Boundaries of four territories around an English farm, carved out by rival cock robins

Territory

Chir'ri-tew! Ir'ri-tew! Wis'-yoo, Wis'-yoo!
Wee'! – Swee'! – Tew-ay'! Tew, tew', tew, Psee'!
Chirri-wee'! Tyo-to'! Se-Wis'sy-wissy, Wis'sy-wissy, Wee'!

Some years ago an English zoology professor, Walter Garstang, wrote an odd and charming little book, *Songs of the Birds*. This was one of his versions of the fall song of the darting, bobbing, bold and tame little bird that all English-speaking Europeans call robin; not to be confused with that bigger thrush, the American robin.

The sweet song of cock robins begins at Christmas, trickles and tinkles like flickering waterfalls on a pebbly streambed nearly every day from late February to the middle of June. July is a silent month; but from August to October the song is doubled – hens sing as well and as strongly as cocks. November, again, is a rather silent time; but the robin probably sings on more days in the year, altogether, than any other European bird.

The red breast of the robin is its banner, and its liquid song its trumpet; for at seasons the robin is very warlike. It struts and sings to claim its possession of land. 'One bush cannot harbor two robins' is an old saying.

Aggressive European robin inflates throat and breast

Most birds hold territories in the spring, at the start of the breeding season. Many small garden birds have one or two acres to each warlike cock bird or mated pair. Rather few birds also have fall territories: but the robin is one, and among the browning leaves cocks and hens alike maintain their acres, by threat and song.

In the spring the hens hardly sing at all. But the cocks sing, chase, bob and wave with puffed red breasts at each other, until eventually each has carved out an acre or so for himself, with boundaries that mark where the aggressiveness of his neighbors is about equal. The red breast of the robin is not a courtship banner; a cock robin courts a hen by feeding her.

Birds mark their landowner's rights in many different ways. Hummingbirds often fly in flights so curved that they appear tied to their headquarters by invisible thread, their metallic throat-gorgets a signal of war to rival males and, in special short dives and swoops, of courtship to their females. Many wading birds have special territory-flights; and snipe fly to a height from which they plunge in a fast fluttering dive, their outstretched tail-feathers sounding a humming, bleating war-cry – or rather, war-drum, for it is not a vocal sound.

The territory system is, of course, useful to birds – a kind of land agency. It spreads the breeding pairs and eventually their new families evenly over the kind of land that suits them.

Spring battles of cock robins are often rough; but the rivals seldom fight to the death

Robin courtship; hen begs like a newly flown fledgeling, cock feeds her

Pair of satin bower birds at male's bower in heart of his territory

Air-fight of male ruby-throated hummingbirds

Some birds have such elaborate territory rituals that scientists often wonder whether the system can sometimes go beyond its usefulness. The male satin bower bird of Australia stakes a territory when the breeding season comes, selecting a high branch from which he advertises ownership with a ringing *ee-oo* cry. In the territory he then quickly builds an extraordinary structure (usually north and south) of two parallel walls of arched dry twigs. Near one entrance of this he puts his collection of objects; for he will collect almost anything, particularly if it is blue or bluish – parrot feathers, blue or violet flowers of many kinds, bits of blue glass bottles or blue plates, blue paper, blue cloth, bluish or brownish snailshells, and even blue animals if any are around. He may steal blue-bags from laundries. He may also plaster and paint his bower with fruit pulp.

Now at the bower the male displays to the duller-colored female, with a whirring leaping display, with a specimen from his collection in his beak. But the bowers have a great attraction for the rival neighboring males. They raid. They steal. They sneak in and out by special hidden routes. Out of a hundred bits of blue bottle put (by bird watchers) on runways and bowers, 76 were found in the collections of *neighbors* by noon next day!

Social sea birds' territories. Space between nests is settled by distance these elegant terns can stretch their beaks to

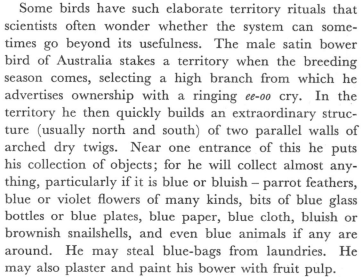

Snipe drumming; outer tail-feathers vibrate

Male mallee fowl tests temperature of incubation mound with beak; opens it up if it is too hot, piles more leaves or loam on if too cool

Male silvery-cheeked hornbill coughs up pellets of mixed earth and saliva; female uses them to plaster nest-hole entrance

Nests

From his bathroom window in England one of us has watched a hen goldfinch weave her perfect bowl-shaped nest on a big side-branch of an old sycamore.

The open cup is perhaps the commonest type of bird's nest. In the North American West the rufous humming-bird builds one of the most delicate bowls of all on a downward-bending branch, of cottony willow down all mixed and covered with green moss, cemented with spiderweb and decorated with bits of leaves and bark.

The long-tailed tailor bird of Asia also builds a typical deep soft nest-bowl of stems, wool and down. But this nest is slung in a cradle of two or more large hanging leaves, which the bird sews together with thread. It steals the thread from spiders, moth-cocoons or human house-wives, punches holes in the leaves with its sharp beak, somehow ties stop-knots on the threads and draws them through until they are tight.

Remarkable among bowl nests are those of a curious small family – the tree swifts, of Asia and the East Indies. A tree swift's nest is a tiny cup of bark and feathers into which the single egg fits like an acorn: it is gummed together, and to a horizontal branch, by the bird's own saliva. When sitting the bird grasps the branch with a foot on each side of the nest and egg, which fit snugly among its belly feathers.

Many birds of many families nest in burrows or holes. In France we have watched pairs of common bee eaters quickly excavating their nest-holes in a sandbank. The birds dug with their bills and kicked spurts of sand out every few seconds. When finished, the burrow may run up to 9 feet horizontally, and at the end of it the birds incubate on the bare sand.

In high trees in Africa the female silvery-cheeked horn-bill finds her nest-site in a hole. To her the male flies with plaster for the entrance, with which she imprisons

Above: rufous hummingbird's nest. Inner diameter of rim: one inch
Below: pair of bee eaters excavate nest-burrow

Goldfinch's nest-cup is woven of stems and roots with
moss and lichens, lined with plant-down and wool

*Above: eastern crested tree swift (l.)
& long-tailed tailor bird (r.) at nests*

*Below: ringed plover's 'nest' is simple
scrape on pebbly barren ground or beach*

*The tiny elf owl of the American desert
breeds in old woodpecker holes*

herself for a period of up to $4\frac{1}{2}$ months! During this time
she incubates her clutch and feeds her two young on
fruit regurgitated by the male.

Some birds use second-hand holes. In the Arizona
desert we have seen the world's smallest owl (no bigger
than a sparrow) rearing its young in old woodpecker
holes in the huge, stately saguaro cactuses.

In Australia at least 3 parrots and 5 kingfishers regularly burrow into occupied termites' nests. There are
termite-hill-nesting birds, too, in South America. In
Africa the red-and-yellow barbet is also an example.
Oddly, the termites do not seem to molest the birds, and
we have no evidence that the birds eat their hosts.
Possibly the birds get some protection from enemies from
this curious association.

Largest of all birds' nests are those of a family of game
birds known as the mound-builders or megapodes. Each
pair of mallee fowls in the Australian bush owns a vast
mound of soil and loam scratched up mainly by the male.
In this mound are many egg-chambers filled by the birds
with fermenting leaves; and in the breeding season the
males dig these out, the females lay in them and the
males cover them up again. The eggs are incubated by
the heat of fermentation, which is controlled almost entirely by the male. When the chicks eventually hatch
they are, though small, almost able to fly, and their
parents do not look after them at all, but continue busily
attending to the mound.

Some birds have no nests at all, or practically none.
The king and emperor penguins rest their eggs on their
feet and cover them with a pouch. Some of the auk
family have single eggs which they sit on upon bare rock.
Many waders, like plovers and oystercatchers, lay their
clutch on a simple scrape in the open; their eggs (p. 87)
are protected by concealing coloration.

*The red-and-yellow barbet may excavate its nest in termite-
hills in the semi-desert East African bush*

Hen common pheasant lays an egg a day till clutch is full, then incubates 3–3½ weeks

Laughing gull's clutch of 3 eggs fits its mid and side incubation patches

Eggs

The largest egg known (14½ inches long, around 27 pounds) was laid by the largest extinct bird known, the elephant bird. In a good sense, though, it was a small egg, for it probably weighed under 3 per cent of the bird that laid it, far below the average. Yet smaller (1·7 per cent) is the egg of the ostrich, even if, at around 3 pounds, it is the largest now laid. In proportion, it is nearly the smallest: the smallest egg and egg output of any bird known are those of the emperor penguin, whose single annual egg weighs but 1·4 per cent of its body.

The emu's egg (1·5 per cent) is nearly as small: but the quite closely related kiwi lays an egg that weighs one third of its body – the largest known, in proportion. Though the eggs of hummingbirds are the smallest known, they are above average in proportion (usually 10 per cent). A bee hummer's egg-weight is, we believe, unknown; but, judging by close relations, should be about 0·15 grams, or around five thousandths of an ounce.

Hummingbirds lay clutches of two: but most small birds lay many more, producing one a day and usually starting to sit when all are laid. In the wild, the mass-output record seems to be held by the little goldcrest, which produces 144 per cent of its own body weight in a ten-egg clutch. Most eggs in a year are probably laid by the common pheasant and partridge; if they lose their first clutch they can lay in all nearly 30.

Nearly all female birds have bare patches in the breeding season among their breast-feathers, to warm their clutches next their skin: and if the males share in the incubation most have brood-patches too.

Many small birds regularly lay two, and some even three, clutches in the year. The early and late clutches tend to be smaller than those in the full season. The size seems to depend on the food available.

There is enormous variation in the incubation period of birds – the time to hatching from the laying of the last

Variation in the average clutch size of eggs of the European robin: increases with day length northward and also eastward where May and June are warmer and there is probably more food

egg, when most birds start to sit. Smaller singing birds and most woodpeckers usually hatch their eggs out before the end of the second week of sitting. Groups whose eggs mostly hatch in week 3 include rails, pigeons, nightjars and crows: in week 4 grebes, divers, game birds, cormorants, gulls, waders, herons and ducks: in weeks 5 and 6 ostrich, rheas, storks, falcons, most hawks, cranes, flamingos, larger geese, swans, auks and owls: in 7 and 8 cassowaries, penguins, petrels, gannets, vultures and eagles: in 9 and 10 emus, most albatrosses and the Andean condor. The longest incubation periods so far reliably recorded for any birds are 73 days for the wandering albatross, 80 days for the kiwi and 81 days for the royal albatross.

The array of eggs in the photograph opposite belongs to 41 species in 34 families. Coloration is laid upon a bird's eggshell by glands as it passes down the oviduct; the four main pigments are oocyanin which produces a basal blue; oochlorin, yellow; ooxanthin, red or purplish (as on tinamou eggs); ooporphyrin which often produces fine patterns, as on the eggs of waders. Most eggs tend to be oval with one end rounder than the other. The most pear-shaped form is found among the eggs of auks, which can roll in a small circle and are not likely to fall off a ledge. The purest ovals are perhaps those of game birds, loons and some birds of prey, and most round are those of owls. The eggs of emus and tinamous are 'biconical', tapering rather evenly towards each end.

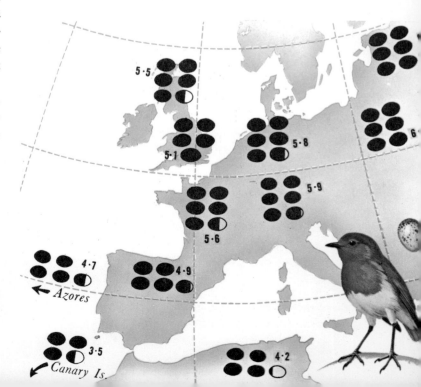

Osprey

Brown booby

Steller's eider

Red-throated loon

Chilean tinamou

Madagascar sparrow hawk

Peregrine

Great horned owl

Ptarmigan

Great bustard

Boat-tailed grackle

Little bustard

Sharp-tailed grouse

Common murre (guillemot)

Senegal dove

American black vulture

Incubator bird

Guira cuckoo

Emu

Clapper rail

Catbird

Red-billed tropic bird

Black-headed jay

Common grackle

Yellow-bellied tyrannulet

House wren

Black-bellied (gray) plover

Ovenbird

Calliope hummingbird

Eastern kingbird

Veery

Great blue heron

Painted bunting

White-breasted nuthatch

Water pipit

Jaçana

Western tanager

Gray kingbird

Common nighthawk

Crissal thrasher

Martinetta

87

Brood parasites

About 78 birds – less than one species in a hundred – lay in the nests of others and leave their eggs to be hatched and their young to be reared by fosterparents. The habit has probably arisen at least six times quite independently in the course of evolution, for the known brood parasites belong to six different families.

Birds of many kinds may casually drop eggs in the nests of others. The habit is common among the ducks, specially so in the tribe of ruddy ducks and their allies, whose eggs need little incubation after the first few days. The shy parents leave their nest on slight provocation; and the nest itself is poorly made. One member of the tribe, the white-headed duck of Europe, very often lays in the nests of coots. Another, the black-headed duck of southern South America, is a full brood parasite: no nest of it has ever been found. Its eggs, though, have been found in the nests of an ibis, a screamer, the swan-like coscoroba, other ducks, a caracara (a relative of the falcons!), the limpkin, rails, coots and gulls.

It is probable that all the 14 members of the honey-guide family (all but one of which live in Africa) are brood-parasites of hole-nesting birds like barbets, woodpeckers

In México giant cowbird, outside entrance to nest of Montezuma oropéndola, parasitises birds of own Icterid family

Paradise wydah pair, cock melba finch:
hen wydah lays in nest of 'finch' (a waxbill)

In Argentina yellow-billed coot is among
the many hosts of black-headed duck

and starlings. Wholly African is the widow bird or wydah family, all eight of which parasitize waxbills, and some of which have other hosts. The wydahs are quite close to the weavers in relationship, but only one of the 95 true weavers is a parasite – the African cuckoo finch, which specializes in warblers as hosts.

The most important parasitic birds of the Americas are the cowbirds, eight members of the specially American icterid family. The bay-winged cowbird of Argentina shows how the habit may evolve; for its pairs look for (or oust the owners from) nests of other species in which they lay eggs and feed and rear their own young. Next most primitive are the screaming cowbirds, which pair up in the spring as usual, but hold egg-laying until their bay-winged cousins' nests are ready, when they lay their eggs exclusively therein and leave the bay-wings to rear the young. More advanced are cowbirds which have entirely or largely lost their monogamous and territorial habits: some, like the giant cowbird, specialize largely in other icterids as hosts, but others have adopted a large variety of species, mostly smaller than themselves.

About 200 different fosterers have been recorded for the North American cowbird: its females watch hosts building and sometimes lay four or five eggs on successive days, each directly into a chosen nest, usually just after the first egg has been laid by the host.

Forty-seven out of the 126 cuckoos are parasites; though only the striped cuckoo is so in the Americas. The other 46 comprise a whole subfamily in the Old World. Most widespread and successful of these is the common cuckoo, for which at least 300 hosts are known.

The female common cuckoo seems to be an even better nest-finder than the North American cowbird, for she can lay more than 15 eggs in a season, usually at 2-day intervals, timing each to a fosterer's first egg. She holds this fosterer's egg in her beak while she lays direct into the nest, flies off and eats the stolen egg. Her own egg has an incubation period of but 12½ days, usually as short as or shorter than that of the host; and when the young cuckoo is quite newly hatched it wriggles in the nest until it has shoved the fosterer's eggs or young out.

Cuckoos tend to lay in the nests of the host species by which they were reared, and by natural selection many *gentes* (that is, hereditary lines) have developed, each with eggs closely resembling those of their fosterers: some beautiful examples are shown on this page.

In Africa gray woodpecker pair, host-birds for the scaly-throated honeyguide, mob intruder at nest-hole

In Europe meadow pipit is one of the most regular hosts of the common cuckoo

Meadow pipit	Brambling	Rufous-bellied niltava	Meadow bunting	Streaked laughing thrush	Great reed warbler
Cuckoo	Cuckoo	Cuckoo	Cuckoo	Cuckoo	Cuckoo

Through its range cuckoo has gentes *that lay eggs (lower rank) wonderfully resembling those of hosts*

Pulli

The heading above means, in Latin, young animals. Pullus has been adopted as the official word to represent a bird that has hatched but cannot yet fly. As soon as a bird can fly it is a juvenal. Pullus is the only word we can use for both nestling and chick: a fledgeling is a bird that has just flown and is therefore juvenal.

Pulli are of two main sorts, if we exclude the young of flightless birds, whose transition to juvenals is hard to define. Most pulli are altricial, that is, helpless and often naked when hatched: these are also called nidicolous – staying in the nest – or simply nestlings. But many birds have precocial pulli fully downy when hatched, often called nidifugous because most run away from the nest when dry – in short, chicks, ducklings or goslings.

If we call (as most do) the period between hatching and fledging the fledging period, then some precocial birds have short fledging periods indeed. Megapodes (p. 85) can practically fly when hatched, and spend the early juvenal stage in further growth. Other game birds like ptarmigan have fledging periods as short as ten days, and nearly all continue to grow after they can fly.

Many small singing birds fledge in under a fortnight; the majority of passerines in under three weeks; pigeons, nightjars, hummingbirds, trogons, bee eaters and most woodpeckers in under four. Bustards, most owls, motmots and some kingfishers, icterids and crows take up to five; most waders up to six; herons, falcons, skuas, gulls, auks and some toucans up to seven, though murres and razorbills (auks) flutter from their cliffs at about a fortnight. Storm petrels, some cormorants, darters, some bitterns, storks, most rails and some large owls and hornbills cannot fly

Directive and recognition marks in the mouths of nestlings: l. to r., croaking cisticola, a warbler; yellow-throated longclaw, wagtail-pipit family; speckled mousebird. All African

Young razorbills a fortnight hatched flutter from cliff when primary feathers are mere buds, continue growth at sea. Below, eider ducklings leave nest when dry, tumble after ducks down steep rocky moors to the sea

until they are nearly eight weeks old. The tropic birds, pelicans and secretary bird may take a week longer.

The birds with really long fledging periods embrace rather few families. Swifts may not fledge for nearly ten weeks in years of insect scarcity: other ten-week birds are cranes, the smaller New World vultures, the osprey and caracaras. Petrels, gannets, most eagles and barn owls seldom fledge in under eleven. Big Old World vultures, like the griffon, may not fledge in under twelve.

With quite a different order of fledging time are the albatrosses, the largest penguins and the condors. The smaller albatrosses and mollymawks have fledging periods of 20 or 21 weeks. The three North Pacific albatrosses and the three smaller Antarctic penguins spend almost exactly half a year in or near their nest. The California condor certainly, and the Andean condor very probably, cannot fly until 26–30 weeks hatched. The emperor penguin is fed by its parents on the antarctic sea-ice for 35–39 weeks before it swims off.

The longest fledging period absolutely proved is that of the royal albatross at 36 weeks, though there is evidence that its close cousin the wanderer may go to 44 or 45. But the king penguin spends from 10 to 13 months as a pullus; at times its parents cannot find much seafood and it has to live on stored fat and does not grow.

The pullus period of a bird has adaptations of color and organ special to it. The young of many nidicolous birds have colored mouth markings which elicit parental feeding responses when they gape. Pulli of hole nesters often have horny spiked heel pads to grip the walls. Nidifugous pulli are almost all colored with patterns that conceal them from enemies when they lie still.

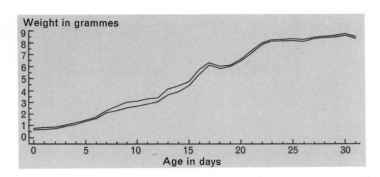

In distraction display yellow-throated sand grouse parent raises wing, drops other, flutters as if injured, distracts predator from neighborhood of young, which can then rely on cryptic 'freezing' for protection

Most hummingbirds rear twins. Weight-chart of two Estella hillstars through fledging period shows even growth of both and drop in weight when feather buds sprout in third fortnight

Nidifugous young of yellow-throated sand grouse seem quite boldly patterned against plain background; but when they 'freeze' in grass cover outline-breaking coloration effectively blends them with surroundings

Wandering albatross: air, stages from first year (r.) to male of 9 or more (l.): ground, Campbell I. adults with egg and advanced young

Adolescence

Most birds have a short adolescence, for they breed in the first season after that in which they are hatched, at a little under a year old. But quite a number breed later.

Second-year breeders include the emu, diving petrels, geese, many hawks and owls, smaller gulls, some swifts, a few large passerines. Frigate birds first breed in their second or third, the smaller penguins and storm petrels in their third, and the ostrich, pelicans, king vultures, most terns and gulls in their third or fourth year.

Typical fourth-year breeders are gannets, the larger gulls, the Adélie penguin. Storks breed in their fourth or fifth; many petrels and large birds of prey in their fifth; the king penguin in its fifth or sixth; the California condor in its sixth.

All birds so far known to breed first at seven or older are petrels and albatrosses. Male short-tailed shearwaters breed first at seven, females at five. The fulmar probably does not come to land until three or four, or breed till seven. No royal albatross known to be in less than its sixth year was seen at the colony watched by L. E. Richdale, and none provedly bred before its eighth year. One male did not breed until its eleventh.

Longest-lived wild bird yet known, this black-browed albatross joined the gannet colony on Mýkines in the Faeroes in 1860, was shot in 1894 when at least 34, probably 40

What is this long adolescence for? Some ornithologists have suggested that it is inherited as a method of limiting the population: but we doubt this. We believe it is long for learning, just as human adolescence is long. The slow maturers have to learn a lot: the great vultures must get to know the topography, and all the air-currents, thermals and winds of thousands of square miles: the great albatrosses need nine years of experience to become masters of the trackless stormy oceans and fit for parenthood.

The longest adolescents are the slowest of breeders. All lay but one egg. The king penguin, with its year-long fledging period, breeds only twice every three years. Condors and the two great albatrosses breed every other year.

Birds that have lived longer than any others known, all in captivity. Above: eagle owl, 68 years; Asian white crane, 59. Below: Andean condor, 65; greater sulfur-crested cockatoo, 56; bateleur, 55. Parrot records of 69, 79, 80 and 120 years are not provable through lack of reliable documents

Longevity

In spite of half a century of banding, we still know rather little about how long birds can live in the wild. But the records of some zoos and aviaries go back a century and a quarter; and from the studies of the late Stanley S. Flower and others we can say that the longest-lived birds proved are probably the five figured above.

The only lives the banding records can so far give us over 30 are herring gull (nearly 32), curlew (31½) and black-headed gull (31¼). But if banding cannot yet find maximum wild longevity for us, it can already tell us the average *expectation* of life of wild species.

All birds have a relatively high mortality rate when juvenal, and a lower mortality rate when adult. Once a bird is mature its expectation of life is about constant.

It may be independent of its age, or in some cases actually improve with it from experience of life.

The expectation of life is a calculation of the length of time that, on an average, animals *do* live in nature. It has little to do with how long individuals *can* live. In nature it is probable that only top-of-the-pyramid birds, like vultures and albatrosses, can die of old age. The rest die by being killed and eaten, of starvation, by drowning on migration, by accident, or from disease.

But one bird has been found with a life expectation less than a year: the mallard in Britain, where it is a major shooters' prey and rates 11 months. Apart from sporting birds, small birds rate lowest. Good figures are European robin, redstart, swallow, 12 months; American robin and European song thrush, 17; European starling, 18; European blackbird, 19; blue jay, 20. Over 2 years are European woodcock, lapwing, heron, marsh hawk, night heron. Some cormorants, geese, gulls and owls can expect over 3, swifts over 4, several terns over 5. Banding has not gone on long enough to produce figures for really long-lived birds. We guess, though, that one day albatrosses, and a few other great birds, will be *proved* to be able to live as long as a man, and to have a better life-expectation than man in middle age.

Pied flycatcher feeding young. Past juvenal stage, average expectation of life is 18 months

Jackdaw opening correct box according to number of dots on key card. In another Köhler experiment this bird also learned to associate each number from 1 to 5 with one of 5 plain boxes differently colored

Instinct and intelligence

Birds are creatures of instinct. They have a lively intelligence that operates in a field more limited than that of high mammals, and quite unlike that of man. Their learning and memory abilities can be marvelous: a budgerigar can learn nearly as many English words as some Englishmen, and can even associate some of them with objects, sounds or times in its environment. But it cannot ever understand the true meaning of them.

An instinct is a capacity to respond with special and often clear-cut patterns of behavior to stimuli in the environment – a capacity which is inherited, is innate, does not have to be learned. In any bird there is a whole complex of innate drives which lead to what behavior students now call appetitive behavior. Under the appropriate stimuli birds express urges or appetites for certain kinds of activity, ranging from simple random searching to activities of extreme complexity (like starting breeding) which involve more than one instinct. Eventually the appropriate environmental circumstances (usually simple and special in pattern) may release the final consummatory act, the satisfaction of the appetite. A bird, W. H. Thorpe says, is 'tuned to recognize without previous experience the goal of its instinct'.

Birds fight their way out of their egg by instinct, hide by instinct, flock and forage by instinct, scratch and preen by instinct, sing and cry by instinct, migrate, orient themselves and navigate by instinct, take territories and

Köhler hid food in one of 5 boxes numbered by irregular blobs. Raven was shown key of 1 to 5 differently irregular bits of plasticine. Arrows link keys with boxes with same number, always correctly opened

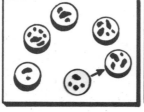 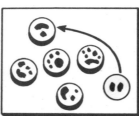 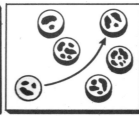 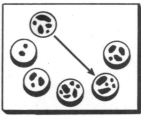 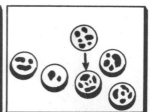

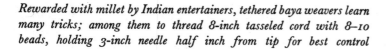
Blue tits can beak up over 2 feet of baited string to perch, placing foot on loops. At least 6 other families can solve problem; ability varies. Solution may come from insight, not trial-and-error learning

Rewarded with millet by Indian entertainers, tethered baya weavers learn many tricks; among them to thread 8-inch tasseled cord with 8–10 beads, holding 3-inch needle half inch from tip for best control

display by instinct, build nests and feed and protect their young by instinct. Nearly all these activities can be, and often are, improved by experience, by learning.

Intelligence is still rather a loose word, so to tighten it a little let us confine the realms of birds' intelligence to those abilities of theirs which involve learning and insight. First, birds have a large capacity for habituation; for learning not to respond to things in the environment that may frighten them at first but are found by experience not to be unfavorable. Habituation sorts and simplifies a bird's mental pictures of the real and the bogus dangers around it, and saves energy.

A large element of trial-and-error enters into the learning of birds. Chicks peck by instinct, learn much about what is rewarding to peck by trial. Pigeons go through drinking motions by instinct, but have been proved to have to learn by several trials that water is the stuff to drink. Some (but by no means all) nest-builders are incompetent the first time, and have to learn the right sizes and shapes of twigs before they can do the kind of job their innate drive prescribes.

Individual birds vary greatly in their capacity for successful trial: though tits have a natural drive to make trials of all kinds only a few 'genius' tits found out how to open milk-bottle tops and steal the cream when modern bottles were first introduced in England, and the habit spread in a very orderly way from rather a few original centers by imitation. Birds generally have a fair capacity for imitation, and a few families a propensity for the vocal mimicry of other species which is as remarkable as it is (at present) inexplicable. Birds

also are very fond of play, adults more so than young; play probably enhances their capacity for trial learning.

Experiments have shown that birds learn some lessons by insight. Presented with new problems, they sometimes appear to find the answers by a quick reorganization of their previous experience, without trials. Put another way, birds have an inherent curiosity which sometimes enables them to cut corners, and meet new situations with a kind of drill that has been set up by old ones.

A few birds use tools: woodpeckers have their favorite anvils where they wedge acorns to split them; the woodpecker finch of the Galápagos Islands uses a long cactus spine to poke insects out of holes. Some birds learn tricks in the wild and captivity – string-pulling, drawer-opening, needle-threading, pulling sticks away to release nuts – which have no relation to natural problems and must be at least partly based on insight.

The counting ability of birds is about as good as that of a man deprived of the abstract concept of number: shown groups of marks on a screen for too short a time for deliberate counting, man can nearly always distinguish between four and five, only sometimes distinguish between seven and eight. Birds, which cannot name the numbers, get about as far – pigeons up to five, ravens and jackdaws to six or even seven.

Birds live in a world of which they themselves can have no abstract concept. Within it they have wonderful skills, based on a network of complex instincts, fine learning capacity and memory, a dash of insight. No philosophers they, they live and die in a drama of colors and shapes and music that makes philosophers of us.

MALES

BLACK-CHINNED VIOLET-CROWNED BUFF-BELLIED WHITE-EARED BROAD-BILLED

CALLIOPE LUCIFER COSTA'S RIVOLI'S BLUE-THROATED

ANNA'S BROAD-TAILED RUBY-THROATED ALLEN'S RUFOUS

FEMALES

BLACK-CHINNED RUBY-THROATED COSTA'S (similar) LUCIFER BROAD-TAILED CALLIOPE RUFOUS

ANNA'S BROAD-BILLED RIVOLI'S BLUE-THROATED WHITE-EARED

TALGOXE SVARTMES BLÅMES

KÄRRMES TALLTITA AZURMES

Kontinental Skandinavisk

BALKANMES LAPPMES TOFSMES

Kontinental

SKÄGGMES STJÄRTMES PUNGMES

Skandinavisk

ROLLIER HUPPE

GUÊPIER

MARTIN-PÊCHEUR

COUCOU GRIS COUCOU GRIS
Phase rousse
(♀ seulement)

COUCOU-GEAI

96

ENGOULEVENT D'EUROPE ENGOULEVENT A COLLIER ROUX

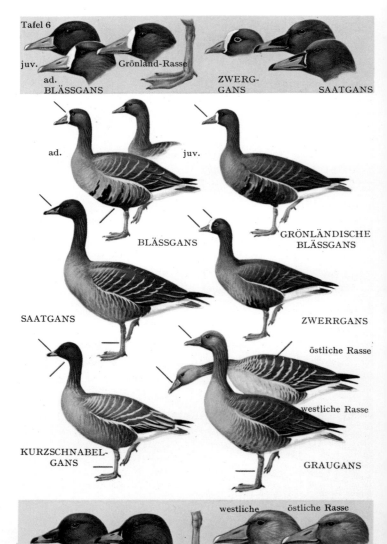

Tafel 6

juv. ad. BLÄSSGANS Grönland-Rasse ZWERGGANS SAATGANS

ad. juv.

BLÄSSGANS GRÖNLÄNDISCHE BLÄSSGANS

SAATGANS ZWERRGANS

östliche Rasse

westliche Rasse

KURZSCHNABELGANS GRAUGANS

westliche östliche Rasse

KURZSCHNABELGANS GRAUGANS

CHAPTER VII

Bird Watching

Identification

All over the world some hundreds of thousands of bird watchers are using instruments specially of the twentieth century: field guides, and field identification drills.

We write of field guides as new because in their modern form they are indeed so. 'What's hit's history, what's missed's mystery', said the gun collectors of the last century. They had sense on their side in rejecting sight records in times when there was no proper code of field drill worked out – and no published study of the appearance of all birds in all their plumages and molts critical enough to enable a field worker to identify every bird he saw without shooting it.

Whole continents and subcontinents are now, or shortly will be, served by pocket or semipocket field guides to their birds, illustrated by pictures showing the essential recognition points, with a back-up text which describes style, habit and voice.

Roger Peterson has been preparing such bird guides for nearly thirty years. At present there are effective *field* books in existence (in some countries several excellent rival alternatives) to the birds of the whole of North America including Texas and Hawaii, México, the West Indies, Trinidad, the Argentine Republic, Europe, Russia, Japan, large parts of Africa, large areas of Asia including parts of India, Malaysia, the Philippines, the south-west Pacific, New Zealand, Tasmania and the world's oceans. New guides to México, parts of Australia and the sea-birds of the world are in project.

Figured here are illustrations from RTP's own field guides to the birds of western North America and (in three different editions) Europe. The Peterson system, as it is often called, is based on patternistic drawings that indicate the key field marks with arrows. These pointers and the comparisons between similar species are the core of the system. Field books are not textbooks: they cover essentials for the field worker only: and they must not be used without the proper drill. Used with drill they have advanced our beloved science amazingly in one human generation. The watcher should use his pencil during and after his observation, and before his field guide check; and write his notes as fully as possible.

Opposite: plates from Peterson field guides in four languages. The formal arrangement of similar species near each other facilitates quick comparison of patterns. Short arrows point out key field marks of each species

Upper left: hummingbirds; A Field Guide to Western Birds. *Upper right: tits (Paridae); Swedish edition of* European Field Guide

Lower left: some of the most colorful European birds; French edition. Lower right: gray geese of Europe; German edition

Below, we offer our field drill. Some people like mnemonics – artificial aids to memory – and to this end we start each heading with a bold face capital. These spell out our objective: **WHICH IS IT?**

Where and when? (Locality and date.)

Habitat: is it in a wood, marsh, meadow?

Impression: what does the bird look like at rest, in movement? Note the general appearance.

Comparison: what is its size? Note this in relation to some well-known species, or better still some known species that your bird is in company with, if any.

Habits: how does the bird behave, move, when standing, walking, running, flying?

Identification flashes or field marks: many birds have diagnostic bars, patches or contrasting marks that readily identify them. The birds use them for the same purpose as bird watchers – for recognition. See the amplification, below, of the important subject of *field marks*.

Sounds: hear your bird. Write down all you can of what it cries or sings. Listen to published sound recordings if you have any.

Important details (size, shape, color) of legs, feet, bills and, if possible, eyes.

Tail and wings: their shapes, length and patterns. (Identification flashes are often here.)

Each of the above headings which deal directly with identification may demand an entry in the notebook if the record is to be reliable. To supplement them we suggest a secondary drill with the code: **DO IT!**

Distance: how far were you from the bird?

Optics: binocular or telescope; what power? Comment also on the light and its direction.

Instant of observation (time and duration).

Team: log the names of your companions, if any. Somebody may want to check with them.

Field marks: these have also been called 'trade marks of nature'. Below we offer a basic outline of the things to look for.

(1) *Breast:* is it plain (unmarked), spotted, or streaked or striped?

(2) *Wings:* does it have wing-bars (one or two) or are the wings plain? Wings of water birds may have: (a) patches, (b) stripes, (c) solid color, or (d) black tips.

(3) *Tail:* does it have a band at the tip, bands across it, white sides, or spots in the corners?

(4) *Rump:* does it have a conspicuous rump patch?

(5) *Head:* does it have (a) a stripe over the eye; (b) a ring around the eye; (c) stripes on the crown, or (d) a patch on the crown?

The notebook

'The notebook', said Dr. James T. Emlen Jr. in a presidential address to the Wilson Ornithological Society, 'is not just a record book for the archives; it is a work book in which observational skills are repeatedly and continuously tested and sharpened'.

There are of course as many note-taking systems as there are note-takers: and we know of no ornithologist of experience who has not changed his ways several times. Basic to us all, though, is the pocket field notebook; small and cheap with pencil in attached tube or on a string. Plain card binding is best; colored covers run in wet weather. In rain or snow many people carry their pocket books in tobacco pouches or plastic bags.

As the note-taker gains experience he will find his drills improving, becoming second nature. The identification drill already discussed is the root of all bird watching: but many others must be obeyed before observation pays dividends, and something new and valuable finds its way from the notebook into our science and sport. An important drill is neatness; another consistency of style; paramount are completeness, truthful accuracy and objectivity.

Dr. Emlen made a neat demonstration of the value of objectivity when he quoted two hypothetical notebook entries, each of the same number of words: 'Male redwing [red-winged blackbird] No. 16 sighted a hawk circling high in the sky and responded with a series of alarm calls'. And 'Male redwing No. 16 tilted its head as a hawk passed high overhead, then uttered a series of shrill hissing notes'. The second entry contains no unprovable assumptions: the first, three – that the redwing saw the hawk, that it responded to the hawk, and that calls it made were alarm calls.

Adequate field recording requires a routine entry of time, place, ecology, climate, companions and often geology, too. An ornithologist is a good map reader, uses large scale maps and understands all the symbols. Most popular maps, when available, are 1:100,000, inch to mile, 1:50,000. Britain is blessed with a wonderful 2½-inch series which even shows field boundaries, and a National (kilometer) Grid on all its maps which on the inch-to-miles and large scales enables anybody to pin a point within a hundred meters and log it as a six-figure reference. Many continental European maps at the 100,000 scale have kilometer grids; pinpointing upon these is quicker than recording latitude and longitude. Some ornithologists we know carry geological maps naming the underlying rocks and showing glacial drift, and carefully note the avifauna in relation to these features.

Now that the botanists in most civilized countries have so neatly sorted out and classified the zonation of plants the bird watcher has little reason to mis-identify a bird's habitat or biotope. Most regions now have published habitat classifications; and many note-takers have developed semishorthand symbols for logging them. Semishorthand is widely used for noting climate – an essential daily, sometimes hourly drill: bird watchers can usefully learn the cloud coverage symbols, or Beaufort letters; the Beaufort wind scale; the international visibility scale. Too many often neglect the simple logging of at least the morning temperature (preferably in Centigrade), barometric pressure, and (if they have wet- and dry-bulb thermometers) the humidity, and we have ourselves often forgotten to write down such elementary episodes as a shower or snowfall. Times should always be noted on the Continental system, i.e. 0630 for 6.30 a.m., 1750 for 5.50 p.m. and referred to GMT, Greenwich Mean Time, CDST, Central Daylight Saving Time, or whatever the local setting is. Notes on abundance are almost useless when logged as 'common', 'scattered', 'a few': but an observer with no time for strict census work can often get useful comparisons by logging birds encountered in single figures (under 10) as 'order 1', double figures order 2, treble figures order 3, etc. All doubts and hearsay information should be written down critically.

Field book notes should be transferred to the permanent record *as soon as possible*, before the observer has forgotten his own abbreviations. What this permanent record consists of is a matter of taste and experience. On an expedition it is perhaps best to have a hardbound quarto or foolscap journal for the permanent record: as daily entries will vary, a day to a page diary is no good. Good books are one side of a page plain, the other ruled. Species and places can be underlined in different colors and indexed when the book is full or the job is over.

Many ornithologists keep permanent records on quarto or foolscap ($12\frac{1}{2} \times 8$ in.) paper in loose-leaf binders; but a lot of people are coming round to files of smaller slips and cards. Cards usually measure 3×5, 4×6 or 5×8 in.; slips (which make up into neat and portable little binder-books) $3 \times 6\frac{1}{4}$ or 5×8. One of us started with an over-elaborate 4×6 card index system with many colors and tabs, but long ago gave it up and went over to 5×8 slips in binders. Two binders holding well over a thousand slips can be stowed in a briefcase; but a card index is a real bore to hump about. Both sides of a 5×8 slip have room for about 350 words of ordinary handwriting: slips of this size are perfect for noting a scientific paper or book and making an abstract of its contents, and can be quickly shuffled to make up a bibliography.

Nearly every civilized country or state, and many counties and lesser units, have their own check-lists of birds arranged in a systematic order. Most bird watchers will be happy to classify their slips, cards or leaves by its system. Those of us who cover a lot of subjects need other systems, too: and here two great allies can be recommended among the numerical classifications of knowledge available. These are the system of the Library of Congress in the U.S.A., and the Universal Decimal Classification, more widely used in Europe.

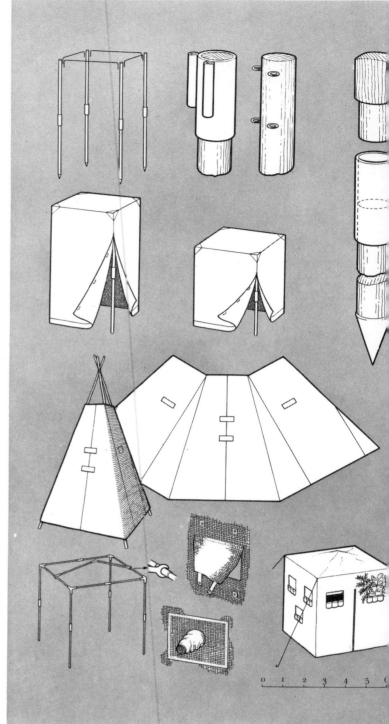

Left: red kite's nest in Spain was photographed from this 35-foot pylon hide by Eric Hosking, George Shannon, RTP

Above, top: Hosking hide, 6-ft. and 4-ft. styles, with detail of alternative metal tube and screw eye fixings for wire, hardwood peg for driving bottom half of pole

Middle: Skutch wigwam hide, showing method of cutting four 2×1 pieces. Three supporting poles can be cut on the site

Bottom: Tinbergen hide; note pockets, detail of frame flaps (to prevent birds lining up observer through opposite peepholes), camera sleeve

Field glasses and blinds

One fairly expensive piece of apparatus, and one only, is an absolute necessity for the bird watcher: field glasses.

Looked after properly, famous-name instruments by such craftsmen as Barr and Stroud, Bausch and Lomb, Hensoldt, Leitz, Ross and Zeiss are practically immortal. It pays a beginner to buy a top quality instrument for at least £30 or $85 and insure it; or to go for a good name at a second-hand dealer.

Consider the 'exit pupil' of a glass. This is found by dividing the diameter of the object lens (the lens furthest from the eye) by the magnification. The light gathering power varies as the square of the exit pupil. No ornithologist we know uses a glass with an exit pupil less than 3.8 (e.g. that of the popular 8×30 binoculars); and some who do night or dusk or dawn work prefer exit pupils of at least 5 (as with 8×40 or 10×50). We both use 9×35s, that is binoculars with a magnification of 9 times, and an object lens diameter of 35 mm.; and believe that the best magnification range is from 7 to 9 for general work. Few glasses with magnification over 9 give a field of view of over 120 yards at a thousand, and most weigh around 30 ounces. Ours weigh not much more than 20. Few glasses with magnifications of $10 \times$ or more can get objects nearer than 25 feet into focus.

All glasses should be checked for chromatic aberration – apparent rainbows round bright objects in the field of view, which should be confined to the edge of the field. All glasses should have their inner lenses and prisms bloomed with a bluish-looking mineral film: this can put the light transmission up by nearly a quarter. Most people prefer a central focusing screw that works both eyepieces together.

An important auxiliary for the advanced bird watcher is a telescope. Almost everybody in the sport and science does better to carry a 7–$9 \times$ binocular and a fairly powerful 'scope than just a 10–$12 \times$ binocular. All telescopes of any value have a magnification of at least $20 \times$; compared to binoculars they have a correspondingly small field, with fields of view of from 23 to 44 yards at 1,000 yards for 20–$25 \times$, 15 to 25 yards for 30–$35 \times$, 11 to 20 yards for $40 \times$ and over. All need stands; the lower magnifications work quite well on monopods (the telescopic tubular Newman Sinclair version weighs under a pound and folds to a walking stick), the rest on bipods or, better, tripods. For all, car-window clamps are marketed.

Some of the finest and most compact telescopes now on the market are, in fact, glorified prismatic monoculars, with no pull-out and quick eyepiece focusing. Many have interchangeable magnifications; one of the best of these, the German Hertel & Reuss Tele-vari, works on the zoom principle, as does the latest in the U.S. Balscope range made by Bausch and Lomb. The good new 20×60 English Ross prismatic Spottingscope weighs under two pounds and has a wide field.

The art of hide or blind making has been reduced by long trial and error to simple principles. Standard portable hides which can be readily made at home are in use all over the world; those we figure here are designed by two experienced life history and behavior students, who are also photographers, and a world-famous bird photographer who is also (naturally) a behavior student.

The wigwam hide was designed by Alexander F. Skutch for tropical nest watching in Central America. Its basis is about 8 yards of khaki shirt material of standard yard width and 3 slender poles about $9\frac{1}{2}$ feet long cut on the site. The three-sided wigwam has a double elongated slit (the lower for a camera) in front and slits on the other sides, each slit with a press-stud flap; the open top can be covered with a triangle of impermeable cloth. Niko Tinbergen's 4-foot-cube watcher's hide is based on $\frac{3}{8}''$ aluminum alloy tubing jointed by bits of electric insulation tubing. The cover is of 5 or 6 yards of canvas at least 4 ft. wide. The hood has a back zipper, 2 windows at the back, 3 windows on each other side, the lowest for cameras. Inside flaps shut by press-studs; outside pockets below the windowsill take stalks of small foliage to break outline and conceal the observer.

The Hosking hide is made of yard-wide fawn or green gaberdine, sewn in the form of a cross to give a double roof. Its horizontal cross-section is thus three feet square. In wet country, Eric Hosking substitutes or adds a rubberized roof square. He uses a 4-foot height for some nests, 6 feet for others, and has a dozen in use every season, with a selection of half-poles, the bottom ones of which can be hammered into the ground by striking a hardwood peg placed in their upper sockets. The roof is stretched by angled members of stiff wire. Guy lines are seldom necessary; but corner reinforcements are padded on to the gaberdine, and Hosking fits at least one flexible camera sleeve and several peepholes on all sides (with inside cover flaps) and pockets for notebook, lenses and (around the outside bottom) for anchoring stones or turves.

Left to right: modern Bronica; Leica M3 with Visoflex II reflex attachment, on robust tripod with universal head; Kenyon stabilizer KS-4, whose twin gyroscopic wheels reach 20,000 r.p.m.; modern Exakta; 300 mm. Kilfitt f5.6 telephoto lens on reflex miniature 35 mm. camera; Honeywell Futuramic II strobonar electric flash 65A, gives 1/1500 second of intense light

Photography

As early as the 1880s, birds were recorded photographically, but incidental to landscapes – sea birds on cliffs, gulls over the waves. The first nest, that of a song thrush, was pictured in 1892 by the Kearton brothers; the first close-up of a wild bird, a lapwing on a nest, was taken in 1895 by R. B. Lodge. Charles Kirk, O. A. J. Lee and Oliver Pike joined these British pioneers in bird portraiture before the turn of the century, to be followed not many years later in North America by Herbert K. Job and Frank M. Chapman and in Sweden by Bengt Berg.

Since the days of these masters, and specially in the last quarter century, color film has had its rise; film speeds have been stepped up again and again and so has film quality. High-speed strobes have largely replaced the flash bulb (but not entirely). Lenses of great focal length and highly critical definition have proliferated, forming glittering galaxies on the dealers' shelves. Cameras so sophisticated that they almost think like computers, Polaroid cameras enabling instant development, ingenious systems of synchronization and remote control, zoom lenses, fluid tripod heads, gyroscopic stabilizers, filters innumerable and hundreds of other accessories have revolutionized photography.

The skilled photographer of today must aspire to be an artist as well as a reporter. But he must remember that, unlike a painting, a photograph is not a composite of past experience; it is the record of a split second, an arrested moment – or, in the case of motion pictures, the record of a few seconds or minutes. Therefore photography is perhaps more useful than sketching for some facets of ornithological research. For the behaviorist, its products are raw visual data that can be re-interpreted long after the event. The ecologist, with photographs, can tell his readers far more about an environment than he could with words alone. No field biologist these days is without a camera. Professor Arthur A. Allen of Cornell University, the first of 37 universities in the U.S.A. to offer advanced work in ornithology, years ago gave his many graduate students a thorough groundwork in photographic techniques.

There are four basic ways to get pictures of birds: (1) shooting from a distance with a long lens (up to 600 mm. or even longer) using a heavy tripod, either with or without a blind; (2) stalking, with a lens of moderately long focal length (300 mm. is perhaps the ideal); (3) working close from a blind, using either available light, strobe or flash; and (4) remote control, wherein the camera may be close to the subject while the photographer waits, concealed, at a distance.

The disadvantage of most remote-control devices is that the photographer must reveal himself when he resets the camera. There are, however, at least three

35 mm. reflex cameras – the Minolta, the Nikon and the Praktina – wherein this problem is solved by a solenoid and motor unit which not only trips the shutter but rewinds for the next shot. It is even possible to rig up a walkie-talkie radio unit that will operate the camera at a distance of a mile.

In the days before the advent of color transparencies, most bird photographers preferred a film area of 4 by 5 inches. Allan Cruickshank still does and employs both a Graflex and a Speed Graphic. Eric Hosking shoots most of his close-ups with somewhat smaller 'quarter plate' (3¼ × 4¼ in.) field cameras equipped with a German-made 'LUC' shutter for quietness.

In recent years, however, there has been a swing to the convenient smaller sizes, especially 35 mm. Eric Hosking favors the fabulous Zeiss Contarex. RTP has a Leica M3, an Exakta and a Nikon. Using a reflex housing on the Leica and adapters on the Exakta and Nikon, all three take his favorite lens, an f4 300 mm. Kilfitt which he regards as the most useful lens for wildlife photography. Lenses of shorter focal lengths do not produce large enough images and those of longer focal lengths cannot really be used close enough to small subjects. The f5.6 300 mm. Kilfitt focuses down to 10 or 11 feet and the bulkier f4 model can actually be used at 5 or 6 feet, enabling one to get a frame-

filling image of the smallest bird. Many wildlife photographers who wish a somewhat larger film area for making black and white enlargements of exhibition quality, but who would avoid the bulkier cameras, compromise on the Swedish-made Hasselblad or its excellent Japanese counterpart, the Bronica. We have mentioned only a few of the more ideal items of equipment here – none of them is cheap. Space does not allow us to discuss the merits of the myriads of less costly cameras and lenses.

During the past half century many books and pamphlets dealing with the techniques of wildlife photography – the tricks of the trade – have been written, starting with the works of Oliver Pike, A. Radclyffe Dugmore, L. W. Brownell and others. But the whole field is evolving so rapidly that we will suggest only two of the latest (1962) as basic reading – *Bird Photography as a Hobby* by Eric Hosking and Cyril Newberry, and *The Complete Book of Nature Photography* by Russ Kinne. These two books offer the best blueprints for success.

Nearly all of the species of birds of North America and Europe have now been recorded on film with pinpoint fidelity. The era of the bird portrait is waning; there is a growing demand for pictures with more meaning – sequences of behavior, pictures illustrating points of biological significance and, of course, pictures that are simply beautiful and evocative.

Motion-picture photography

Birds are creatures of movement. The ciné camera translates this movement more accurately, more excitingly, than the still camera, which by its very principle freezes action. In still photography the initial investment is the major item; in ciné it is the upkeep. Therefore, standard theater-size 35 mm. is ruled out for non-professionals; 16 mm. is the practical size, acceptable not only for home use but also for the lecture hall and even the theater and television. The cost of shooting 8 mm. is less than one third that of 16 mm., but this miniature film leaves much to be desired.

Currently, we are using three ciné cameras. Two have reflex systems that allow viewing through the lens while shooting: (1) the Arriflex, the aristocrat of 16 mm. cameras, and (2) the Bolex (photograph right) which costs scarcely one fourth as much, yet approaches it in performance. Through-the-lens viewing is essential when filming wildlife, because of the problem of parallax and the necessity of following action, changing focus, etc. However, in certain situations we also find the rugged, dependable Bell and Howell most satisfactory. Mounted on a Borden camera gun with a Nydar gunsight (large photograph) it does a superb job on flying birds in slow motion. First the focus must be pre-set (anywhere between 30 and 60 or 70 feet) and the speed put at 48 or 64 frames per second. When the bird is centered in the bull's-eye, the trigger is pulled and held there until either the bird or the film has 'run out'. Out-of-focus footage may be eliminated later in the cutting room. However, a sequence is more effective if the bird is allowed to fly out of the picture at the close.

Although some ciné photographers, for the sake of economy, shoot and project at 16 frames, we recommend 24 as the basic speed. This reduces flicker, allows the addition of a sound track, and is required by television studios (which project at 25). Small birds with quick, incisive movements come through better when filmed at

32 frames and projected at the usual 24. Flight shots should never be taken at less than 32, and if slow motion is desired the setting should be 48 or 64 – even though at 64 the camera is racing at nearly three times the normal speed and consuming film at a ghastly rate. John Storer and Richard Borden both use Bell and Howells modified to shoot at the extreme speed of 128.

In using the camera gun or a pistol grip when tracking

flying birds, the 2-inch lens is the easiest of the longer lengths to handle; a 6-inch lens is harder to keep on target. The 4-inch is a good compromise, pulling the bird in and allowing enough control.

Recently, a new gadget has been added to the growing arsenal of the affluent photographer, the Kenyon stabilizer. This small gyroscope, powered with a battery pack, gives virtually tripod-stability to hand-held pictures even with 4- and 6-inch lenses. Admittedly costly, it is not just an expensive toy; it should be investigated by any ciné photographer who does much work from boats or planes or who films birds in flight.

The choice of the tripod is especially critical in ciné work. It must not be light, but solid enough to prevent wind vibration, particularly when long lenses are used. RTP uses heavy wooden legs equipped with a Miller fluid-action pan-head. There are other fluid heads as well as geared pan-heads, but the Miller, an Australian make, is a general favorite.

A word about 'panning' – swinging the camera horizontally: avoid panning with a long lens unless the subject is moving with the pan. Even with a lens of short focal length, pan very slowly and evenly.

The Miller head facilitates this. So does the Kenyon stabilizer.

Among the glittering array of lenses available for wildlife work in ciné perhaps the most ideal is again the 300 mm. Kilfitt. RTP prefers the f4 model which, by means of adapters, is interchangeable with his Arriflex and Bolex as well as his still cameras. If a lens longer than 300 mm. is to be supplemented, it is best to jump to 500 or 600. Lenses longer than 600 are unwieldy and well-nigh impractical under field conditions. Actually, a 300 mm. lens on a 16 mm. ciné camera covers slightly more of the film area than a 600 mm. does on a 35 mm. still camera. In other words, one need not be half as close to a bird to get a picture-filming image.

Editing can make or break a film. In shooting sequences, start with an establishing shot which gives the setting, the environment; then a middle-distance shot of the bird, to be followed by close-ups. This transition can also be accomplished by using a zoom lens, but too many zoom shots in a film are tiresome; half a dozen are enough. If successive close-ups of the same bird are used, avoid 'jump-shots' – with nearly identical poses; change the action or the angle. Also avoid the high sun, cold light and ugly shadows of noon, especially in the middle latitudes of the world. There is more pleasing color saturation before 10 a.m. and after 3 p.m. Take a siesta, bring the field notes up to date, catch butterflies – or do anything else during the mid-day.

When scientific analysis is more important than public showing, use black and white. Niko Tinbergen shoots most of his long behavior sequences in black and white at 16 frames, thereby keeping his costs within a reasonable budget. But even in black and white, ciné work is not cheap. In color, costs can run sky-high. The skilled ciné photographer may use only one foot in four or five when he edits his finished film. Then, if he values his labors, he makes a copy and stores the precious original in a temperature-controlled, fire-proof vault.

For slow-motion flight pictures, Roger Peterson shoots at 64 frames per second, using a gunstock. A Nydar gunsight makes accurate tracking easier

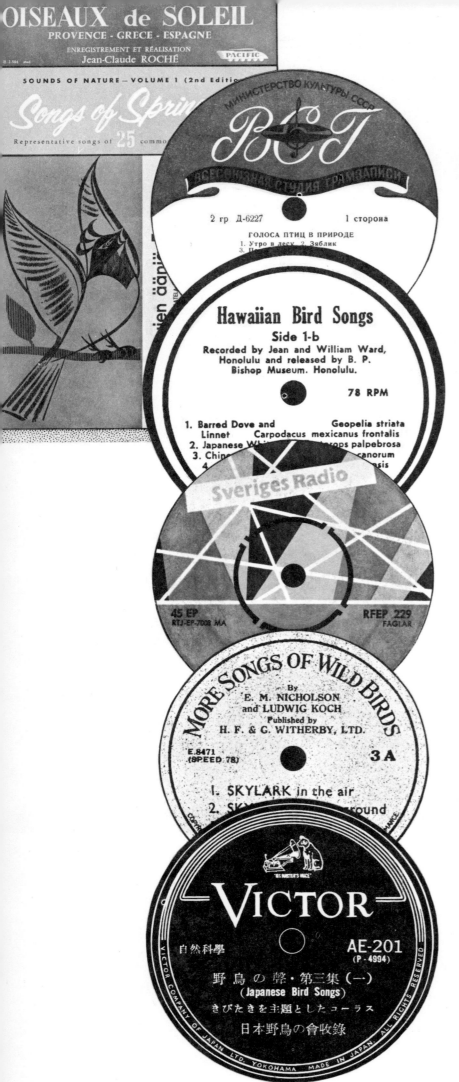

Sound recording

The voices of about 2,300 wild species of birds had been recorded by 1962: well over a quarter of all the living species. The sounds of over half these are available on published discs. About three-quarters of the regular European and North American birds are at least on tape in some laboratory archive, if not on processed disc.

Some further measure of the revolution in our midst can be understood from the number of bird-sound and bird-song discs offered for sale in Europe and Japan. The first (indeed the world's first), of which no copy appears now to exist, was published in 1908 by HMV in London: it was the voice of a captive nightingale hand-reared in Germany, recorded acoustically by a horn-microphone. The first published disc of wild birds, about ten species recorded by Ludwig Koch, was issued in Berlin in about 1910: no copy of this can now be found, either. No other known record was published till 1922. According to the careful research of our discographer friend, ornithologist Jeffery Boswall, about 9 different discs had been put on sale by 1932, over 50 by 1942, about a hundred by 1952, and nearly 250 (including LPs) by 1962.

All this hobby, art and science has developed within the lifetime of the first known bird recordist – Ludwig Koch, who as a boy made the first bird recording known still to exist on an Edison wax cylinder phonograph in 1889: a common shama. At the time we write, Koch is still active in and around England, where he has lived for the last thirty years, during which he has inspired a whole movement and founded the magnificent collection of recorded natural sounds of the British Broadcasting Corporation.

Today three other institutions have master collections

of original recordings: Sveriges Radio in Stockholm; N.H.K. – the Japanese Broadcasting Corporation – and the Cornell Laboratory of Ornithology in the United States; the last has voices of well over 1,500 species. One private freelance, Dr. W. W. H. Gunn of Canada, has a collection that ranks with these.

Apart from Koch and Gunn, patient recordists of vast experience and skill have worked or are now working, and have published records, all over the world: in England John Kirby and Eric Simms; in France Jean-Claude Roché; in the U.S.S.R. Boris Veprintsev; in Denmark Carl Weismann; in Switzerland Hans Traber; in Sweden Sture Palmér; in Germany G. Thielcke; in Africa Myles E. W. North; in Japan the brothers Kabaya; in the U.S.A. Albert R. Brand, Peter Paul Kellogg and Don Borror. There are fine artists working now also in Australia (Peter Bruce), New Zealand (Kenneth and Jean Bigwood), Hawaii (Jean and William Ward), México (L. Irby Davis), Venezuela (Paul A. Schwartz) and Brazil (Johann Dalgas Frisch).

The pioneer work of Ludwig Koch before World War II was all done with the cumbersome equipment of the day. His microphone cables ran from marsh, bush and woodland to a great van in which sound engineers crouched over generator-driven wax recorders. His recordings were cut directly on master discs, and the sounds selectively dubbed later in the studio. Albert Brand, the American pioneer, used much the same technique.

With the war, and the coming of the magnetic tape recorder, techniques got lighter and better. The best results still come from custom-built recorders operating from jeeps or Land-Rovers with vibrator converters, portable generators or extra dynamos and batteries. These can get almost perfect recordings down hundreds of feet of cable. But miniature portable battery sets have reached a wonderful technical efficiency: and a modern amateur can hump his own battery set, with a portable parabolic reflector for his microphone, for miles through the bush, and get tapes (at the hi-fi speed of 15 inches per second, which can deal best with steeply changing frequencies) that can stand up to the best, and provide material adequate not only for broadcasting and hi-fi disc dubbing and reproduction, but for scientific analysis by oscillograph and (now more usually and usefully) spectrograph – instruments which make a visual picture of the sounds themselves which can be both harmonically analyzed and compared with those of other birds.

Bird song, then, is not something which we can merely collect, but something which, like eggs and skins and photographs and facts, we can analyze. Amateurs need money, a touch of electronic training, time and opportunity to make a satisfactory hobby as recordists: but many are joining the ranks and multiplying (rather than merely adding to) the material available to us all. Scientists in many laboratories, with scientifically-minded musicians as colleagues, are finding unexpected and interesting things out, from tapes, about the anatomy of bird song; are discovering new evidence about the learning-power and instincts of birds, even pointers to their evolution.

The field man, blessed by the deluge of discs, has now a good, new, vital weapon in his eternal striving toward quick, accurate identification. Few of us, however experienced, have not had to learn some of even the commonest songs again the hard way, by hearing them anew, and then finding their singers, each spring. Now it is armchair and disc; so that when the warblers, the thrushes, the other migrants come, we are ready for them and wise before the event.

Pied kingfisher

Dabchick

Demoiselle crane

Little egret

Egyptian goose

Common crane

Shoebill

Upper left: Lascaux's 'prehistoric tragedy'
Lower left: some of the birds of Tajo Segura
Above: From Ti's tomb, 5th dynasty of Egypt

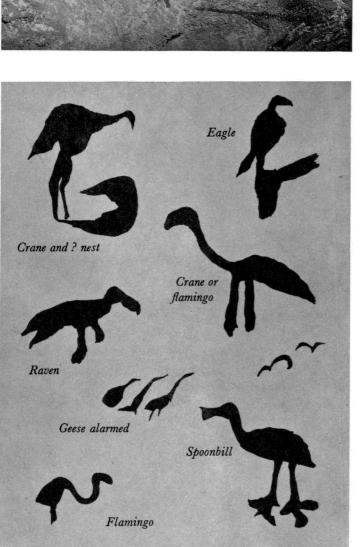

Eagle

Crane and ? nest

Crane or flamingo

Raven

Geese alarmed

Spoonbill

Flamingo

Tally ho!

In the wonderful cave of Lascaux the ancient hunters of Périgord in France portrayed their prey, inspired by the needs of magic, education and perhaps even science.

The Stone Age hunters who decorated the walls of caves made what are probably the earliest lists of animals known to us. Most authorities have thought that the Lascaux master artists worked from 25 to 15 thousand years ago. At that time, however, the local fauna was boreal in character; with mammoth, reindeer, saiga antelope, woolly rhinoceros and a race of wild horse close to Przewalski's race that still inhabits Outer Mongolia. Neighboring decorated caves show this fauna.

None of these animals is figured at Lascaux. The cave paintings include a wolf, cave bear, cave lions, red deer, aurochs (urus, the ancestor of domestic cattle), and ibex. Instead of the Przewalski horse the many horses on the walls are tarpans – forest horses; we can also be sure that the Lascaux bison belong to an earlier race or species (with sharp ascending horns), larger and grander than the surviving European bison; and the late F. E. Zeuner was convinced that the single rhinoceros is not the long-horned, high-withered woolly rhino but a tubbier, stubby-horned woodland species known as Merck's rhinoceros. This last flourished in a fauna of about a *hundred thousand* years ago – a warm time between a big retreat of the ice and its next advance.

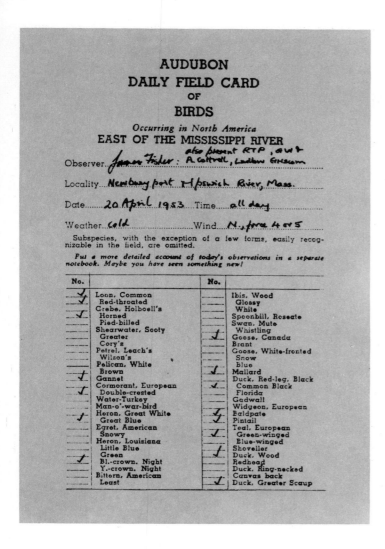

We dwell on Lascaux at some length – for between the famous rhino and a magnificent bison reposes the world's first known essay in ornithology: a dead hunter with a bird-mask, and by him a bird-crowned stick.

One of the earliest known biggish bird lists was depicted by a New Stone Age artist or artists on the walls of the Tajo Segura, a cave in southern Spain, about six thousand years ago. The ornithologists concerned had little skill, but enough to assure us that the bird fauna then was much the same as now.

When the Tajo Segura bird watchers or bird hunters were making their scrawls on the walls the world's first civilization was already established in the Near East. By 3100 B.C. a Sumerian building near Ur had doves and eagles on its friezes; by 3000 B.C. some of the most lovely geese ever painted (of identifiable species) adorned Egyptian tombs. One famous early tomb, that of Tí (c. 2500 B.C.), figures quite a list of species, of which one, the shoebill, no longer lives in lower Egypt. No less than ninety species of birds are among the mummies, drawings and hieroglyphic records of ancient Egypt.

The Ancient Greeks were the first people to make the proper kind of lists we use in science: and the world's first great biologist, Aristotle (384–322 B.C.), made the first one of birds. He mentions about 170 species, of which about 126, whose habits are described in some detail, are recognizable.

Aristotle's work was improved by other, later classical minds – notably that of a Roman army officer and naturalist, Pliny the elder, who was killed in the Vesuvian eruption of A.D. 79 and must have known and dined with the 'Campanian Audubon', the great artist whose 'list' of the birds of Pompeii (p. 142) is almost as fresh now as when he laid the final varnish of white Punic wax mixed with oil and put away the last silken brush.

Since those times of classical glory, the civilization of the West had its long ages of slow progress, but never shed its inheritance of intellectual order. Lists accumulated, for a thousand years and more stuffed with uncritical quotations from unverified teaching, fable and nonsense. Before the Reformation and the first printed bird book in 1544 there were, it is true, some fine Arab improvers of natural history, some royal naturalists and falconers, and many poets like Chaucer and Holland, and some artists who gradually built up the lists. After William Turner's treatise on 130 mainly European species (1544), our science grew wings, spurred on by inquiring minds like those of Gesner (Swiss), Longolius (Dutch), Kay, Browne, Merret, Willoughby, Ray and White (English); Sibbald and Martin (Scottish). By the mid 18th century a scholar could have a good library of printed books, among them editions of the greatest, standard scientific lists of all time, the immortal *Systema Naturae* and *Species Plantarum* of Carl Linné, Carolus Linnaeus of Sweden. In the tenth edition of the *System of Nature* (1758) Linnaeus listed 564 species of birds from all over the world, of which well over 500 are identifiable. This, by universal agreement (and now rules) is the basic list to add to, and contains the basic system for all scientific naming.

Most bird-watching nations around the world now have a standard list of birds for every country or state, most counties and some parishes and special districts.

Lists, of course, have cast a certain competitive spell on their makers, which we would be the last to deprecate: most English bird watchers cry *tally-ho* when they log a new bird for the area or a Life Bird. Tally records are scorned by some: but their pursuit sharpens field skill and gives a lot of useful pleasure. The North American year record of species seen or heard belonged to Guy Emerson in 1939 (497), to RTP in 1953 (572), and since 1956 has belonged to Stuart Keith (594). JF logged 713 species in the Holarctic Region and México in 1953.

A single day's count of 230 species was set up by a party led by L. Irby Davis in México in 1950. In the U.S. single parties have reached or exceeded 200 in Texas, Florida and California. In Europe Big Days with much over 100 are rare.

Nobody knows for certain who has seen the most species of birds alive and wild, though the late Ludlow Griscom's life list, over 2,000, is among the world's larger lists.

Local records

Gilbert White, the tender, wise and inquiring curate of Selborne, dreamed of the day when every kingdom, every province might have its own monographer.

Local avifaunas can be defined as systematic catalogues of birds which attempt to be comprehensive, embrace previous work critically reconsidered, and deal with the birds' status, habits, movements and history in the area. Such books or papers have now been published for (for instance) all the provinces of Canada, all the United States of America, all the modern departments of France and all the counties of England.

In countries so advanced, ornithologically, we can choose an early pioneer master-work which set the style and standard. In what is now the U.S.A. the Englishman Mark Catesby spent the years 1712–19 (in Virginia) and, backed by wealthy patrons, returned to colonial America in 1722 and worked as collector, recorder and artist until 1726. He spent most of the rest of his life in England writing and illustrating the magnificent *Natural History of Carolina, Florida and the Bahama Islands*, published with 109 plates of birds. Linnaeus and later Linnean namers based the designations of at least 75 species of birds on the illustrations and descriptions of the hard-working and brilliant Catesby.

Catesby's book was the only attempt to give the whole natural history of an American colony in colonial times. Thomas Jefferson himself published what perhaps rates as the first bird list of the United States in his *Notes on the State of Virginia* in 1787. But though this President listed over 100 birds, he knew but 60 or 70 well, and his list scarcely rates as an avifauna. The first scientific regional avifauna of the United States was published in 1844 – James Ellsworth DeKay's volume on the birds of the state of New York. At least one avifauna now exists for every one of the fifty states, and half published their first in the 23 years between 1889 and 1911.

In France the pioneer local faunist (and avifaunist) was Pierre Joseph Buc'hoz who published a fine catalogue of the animals of Lorraine in 1771. Since his day every one of the 87 departments of France has produced one or more avifaunas. Half of them published their first in the 50 years between 1828 and 1887. England started earlier than France – with Dr. Robert Plot's natural history of Oxfordshire published in 1677 – but consolidated rather later. All the major counties now have avifaunas, and half of them produced their first in the 72-year period 1829–1901.

In their search for historical material modern avifaunists must cover previous literature exhaustively, dig deeply into private files, old notes of bygone naturalists. Important sources have quite often been overlooked. For instance, between 1880 and 1893 Lord Lilford, the reigning ornithologist of JF's own county of Northampton, published a county avifauna in parts in the county naturalists' journal. It paid no attention whatsoever to a county genius, the poet John Clare.

Clare was working at his best between 1820 and 1837, when only about 70 species of Northamptonshire birds had been recorded in print, most by John Morton. Clare nearly doubled the list. Lovely descriptions and accurate notes exist in his published poetry and prose of no less than 119 bird species, of which 65 had never been previously recorded for the area by anybody else.

Some particular areas, through proximity to an ancient university or through chance, have had a specially long and complete succession of bird recorders and bird records. Concord in Massachusetts has the reputation of being the best-birded place in the New World. Its pioneer was another poet; though David Henry ('Henry D.') Thoreau does not appear to have had Clare's bright sensitivity to birds, and never learned many songs, he had a crude optical glass and made many 'first records' for the Concord area.

Some of Thoreau's notes go back to 1832, when he was only 15. He died in 1862; but in 1868 William Brewster began to visit Concord and to amass skins and an incredible collection of notes, by no means all of which had been published when he died in 1919. Fortunately this paragon of North American field skill had a successor and editor of equal caliber – the late Ludlow Griscom whose *Birds of Concord* was published in 1949. Since Griscom's time the continuity of observation has been assured by the field station at Drumlin Farm in nearby Lincoln, managed by Wm. Drury Jr. There are now nine decades of matchlessly complete bird data available for Concord.

In Europe few areas can vie with Concord for their succession of local recorders, though the forest of Fontainebleau near Paris, the Norfolk Broads, the London parks, the Oxford meadows, Linnaeus's fields and meadows near Uppsala in Sweden are among the good ones. Some well-watched spots have attracted generations of chroniclers by virtue of their remoteness or special interest – like the Camargue marshes in southern France, or Germany's Heligoland. Perhaps the most remarkable history is that of the archipelago of St. Kilda, the westernmost islands of Scotland. This national nature reserve houses one of the finest sea bird communities in the world. The islands were first scientifically investigated by the great Scottish naturalist Martin Martin in 1697, who made a fine catalogue with notes on their birds. Since Martin's time St. Kilda has had more books and scientific papers written about it than any comparable area in the whole of Europe. Of the last 134 years only the odd 34 seem to have gone by without the making of some valuable natural history observation by some resident of or visitor to St. Kilda.

Below: Title pages of early British works with good local avifaunas; and (lower right) blackcock (1), spoonbill (2), bittern (3), mallard (4) and barn owl (5) in John Ray's Ornithology of Francis Willughby *(1678)*

Above: Hundreds of regional books have been written dealing with the birds of nearly every part of the world.

Censuses

Thomas Pennant and Gilbert White, close friends and pioneer English naturalists, did, we know, make a few casual bird counts in 1768 and after: but the first great bird census was made by the immortal American pioneer ornithologist Alexander Wilson. Watching a great flight of passenger pigeons in Kentucky in 1806, Wilson wrote: 'if we suppose this column to have been one mile in breadth (and I believe it to have been much more) and that it moved at the rate of one mile a minute; four hours, the time it continued passing, would make its whole length two hundred and forty miles. Again supposing that each square yard of this moving body comprehended three pigeons, the square yards in the whole space, multiplied by three, would give two thousand two hundred and thirty millions, two hundred and seventy-two thousand pigeons! An almost inconceivable multitude, and yet probably far below the actual amount.'

A. W. Schorger's guess at a 3 to 5 billion total population of the passenger pigeon in the world before its decline and crash stems from similar calculations. It is quite likely that Wilson's huge flock embraced more than half the total population of his day.

Nobody seems to have counted a sea bird colony before Friedrich Faber noted 13 to 15 occupied gannets' nests on Grímsey, off north Iceland, in 1819. Nobody seems to have thought of censusing a common colonial land bird until J. A. Harvie-Brown wrote round in 1875 to all the lairds in Caithness, Scotland, for returns of the numbers of rooks' nests on their estates. Nobody started plotting birds on large-scale maps until L. Jones made a census of the wintering birds of about 1¾ square miles around an Ohio town in 1898, or F. L. Burns made a breeding bird census of a square mile of Pennsylvania in 1899, 1900 and 1901. But after the turn of the century several workers in both U.S. and Britain began to awaken to the possibilities of measuring and comparing bird density. Refined and elaborated, the bird census is now growing as a research of the first importance, which enables us not merely to measure the numbers of birds, but to compare them, and from the comparison to learn a host of ecological and evolutionary principles.

The census can tell us how fast birds can increase, the speed of recovery of birds after natural catastrophes and the success of species new to areas; the seasons of greatest mortality and migration; the extent of periodic fluctuations in number and how far these are regular; changes in distribution and the extent and speed of colonization of new land; the ability of birds to withstand the competition of other species newly introduced into their habitat by man or by natural colonization.

The results of sample habitat breeding censuses are usually given in Europe in individual birds, in North America in pairs (or occupied territories), to the hundred acres. Here we use the former. While American tundra and woodland seem somewhat richer than European, the following density figures reflect populations in both countries. True tundra in the full arctic rates from none to under 30 birds per hundred acres; but some Alaskan and Canadian rich tundras may support from 200 to 530. Heath and moor populations run from very little to about 220; brush and scrub 200–600; ponds and lakes to about 225; marsh 100–540; sage semi-desert only around 10; open simple grassland 40–220; agricultural land (tilth, hedges, leys, meadows, orchards) anything from 30 to about 720, depending on the richness of the soil and the variety of the crops.

The densest bird populations are found in woodland and in parkified urban suburbs and gardens. It is true that virgin northern woodland far from clearings or rides carries under 100, often under 50; but normal woodland supports anything from 100 to 1,500 or exceptionally over 2,000 birds per hundred acres. The progression of density in different countries follows much the same pattern, with conifers (spruce-pine) low – 150–200 Finland, 100–500 central Europe, 190–660 N. America and México – and deciduous woodland higher – 430 Finnish birch, 640–1,200 various central European forests, 200–1,540 various N. American woodland samples. Mixed conifer-deciduous samples often give higher figures than pure deciduous woodland stands. In both continents the highest density of over 1,000 is mainly found in bottomlands and flood-plains, for example the poplar-willow-ash woodland of the Danube, or the mixed valley hardwoods of Maryland, or the live oaks of the Californian river courses.

The city park and suburban or rural garden – widespread habitats made entirely by man for his aesthetic pleasure and spiritual satisfaction – probably support the most consistently dense avifauna in the world. When they contain colonies of social nesting birds like martins or rooks they can occasionally have over 10,000 birds to the hundred acres, or even more.

We have already dwelt (p. 72) shortly on the methods and results of making censuses of individual species of birds, and ways by which figures for the total land bird population of whole countries can be estimated. There are many refined techniques now in operation. Even banding returns can be used to arrive at figures for whole species populations. But the firm foundation of most census work remains the nest count or territory count. We have spent hundreds of happy days in the field counting the numbers of apparently occupied nests in sea bird colonies. On one of our trips JF took this photograph of the largest massed colony of breeding common murres in the North Atlantic. About a million now breed each year on the flat rock slabs of Funk Island off Newfoundland's east coast; and a large section of the colony is embraced by the photograph opposite.

Murre colony, Funk Island, Newfoundland

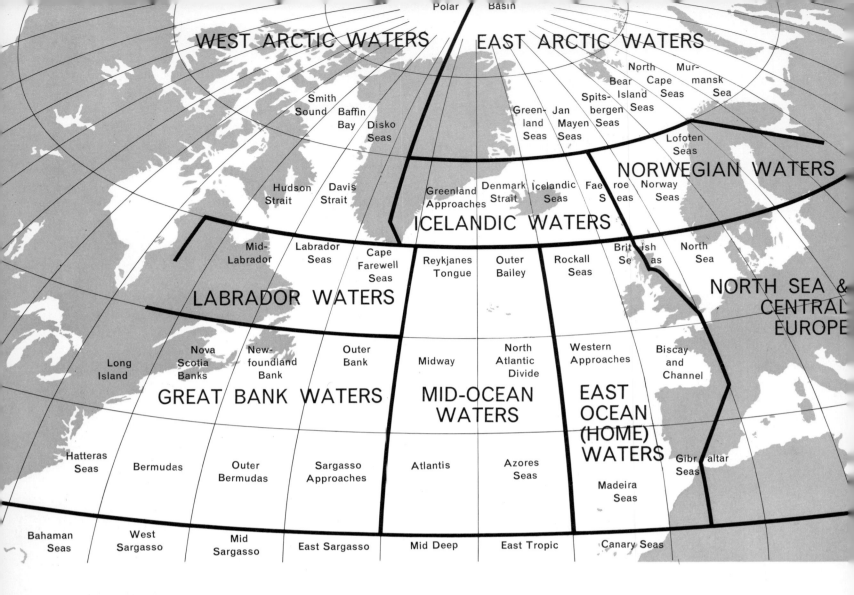

The map shows ocean regions with the following labels:

Polar Basin

WEST ARCTIC WATERS — EAST ARCTIC WATERS

North Bear Island Seas, Murmansk Sea, North Cape Seas, Spitsbergen Seas, Greenland Seas, Jan Mayen Seas, Lofoten Seas

Smith Sound, Baffin Bay, Disko Seas

NORWEGIAN WATERS

Hudson Strait, Davis Strait, Greenland Approaches, Denmark Strait, Icelandic Seas, Faeroe Seas, Norway Seas

ICELANDIC WATERS

Mid-Labrador, Labrador Seas, Cape Farewell Seas, Reykjanes Tongue, Outer Bailey, Rockall Seas, British Seas, North Sea

LABRADOR WATERS

NORTH SEA & CENTRAL EUROPE

Long Island, Nova Scotia Banks, Newfoundland Bank, Outer Bank, Midway, North Atlantic Divide, Western Approaches, Biscay and Channel

GREAT BANK WATERS — MID-OCEAN WATERS — EAST OCEAN (HOME) WATERS

Hatteras Seas, Bermudas, Outer Bermudas, Sargasso Approaches, Atlantis, Azores Seas, Madeira Seas, Gibraltar Seas

Bahaman Seas, West Sargasso, Mid Sargasso, East Sargasso, Mid Deep, East Tropic, Canary Seas

The sea log

Practically nothing was known about sea birds, by anybody who could record it, until about a thousand years ago.

It is true that there are a few sea birds in Stone Age etchings and paintings, notably some veritable great auks in the Magdalenian cave of El Pendo, which has been dated about 8000 B.C. The home of civilization was the Mediterranean, and all we hear about from the artists and authorities before the time of Christ are a handful of its salt-water birds: pictures of cormorants and a pelican in Egyptian tombs of about 2500 B.C.; gull, tern and shearwater in the poems of Homer (whoever he was or were) around the 12th to 9th centuries B.C. The Old Testament adds nothing, for it mentions only the pelican and cormorant in *Deuteronomy* (7th century B.C.) and later books. The great Aristotle (384–322 B.C.) separated the cormorant and pigmy cormorant, but added no further sea birds to the Mediterranean list.

Before the Europeans really began to build ocean ships an extraordinary people, from Asia and the East Indies, began to colonize the scattered islands of the vast Pacific Ocean in small catamarans and later in great double sailing canoes that could carry up to a hundred people for many weeks. Not until the West made contact with

the descendants of these heroes in the 18th century was it discovered that the Polynesians had become fine navigators through knowledge of the stars, through the use of stick-net charts of islands and currents, and through knowing and following the birds.

It is a moot point whether the Polynesians or the Irish or the Viking Norsemen were the first marine ornithologists. All used bird watching to help their navigation out of sight of land: and a pretty crude navigation it was, for in the Pacific great islands like Tahiti and Hawaii were almost certainly discovered by ships' companies blown off course; and the first Viking discoveries of Iceland, Greenland and North America were all made by ships astray. When the Norsemen reached Iceland first in about 865 they found Irishmen already there: and it is credibly recorded that the first Irish explorers (mostly monks and priests) had island-hopped in skinboats or curraghs to Iceland, by Scotland and the Faeroes, on the trail of the migrating geese in spring.

Three weeks before Columbus sighted a light on Watling Island in the Bahamas and rediscovered America his crew had been aware of the neighborhood of land by watching birds: particularly boobies. The early sea explorers of post-Columbian times seem to have known their birds quite well, and to have used them as land-guides. Some like Cartier (St. Lawrence) and Barents (Spitsbergen etc.) of the 16th century, the Tómasson brothers and Jón Guðmundsson (Iceland), du Tertre (West Indies), Worm and Debes (the Faeroes), Martens (Spitsbergen) and Martin (Scotland) of the 17th century, and a good crop of 18th century travelers and voyagers – particularly Captain James Cook's naturalists (the Forsters, father and son) – had the urge or even the commission to watch sea birds for the sake of pure record.

Just over 260 full species of sea birds are now recognized. The species in most families were discovered and described later than those in the important land bird families. Only 28 were known to Linnaeus in 1758, though by 1766 the great first scientific namer had described seven more. By the end of the 18th century only a hundred (exactly) were known. Only half the species were known by 1822, only three-quarters by 1844. After then progress was steady; and all but a dozen species were named by 1900. Since 1916 only two new sea birds have been discovered: Murphy's petrel, described by R. C. Murphy in 1949 and now known to breed in fair numbers in the remotest islands of the South Pacific; and Jouanin's petrel, described by C. Jouanin in 1955, which is not uncommon in the Persian Gulf and the north-west Indian Ocean but whose breeding grounds have not yet been found. Incidentally, nobody has yet found the nest of the magenta petrel, MacGillivray's petrel or the sooty storm petrel: all these are Pacific birds.

Over a fifth of our sea birds are named scientifically or in the English vernacular (or both) for some ornithologist-discoverer or describer or other pioneer. This reflects the fact that a big minority of sea birds live, or lived, in areas where there were no men to give them proper native names.

Of the living sea bird families, the majority are wholly marine, repairing to coastal land only to breed. But some have wholly or partly deserted the open sea in the course of evolution and have become estuarine or fresh-water birds. Most of the living pelicans are birds of river deltas or inland lakes, and some cormorants have a broad range on continental fresh waters. A substantial minority of gulls and terns are likewise inland birds and a few species may reach a coast only by accident. The small snake bird and skimmer families are estuarine or fresh-water birds, never properly marine. All but one of the skuas are true sea birds only in winter, as are the delicate phalaropes. The two sheathbills of the south are parasites on sea bird colonies and scavengers. Some birds of families not fundamentally marine have, on the other hand, taken to salt water; thus among the wildfowl the eiders, scoters and steamer ducks are really sea birds, and most divers and several grebes winter at sea.

To this day the list of sea bird breeding places, especially in the Pacific, is far from complete; and ornithologists are only just beginning to collect world-wide accurate information about their distribution at sea. Organized plots of birds against latitude and longitude were rare until the early years of the present century, though Nansen and his companions on the famous attempt on the North Pole in *Fram* in 1893–96 kept recording under the greatest hardship. But pioneers like M. J. Nicoll (1904 on), R. Pässler (1911 on), and J. T. Nichols (1913 on) had worked out a good sea-log system and discipline before World War I; and after it methods were refined by Poul Jespersen of Denmark, and by W. B. Alexander of England who gave the sea-loggers their first real tool in 1928 with the publication of his classic *Birds of the Ocean*, the first identification book for sea-going bird watchers. In the 'thirties transects, or running sea logs from ships, became a more normal routine for the voyaging ornithologist. R. C. Murphy's *Oceanic Birds of South America* was published in 1936, and is still the greatest work of research and scholarship in marine ornithology; and in the previous year V. C. Wynne-Edwards showed most elegantly how an analysis of the results of accurate transects could produce a real picture of the at-sea distribution (with seasonal changes) of the birds of a particular ocean, the North Atlantic. The map reproduced here represents the ten-degree classification of part of the North Atlantic propounded by another pioneer sea-logger, E. M. Nicholson, in 1951, refined by JF in the subsequent year for his monograph on the fulmar.

During World War II standing orders at sea to officers and men of Britain's Royal Navy (no doubt as a means toward alertness) included advice on making bird logs at sea for analysis by the British Trust for Ornithology. In 1946 the Royal Naval Bird Watching Society was formed; in 1956 members of Britain's merchant navy were admitted; in 1961 the Netherlands Seafarers' Bird Watching Society was established. Lately the R.N.B.W.S. has devised good sea-log forms which when filled in are analyzed in the Natural History Museum in London, by Dr. W. R. P. Bourne and other marine ornithologists.

The identification of birds at sea remains most difficult. The systematics of many species and groups is being rapidly improved, and new field (or rather, ocean) guides are badly needed. Many marine bird watchers hope that the whole business of analyzing the distribution of ocean birds, which cross no national boundaries, may become an international obligation, based on some new institute in a seafaring country. With new and comprehensive identification guides, and a swift charting drill, the next generation of sea-loggers may bring as much precision to the sea-bird species plot and its changes as the landlubbers have already attained with their less mysterious and more easily mappable birds.

The watchers and the flyways

About half the birds of the world have two addresses, quite often thousands of miles apart, and twice a year travel between them. They travel alone, or in stately flocks, by night and day, navigating by the heavenly bodies, stopping to refuel at favorite feeding grounds. Many migrate on broad fronts, as many or more along traditional flyways – valleys and coasts.

As the migrants go, so has man watched them since his early times as the inheritor of the earth. It is not to be believed that Stone Age hunters were unaware of the passage of the storks and cranes, the clanging wildfowl, or of the musical arrival of the little spring singing birds around their homes. The common people, and the earliest poets whose lines come down to us, like Homer, were perfectly well aware of the twice yearly tides of bird migration.

The present study of migration occupies much of the time of more than half the professional and sub-professional ornithologists of the world, and the vast majority of its thousands of active amateurs. To us it is a spring routine to log the first arrivals and first songs, a pleasant autumn chore to man an observation station at banding time. Our standard books are full of meticulous and detailed maps of birds' summer and winter quarters, and the routes they take between them – maps based on direct observation by hundreds of different people and on the recoveries of some tens of thousands of marked (banded or ringed) birds.

It is hard to believe that most of this information has been collected in just half a century, and nearly all of it in a century. Great authority on swallows and swifts as he was, Gilbert White of Selborne could never divest himself of the idea that they must sleep in the winter somewhere in bank, bush or building in their summer haunts. Quite late scholars, taking a suggestion that appears to have originated 23 centuries ago with Aristotle, believed that migratory birds hibernated: the last important one was Georges Cuvier in 1817. (So far only one bird (p. 66) has been discovered to hibernate truly.) As late as 1702 one Morton in an anonymous pamphlet actually suggested that swallows migrated to the moon – or that if they did not, some other place would have to be provided for them.

The serious scientific study of bird migration did not really begin until the eighteen fifties. Its pioneers were a German, Heinrich Gätke, and a Russian, A. von Middendorff. Von Middendorff read a paper to the Imperial Academy of Sciences in St. Petersburg in 1855, which coordinated the observations of a group of his correspondents all over European Russia from which he was able to make maps, with isochronal lines, showing the advance of various spring migrants across the country. Gätke was inclined to make wild guesses and statements, and remained puzzled about the causes and methods of migration all his life; but he took up residence on the island of Heligoland (27 miles off the mouth of the Elbe) in 1837 as a young artist of 23, and during the 'fifties and onwards started to contribute articles on migration to German and English journals which established Heligoland as an important flyway 'bottleneck' and as the first unofficial bird observatory. His classic *Heligoland as an Ornithological Observatory*, first published in Germany in 1891, inspired workers all over the world to pay attention (perhaps, in the long run, almost too much attention) to islands and coasts and led very soon to the establishment of the first of what is now a great network of official observatories and migration-watching points.

By the time Gätke's book came out the recognition of the flyway, or concentrated migration route, had emerged

in both Europe and North America, stimulated in North America by some early notes of Audubon's friend John Bachman (1836), much thoughtful material in Audubon's own *Ornithological Biography* (1831–49), an important paper by S. F. Baird (1866) and the observations in the Mississippi Valley published by W. W. Cooke in 1884–85, which were the first to link spring immigration with temperature and pressure. In Europe in the 'seventies much was pondered on rather little evidence by J. A. Palmén of Finland, F. L. A. Weismann of Germany and A. de Brevans of France, in works which are now of historical interest only,* but which served to create enthusiasm and convince students that they needed a new, comprehensive and coordinated program of field observation. Britain was first in the field with such a program: organized by J. A. Harvie-Brown and John Cordeaux, keepers at a number of British lighthouses and lightships sent migrant bird notes for central analysis from 1879 to 1887. After this, observations at Irish lights were collected by R. M. Barrington, and lights were used as unofficial bird observatories also in Denmark, Germany and U.S.A. Between 1905 and 1913 the British Ornithologists' Club cast a network of observers over England and Wales, inland as well as coastal, and published nine detailed reports. Similar networks in the earlier years of the present century were set up in Hungary, Switzerland and U.S.A.

These early pioneers of direct observation were groping for a system by which the extent and direction of bird migration could be identified and understood, matched with seasons and weather movements. They were avid

*The three standard modern works on bird migration, those of Sir Landsborough Thomson of Scotland (1926 and later editions), the late F. C. Lincoln of U.S.A. (1939 and later editions) and Jean Dorst of France (1956 and later editions), have excellent historical chapters; and W Rydzewski of Poland published a useful history of bird marking in 1951.

Adélie penguin with U.S. Antarctic Research flipper band, now adopted by expeditions of other nations

collectors of data, and, like many pioneer data collectors, not certain of its value until they started to analyze it. They were moving toward the present system in Europe and North America: the observatory system. Early in their work they were furnished with a key tool: the bird band.

The earliest man known to have marked a bird – according to Professor Rydzewski's scholarly researches – was one Quintus Fabius Pictor. Sometime between 218 and 201 B.C., when the second Punic War was on, this Roman officer was sent a swallow taken from her nestlings, by a besieged garrison. He tied a thread to its leg with knots to indicate the date of his relief attack, and let the bird fly back. In the later Roman days of Pliny (1st century A.D.), a certain knight fond of chariot racing in Rome used to take swallows with him from Volterra, 135 miles away, and released them with the winning colors painted on them, no doubt enabling his friends at home to confound the local bookmakers.

The earliest use of a modern style band dates from the Roman occupation of Britain; a metal ring was found on the leg bone of a guineafowl dug up at Silchester.

Many early falconers marked their birds with name plates or bands: Marco Polo encountered such marks in Asia between 1275 and 1295. There are quite a few early records of fast journeys by marked falcons, and of allegedly very long-lived herons marked by the nobles whose falcons brought them in unharmed (some of which are probably fakes). Swans and ducks were marked with metal collars by landowners in the 17th and 18th centuries. In the middle of the 18th century J. L. Frisch tied threads to swallows' feet dyed in water color, to test whether (as a fashionable theory of the time held) they hibernated under water. They came back next spring with the dye not washed out. A woodcock caught in a rabbit net in England in 1797 was marked with a brass leg-ring and shot in the same place twelve months later.

In the 19th century deliberate marking of albatrosses, geese, ducks, eagles, falcons, storks, buzzards, gulls, terns, guillemots, swifts and passerines was tried, in more or

Below: rings and wingclips (natural size) used by Switzerland, U.S.A., Britain, the Falkland Islands, U.S.S.R., Portugal, Denmark, Norway, Spain, Sweden, Belgium, Czechoslovakia, Iceland, Finland and the Netherlands

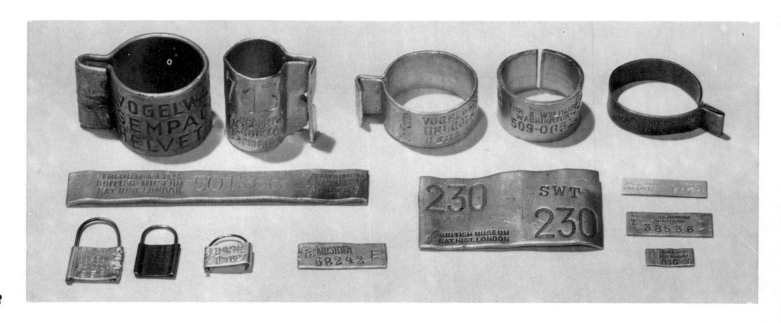

less haphazard ways, by many people, most of whom were interested in migration; among them the Americans Audubon and Bachman, the German ornithologist J. F. Naumann, the English scientist Dr. Edward Jenner, the Finnish ornithologist A. Nordman, the English ornithologists Lord William Percy and H. W. Feilden, the Scottish explorer W. S. Bruce in the arctic.

The pioneer of modern scientific banding was Hans Christian Cornelius Mortensen of Denmark. In 1890 he marked starlings around his home at Viborg with thin zinc rings inscribed in ink with VIBORG and the year of marking; but gave his experiments up as unsatisfactory. But in 1898, when aluminum was available at a reasonable price, he banded a red-breasted merganser (which was recovered) and in the following year banded 164 starlings with the first rings which were marked with a return address *and a serial number*. It was because of the introduction of the all-important serial number, which for its lifetime identified the individual bird, that Mortensen became the father of modern banding. The Frenchman C. Millet had suggested the use of serial numbers as early as 1866; but his scheme (involving colored neck collars) was never carried out.

Unnumbered banding was carried on by several workers long after Mortensen's time, the most spectacular scheme being that of Jack Miner of Kingsville in Ontario, who started ringing ducks in 1909 with bands stamped with 'Box 48, Kingsville, Ontario' and a verse of scripture. The Jack Miner Migratory Bird Foundation has now marked over a hundred thousand birds, mostly ducks, geese and mourning doves. But the world's great banding workers and organizations have all followed the 1899 Danish lead with rings with terse, clear addresses and serial letters and numbers, pioneer schemes (pre-World War I) starting in North America in 1902, Germany in 1903, Hungary in 1908, England and Scotland in 1909, Russia and Jugoslavia in 1910, Sweden, Holland and Switzerland in 1911, Australia in 1912, Austria and Finland in 1913, France and Norway in 1914. Today wild birds are banded in about 50 different countries from Antarctica to Greenland. In the whole world over two million have

been marked in each recent year, and over thirty million since 1899 (of which over a million have been recovered). By 1961 estimates and a count give North America the record banding total of about 13 million; Germany comes next with about 3,600,000, then Britain and Ireland with 2,881,619, Russia with about 2,300,000, and Sweden with just over a million. Close on three hundred permanent or semi-permanent banding observatories are now in operation, with their own finances and staff.

The need for bird observatories, most importantly at nodal points on flyways, was foreseen before the invention of the numbered band; and indeed the pioneer Gätke on Heligoland considered his headquarters an 'observatory' a century ago. The first official scientific bird observatory was also set up in what was then Germany, at Rossitten in the Baltic in 1901 by J. Thienemann. This worked with its own bands from 1903 until 1945, when all its records were destroyed in the war. In 1956 it was re-established as a station (now Rybatschi) by the Russians. In 1910 the present official Vogelwarte Helgoland was started in Gätke's old island under H. Weigold. Damaged in World War I, and totally destroyed in World War II, the observatory has now moved to neighboring Wilhelmshaven; but birds are now banded on the island itself again in vast numbers – indeed, the total of 16,123 for 1959 was an all-time record. The Rossitten observatory now has a successor at Radolfzell on the shores of Lake Constance, and the two German schemes each issue their own rings. With substations, about 20 observatories are now manned yearly in Germany; and banders in Luxemburg and Austria use Radolfzell rings.

In Britain the great migration student W. Eagle Clarke pioneered Fair Isle, between Orkney and Shetland and at a real flyway bottleneck, as early as 1905, and worked there with companions for several springs and autumns. Many unofficial banding stations were established after what is now the national Ringing Scheme for Britain (with which Ireland collaborates) was set up by H. F. Witherby in 1909. The first 'official' British observatory was founded by R. M. Lockley on the island of Skokholm off the Welsh coast in 1933. In the following year the

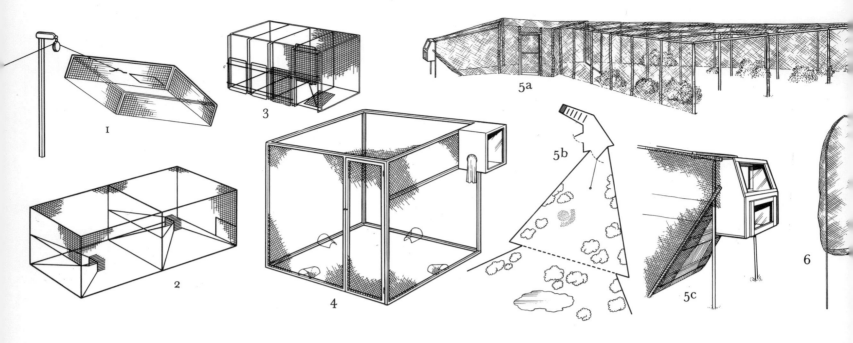

first in Scotland was opened on the Isle of May in the Firth of Forth. Fair Isle became an official station in 1947; and in that year England's first bird observatory was established on Lundy. There are now 17 bird observatories in Britain and Ireland represented on the Bird Observatories Committee of the British Trust for Ornithology (which now runs the Ringing Scheme), which means that each must be able to find accommodation for banders in or near the station. With other stations manned at migration time but not represented on the committee England can now boast over 40 permanent or semi-permanent ringing points, Wales and Scotland each five, Ireland six, the Isle of Man and Jersey each one. In proportion to its size and population, Britain has the best migration station coverage in the world.

However, Britain has plenty of friendly competition in Europe. Sweden, which now has one national scheme, rings more birds per human head than any other country in the world, and two of its observatories, Ottenby and Falsterbo, are models to all. France has been developing observatories lately (most important, the Tour du Valat in the Camargue), as has Spain; Italy has at least 28 regularly manned banding points. In Holland up to 14 observatories and banding points are regularly operated. Switzerland has a magnificent banding organization based on the observatory at Sempach. The U.S.S.R. reorganized its Bird Ringing Bureau in 1951 and now rings twice as many birds a year than all she ringed before World War II. Belgium has an excellent scheme, as has pioneer Hungary, and Poland – where a fine magazine, *The Ring*, edited by Prof. W. Rydzewski, is the organ of the International Committee for Bird Ringing, which meets every fourth year. Intensive banding is operated by the Czechs, the Norwegians and the Finns.

The first serial bands in the United States were placed in 1902 on young black-crowned night herons near Washington, D.C., by Dr. Paul Bartsch of the Smithsonian Institution. In 1909 the American Bird Banding Association organized a national scheme, which was in turn taken over in 1920 by what is now the U.S. Fish and Wildlife Service. The Canadian Wildlife Service cooperates, uses the same bands and receives duplicate microfilm of all records. There were 55 official banding stations in 1960 in the U.S.A. alone, and many other unofficial stations and manned ringing points.

Banding goes rather slowly in Central and South America; but in Asia it has been re-started in Japan, which had a fine record before World War II, and is being developed in India (by Dr. Sálim Ali), Malaya, Indonesia and Borneo. Australia and New Zealand have shown great new enthusiasm lately, with programs organized by the government and by the national ornithological society respectively. South Africa now has its own excellent scheme and at least three observatories; and banders are working in Nigeria, Ghana, the Congo and East Africa. In the last 18 years a big ringing and penguin flipper banding campaign has been organized at the many research stations in Antarctica, as a consequence of which our knowledge of the lives and movements of several sea birds has been quite revolutionized.

Birds banded in the nest, or before they are fledged, are now outnumbered by birds banded after trapping in most areas of the world. Each technique gives us different but complementary information about longevity, life-expectation, the permanence of mating partners and summer and winter territories, the coherence of families, communities and flocks (like those of geese which migrate together), whether young or old birds tend to pioneer

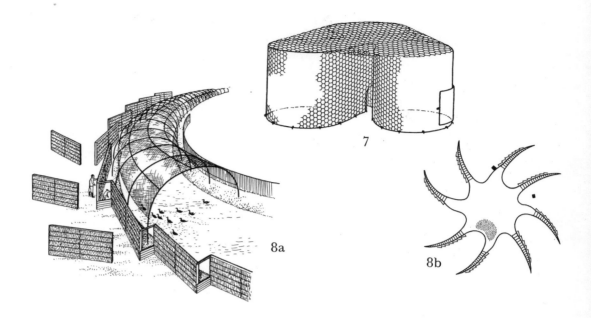

Some trapping gear of the modern bander:
1. Beals actuated drop trap; 2. Modified
Government sparrow trap; 3. Potter trap;
4. House trap; 5a. Heligoland trap, also
showing plan (b) and detail of catching
box (c); 6. Bat fowling net; 7. Clover-
leaf trap; 8. British duck decoys operated
by the Wildfowl Trust: (a) pipe at Berkeley
New Decoy, Slimbridge; (b) plan of Bor-
ough Fen Decoy

new range – quite apart from the actual geography and season of migration flights, and the effects of climate and weather upon them. Moreover, with the rise of trapping and the use of special colored bands as well as metal serial bands refined field studies of individual birds and their descendants through generations have been and are being made on a most elaborate scale.

Long before the sport, hobby and science of bird banding was invented man had been a fowler of the living bird for food or cage. Duck decoys, clapnets, spring nets, bat fowling nets, drop traps, aerial (curtain or trammell) nets across forest rides or canyons or under bridges, fleygs (the racket-like sea bird net independently evolved in the Komandorski Islands of the North Pacific and in North Atlantic islands), and all manner of snares, had been in use by hunters for centuries. Very little attention was paid to most of these efficient bird-catching techniques by the early ringers. Indeed, in 1923, an early year of the present banding régime in the United States, the famous California ornithologist Joseph Grinnell got an official flea in his ear from the State Fish and Game Commission for even suggesting that banders might be trained in aerial net techniques by local (illegal) bird-netters using ancient Italian methods. Mist nets (p. 124) did not come into operation until after World War II.

In America trapping was encouraged in the early days of banding, it is true: but anything as straightforward as a clapnet, a batfowling net, a canyon net or a Heligoland trap was ruled out of court for a long time. Instead a spate of original invention was based only in a few cases on traditional designs like the drop trap. Most of the banders' traps of the 1920s were designed on the trip-door principle, actuated either by bander or bird, or on the funnel-entrance principle where birds are

baited into a cage and cannot find their way out again.

All sorts of traps, among them special traps for special birds, were invented by ingenious American pioneers like A. W. Higgins, William I. Lyon, Miss Jessica Potter, E. A. Everett, F. J. Lurvey, S. Prentiss Baldwin and Jack Miner; and pioneer trap-banders in Europe, notably R. M. Lockley, had their share of inventions. Perhaps the most important banders' inventions or adaptations that have come into general use since the first comprehensive U.S. *Manual for Bird Banders* by F. C. Lincoln and S. P. Baldwin (1929) are the modern forms of drop trap and house trap, the Potter trip trap, various funnel traps and specialized duck traps, and the Heligoland trap.

The Heligoland trap was in general use in Europe a long time ago but has only lately come into any use in the United States. It is based on a method used by the local thrush catchers on Heligoland noted by Gätke in his pioneer days of observation there a century ago. An old Heligoland *troosel-goard*, or thrush bush, consisted of a fence of 10-foot brushy branches stuck upright in the ground in a 20-foot row, with a parallel fence stuck in the ground with its branches' bases about 7 feet away but their tops slanting over to close with the tops of the upright row. The slanting side is covered with a net which bellies out behind it in a semicircle. Cover on the rather exposed island of Heligoland is scarce, and the birds are attracted to the trap for cover's sake alone, and can be easily driven into the catching net from the upright side.

When Vogelwarte Helgoland was established in 1910 under Hugo Weigold the famous *Fanggarten* or walled trapping garden was established in abundant living plant cover, such as is inevitably sought by tired migrants, with several funnel traps disposed over the bushes, on the thrush-bush principle, so that the best cover was at or just within their entrances. Birds driven in by beaters inevitably flew up the tunnel, round a bend, and into what appeared to them to be an open window but was in fact a glass-backed catching box.

The Heligoland trap caught on rapidly in Germany and other parts of Europe. The first in Britain were erected on Skokholm by Lockley in 1933 and on the Isle of May by the Midlothian Ornithological Club in 1934. Nowadays all bird observatories in Europe have them, and quite a number of private stations; and all sorts of ingenious modifications of them have been invented to fit walls and natural gullies and canyons: and many European clubs have portable Heligolands which can be quickly erected.

The Heligoland trap works on much the same funnel principle as the duck decoy. This was invented in Holland, and was introduced in England in the 17th century, and until recent years was a purely commercial apparatus, extremely expensive to build, and with the marketing of highly edible winter food as its sole object. Nearly all duck decoys are artificial shallow ponds of about three acres cleared and dug in wet woodland cover. From each pond usually at least four and sometimes many more 'pipes' curve into the surrounding woodland. A pipe is a ditch that tapers and shallows toward its far end, which is invisible from the main pond; and it is covered by netting supported on semicircular hoops usually of metal which decrease in size toward the catching net at the end of the ditch, which is actually on dry land. One side of the curved pipe is solidly screened by brushwood; the longer side is screened by a series of staggered overlapping head-high hurdles of straw or reed behind which the decoyman can crouch and through holes in which he can observe the ducks.

Many decoys entice ducks into the pipes by food or by pinioned or tame decoy ducks or both; but the usual decoy is a dog. Ducks have the insatiable curiosity of Kipling's elephant's child and when swimming always tend to 'mob' a dog on the bank, following it if it appears to run away. A decoy dog is trained to show itself at a gap between the staggered hurdles, disappear, and show itself quickly at the next gap up the pipe. The ducks follow up the pipe until they are far enough for the decoyman to show himself to begin with near its entrance, and later further up, and thus drive them to fly up the pipe, round the curve and flutter into the blind alley catching net at the end.

Thousands of ducks – probably the majority now banded in Europe – are banded every year now in Dutch, Danish and British duck decoys, and in the special duck traps at Abberton in Essex built and operated by Major-General C. B. Wainwright. In 1951 the first duck decoy

in the New World was operated at the Delta Waterfowl Research Station in Manitoba, Canada; it captured 1,600 ducks for banding in its first season.

Two important and very similar waterfowl catching inventions were independently pioneered in 1948 to band wild geese. In February of that year a rocket-propelled net made its first goose catch in Gloucestershire, fired by the man who thought it up, our old friend Peter Scott, Director of the Wildfowl Trust; his fellow Trust council member James Robertson Justice had the same idea during World War II. In December of the same year, quite unaware of what was going on in England, Hubert H. Dill and William H. Thornsberry caught their first geese at Swan Lake National Wildlife Refuge in Missouri with a mortar-propelled net, the American boom net. These inventions have now been highly developed, and have caught thousands of geese for banding – with most valuable results considering that the recovery rate is now 15 per cent or more.

We can give an example of the value of rocket-netting, combined with other new banding methods, by reporting the Wildfowl Trust's pink-footed goose campaign of the early nineteen fifties.

The pink-footed goose nests only in East Greenland, central Iceland and Spitsbergen. The smallish population breeding in the last archipelago winters in Denmark, Germany and Holland: and the rest virtually only in Britain.

In the winter of 1950–51 the earliest big rocket-netting campaign in Scotland and England caught 629 pinkfeet. In the next summer an expedition led by Peter Scott, with his wife Philippa, Finnur Guðmundsson of Reykjavík and JF went with a horse-train to the Þjórsarver við Hofsjökull, an oasis in the central desert of Iceland, discovered that – as Finnur had suspected – it supported the headquarters of the Iceland breeding population, about 5,500 breeding adults in that year, and caught (with the help of rabbit-netting) 384 individual adult pinkfeet during the month-long period when they run with their growing goslings in flightless molt. Two of these had been banded in Scotland the previous fall: the rest, with 769 goslings (a total of 1,151), were marked. To catch them we found ourselves re-inventing a driving technique that may date back in the area to the Viking days of the 11th century; for we visited stone-catching-funnels in nine different places in the oasis, some of which had probably been in use until the 17th century, possibly later.

In the fall of 1951 525 more pinkfeet were marked by rocket-netting in Scotland and England: and recovered were eight more that had been banded in Britain in the fall of 1950, nine in Iceland in the summer of 1951, two already in Scotland in the same month.

In the fall of 1952 1,129 more pinkfeet were 'rocket-banded' in Scotland and England: of the additional

In 1951 a Wildfowl Trust expedition rediscovered the central Icelandic breeding
grounds of the pinkfoot, and the technique
of catching goslings and adults at the flightless stage. L. to r., Peter Scott, Finnur
Guðmundsson, Philippa Scott and Valen-
tínus Jónsson netting 114 birds on 31 July

Below: rocket-netting; a successful catch of
Icelandic pink-footed geese by the Wildfowl Trust in Britain, October 1955,
photographed from firing hide

recoveries eleven had been banded in winter 1950–51, six in Iceland in summer 1950, seven in fall 1951, twelve in the same or the previous month.

Armed with all the techniques worked out in 1951, Peter Scott led a triumphant expedition back to the Þjórsarver in 1953 which found a breeding population of about 8,200 adults, banded no less than 3,614 adults and 4,861 goslings, 8,475 in all. Among their recoveries were 53 1950–51 British marked birds, 108 1951 Iceland birds, 30 fall 1951 British birds and 72 fall 1952 British birds.

In the fall of 1953 1,558 pinkfeet were rocket-netted in Scotland and England, of which 15.4 per cent were already banded. The major campaign ended in the fall of 1954 when 1,572 more were rocket-netted, and of their 1,049 adults about the same percentage were already banded. In the course of the whole research program 14,800 pinkfeet in all were ringed and about 1,900 recaptured or recovered. One bird (REYKJAVIK 21152) was ringed as an adult on a hill in the Þjórsarver oasis called Oddkel-salda on 20 July 1951, rocket-netted in Midlothian, Scot-

land, on 25 November 1952, caught again in flightless moult on Oddkelsalda on 26 July 1953, and rocket-netted again near Annan in the Scottish Lowlands on 26 October 1954. Five others were caught three times in the sequence Britain–Iceland–Britain and one in the sequence Iceland–Britain–Iceland.

From the recapture figures a mathematical estimate of the British wintering population of late 1953 was 43,000; this was certainly over 90 per cent of the world population, and by the end of the rocket-netting that fall about 8,000 living pinkfeet – nearly one in every five – carried bands, most of them personally put on their legs by Peter Scott.

This great banding campaign was not only able to measure nearly the whole world population of the pink-foot, but make a model of its annual and seasonal fluc-tuations over three and a half years estimated from death rates and recovery rates. Between 1950 and 1953 the death rate (October to October) of adult pinkfeet was about 26 per cent and that of yearlings about 42 per cent. Of the 14,000 that died in 1953 it is likely that 12,000 were shot: the pinkfoot is a top sporting bird to British wild-fowlers, who are, in a very real sense, its chief natural predators; and the crop of geese they take, though it is between a quarter and a third of the entire fall population, does not appear to endanger the status of the species, which reached a high peak in the breeding season of 1953.

The pinkfoot campaign also established that these geese probably pair for life, and remain in some sort of association with their families beyond the normal first year. But its chief triumph was the assessment of population, and its demonstration that scientific measurement can solidly establish the legitimacy of a traditional sport. There can be no ecological objection to pinkfoot hunters as long as their crop remains within the replacement capacity of the goose.

We have dwelt at some length on this classic campaign because it was based on a new technique (rocket-netting) and a rediscovered old technique (flightless goosedriving). There is still, throughout the realm of banding, scope for new techniques, and on both sides of the Atlantic workers have been rather slow to adopt each other's methods, or older fowling techniques. Take the mist net. A curtain net for woodland rides, gullies, gaps and bridges so fine that it was practically invisible to flying birds is believed to have originated in Honshu, Japan, over 300 years ago. It reached a high degree of refinement and skilled use nearly a century ago. Mist netting spread widely over Japan.

In the present century, though licensed, Japanese fowlers took over 7 million birds annually in mist nets between 1924 and 1942; in a peak year, 1928, no less than 16,000 fowlers had permits. The Japanese are now paying serious attention to limiting what has become an excessive toll of life. What in the hands of fowlers can be too murderously efficient a source of wild food was not recognized as a boon to Western banders until as late as 1947 when our friend Oliver L. Austin Jr., with the U.S. occupation forces in Japan, shipped some mist nets to America. They quickly caught on in Britain and the rest of Europe, as well as in North America, where they are mostly in use under license: for the very strictest rules are necessary in their operation. The British Bird-Ringing Committee, which enrolls no banders without the most careful vetting, requires by rule that no mist net be left unattended for more than half an hour.

Trapping and netting rules, indeed, are vitally necessary in modern banding. Gone are the days when banding authorities issued rings haphazard and without inquiry, and enthusiastic but inexperienced youths could, unsupervised, mark birds in the nest too young for ringing, or leave traps unvisited for hours in the breeding season. We do not mean that ringing has ever resulted in a serious mortality of the ringed: but all our modern ring-

ing authorities have realized that the science, hobby and sport must be totally free of mistakes and unconscious cruelty. That is why in every important national scheme we know of, the tyro has to learn from an experienced ringer, preferably and of course most quickly at an observatory, before he is allowed a permit.

It is not easy to put the right kind of ring on the right bird rightly; it is even less easy to take a ring off. An inexperienced or fumbling operator can easily kill a small passerine by pressing its diaphragm if he has no inkling of the proper way to hold it. The economy of science requires, too, that birds when banded should in many cases be weighed, sexed and measured, and that notes should be made on their molt and condition, and that (at least at some well-organized observatories) their parasites should be collected. This means that their release must be delayed for quite some minutes, and that methods of keeping them healthy and calm must be followed.

What we are trying to say is that banding is no idle hobby, but a severe and complex scientific discipline with scores of written and unwritten rules. A bander must be prepared to spend a season learning the game before he can turn himself loose, and must be able to quote his manual or banders' guide more accurately and easily than a motorist passing his license test. Nobody can be trusted to handle wild birds alone, or instruct others, until he has proved himself by tender deftness, dexterity and practical common sense to be familiar with every problem that comes his way, to be an impeccable identifier foremost, but beyond that to know what to expect about the

A whinchat, trapped at a British migration observatory, held in the ideal position for banding; head comfortably between first and second fingers, breast not pressed. Special pliers squeeze band gently round leg

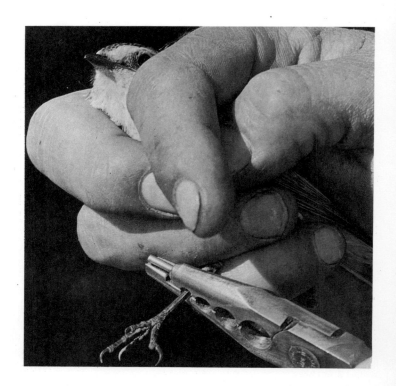

in-the-hand behavior and psychology of every kind of bird he handles, and, having handled his bird, to make his records as accurately as a computer programmer and nearly as promptly as a computer.

So much for banding. Banding has provided a new core to our study of bird migration. But new techniques have brought direct migration 'watching' back into equal favor. A successful tool like the band gets perhaps a little over-fashionable. Its limitations get lost in the fascination of using it. It is a tribute, then, to the broad thinking of a handful of post-World War II ornithologists that they have exploited some advances in other sciences refined by that war to branch out into new fields, cross new thresholds. It always pays to rub sciences together, especially if one or both are new. What have been rubbed with ornithology since the middle 1940s, are (as far as bird migration is concerned) the new, refined meteorology and weather-prediction, the new techniques of sound recording and the war-born applied science of radar.

In Britain Kenneth Williamson, first director of the Fair Isle Bird Observatory (between Orkney and Shetland) when it was established in 1947, applied his skill and experience not merely to building up a fine banding record for Britain's most northerly bird station but to analyzing the rushes of immigration in terms of the by then very accurate daily weather charts of the British Meteorological Office. Thirty years previously Fair Isle pioneers like W. Eagle Clarke and the formidable pioneer Scottish bird recorders Evelyn Baxter and Leonora Rintoul had suggested that the main influxes of autumn migrants

in Scotland were linked with easterly and south-easterly winds. In a series of masterly analyses Williamson proved that these influxes were, in a sense, abnormal. He developed his important theory of 'migrational drift' by linking each rush and influx of birds at the Fair Isle with the local conditions in Scandinavia. He found that the normal migratory route of Scandinavian migrants in fact was southerly and that the main flyway was along the eastern North Sea coast. But when the prevalent fall anticyclone over Scandinavia was very powerful, pronounced easterly winds swept coasting migrants along western Norway and Denmark to sea and out of sight of land.

The British influx of such migrants, he believes, are 'drifters'. Once at sea and out of touch with their eastern lead-line coastal flyway such westerly-driven birds probably fly down-wind 'deliberately' – possibly getting a drift from the wave formation of the sea, at least by day – and make their landfall anywhere from Shetland south, to pick up the western lead-line of the eastern British coast and rejoin their basic flyway in the Channel area. Williamson's original theory of drift-migration has been much refined by recent studies but still stands in essence.

As long ago as 1881 the American ornithologist W. E. D. Scott published observations of birds crossing the moon and thus pioneered a technique of measuring the nocturnal migration of birds. But serious scientific moon-watching did not really begin until 1945 and its results were not fully published until 1951 when George H. Lowery Jr. at Kansas University brought out his *Quantitative Study of the Nocturnal Migration of Birds*. By setting up a chain of observation stations, working with superior optical instruments mainly during the five days when the moon was full, Lowery established that telescope observations of moon-crossers could be relied on to produce a good measure of the volume and direction of nocturnal migration, could prove that night migrants fly more often singly than in flocks, move most heavily up to midnight and on a broad front more than by special skyways, and are very susceptible to the local meteorological system, particularly to barometric pressure.

Later in America Stanley C. Ball realized that considerable dividends could be gained simply by recognizing and logging the calls of night migrants and the apparent direction of their movement; and this technique was mechanized by 1959 when Richard R. Graber and William W. Cochran published the results of a study in which night migrants recorded themselves on a tape-recorder *via* a permanently fixed upward-ranging microphone-fitted parabolic reflector, for subsequent analysis in the laboratory.

We have already mentioned (p. 117) that in the late 1870s questionnaires were circulated to lighthouse-keepers

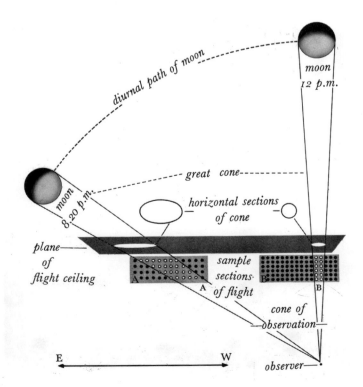

Lowery's diagram showing that twice as many birds may fly at midnight (B) when moon is at zenith, as at 8.20 p.m. (A), but only half as many are visible against moon through contraction of cone of observation

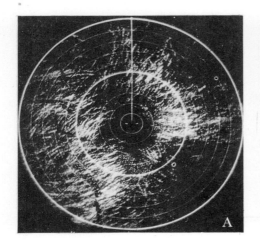
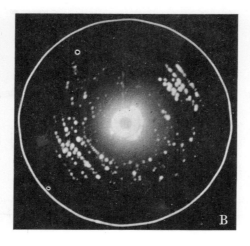

A. *One of the first photographs to be published of radar 'angels'; strong and complex echoes from flocks of birds migrating at low to medium height over n. Switzerland, 0659 hours 21 Oct. 1956; from Ernst Sutter's study.*
B. *Illinois N.H. survey photo; spot rows show waterfowl flocks' tracks repeatedly intercepted by radar beam.*
C. *London area 29 Mar. 1958. Scatter of 'angels' represents night migrants. N. of mid-point five distinct w.-e. clumps, and a faint sixth, identified by W. G. Harper as waves of starlings leaving roost for n. Europe at 45 m.p.h. air speed.*

in Britain. The great pioneer William Brewster of U.S.A. had the same idea at about the same time: and from both surveys it emerged that there was quite a considerable mortality of night-migrating birds at lights. Dazzled by the light, passage birds destroyed themselves against the superstructure of the lighthouses. Since those days it has been gradually realized that all high man-made structures, whether illuminated or not, are a death-trap to night-migrants on their course – among them not only light-houses but skyscrapers, monuments (like the George Washington monument in the U.S. capital) or the more recent radio and television towers, which multiply fast and are often 1,000 feet tall. Oddly, ornithologists have until recently seldom analyzed the accidental kill at such obstructions, which in a rather horrifying way provides a natural sample of the bird numbers and species involved in night passages. However, Harrison B. Tordoff and Robert M. Mengel of Kansas University made an important study in the fall of 1954. They examined, with the help of members of the local Audubon Society, the 1,090 birds killed by colliding with the newly-erected 950-foot tower of station WIBW-TV at Topeka between 25 September and 23 October of that year.

At the Lake Iamonia television station in Florida Herbert L. Stoddard Sr. converted the surrounding area in 1955 into a sward of grass as smooth as a golf green so that dead birds could be easily spotted from a cruising car. He or his assistants patrolled the area virtually every day for nearly eight years! From his analysis of tens of thousands of birds Stoddard found that night movement takes place in every month of the year, and involved no less than 129 species at this particular station, some of which had hitherto been thought only day flyers.

In the summer of 1941, working with what was then a new and at the time vital British invention, the radar scanner, Dr. E. S. Shire discovered that birds can reflect radio waves with sufficient echo to be detected. In September of the same year the zoologist George C. Varley (now Hope Professor of Entomology at Oxford but at that time a radar boffin) proved by direct visual checks that echoes on a scanner at the Straits of Dover came from gannets flying singly above the sea.

Though the radar physicists were reluctant to accept it at first, it soon became clear as defensive radar came into use in the Mediterranean, Australasia and North America that birds could indeed be detected even on the crude early sets. It was first formally proved that this was so when J. A. Ramsay of the British Coast and Anti-Aircraft Experimental Establishment suspended a gull from a balloon and got separate echoes from both. When high-powered transmitters came in early in 1943, bird echoes, in the words of Dr. David Lack and Dr. Varley, 'became such a menace on British coast-watching equipment that we specially trained radar operators to distinguish them from echoes of operational importance'. Birds, indeed, gave rise to several E-boat scares and to at least one invasion alarm; and it was soon realized that starlings and even small passerines could produce the hitherto unexplained small blobs of echo on a plan-position radar display-screen – blobs that had their own varying populations and movements and were known as 'angels'. 'Angels' were known to increase markedly around sunset (roosting birds) and in spring and autumn (migrants) and presented quite a hazard to airfield control and the operation of all high-powered sets.

In 1952 W. G. Harper, in 1954 J. G. Tedd (later joined by Dr. Lack, the Director of the Edward Grey Institute of Field Ornithology, who was a radar scientist in World War II) and in 1955 Dr. Ernst Sutter of Basel, all began working independently on bird echoes – with the high-powered centimetric radar scanners of Britain's Meteorological Office at East Hill in Bedfordshire; of the Royal Air Force's various stations; and of Zürich airport. In 1957 Dr. Sutter published the first scientific radar analysis of bird movements, Harper, Tedd and Lack following with interesting papers in the subsequent year.

Sutter's paper and published photographs showed most beautifully the October flights of migrating birds across a circle of northern Switzerland with a 20-mile radius. Harper's work confirmed that inland migration in England was generally on a broad front, at nights normally up to 5,000 feet and sometimes up to 10,000, very occasionally to 16,000. Tedd and Lack, whose apparatus could detect 'angels' at a range of over 60 miles, found an angel

D. *Radar screen photo during a movement described later. (See diagram G.)*
E-F. *Drawings from radar films of migration over e. England by D. Lack and E. Eastwood; (E) 1200 9 Jan. 1959, departure large lapwing-type echoes ahead of snow (hatched) moving s.; (F) 2100 24 Aug. 1959, huge s. exit warbler-type echoes and small sw. wader-type movement Channel; anticyclone, wnw. wind.*
G. *Morning 6 Oct. 1959, small movement ssw. from Scandinavia; and dense w. departure from Continent, presumed mainly chaffinches; anticyclone in s. Scandinavia, se. wind*

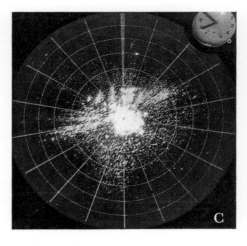

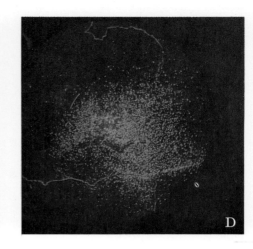

C

D

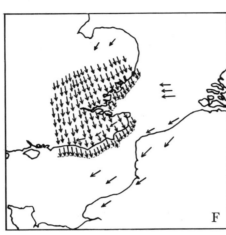

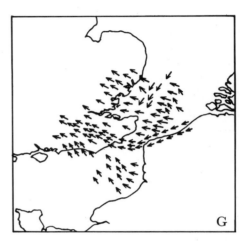

E

F

G

pattern in Norfolk that precisely reflected the flock movements of fall migrants that they themselves watched in the area covered by the set. In the same way angels around Cambridge, Massachusetts, where A. W. Friend had noted up to 200,000 in a 20-mile radius on his scanner, were correlated with flocks of migrant birds.

Soon these and other workers had established many things by radar. Lack deduced that overseas (North Sea) migrants out of sight of land in clear weather kept a constant heading (presumably by sun and stars) and did not usually correct for wind drift. Caught in overcast, at least some flew around irregularly with repeated changes of direction. Lack also confirmed that the common passerine winter visitors to Britain normally fly below 5,000 feet, but tend to fly higher in spring than in autumn, and higher by night than by day. In favorable weather in September 1959 Lack found small passerines that had left Scandinavia early at night making a dawn landfall in Britain at heights of up to 21,000 feet. Waders (like lapwings), Lack found, travel at a more constant height than passerines, usually between 300 and 600 feet.

It had been known for some time that in mountain areas birds could reach the height of Everest: but Lack's passerine record of four-mile altitudes over the comparatively low British countryside has prompted him to ponder whether birds have special adaptations to the physiological strain of such vast height changes – in a flight which no aviator could stand in an unpressurized craft; and adaptations also for gauging their height.

Later, with E. Eastwood, Lack actually filmed bird migration within a radius of 80 miles on the Marconi radar scanner near Chelmsford in Essex. Each 15-second scan of the antenna was photographed as one frame of a cinematograph film and from the projected film (which showed events speeded 240 times) the speed of migration, and changes in direction, could be accurately and quickly observed and measured. It was even possible to discover that wintering starlings sometimes migrated, by day or night, back to their Baltic breeding-places by direct flights from their huge English roosts.

These studies with giant, powerful radar are being continued and collated with much observatory work; and many mysteries of bird navigation and of weather stimulus to and control of migration will soon be solved. Of course new mysteries will then arise. But small radar sets, as used in aircraft, are also proving useful, even though they have relatively low power and small ranges. Thus recently Richard R. Graber and Sylvia Sue Hassler worked with such a set at the University of Illinois airport and were able to measure the actual density of night-migrating birds in terms of individual birds crossing a mile line every hour. Radar cannot name the angels for us (we can sometimes name the birds on radar – especially if they are abundant birds like starlings and big corvids which have big roosts), but it can, in suitable conditions and if well interpreted, give a much broader and more accurate picture of their movement and density than any scatter of day-watching or moon-watching ornithologists.

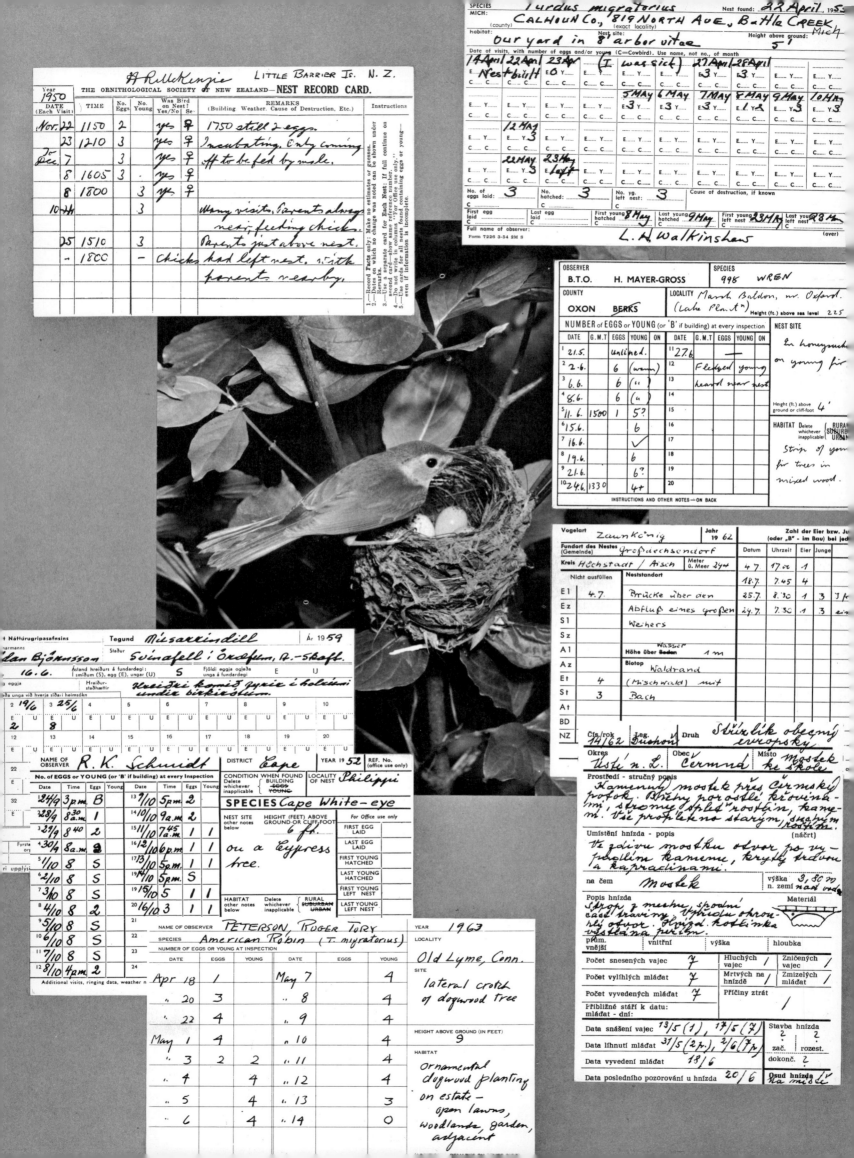

Turdus migratorius   Nest found: 22 April, 1955
MICH:
CALHOUN Co., 819 NORTH AVE., BATTLE CREEK
(county)   (exact locality)   MICH
habitat: **Our yard in 8' arbor vitae**   Height above ground: 5'

Date of visits, with number of eggs and/or young (C=Cowbird). Use name, not no., of month

14 April	22 April	23 April	(I was sick)	27 April	28 April		
E Nest built	E 0	E Y	C	E 3 Y	E 3 Y	E Y	E Y
		5 May	6 May	7 May	8 May	9 May	10 May
		E 3 Y	E 3 Y	E 3 Y	E 1 Y 2	Y 3	Y 3
	12 May						
	E 3						
	22 May	23 May					
	E 3	E Left					

No. of eggs laid: 3   No. hatched: 3   No. yg. left nest: 3   Cause of destruction, if known

First egg laid: Last egg laid: First young hatched 9 May   Last young hatched 9 May   First young left nest 23 May   Last young left nest 23 May

Full name of observer: **L. H. Walkinshaw**

Form 7226 3-54 2M S   (over)

A. R. McKenzie   LITTLE BARRIER Is. N.Z.
THE ORNITHOLOGICAL SOCIETY OF NEW ZEALAND—NEST RECORD CARD.

Year 1950

DATE (Each Visit)	TIME	No. Eggs	No. Young	Was Bird on Nest? Yes/No	Se.	REMARKS (Building Weather. Cause of Destruction, Etc.)	Instructions
Nov. 22	1150	2		yes	♀	1750 still 2 eggs.	
23	1210	3		yes	♀	Incubating. Only coming	
Dec 7		3		yes	♀	off to be fed by male.	
8	1605	3	.	yes	♀		
8	1800		3	yes	♀		
10-11			3			Many visits. Parents always nest, feeding chicks.	
25	1510		3			Parents just above nest.	
-	1800		-			Chicks had left nest. With parents nearby.	

Instructions column: 1—Record Facts only. Make no estimates or guesses. 2—Dates on which no change was noted can be shown under Remarks. 3—Use a separate card for Each Nest. If full continue on second card—same reference number. 4—Do not write in columns "For Office use only". 5—Use cards for all nests found containing eggs or young even if information is incomplete.

OBSERVER B.T.O.   H. MAYER-GROSS   SPECIES 998 WREN
COUNTY   OXON   BERKS   LOCALITY Marsh Baldon, nr. Oxford ("Lake Plant'n")   Height (ft.) above sea level 225

NUMBER of EGGS or YOUNG (or 'B' if building) at every inspection   NEST SITE

	DATE	G.M.T	EGGS	YOUNG	ON		DATE	G.M.T	EGGS	YOUNG	ON
1	21.5.		unlined.			11	27.6		—		
2	2.6.		6	(warm)		12			Fledged young		
3	6.6.		6	(")		13			heard near nest		
4	8.6.		6	(")		14					
5	11.6.	1500	1	5?		15					
6	15.6.			6		16					
7	16.6.			✓		17					
8	19.6.			6		18					
9	21.6.			6?		19					
10	24.6.	1330		4+		20					

En honeysuckle on young fir
Height (ft.) above ground or cliff-foot 4'
HABITAT Delete whichever inapplicable (RURAL SUBURB URBAN)
Strip of young fir trees in mixed wood.

INSTRUCTIONS AND OTHER NOTES—ON BACK

Vogelart **Zaunkönig**   Jahr 1962   Zahl der Eier bzw. Ju (oder "B" - im Bau) bei jed

Fundort des Nestes (Gemeinde) **Großaechsendorf**
Kreis **Höchstadt / Aisch**   Meter ü. Meer 244

		Neststandort	Datum	Uhrzeit	Junge
Nicht ausfüllen			4.7.	17.00	1
			18.7.	7.45	4
E1	4.7.	Brücke über den	25.7.	8.30	1 3
E2		Abfluß eines großen	24.7.	7.30	1 3
S1		Weihers			
Sz					
A1		Höhe über Boden 1 m			
Az		Biotop Waldrand			
Et	4	(Mischwald) mit			
St	3	Bach			
At					
BD					
NZ					

Čís./rok 14/62   Leg. Duchoň   Druh **Střízlík obecný evropský**
Okres Ústí n. L.   Obec Čermná   Místo ke Mostek škole

Prostředí - stručný popis
Kamenný mostek přes Čermský potok. Břehy porostlé křovinami, stromy, stlej rostlin, kamem. Vše propleteno starým, suchým rostlin.

Umístění hnízda - popis (náčrt)
Ve zdivu mostku otvor po vypadlém kameni, krytý travou a kapradinami.

na čem Mostek   výška 3,80 m n. zemí nad vodu

Popis hnízda: Strop z mechu, spodní část traviny. Vchodu ohronhlý otvor. Hnízd. kotlinka vystlána peřím.

Materiál

	vnější	vnitřní	výška	hloubka
Počet snesených vajec	7		Hluchých vajec 1	Zničených vajec 1
Počet vylíhlých mláďat	7		Mrtvých na hnízdě	Zmizelých mláďat
Počet vyvedených mláďat	7		Příčiny ztrát	

Přibližné stáří k datu: mláďat - dní:
Data snášení vajec 13/5 (1), 17/5 (7)   Stavba hnízda zač. 2 rozest. 2
Data líhnutí mláďat 31/5 (2 r.), 2/6 (7 r.)   dokonč. 2
Data vyvedení mláďat 18/6
Data posledního pozorování u hnízda 20/6   Osud hnízda na místě

+ Náttúrugripasafnsins   Tegund **Músarrindill**   Ár 1959
...armanns ...dan Björnsson   Staður **Svínafell í Öræfum, A.-Skaft.**
16.6.   Ástand hreiðurs & fundardegi: í smíðum (S), egg (E), ungar (U) 5   Fjöldi eggja og/eða unga á fundardegi E U

Hreiður staðhættir: Hreiðri komið fyrir í holtúni undir birkirótum.

...eða unga við hverja síðari heimsókn:

2 19/6	3 25/6	4	5	6	7	8	9	10
U 2	U 8	U	U	U	U	U	U	U
11	12	13	14	15	16	17	18	19	20
	U	U	U	U	U	U	U	U	U

NAME OF OBSERVER **R. K. Schmidt**   DISTRICT Cape   YEAR 1952   REF. No. (office use only)

No. of EGGS or YOUNG (or 'B' if building) at every inspection   CONDITION WHEN FOUND Delete whichever inapplicable BUILDING EGGS YOUNG   LOCALITY OF NEST Philippi

Date	Time	Eggs	Young	Date	Time	Eggs	Young
24/9	3 p.m.	B		13 9/10	5 p.m.		2
28/9	8.30 a.m.	1		14 10/10	9 a.m.		2
27/9	8.40	2		15 11/10	7.45 a.m.	1	1
30/9	8 a.m.	2		16 12/10	6 p.m.	1	1
1/10	8	S		17 13/10	5 p.m.	1	1
2/10	8	S		18 14/10	5 p.m.	S	
3/10	8	S		19 15/10		5	1
4/10	8	2		20 16/10		3	1 1
5/10	8	S		21			
6/10	8	S		22			
7/10	8	S		23			
8/10	4 p.m.	2		24			

SPECIES **Cape White-eye**
NEST SITE other notes below   HEIGHT (FEET) ABOVE GROUND OR CLIFF FOOT 6 ft.
on a Cypress tree.
HABITAT other notes below   Delete whichever inapplicable (RURAL SUBURBAN URBAN)

For Office use only:
FIRST EGG LAID / LAST EGG LAID / FIRST YOUNG HATCHED / LAST YOUNG HATCHED / FIRST YOUNG LEFT NEST / LAST YOUNG LEFT NEST

Additional visits, ringing data, weather...

NAME OF OBSERVER **PETERSON, ROGER TORY**   YEAR 1963
SPECIES **American Robin (T. migratorius)**   LOCALITY Old Lyme, Conn.

NUMBER OF EGGS OR YOUNG AT INSPECTION

DATE	EGGS	YOUNG	DATE	EGGS	YOUNG
Apr 18	1		May 7		4
" 20	3		" 8		4
" 22	4		" 9		4
May 1	4		" 10		4
" 3		4	" 11		4
" 4		4	" 12		4
" 5		4	" 13		3
" 6		4	" 14		0

SITE lateral crotch of dogwood tree
HEIGHT ABOVE GROUND (IN FEET) 9
HABITAT Ornamental dogwood planting on estate — open lawns, woodlands, garden, adjacent

Nest-records

During the breeding season of 1936 E. A. Billett, a keeper at Whipsnade Zoological Park in Bedfordshire, England, kept a record of the fortunes of every nest in the nearly six-acre bird sanctuary in this famous park, the open country zoo belonging to the Zoological Society of London.

The bird sanctuary at Whipsnade was at that time (and indeed still is) liberally provided with nest boxes; and all except those occupied by wrens could be easily examined. Out of the 173 nests of 23 different species discovered in the sanctuary – giving it the very high density (compare p. 112) of at least 5,864 breeding birds to the hundred acres – 38 were in nest boxes, and were those of blue tits, great tits and starlings. Billett recorded the results of almost daily visits to these nests; the precise numbers of eggs laid, and young hatched and fledged. As analyzed by Julian Huxley, the breeding efficiency in this protected place was rather high; of 265 eggs laid 210 (79%) hatched and 196 (74%) fledged. In the following season, with bad weather, there were fewer nests and eggs of these three species, and a smaller percentage of eggs laid became fledgelings.

After this pilot-survey Huxley realized that the meticulous recording of all or part of the fate of nests could, when spread widely over the years, seasons, latitudes and species, provide most valuable statistical data about clutch-size, breeding season and breeding efficiency all over the world. With JF, who was his assistant at the time, he designed what we then called Hatching and Fledging cards for the British Trust for Ornithology to circulate among their members in 1939.

Today over ten thousand nests are annually watched in Britain alone and recorded on improved cards (now known as nest-record cards) which the observers send in for central analysis. By 1961 about 130,000 nests had been recorded, and a thousand nest-histories or more were on file for each of no less than 25 species, blackbird nest-records leading with no less than 22,683. In less than a decade (by 1948) the idea had spread to seven other countries, and at present at least two dozen nest-record schemes are run in countries and states from Spain, Italy and Hungary to Finland, from Iceland to Estonia and Czechoslovakia, from Alaska and British Columbia to Massachusetts and Michigan; and in Rhodesia, South Africa and New Zealand.

With their early start, the British records have so far provided the best material for analysis. Indeed, so important is the inquiry now regarded in the United Kingdom that the Nature Conservancy has recently made a grant to the BTO to support a whole-time organizer, H. Mayer-Gross, who himself recorded the fate of no less than 2,280 nests in the two years 1960 and 1961; which was no mean feat.

Rather over five thousand cards were available under the BTO scheme after its first ten years: the number doubled again in two more, redoubled in another, redoubled in two more, redoubled in four more. This meant that a quarry of nest-records for some species was available as early as 1946, when Dr. David Lack made the first use of them for his work on the clutch-size of the European robin (p. 86), and with R. Parkhurst established valuable statistical information about the yellowhammer's English breeding season and clutch size and compared them with those in Europe.

The first full nest-record analysis was published in 1949 by Miss E. T. Silva (now Mrs. Lack), who was able to compare 484 BTO song-thrush cards with many records of the same species from other sources, including Europe. It is worth quoting her results as they show that positive and useful statements can be made from analysis of what by later standards is regarded as a rather small sample. It was quite clear after the analysis that the British song-thrush's usual laying season was from mid-March to mid-July, with at least two broods, and that it laid four eggs more often than not, and five more often than one to three. Its clutch-size varied seasonally with a peak in May (in June in Finland); and was, on average, smaller than in Holland, smaller still than in Finland. Brood-size and nesting success varied from year to year. On average, of 100 eggs 71 hatched and 55 left the nest; predation was the usual cause of any lack of nesting success, which did not vary with clutch-size or season. The mean incubation and nestling periods were established at 13.4 and 13.2 days respectively, and both tended to be slightly longer early in the season than late.

Since then many common British birds have had such nest-card analysis, which has truly linked their seasons and fortunes with climate and food-supply. Refinements have been introduced into the analysis to allow for the fact that more observations tend to be made in the early half of the breeding season; even the keenest observer's enthusiasm can wane a little. A new song-thrush sample based on 3,500 cards by Myres and Snow confirmed Mrs. Lack's earlier results in more particulars; but they brought in for further comparison the facts from 5,700 blackbird and 350 mistle-thrush cards. Adams has got results from 1,445 (barn) swallow cards in Britain which show an average breeding success of 72% – as high as that of a true hole-nester, though the swallow builds an open nest under cover. Great tit and blue tit records have been used by several workers and compared with the results of special team programs in the field. Spotted flycatcher, greenfinch, coal tit, willow warbler, meadow pipit and wood pigeon are among the other birds whose six by four cards have been put to use, to the eventual transformation of the sections on breeding in the new editions of the standard works.

Life-history studies

'Five or six or more feet down the chimney does this little bird begin to form her nest about the middle of May, which consists, like that of the house-martin, of a crust or shell composed of dirt, or mud, mixed with short pieces of straw to render it tough and permanent; with this difference, that whereas the shell of the martin is nearly hemispheric, that of the swallow is open at the top, and like half a deep dish. This nest is lined with fine grasses and feathers, which are often collected as they float in the air'.

'Generally nests on rafters in sheds and outhouses, also on flanges of iron girders: but in some districts many pairs breed inside chimney stacks. Exceptionally nests in roofs of caves, and very rarely on branches of trees. Nest.—Built by both sexes of mud with bits of straw worked in to hold material together: more saucer-shaped than that of House-Martin, open at top and resting on support of some kind as a rule, but has been known to build on side of wall under eaves, like House-Martin, but nest open above'.

The first of these accounts of the nesting of the swallow, which North Americans love as the barn swallow, was written by Gilbert White of Selborne to his friend Daines Barrington on 29 January 1774. The second was published by an equally tender and accurate naturalist parson, Francis Charles Robert Jourdain, in October 1938. It is a remarkable tribute to and commentary on the world of the curate who has rightly been called the father of field natural history.

The particular passage of White's that we quote was not actually published until late in December 1788 in the *Natural History of Selborne*. But the gist of it was published rather earlier, in the *Proceedings of the Royal Society of London* of 1775, in the second of two papers on hirundines (and the swift which White thought *was* an hirundine) which are the first great ornithological life-history studies the world has known. In both the scientific – Royal Society – and discursive – Selborne – versions of his swallow study White, the great enthusiast, betrayed a passion for and devotion to observation and elucidation that was not paralleled, in our opinion, for more than a century – not until Edmund Selous, in his less literate, more obscure yet equally enthusiastic way, after years of watching, began to write, in 1899, of nightjars, waders, grebes, blackcock, divers, crows and other birds with the same curiosity and fire.

Every ornithological professor, institute director or leader of today usually has, amongst the advice he gives pupils, a bird to offer. 'Take a bird', he says, 'a well-worked bird, a neglected bird, a common bird, a rare bird – *some* bird you can get on terms with; and learn it, learn more of it, set a program for it – learn what is known, what is not known'.

In short, a straight way to ornithological delight and fulfillment is to become a monographer (or at least pos-sibly a future monographer) of one or a few particular species. There are, after all, about 8,550 living species to go round, quite apart from the extinct ones which scholars like Newton, Grieve and W. Blasius (great auk 1861, 1885, 1903), Strickland and Hachisuka (dodo 1848, 1953) and Schorger (passenger pigeon 1955) have monographed. So far, by our rough reckoning, not much more than a hundred birds have been monographed to the Gilbert White standard: that is to say with a completeness which embraces some years of observation, a wide coverage of life-history, behavior, distribution and ecology, and with an exercise that White had little trouble with, but modern workers must practice over months or even years – a thorough ransacking of the existing literature, ideally not merely that in scientific journals but also scattered observations in books, whether they be bird books or not: for no animal is complete in a monograph without its own biological history in relation to its relatives living and extinct.

In Wales, where many share rather few surnames, men and women are trade-named Evans the post, Morgan the fish, Jones the bread. We think with respect and affection of many of our late and living ornithological friends in this style. As we cannot mention all, we name one for each letter of the alphabet: Armstrong the wren, Buxton the redstart, Chance the cuckoo, Davies the reed warbler, Eckstein the canary, Friedmann the cowbirds, Gordon the golden eagle, Hochbaum the canvasback, Ivanov the snow cock, Jameson the wandering albatross, Kendeigh the house wren, Lack the robin, Mayfield the Kirtland's warbler, Nice the song sparrow, Owen the heron, Paludan the razorbill, Queeny the ducks, Richdale the mollymawk, Stoddard the bobwhite, Tuck the murres, Uspenski the brent goose, Vogt the guanay, Walkinshaw the sandhill crane, Yeates the rook and Zimmer the hepatic tanager.

One of us has had more than half a life-time of joy, wonder and sweat in the pursuit of a beloved species, the fulmar. Over ten years ago JF found some fact of value for his monograph on this oceanic sea bird in each of 2,378 separate published papers or books, and collected at least one other unpublished fact from each of 575 informants by correspondence. Ten years later new materials bring the totals up to about 3,000 and 1,000. An historian of a species is lucky if he gets 10 per cent of his time in the field collecting data. About 30 per cent is spent in libraries (including his own) reading what others know. Over half is spent analyzing data and working it up.

Nevertheless there is a special thrill to the challenge of mastering one bird or a few, and about sixty of the happiest naturalists we know or have known are those who have succumbed to it and written a treatise. A bibliography of some of the more important species monographs is cited on pp. 279–81.

Top shelf (left to right):

THE WREN — Edward A. Armstrong — Collins
THE YELLOW WAGTAIL — Stuart Smith — Collins
THE GREENSHANK — Desmond Nethersole-Thompson — Collins
THE FULMAR — James Fisher — Collins
THE HERRING GULL'S WORLD — Niko Tinbergen — Collins
THE HERON — Frank A. Lowe — Collins
THE HAWFINCH — Guy Mountfort — Collins
19 THE HOUSE SPARROW — J. D. Summers-Smith — Collins

ÉCOLOGIE DU MANCHOT ADÉLIE — ÉLEK

THE EMPEROR PENGUINS — Jean Rivolier

A POPULATION STUDY OF PENGUINS — OXFORD

Penguin Summer — Eleanor Rice Pettingill

Darling

The Wandering Albatross — William Jameson

SHEARWATERS — R. M. Lockley

THE GANNET — J. H. Gurney — LONDON WITHERBY

THE HOME LIFE OF THE SPOONBILL — Bentley Beetham

THE HOME SUCH — ALLEN

THE FLAMINGOS — Robert Porter Allen

The Mystery of the FLAMINGOS — COUNTRY LIFE

The Mute Swan in England — N. F. Ticehurst

A THOUSAND GEESE — Peter Scott and James Fisher — Collins

Middle shelf (left to right):

EAGLES — Leslie Brown

BENGT BERG DIE LETZTEN ADLER

The Golden Eagle — Seton Gordon — Collins

THE HOME LIFE OF THE OSPREY — C. G. Abbott

The Return of the Osprey

RENZ WALLER · DER WILDE FALK IST MEIN GESELL

СОКОЛ · КРЕЧЕТ

In Search of the Gyr-Falcon — Ernest Lewis — Constable

The Taming of Genghis — Ronald Stevens — Faber and Faber

THE PEREGRINE AND GYRFALCON POPULATIONS IN ALASKA — CADE

THE GROUSE IN HEALTH AND IN DISEASE — POPULAR EDITION — SMITH, ELDER & Co.

THE CAPERCAILLIE IN SCOTLAND — J. A. Harvie-Brown

THE BOBWHITE QUAIL · ITS HABITS PRESERVATION AND INCREASE — STODDARD — SCRIBNERS

A PARTRIDGE YEAR — Esmond Lynam-Allen & A. L. W. F. Robertson — ELBE

MOULTS IN THE ROCK PTARMIGAN &c. — FINN SALOMONSEN

The Sandhill Cranes — Walkinshaw — 29 CRANBROOK

THE LAPWING IN BRITAIN — K. G. Spencer

A PAINTER'S YEAR

CLAUDE GREY DIE GEFIEDERTE WELT

GEOGRAPHIC VARIATION IN LIMICOLINES · PITELKA

A BOOK OF THE SNIPE

BIRD BEHAVIOUR — W. Bickerton — F. B. Kirkman

THE HOME LIFE OF THE TERNS — W. Bickerton — NELSON

SEA TERNS or Sea Swallows — George Marples — Anne Marples — Illustrated with Photographs, Drawings and Diagrams by the Authors — COUNTRY LIFE

SEA BIRDS CORMORANTS AND OTHERS · STORER

TSCHANZ — ZUR BRUTBIOLOGIE DER TROTTELLUMME

PUFFINS — R. M. Lockley

Bottom shelf (left to right):

The Truth About the Cuckoo — EDGAR P. CHANCE — COUNTRY LIFE

BENGT BERG Eyes in the Night

HELMUT DRECHSLER · UHU-DÄMMERUNG — Reimer

Swifts in a Tower — David Lack — Methuen

Steinmann · Das Jahr mit den Spechten

The California Woodpecker and I — MacMillan

THE IVORY-BILLED WOODPECKER — TANNER

N. Y. STATE MUSEUM BUL. 326

LIED UND LEBEN DER DROSSEL UND DROSSELN · URNER A. T.

Eric Hosking & Cyril Newberry — SONG OF THE WOOD THRUSH

THE ADVENTURES OF COCK ROBIN AND HIS MATE — KEARTON

ROBIN RED-BREAST — DAVID LACK

THE LIFE OF THE ROBIN — DAVID LACK — OXFORD

A STUDY OF BLACKBIRDS — R. K. MOON

THE BRITISH WARBLERS — Robert Sweet — H. Eliot Howard

REED-WARBLERS — BROWN & DAVIES — 101

SITTA PYGMAEA AND SITTA PUSILLA — NORRIS

HINDE · THE BEHAVIOUR OF THE GREAT TIT

ADAPTATION IN THE GALAPAGOS FINCHES — BOWMAN

DARWIN'S FINCHES — DAVID LACK

DISTRIBUTION AND VARIATION OF THE BROWN TOWHEES — DAVIS

SPECIES FORMATION IN THE BELDING STORES OF MEXICO — SIBLEY

SONG SPARROW — NICE

ANNUAL CYCLE, ENVIRONMENT, AND EVOLUTION IN HAWAIIAN HONEYCREEPERS — BALDWIN

MAYFIELD · The Kirtland's Warbler — CRANBROOK

U. S. National Museum Bulletin 223

Latin, the Language of Zoology

The Redwinged Blackbird — ALLEN

The Popular Waterfowl

SOLD FOR A FARTHING — CLARE KIPPS

CANARY — BY GUSTAV ECKSTEIN — Faber and Faber

BOWER BIRDS — MARSHALL — OXFORD

1

2

3

4

5

6

7

1–7. *Great crested grebe displays and rituals, mainly after the pioneer study of Julian Huxley (1914). 1. Seeking attitude of either sex; 2. Female assuming hostile attitude; 3. Pair in 'cat' position; 4–6. Pair in stages of the shaking ritual; 7. The 'penguin dance', a bond-cementing ritual involving presentation of nest material*

8–10. Aggressive display; birds with strong attack, weak escape motivation. 8. Hermit thrush (after Dilger 1956); 9. Common jay (after Goodwin 1952); 10. Threat posture of male roseate tern

11–13. Distraction display. Kentish (or snowy) plover 'injury feigning' to human intruder; 11. Static display; 12. Mobile display (after Simmons 1951); 13. Distraction display of avocet (after Simmons 1955)

14–16. Displacement activities. 14. 'False' brooding by oystercatcher (after Simmons 1955); 15. Grass-pulling by herring gull (after Tinbergen 1953); 16. 'False' preening of courting mandarin drake

Studying bird behavior

Birds, as the most observable and colorful of all the higher animals, have been for over a century the constantly favored tool for the ethologist: the student of animal psychology, behavior and mind.

As early as 1778 A. J. Lottinger published in France the results of one of the earliest known experiments on bird behavior: unlike a cuckoo he took all of the eggs from each of 17 small passerines' nests and substituted one egg of another species to represent a cuckoo's. All the birds deserted. He was, without really knowing it, proving the adaptive value of the cuckoo's habit of taking but one, and substituting its own. He might have guessed this from the result of another experiment in which he took all the birds' eggs save one of their own clutch: they still deserted.

This experiment (ineffective as it was to its perpetrator, who simply concluded that the result was the effect of some divine decree) was a freak before its time: there was little if any *experimental* work on bird behavior until the present century. But there was plenty of obser-

vation in the middle years of the nineteenth century, accompanied by thoughtful speculation. Psychology had been more-or-less a science since the 17th-century years of the French philosopher Descartes.

Eighteenth-century naturalists like Gilbert White and Oliver Goldsmith had pondered in a literary way upon the minds of birds and their emotions, in particular the kind of drive (which we might now call agonistic behavior) which led them to take up territories in the breeding season. But a German ornithologist, Bernhard Altum, has perhaps the honor of being the first modern bird ethologist; he published a book in 1868 about birds' habits in which he thought that the possession of territories assured birds a guaranteed food supply – a suggestion which, as far as we know, is the first identification of a biological advantage for a prominent bird behavior pattern and is still generally held to be valid, though modern ethologists like Niko Tinbergen would attach as much importance to the rôle of territory-holding as a dispersal mechanism. Paradoxically, it is also an attraction mechanism, guiding rivals to good neighborhood.

8

9

10

11

12

13

14

15

16

By the time Charles Darwin published his second most important book, *The Descent of Man, and Selection in Relation to Sex*, in 1871, he was well-armed with succinct and accurate descriptions of bird behavior from many sources. He freely used the word 'display' in the accounts of courtship (and aggression) that he quoted to support his thesis that the bright plumage and courtship adornments of some birds had evolved by a form of natural selection by their mates, a process which he called sexual selection.

A number of displays and adornments which Darwin believed to be connected wholly with courtship have since been shown to be concerned more with rivalry and aggression between members of the same sex: and the great evolutionist does not seem to have paid attention to the numerous birds of which both sexes possess almost equally bright adornments. Of these the display is generally mutual and has as function, as Julian Huxley puts it, 'the provision of an emotional bond for keeping the sexes together during the breeding season' – a necessary adaptation since such birds share in the rearing of the brood.

The description, understanding and explanation of bird behavior is perhaps the most important task of ornithology, in that it illuminates our knowledge not merely of avian evolution and relationship, but of evolution as a whole process, not excepting the evolution and psychology of higher vertebrates, including man himself. It is also the most difficult, largely because its language has for long trailed panting behind its findings. The schools of human and animal psychology have split and sometimes almost foundered in a succession of '-isms' whose history can be only understood by the scholar: introspectionism, intentionalism, functionalism, behaviorism, operationism, each with more-or-less a private language, each often using the same words with different meanings. But as a consequence of several international ethological conferences since World War II, largely inspired by the great Austrian ethologist and ornithologist Konrad Lorenz, the streams of language are running together again.

In a real sense, our understanding of bird behavior has had to follow improvements in language, has had to

1

2

3

4

5

proceed by the succession of *concepts*. A modern systematist, busily trying to improve the family tree of birds by looking at the skull-bones of 'finches' (and nobody is yet certain whether buntings are finches or weaver birds are either), or the distribution of sibling species, does not have to explain what he is doing or coin many more new words now to describe his ideas: and many of the words he uses, like 'allopatric', or 'cline', both explain and describe immediately. Many words of ethology describe, but do not necessarily explain: they are coined, and indeed needed, purely to simplify ideas and make language proper language, so that at least a structure can be provided in or upon which true explanations can later develop.

The behavior patterns of animals can and should be regarded from the evolutionary point of view as of importance just as vital as the anatomical characteristics they are in harmony with. This was realized as long ago as 1874 by the pioneer German psychologist and physiologist Wilhelm Wundt, was developed by the American behaviorist C. O. Whitman in 1899, and has been at the heart of all the work of the last generation. Another principle, propounded by the Welsh psychologist C. Lloyd Morgan in 1894, runs: 'In no case is an animal's activity to be interpreted in terms of higher psychological processes if it can fairly be interpreted in terms of processes which are lower in the scale of psychological evolution and development'. In fact this is an extension of a principle of the Scottish philosopher Duns Scotus promulgated around 1300, and of the English philosopher William of Occam (around 1340), which can be rendered, 'the essentials are not to be multiplied beyond necessity', or, if you like, 'it is idle or false to explain with more what can be explained with fewer'. The average pet keeper or budgerigar owner has unfortunately still to this day no wish to embrace this axiom: doggies, pussy-cats and other pets to most of us are little humans.

We have been trying to show that animal behavior studies must of necessity have a more profound philosophical basis than older studies which have already evolved their own solid rules and methods. The philosopher's job, in a good sense, is to explore intellectually beyond the bounds of science, and return with concepts

Some displays of the herring gull (after Tinbergen 1959). Meeting ceremonies at pair formation may closely resemble hostile encounters between males: 1. Mew call, uttered by birds parallel in pair formation, facing in hostile clash; 2. 'Choking' with rapid downward movements of head; 3. Facing away, an appeasement posture also shown in hostile encounters; 4. Aggressive upright posture, adopted in both boundary disputes and pair formation, and a sequence of it; 5. Anxiety upright posture, often adopted in the facing away (or head flagging) display

and hypotheses which can be later tested. Speculation and wonder, confusion and language controversy are bound to reign when humans tackle the structure, working and function of the super-organ, the brain – the most staggeringly complex organ that evolution has produced, at least on this planet. 'Bird brain' may be a term of opprobrium or fun to most of us; but it is no joke to a working ethologist.

This section of our book is illustrated by drawings of birds behaving, adapted from the classic papers of the past and present of some of the most intellectual and thoughtful stream of workers – professional, amateur, trained and untrained – who have illuminated our science of ornithology, and struggled to clarify our understanding of the bird's mind. The philosophical bird behavior pioneers were watching and wondering and writing long before World War I. Edmund Selous began his passionate, obsessive field notes on what birds did (rather than where or when they were) in or before 1899: they are still difficult for the scholar to analyze because of his furious intermingling of observation and conclusion.

C. B. Moffat, an acute observer, first used the word 'territory' in 1903. F. B. Kirkman, whose thoughtful work is now somewhat neglected, began his black-headed gull watching program in 1905 and field experiments in 1913. J. Porter published his largely-forgotten work on the psychology of the house sparrow in America from 1904 onwards. Oskar Heinroth used behavior to throw light on the relationship of the ducks as early as 1910, and made valuable speculations on the importance of social play in the lives of birds.

Julian Huxley, first great analyst of mutual courtship (among herons and grebes in North America and Europe), was dropping in his footnotes, before World War I, major concepts which began to be widely appreciated years later. Around the same time (from 1908 on) John B. Watson, pioneer observer of and experimenter with American terns, founded what came to be known as the school of behaviorism: he felt and said that much could be learned about human psychology from the study of animal behavior, and little if anything about animal behavior from the pursuit, identification and analysis of 'consciousness'. In the climate of his time, he was right.

In 1907 an English steelmaster, H. Eliot Howard, began publishing (on British warblers) the first of a series of works on the behavior of many kinds of birds which were distinguished by as deep and thoughtful a philosophical and scientifically critical approach as they were in literary style: his *Territory in Bird Life* (1920) is still a classic milestone in ornithology's progress.

In the nineteen twenties there was a considerable spurt in experimental behavior studies largely led by Otto Köhler, first important analyst of insight (p. 95) among birds. Dominating the 'thirties were two new powerful human minds, still active leaders and teachers of modern behavior studies, Konrad Lorenz of Austria, who now works in Germany; and Niko Tinbergen of Holland, now a lecturer at Oxford in England. Lorenz, in 1935, produced the very useful concept of the 'releaser': an inherited behavior pattern brought into play by an instinctive action whose significance to the preservation of the species, as he puts it, 'lies in the sending out of stimuli which are answered in a specific manner by other individuals of the same species'. Releasers are distinguished by their simplicity and unmistakability and, as Lorenz elegantly adds, 'the greatest possible unreality'; and they are of profound value in the study of avian relationship.

Among Tinbergen's many important contributions is the concept of 'displacement activity', which he first published in 1940. Displacement activities are performed by birds when two or more of their drives are opposed, and *appear* to have no relevance to the actual situations they are in. Often they arise in situations unknown in the bird's normal life. In an unexpected or embarrassing situation a man may scratch his head: in displacement activity a bird may likewise preen, or 'falsely' brood, sleep, peck, feed or offer nest material.

Concepts like these, we repeat, describe but only partially explain: but they prepare the way for fuller explanation. All over America and Europe, inspired by Armstrong, Collias, Emlen, Hinde, Huxley, Lehrmann, Lorenz, Marler, Morris, Thorpe, Tinbergen and many others, the students of bird mind, themselves the most active-minded and curious (in the old sense) of the bird watchers, are observing, experimenting, pondering and comparing in the eternal search for explanation.

Experimental field studies of bird behavior (after Tinbergen 1951)

1. Demonstration of herring gull's attachment to its nest site: when eggs are displaced a short distance bird settles to incubate empty site in full view of them

2. Presented with model of giant egg, oystercatcher attempts to roll and incubate it in preference to alternative offerings of its own egg and herring gull's egg

1

2

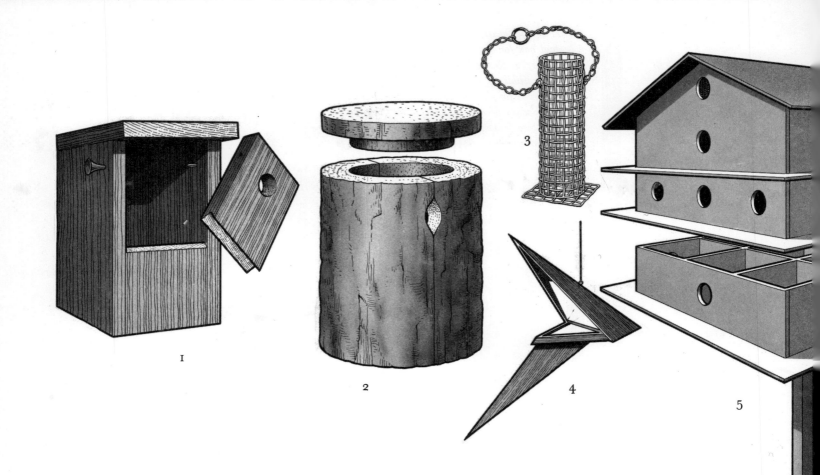

1   2   3   4   5

Prefabs and feeders

We may be sure that the first man-made boxes for birds were not designed by ornithologists but by the kind of bird lovers who liked their birds well-browned and with plenty of bread sauce.*

We know, at least, that the ancient Egyptians of the fifth dynasty (*c.* 2600 B.C.) onwards kept domesticated pigeons and grew wheat; and judging from early figurines pigeons were probably even domesticated by the Halafian Mesopotamians of *c.* 4500 B.C. (p. 250).

Domestic pigeons need nest boxes, dovecots, compact chambers resembling the crevices and holes in the walls of the rocky caves that their ancestor the rock pigeon still nests in around the coasts and hills of the Old World. Quite early on the Egyptians used pigeons not only as food but as carriers, and built huge dovecots: and in the time of Isaiah (who seems to have been three or four prophets and poets, not one), in the sixth or fifth century B.C., dovecots were certainly in use in Palestine and Syria: 'Who are these that fly as a cloud', he, or one of him, wrote, 'as the doves to their windows [=*arubbah*, dove-cots]?' In the time of Varro (1st century B.C.) pigeon lofts, housing up to 5,000 birds, were common on the houses of Rome and the Roman country estates. Dove-cots were built in medieval Europe from early times and were so widely used by 1577 that William Harrison, in *The Description of England*, complained of 'Pigeons, now an hurtful foule by reason of their multitudes, and num-

* To whom a book by our zoologist friend Dr. Leo Harrison Matthews of the London Zoo is notoriously dedicated.

ber of houses daillie erected for their increase (which the bowres [=boors or farmers] of the countrie call in scorne almes houses, and dens of theeues, and such like), whereof there is great plentie in euerie farmer's yard'.

In England in the 16th century the rural poor were short of protein. Pigeons were important in their diet, and we learn that the humble house sparrow was worth catching and even cultivating. In the household books of the le Straunge family of Hunstanton in Norfolk we find that tenants even paid part of their rent in sparrows in 1533 and 1548. Already around this time the people of the Netherlands had invented unglazed earthenware pots to hang under the eaves for sparrows to nest in (to crop the young for food, of course); and we know that these were introduced into England less than a century later when the Dutch came over to drain the Fens.

As far as we can discover, few other prefabs for wild birds were designed before the age of bird protection and advanced bird watching. Not long after the Viking colonization, farmers on Iceland's coasts developed a system of farming the down from the nests of the eider duck colonies. As the down was (and still is) a profitable export great care was taken to see that the birds nested comfortably and safely. On several offshore islands to this day the owners have built cosy sheltered nest sites, sometimes in rows, out of slabs of rock, in which the same individual ducks nest year after year. And for centuries in Europe – especially Scandinavia – hole-nesting ducks of other species have been encouraged to nest in box-like shelters by local farmers and hunters.

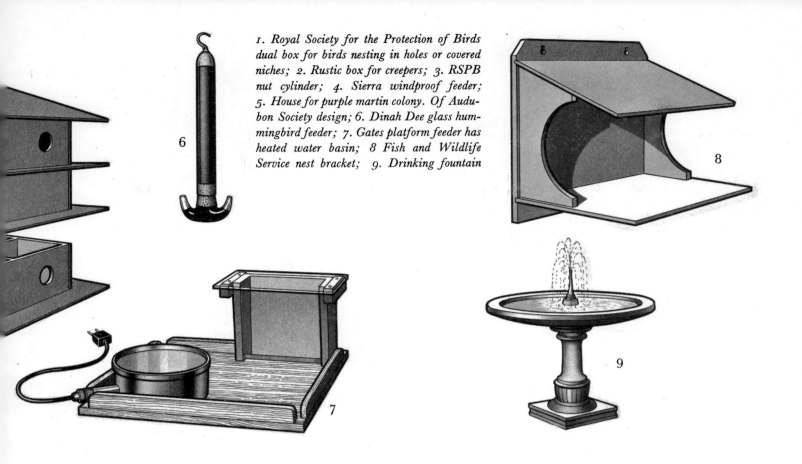

1. *Royal Society for the Protection of Birds dual box for birds nesting in holes or covered niches; 2. Rustic box for creepers; 3. RSPB nut cylinder; 4. Sierra windproof feeder; 5. House for purple martin colony. Of Audubon Society design; 6. Dinah Dee glass hummingbird feeder; 7. Gates platform feeder has heated water basin; 8 Fish and Wildlife Service nest bracket; 9. Drinking fountain*

The first important pioneer of special care for common wild birds by the organized provision of scientifically designed nest boxes and feeding stations was (at least in Europe) Baron von Berlepsch of Schloss Seebach, a castle and 500-acre park in Thuringia, central Germany. The Berlepsch family, which goes back to the 12th century, had for long been forward-looking agriculturists and naturalists; and the baron of the 1880s became obsessed with the care of wild birds, in the interests of insect-control and aesthetics. The account of his improvements in bird culture reads a little strangely now: he had the most rigid ideas as to how nest boxes should be made and sited, and made the most precise specifications for five basic types, carved rather elaborately out of natural logs. He issued the most stringent instructions as to the exact composition of feeder mixtures, and even designed a special cooker for warming up mixtures of meat, bread, grain and fat. He raised the number of nest boxes in his park nearly tenfold, and fed his bird population throughout the year, but especially in cold weather, at a network of stations – 'food-trees' – small fir-trees covered with his fat-based mixture – complex food houses, sticks with holes bored and stuffed with food, food-bells, grain-hoppers, roofed mangers, feeding-houses and boxes which rotated with wind-vanes to shelter the birds as they ate.

Many of the Berlepsch designs are in use today: some of the gadgets advertized in recent numbers of *Audubon* magazine are strangely reminiscent of his 70-year-old ideas, probably by convergence. Most of today's prefabs and feeders are rather simpler and cheaper. They are used in hundreds of thousands in the civilized world. Feeders probably saved at least a million birds in Britain in the appalling winter of early 1963 – a million birds that would otherwise have starved to death. Most feeders and nest boxes are, of course, put up for love; but they are widely used by foresters to encourage insect-eaters; and nest boxes are now used very often by scientific ornithologists with programs of life-history study. We figure here some successful and popular models in use on both sides of the Atlantic.

Most people keep feeders going in fall and winter but leave birds to feed their young naturally in early summer, when even most seed-eaters have a large band of insects in their food-spectrum. However, hummingbirds will feed all through their summer stay in the temperate United States at artificial nectar dispensers. Nowadays many commercial firms produce feeder mixtures in Europe and North America; some have been analyzed for contents and quality and approved by national conservation societies, and are to be recommended.

Nest boxes should be worked over every year. To discourage parasites, old nesting material can be removed from boxes at the annual maintenance check in the fall. In the northern hemisphere it is thought generally best to hang boxes on a northern exposure to shadow them from the midday sun. They should hang vertically or with their upper parts tilting slightly forwards as a protection from rainstorms. It is not desirable to provide a perch under the hole, which could provide a purchase to marauding cats or squirrels.

Sanctuaries

The world's first bird sanctuary was established in Northumbria, an old kingdom which embraced large parts of lowland Scotland and northern England, in about the year 677, by a saint.

We know that in 635 Oswald, King of Northumbria, himself a Christian convert when in exile at Iona, sent for missionaries to convert his barbarous Northumbrian subjects. Aidan, who came from Iona with twelve monks, built a little cathedral on Lindisfarne, the Holy Island of Northumberland, and became its first bishop. By 664 a young man of great piety, who had started life as a shepherd boy in the hills of Scotland, came to Lindisfarne as prior.

Cuthbert lived the simple, contemplative life of a saintly ascetic, always dressed in undyed woolen cloth. In 676 he left Lindisfarne for a solitary hermit's life, at first retiring to a neighboring mainland cell (probably in a cave near the village of Howburn), but soon crossing over to Farne, the largest of a rough and rocky archipelago opposite the royal castle of Bamburgh. The Inner Farne, as it is now called, is but sixteen acres at low water, and on this small uninhabited island, helped by the monks, the anchorite built a circular building, by some accounts 75 feet in diameter (but probably smaller), partitioned into a dwelling place and an oratory. Cuthbert's hermitage was of unhewn stones, timber and turf, low without but deepened within by excavation.

Here Cuthbert prayed and watched, and instructed pilgrims until he was called by King Egbert to the sixth bishopric of Lindisfarne in 684. On Farne (whence he retired and died in 687) he seems to have had a marvelous love for animals: it is reported that otters came to him for blessing, and one historian relates that Cuthbert tamed all the eider ducks (they still nest there to this day, near the southerly limit of their breeding range in England), and rendered them 'subservient to his use, and upon more than one occasion wrought a miracle in their behalf'. Cuthbert watched the gray seals (which breed on the Farnes) and porpoises, and the gannets winging their way to and from their ancient colony of the Bass Rock, which almost certainly existed then, though we cannot prove it.

Cuthbert was buried at Lindisfarne, and was several times reburied since – for the last time in what was then the new cathedral of Durham, whence the see had been transferred, in 1104. His body, which was remarkably little decayed, was reclothed at his re-interment in beautiful episcopal robes. In 1827 his tomb was opened and these robes were found in an excellent state of preservation: on roundels the tender 12th-century nuns had embroidered his favorite mammals and birds as supporters to his episcopal throne.

The earliest bird sanctuary, then, was founded in 677 and vividly remembered in 1104. We know of none other so early; though doubtless many of the early nobles of Europe and Asia became tender to wildlife (beyond the

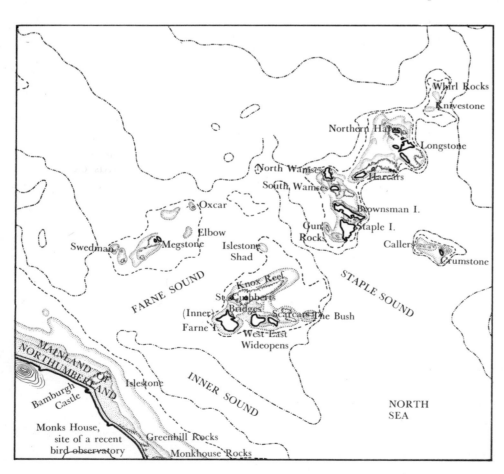

Left: the Farne Islands, scale 1/75,000

Below: St. Cuthbert's robe of 1104, well preserved save for a jagged hole above the episcopal throne. Eider ducks support this throne, below them porpoises; the supporters outside the roundel may be gannets

Right: part of modern city of Oakland, scale 1/c. 22,500, showing Lake Merritt, and flock of pintail drakes photographed by Roger Peterson at this old refuge

huntable, hawkable and shootable) in their parks. Lord Ilchester's family in England, for instance, has protected the Abbotsbury swannery in Dorset for many centuries, and there are records of its existence at least since 1393. In Germany the von Berlepsch barons may have tended common birds for as long.

Apart from private 'estate sanctuaries', bird refuge administration did not get started in Europe until less than a hundred years ago. Indeed, it seems that the citizens of the United States were quicker to grasp the necessity for the conservation of wildlife and scenery than those of Europe. The U.S.A. was, by many years, first in the field with National Parks with Yellowstone in 1872: and to it also goes the honor of making the first wildlife refuges. In 1852 Oakland was a small but growing town on the eastern shore of San Francisco Bay in California: and one of its leading citizens, Samuel Merritt, bought what was then a slough, helped to drain it and form a lake. Today thousands of waterfowl still winter in what is now Lake Merritt in the heart of the downtown business quarter of Oakland, with copious natural food and assured sanctuary from hunters – a lake which became, by a law of the California State Legislature of 18 March 1870, the world's first *official* bird sanctuary. The U.S. was also first in the field with national (federal) wildlife refuges when Theodore Roosevelt signed an order on 14 March 1903, setting aside Pelican Island, near Sebastian in Florida, as a reservation for the protection of native birds.

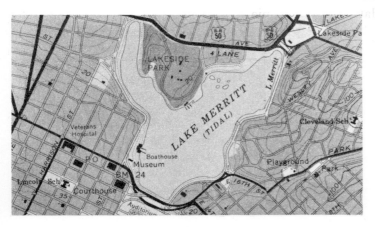

To cut a story short, there now are probably over two thousand separate areas scattered over the face of our planet which are dedicated to the conservation of birds and under some form of management for that purpose. They are private, or belong to charitable, non-government conservation societies, or to local authorities, or to central governments. Some are dedicated mainly to the preservation of habitat. Others are frankly educational. Some – like wildfowl refuges – concentrate largely on the nourishment and support of sporting birds as much in the interests of hunters as of bird watchers. Others protect special species at the edge of their range or for other reasons rare: Aransas refuge in Texas is host to the entire world population of the whooping crane every winter; Havergate Island in Suffolk supports the only British breeding colony of avocets; the Coto Doñana in Spain and the Camargue in France nourish the two magnificent wild herds of flamingos in Europe.

If we take the broad view (which is 99 per cent valid) that every nature reserve is a bird reserve, then today there are well over 700 bird sanctuaries in the United States alone, 261 in Great Britain (180 in England, 32 in Wales, 47 in Scotland and 2 in the Isle of Man), over 200 in Germany, over 200 in Sweden, over 200 in Russia (including some large gardens and small parks), over 100 in Poland, nearly 100 in Holland, and scores in most other European countries. France, Austria, Hungary, Italy and Finland all had sanctuaries over fifty years ago, as did Japan which now has about 500 'monuments' of which over 200 are areas of natural history importance. During the last two generations of bird watchers many dots have appeared on the world sanctuary map in Africa, Asia, Australasia, South America, the West Indies, the Pacific Islands and even some subantarctic islands: and in the more advanced countries, with good nature protection laws, it has become clear that wild bird variety and population can be and is being improved not only in places that are *called* sanctuaries. Birds cannot read notices. A settled housing estate, with parks and gardens and thoughtful inhabitants, is just as much a sanctuary as Selborne Common or Lake Merritt, even if it has no such label – for the recent universal popularity of wild birds makes it so. National Parks may or may not contain official sanctuaries: but by the very fact that they compel a respect for nature become such. Bird observatory islands and areas are – of course – *all* sanctuaries: no field ornithologist could have it otherwise.

The protectionists had good prophets – the early Audubonites in America, the Norfolk naturalists in England, the Berlepschians in Germany. Now they have public opinion on their side, and by virtue of this have big new responsibilities in education, information, research and the advice and persuasion of governments all over the world. The sanctuary network is the visible evidence of their rise to power.

Protection

We have already shown that since 1680 (p. 56) 76 full species of birds have become extinct, and that man is responsible for the extinction of half of them. There are probably over 140 birds now living (pp. 57, 268) with a population of under 2,000; and it is likely that only half as many would be so rare were it not for man.

Man's greatest destruction of birds and other wildlife took place in the second half of the nineteenth century and the early years of the present century: and it was in this period that the conscience of the world began to be aroused. This conscience, moreover, worried also about local rarity, about the destruction and impoverishment of communities, about cruel or overwhelming hunting practices, about the plumage and cage bird trades. Good legislators indeed sometimes proved themselves extremely far-seeing, witness pioneer wild bird laws in the state of Massachusetts in 1818, in Europe in 1834, in Hesse (Germany) in 1836, in Holland in 1837, in Britain in 1869.

We have given some account of the Royal Society for the Protection of Birds, the world's first *national* bird protection society founded in 1889. In Britain there are now several national protection societies, each concerned with a separate branch of nature, which have found a co-ordinative union only since World War II, in the shape of the Council for Nature. In North America progress was in a somewhat different style, toward the same end.

In the United States and Canada the wildlife protection movement started (as it seems to have started almost everywhere) with the bird watchers and bird lovers; in Pennsylvania in 1886. In February that year the dedicated naturalist George Bird Grinnell coined the words 'Audubon Society': a most happy name which all the Western world could use; for Audubon was not only the world's greatest bird artist, but one of America's finest field naturalists, and a European by birth who traveled and observed and published widely in Europe long after he had become an American.

After its foundation the Pennsylvania Audubon Society became dormant for a few years; but it soon revived and was joined by others. By 1904 ten states and the District of Columbia had Audubon Societies; and in 1905 the National Audubon Society was formed (from the National Association of Audubon Societies of 1902). The Audubon movement was early charged with responsibility for the whole of wild nature, though its special love for and interest in birds still shines in its now famous and popular journal, which was started in New York as *Bird Lore* in 1898, before the Society was founded, and changed its name to *Audubon Magazine* in 1941. The National

Audubon Society now publishes a stimulating separate magazine for its ornithological members: *Audubon Field Notes*.

All the fifty present states of the Union (as well as D.C.) now have Audubon groups or clubs affiliated to the National Audubon Society. What is more, these powerful and altruistic private bodies have evolved in a country in which there has been an older sense of government responsibility for wild nature than in any other in the world (the Englishman writes this) – a country which established its first National Park in 1872, years before any other nation did, and whose pioneer Fish and Wildlife Service has been a model to the rest.

To cut a story short, the world began in earnest to put its nature house in order early in the present century. Most Western and some Asian and African and South American countries now have good nature protection laws, though all have difficulty in enforcement. But new problems march with human progress; and private international bodies and full international laws and treaties have had to be made to cope with them.

One of the earliest private international bodies was born at a conference in Paris as early as 1902 and founded in 1922; it is the International Council for Bird Preservation, now commonly known by its French initials CIPO. CIPO meets every two years nowadays and can put very effective pressure on the United Nations and individual governments.

Now closely connected with UNESCO, the United Nations Educational, Scientific and Cultural Organization, is a wider body, the International Union for Conservation of Nature and Natural Resources, IUCN. IUCN was born long before the United Nations: it has excellent and influential Commissions on Survival Service (intelligence on endangered species), ecology, national parks, education, and had a most successful African Special Project in 1960.

One of the nastiest trades, which led to the death of hundreds of thousands of beautiful and often uncommon birds – and on one occasion to the murder of an Audubon warden – was the commerce in 'osprey' plumes, the breeding adornments of several kinds of herons, and in the feathers of terns, birds of paradise and others. By law and public and private enforcement it has by now been virtually stamped out everywhere. But few problems can be wrapped up thus: most need eternal vigilance.

There is a good background of law in the more civilized countries now, protecting at all times nearly all birds but those believed to be pests: but the world needs far more than the thousand (or so) good private or government wildlife sanctuaries and refuges that it has.

Some birds on the Survival Service list need more than sanctuaries to keep them going; thus about half the 432 Hawaiian geese, or nénés, in the world in 1962 were bred

in the grounds of the Wildfowl Trust in Gloucestershire, England.

There are fine agreements, for instance, between the U.S. and Canada, and between a large group of European countries, for the co-ordination of internal laws and the care of the migrant birds that may breed in one and winter in another; but by no means enough laws preventing the importation of birds from one country to another, or the introduction of wild species into countries of which they have never been natives. There is good international legal agreement, now, about the discharge of oil by ships at sea; but it did not come before a million sea birds had come to a dirty end. New insecticides and other pest poisons have surely already killed millions of songbirds in Europe and North America: legal control comes very slowly, and with considerable opposition.

In 1961 the World Wildlife Fund was set up. It shares an office with IUCN at Morges in Switzerland, and is already having fair success in raising the really big money needed for conservation and protection research and action in every corner of the earth. Protection also needs wide, international propaganda. Only a few sportsmen in some educated countries understand, for instance, that their legitimate quarry can safely be shared with a natural population of its natural predators, and that hawks are not 'vermin' to be destroyed on sight.

In 1961 the human population reached 3 billion, having increased by a sixth in the previous decade. By the first decade of the 21st century (within the lifetime of most of our readers) it will have probably doubled. How much room will there be for wild birds and other animals? Enough, we believe; but only enough if the naturalists of the world increase faster, and research and teach as if the fate of the world's beauty and resources depended on them, which it does.

We show here one of Eric Hosking's finest photographs, the first ever taken of the Spanish race of the imperial eagle. It was made from the top of one of his great pylon hides in the Coto Doñana in southern Spain, which has now become an international sanctuary with the help of the World Wildlife Fund. As a race, the Spanish imperial eagle is likely to be on the Survival Service List for some time. Nobody knows exactly what its population is. There were six pairs on the Coto in 1957, and a few others in southern Spain; apart from these no more than a few in Portugal and Morocco: nobody seems to know whether any still breed in Algeria. We can guess that in these countries (its world range) its numbers are very small, probably well under a hundred pairs. 'As it nests on the plains and lowlands', writes our friend Guy Mountfort, 'it unfortunately does not benefit from the natural protection enjoyed by species which breed among inaccessible mountains. Its nest is a tremendous edifice, usually all too visibly located in the crown of an isolated tree'.

Clubs

We suppose that the first bird clubmen were hunters and magicians of the Stone Ages who gathered together in caves to give the birds names, discuss their habits, carve them on wood or bone or rock, or paint them on the walls. They had their special totem birds (or other animals), no doubt, just as some scores of the birds of today's world have been adopted by national, local, school bird-watching societies, bird-protection groups, ornithological clubs. The whole of our beloved science of ornithology stems years back from twos and threes (and then more and more) gathering together, to share ideas, dispute, inform, plan, act, print (when they learned how) and paint.

We may be sure that in the very earliest civilized times there were natural history societies of some sort, based on such great houses as Ptolemy's Museum in Alexandria (3rd century B.C.). Only the other day one of us walked into a room in a newly excavated house at Pompeii (1st century A.D.), which could well have been the headquarters of the local branch of the Naples and District Bird Watching (or perhaps more likely Bird Eating or Bird Hunting or Avicultural) Club, so beautifully were the walls embellished with fine paintings of dozens of different birds most of which still live around there. All were identifiable, including a ring-necked parakeet which must have come all the way from India; and they must have been painted by an Audubon or a Gould of the day, which means a first-rate ornithologist.

Natural history societies of the age of print, of the modern sort, began in the sixteenth century with the founding of the Academy of the Secrets of Nature in Naples. By the early nineteenth century they were legion, and some of these academies and clubs began special publications on birds. The first purely ornithological society seems to have been founded in 1851 – the German Ornithological Society. The second, the British Ornithologists' Union, was founded in 1859. The Nuttall Ornithological Club, founded in 1873, is the oldest in America.

One of us has analyzed the spread of his own hobby in his own country by making a list of the bird societies, and the natural history societies with bird sections or published bird reports. There are now nearly 200 in Britain and Ireland. Starting with a pioneer field club in Belfast in 1821, there were 10 by 1834 (the tenth being the first school natural history society at Bootham, still going strong). The number had doubled by 1853, doubled again by 1867, doubled again by 1888, and doubled again by 1946! There are probably forty or fifty thousand people in England, Wales, Scotland and Ireland who are active, if only in a supporting or subscribing way, in a bird group or bird club. Well over a million people in Britain must have bought a bird book.

Even the old and learned clubs that operate and publish in the most scientific and specialized stratospheres of ornithology in nearly every civilized country are increasing their membership rapidly. Conventions and meetings of bird clubmen have strained the hotel accommodation from Moscow to Caracas, from Regina to Livingstone. In Britain, home of the Old School Tie, the Old Bird Tie is becoming just as popular: on a birding cruise there a year or two ago one of us wore the arctic tern tie of the Royal Naval Bird Watching Society, the other the pink-footed geese of the Wildfowl Trust. Around the saloon table at breakfast friends were discussing plans with us: a crested tit (Scottish Ornithologists' Club), a puffin (St. Kilda Club), an avocet (Royal Society for the Protection of Birds) and a gannet (British Trust for Ornithology).

Bird watchers have many different drives and directions. Some like to work alone, discuss things with few. Some,

like us, have lost count of the clubs we belong to. To be quite clubless is to be on the bank, with the stream of warm companionship, benign freemasonry, scientific criticism and encouragement, flowing ever more deeply by.

The brotherhood of the bird club has contributed more than a little to the cause of international understanding and friendship. Our hobby knows no more political boundaries than the birds. Its devotees exploit nobody, compete only in excellence and thoroughness, take little, give much. In the ninety-odd birding years that we share between us, one or other or both of us has been to meetings in most states of the U.S., most provinces of Canada, Venezuela, the West Indies, Japan, Africa, Russia, Finland, Sweden, Norway, Iceland, Denmark, Germany, Holland, Belgium, Switzerland, France, Poland, Italy, Spain, England, Scotland, Wales, Ireland and the Channel Islands; to the seventy-fifth birthday of the American Ornithologists' Union; to the hundredth birthday of the British Ornithologists' Union; to the first meeting of the All-Union Ornithological Conference of Russia. We have exchanged children with club friends' families for vacations in New England, England, Iceland, Holland and France. All this has given each of us an abundantly happy life.

The secrets of the fellowship of ornithology are not difficult to find. First, all bird watchers love the challenge of discovery, the pursuit of the world's most beautiful and observable animals in every kind of clime. There is no corner of the earth, except the South Pole, where a bird watcher can be bored. Secondly, the bird watcher has friends with the same kind of inquiring spirit and sharing outlook in every country, nearly every town, every place of high learning: the bird-club badge is a passport more universal than the government documents we all have to carry for reasons no bird would ever appreciate.

Left: Old Bird Ties; puffins of St. Kilda Club; arctic terns of Royal Naval Bird Watching Society; pinkfeet of Wildfowl Trust; crested tits of Scottish Ornithologists' Club; avocets of Royal Society for the Protection of Birds: also Audubon Warden Sam Whiddin in uniform

Right: emblems of famous ornithological societies. 1. British Ornithologists' Union's sacred ibis; 2. American Ornithologists' Union's great auk; 3. Royal Naval Bird Watching Society's arctic tern; 4. Society for Ornithological Studies' lark (France); 5. Netherlands Ornithological Union's black-tailed godwit; 6. Danish Ornithological Society's lapwings; 7. Cooper Ornithological Club's California condor (Pacific U.S.A.); 8. Italian Ornithological Association's and Royal Society for the Protection of Birds' avocet; 9. Royal Australasian Ornithologists' Union's emu; 10. South African Ornithological Society's ostrich; 11. Ornithological Society of New Zealand's takahé; 12. Scottish Ornithologists' Club's Scottish crested tit

CHAPTER VIII

The Regiment of Birds

With maps of the families

We here present a classification and geographical atlas of the class Aves with a census of what we believe to be the acceptable genera and species named by 1962. It embraces all fossil, lately extinct and living birds known to us.

This regimentation is pursued in all but three cases down to family level; in the large families Furnariidae (no. 144), Muscicapidae (173) and Emberizidae (181) we have broken down the families into subfamilies.

As far as we know, no bird extinct before 1600 has been acceptably named from any evidence but that of fossil or subfossil bones. Ornithologists know the colors only of birds which lived after this date. We thus take 1600 to be a threshold of modern ornithology, and define birds which survived beyond it as neospecies: all others are paleospecies. Other workers (p. 241) have defined neospecies as those living in and after the Linnean year of 1758, but this involves anomalies since 8 named species based on bones were alive in 1600 but extinct by 1758.

In the classification the symbol † before the name of a family means that it is fossil only and extinct by 1600. An arrow after the name of a geological period (*e.g.* Eocene→) means that the family has persisted from that period to the present. The first known appearance of each family and listed subfamily known from a fossil or fossils, in the geological record, is shown by its number on the chart opposite. We numbered our families in 1961, since when Wetmore (1962) erected the Plegadornithidae, whose single member is included in the census, and Brodkorb (1963) erected the Lonchodytidae and Torotigidae, whose members are not censused, with two exceptions previously held in other families. We have numbered these 40A, 18A and 41A (see under nos. 41, 19 and 42).

'Lately extinct' species lived after 1680, the year before that of the probable extinction of the dodo. We believe that there are 76 of these, of which one is yet to be named and not included in the census. Nine birds recorded as 'extinct before dodo' (one also unnamed and not in the census) were still alive earlier in the 17th century.

The reader can work out the number of paleospecies and neospecies from the figures given under family or subfamily. Thus (family 108) 298 pigeon species are 'known' – that is to say, accepted by us from a study of the literature. Of these 285 are living, 5 lately extinct, 1 extinct before the dodo and 35 fossil. The neospecies are $285 + 5 + 1 = 291$. As 298 are known, $298 - 291 = 7$ are paleospecies, and $35 - 7 = 28$ are neospecies also known as fossils. In the census of genera, the number fossil is of paleogenera (purely fossil genera) only.

The theoretical object of biological classification is to arrange the forms in an order representing their 'natural' relationship. The ideal is to re-create the whole of the family tree, and pick off and name the branches, starting with the oldest, and proceeding only to the next oldest when all the twigs on the former branch have been told off. A classification made thus should end up with a list proceeding from most 'primitive' to most 'advanced'.

This treatment is, indeed, ideal. The trouble is that the fossils are but a tiny sample of the birds of the past. Moreover, when we get a fossil, we cannot study its behavior, physiology and parasites, all of which could give us clues to its true place on the family tree. So we have to make do with what we have got, and arrive at a *practical* classification. Any such classification is based partly on guesswork, but without some system no birds could be arranged, and no decent research could start.

In making this practical regimentation and census of the bird kinds, we have consulted previous classifications, censuses and papers by Amadon, Austin, Berger, Brodkorb, Delacour, Greenway, the late K. Lambrecht, Mayr, the late J. L. Peters, Storer, the late J. van Tyne, Vaurie, Wetmore and Wynne, and revisions of bird families and other groups by other recent authorities. Many experts have generously given us private information.

A summary of the census of genera and species is discussed on page 241, where it is compared with previous censuses. The species is the only unit which is strictly definable; all the other categories from genus up to class are made by man for his convenience, and hallowed by long use and careful judgment. There has been an almost universal measure of agreement for years as to what constitutes an order, a fair one on what constitutes a family.

The layouts and silhouettes are by Roger Peterson. Silhouettes of families now extinct are shown in ghost gray; none has been done for a few based on scanty material.

The maps, researched by James Fisher, have had their presentation designed by Peter Constable Pope, and were drawn by Crispin Fisher assisted by Max Hailstone. The colored circles key what is believed to be the present breeding distribution of the family or group. The colored swords show the sites at which fossils have been found, when these fall outside the present breeding range (if any); some of them, of course, may represent birds that died in their winter range.

Some tropical families have been plotted on Mercator's Projection, but the rest are on equal area maps. Of these the mapnet centered on London, and that centered on the North Pole with the Southern Hemisphere land-masses in petals, were designed by the late Professor Fawcett; and that centered on the South Pole with the northern oceans in the petals was designed on the Fawcett system by James Fisher specially for bird distribution.

The other main maps are on Lambert projections.

Millions of years ago	Period		Taxa
to over 10,000	Holocene or Recent		33, 109, 181d, 181f
to about 2 million	Pleistocene	upper	11, †12, 13, 24, †52, 63, 88, 96, 102, 120, 124, 138, 139, 141, 144a, 144b, 145, 151, 166, 168, 171, 173b, 181b, 181e, 184
		middle	170, 182, 185 and at some stage of the Pleistocene also:- 16, 47, 55, 60, 66, 130, 134, 162, 172, 173g, 173i, 180, 191, 192, 193
2		lower	119, 159, 176, 186
10	Pliocene	u. m.	18, 173a †15, †106
		l. m.	9, 157, 175, 181a 14
20	Miocene	upper	23, †36
		middle	†28, †169, 199
		lower	20, 26, †27, †45, †48, †81, †89, 91, 98, 108, 110, 113, 135, 142, 160, 164, 173e, 189
30	Oligocene	upper	†158
		middle	22, †73, †84
40		lower	29, †34, 56, 59, 64, 71, †79, 80, †82, †83 39, 53, 57, †74, 92, 107, 112, 115, †121, 122, 126, 131
50	Eocene	upper	†10, 41, †44, 46, Eonessa 49, †50, 62, †69, 174, 190
		middle	†8, 21, 32, 51, †58, 85, 90, 129, 136 147
60		lower	7, 17, 25, †35, 37, †43, 54, 61, †68, 70, †87, 94, †95, 103, 105, †114, 127
	Paleocene	upper	Eupterornis 19, Graculavus 31, Telmatornis 75, Gastornis and Remiornis †86, Palaeotringa 93
70		lower	Scaniornis †42
80	Upper Cretaceous	upper	Lonchodytes †18A, Elopteryx †30, Plegadornis †40A, Parascaniornis †42 or †41A, Torotix †41A
90		middle	Baptornis †3, Hesperornis †4, Ichthyornis †5, Apatornis †6
100		lower	
110	Lower Cretaceous	upper	Enaliornis †2
120		middle	
130		lower	Gallornis 49 or †41A
140	Jurassic	upper	Archaeopteryx †1
150			

A classification and census

Class Aves, birds

† Aves *incertae sedis*

Jurassic – Pleistocene
19 species, which have been placed in 12 unique and possibly valid fossil genera and in 6 modern genera, have such fragmentary or obscure remains that they cannot yet be allocated to a family. Included in the census, then, are these 12 genera and 19 species; *not* included are 5 other species in 4 genera known only from fossil footprints, 6 other species in 2 genera known only from fossil feathers, and a few fossil egg shells that have been named.

Subclass † Sauriurae, dawn birds

Order † Archaeopterygiformes

1 Archaeopteryx
Family † Archaeopterygidae, Upper Jurassic
Genus and species: 1 fossil (some authorities hold 2)

The chart above shows the fossil record of birds. In the left column the approximate ages of the periods are given from a consensus of recent radioactive dating. The break between the Pliocene and the Pleistocene simply represents a change in time scale. Of the 202 families we accept (including the 3 new ones of 1962–63) all but 49 (of which 25 are Passerine) are represented by at least one fossil. These (with subfamilies of nos. 144, 173 and 181) are plotted on the chart at the earliest geological stratum in which they have so far been found; also up to the Paleocene every genus is named and plotted in its place.

2 Enaliornis

Family † Enaliornithidae, Lower Cretaceous
Genus: 1 fossil
Species: 2 fossil
May be in loon order, before new family 18A

3 Baptornis and Neogaeornis

Family † Baptornithidae, Upper Cretaceous
Genera: 2 fossil
Species: 2 fossil
Earliest fossil, *Baptornis*, Kansas; may be in grebe order, before family 20

4 Hesperornis and Coniornis

Family † Hesperornithidae, Upper Cretaceous
Genera: 2 fossil
Species: 4 fossil
Earliest fossils, *Hesperornis*, Kansas

p. 42

p. 42

p. 42

5 Ichthyornis
Family † Ichthyornithidae, Upper Cretaceous
Genus: 1 fossil
Species: 7 fossil

6 Apatornis
Family † Apatornithidae, Upper Cretaceous
Genus and species: 1 fossil

7 Penguins
Family Spheniscidae, Lower Eocene→
Genera: 6 living, 21 fossil
Species: 47 known; 15 living, 36 fossil
Origin: probably southern or even subantarctic;
earliest fossil, an as yet unnamed fragment
from New Zealand

p. 42

p. 27

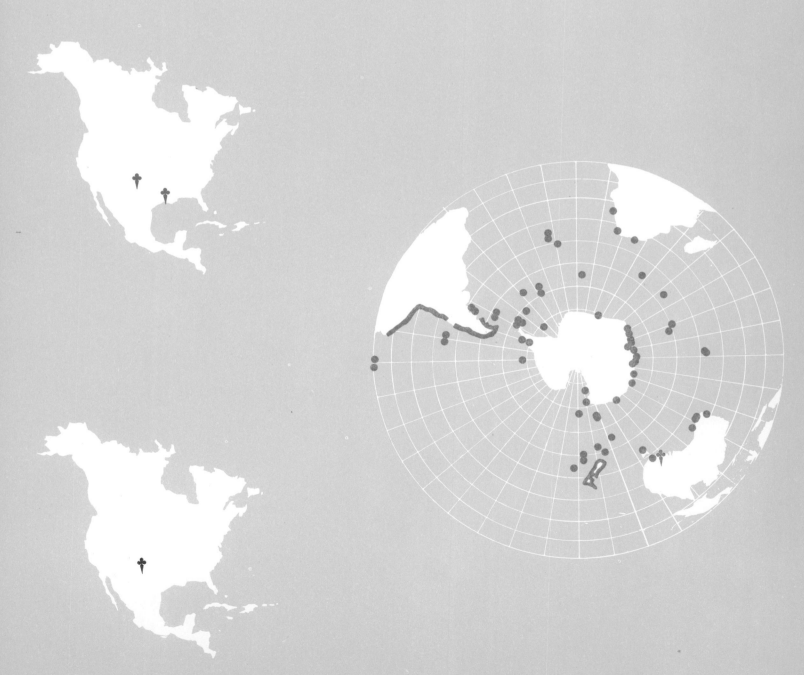

5 Ichthyornis

6 Apatornis

7 Penguins

8 Eleutherornis

Family † Eleutherornithidae, Middle Eocene
Genus and species: 1 fossil
Known from fragmentary pelvis only. May
be in Diatrymiform order, near family 86

9 Ostriches

Family Struthionidae, Lower Pliocene→
Genus: 1 living
Species: 7 known; 1 living, 7 fossil
Origin: possibly Palearctic; earliest fossils
Egypt, Greece, S. Russia, Persia, N. India,
Mongolia

10 Elephant birds

Family † Aepyornithidae, Upper Eocene –
Recent
Genera: 1 extinct before dodo, 3 fossil
Species: 9 known; 1 extinct before dodo, 9 fossil
Origin: possibly Ethiopian; earliest fossil,
Egypt: survived in Madagascar until historical
times

p. 25

p. 25

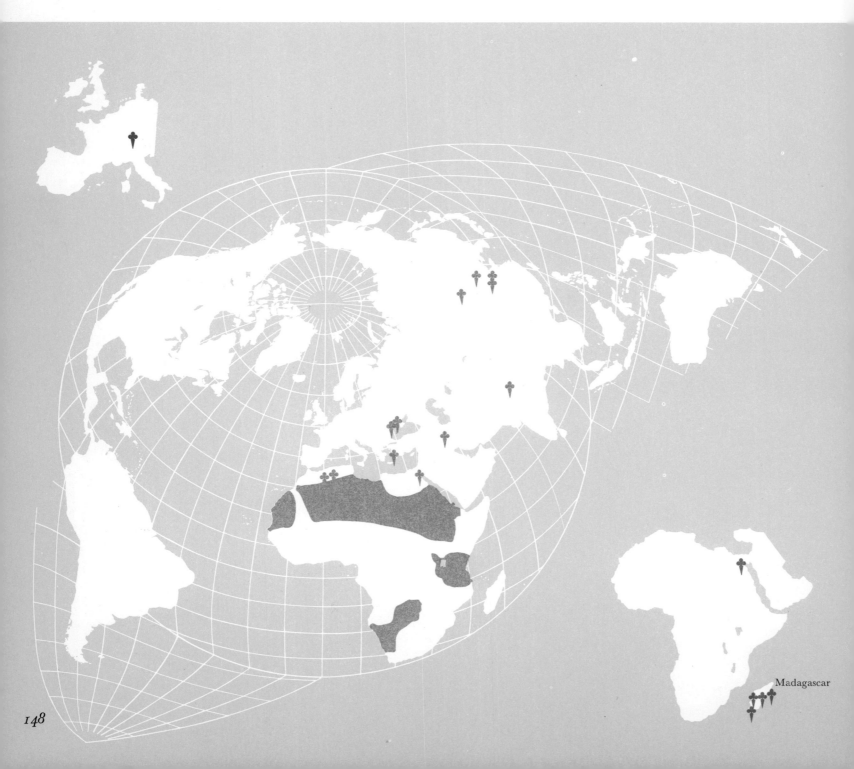

Madagascar

11 Emus

Family Dromiceiidae, Upper Pleistocene→
Genus: 1 living
Species: 3 known; 1 living, 3 fossil
Origin: doubtless Australian

p. 25

12 Dromornis and Genyornis

Family † Dromornithidae, Upper Pleistocene
Genera: 2 fossil
Species: 2 fossil
Origin: doubtless Australian

13 Cassowaries

Family Casuariidae, Upper Pleistocene→
Genus: 1 living
Species: 3 known; 3 living, 1 fossil
Origin: doubtless Australasian; only fossil, race
of living Bennett's cassowary, *Casuarius bennetti
lyddekeri*, New South Wales

p. 25

149

14 Lesser moas

Family: Emeidae, Upper Miocene or Lower
Pliocene – Recent
Genera: 1 lately extinct, 5 fossil
Species: 19 known; 1 lately extinct, 19 fossil
or subfossil
Origin: doubtless New Zealand; survived in
South Island until late 18th century; earliest
fossil, *Anomalopteryx antiquus*, Timaru, S.I.

15 Great moas

Family † Dinornithidae, Middle Pliocene –
Recent
Genus: 1 fossil
Species: 8 fossil
Origin: doubtless New Zealand; survived in
South Island until historical times; earliest
fossil, *Dinornis ingens*, Nukumaru, North Island

p. 25

16 Kiwis

Family Apterygidae, Pleistocene→
Genera: 1 living, 1 fossil
Species: 4 known; 3 living, 4 fossil
Origin: doubtless New Zealand

p. 27

14 Lesser moas

Family: Emeidae, Upper Miocene or Lower
Pliocene – Recent
Genera: 1 lately extinct, 5 fossil
Species: 19 known; 1 lately extinct, 19 fossil
or subfossil
Origin: doubtless New Zealand; survived in
South Island until late 18th century; earliest
fossil, *Anomalopteryx antiquus*, Timaru, S.I.

15 Great moas

Family † Dinornithidae, Middle Pliocene –
Recent
Genus: 1 fossil
Species: 8 fossil
Origin: doubtless New Zealand; survived in
South Island until historical times; earliest
fossil, *Dinornis ingens*, Nukumaru, North Island

16 Kiwis

Family Apterygidae, Pleistocene→
Genera: 1 living, 1 fossil
Species: 4 known; 3 living, 4 fossil
Origin: doubtless New Zealand

17 Rheas

Family Rheidae, Lower Eocene→
Genera: 2 living, 2 fossil
Species: 6 known; 2 living, 5 fossil
Origin: doubtless South American; earliest
fossil, *Opisthodactylus*, Patagonia, may merit
family status, before 17 (16A); if so,
Heterorhea dabbeni, Upper Pliocene,
N. Argentina, is earliest fossil

18 Tinamous

Family Tinamidae, Pliocene→
Genera: 9 living, 3 fossil
Species: 46 known; 42 living, 14 fossil
Origin: doubtless South American; earliest
fossils, Argentina. May be most primitive
typical birds; if so, before family 5

p. 25

p. 27

Tinamous introduced
Easter I.

19 Loons

Family Gaviidae, Upper Paleocene→
Genera: 1 living, 3 fossil
Species: 12 known; 4 living, 12 fossil
Origin: possibly Siberian or North American;
though earliest fossil, *Eupterornis*, France
In 1963 Brodkorb proposed a new family (18A),
the † Lonchodytidae, to precede this; *Lonchodytes*,
2 species, Upper Cretaceous of Wyoming

20 Grebes

Family Podicipitidae, Lower Miocene→
Genera: 3 living, 1 fossil
Species: 22 known; 17 living, 13 fossil
Origin: doubtless Holarctic; earliest fossil
Podiceps oligocaenus, Oregon

p. 61

p. 28

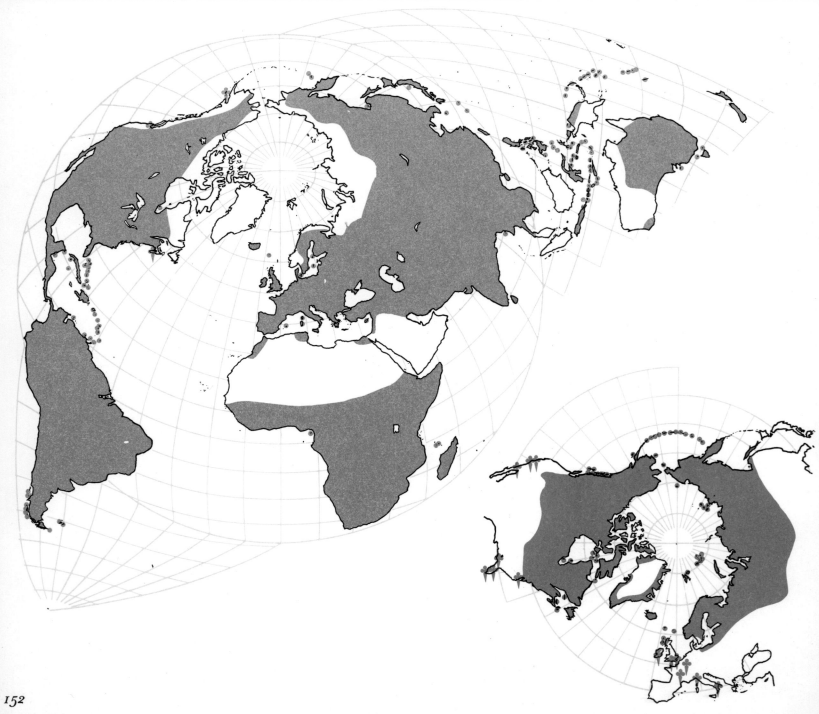

21 Albatrosses

Family Diomedeidae, Middle Eocene→
Genera: 1 living, 2 fossil
Species: 16 known; 12 living, 8 fossil
Origin: probably southern or even subantarctic;
earliest fossil, *Gigantornis*, Nigeria

p. 92

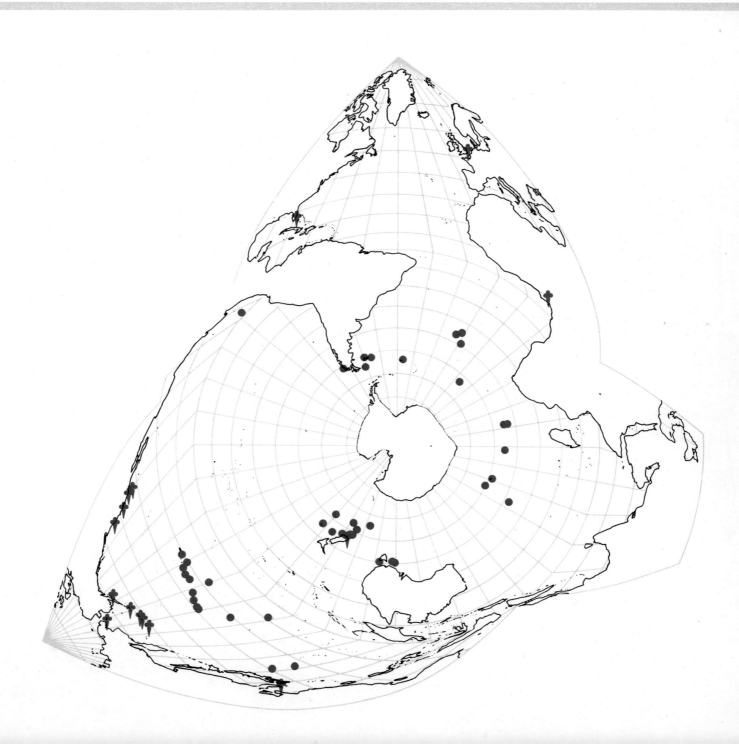

22 Petrels and shearwaters

Family Procellariidae, Middle Oligocene→
Genera: 9 living, 2 fossil
Species: 60 known; 47 living, 25 fossil
Origin: probably southern; though earliest
fossil, *Puffinus raemdonckii*, Belgium

p. 76

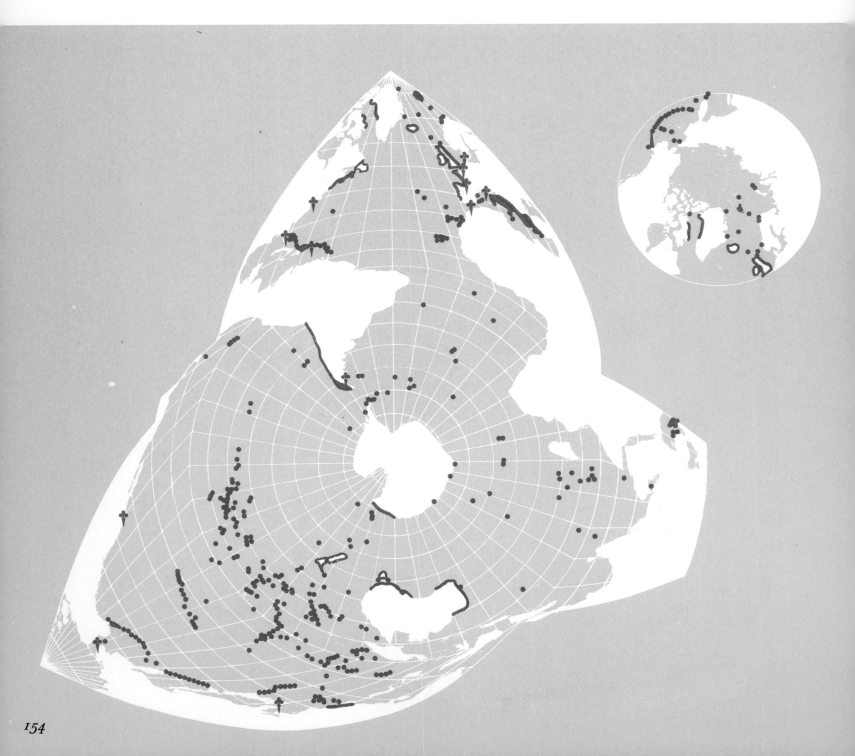

23 Storm petrels

Family Oceanitidae, Upper Miocene→
Genera: 7 living
Species: 20 known; 18 living, 1 lately extinct,
2 fossil
Origin: probably southern; earliest fossil,
Oceanodroma hubbsi, California

24 Diving petrels

Family Pelecanoididae, Upper Pleistocene→
Genus: 1 living
Species: 4 known; 4 living, 1 fossil
Origin: probably subantarctic; only fossil,
Peruvian diving petrel, *Pelecanoides garnotii*,
Perú

p. 30

p. 15

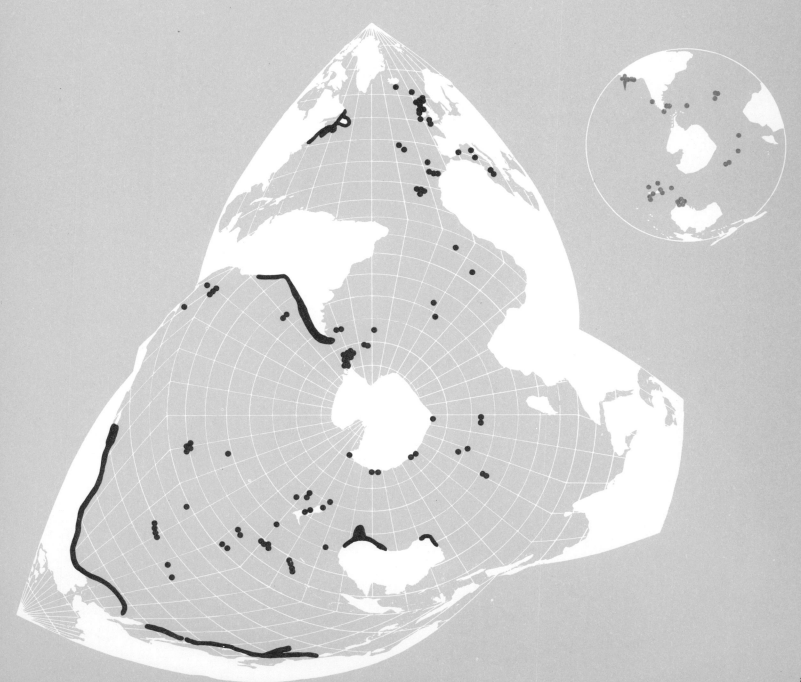

25 Tropic birds

Family Phaëthontidae, Lower Eocene→
Genera: 1 living, 1 fossil
Species: 4 known; 3 living, 2 fossil
Origin: probably tropical; earliest fossil,
Prophaeton, England

p. 30

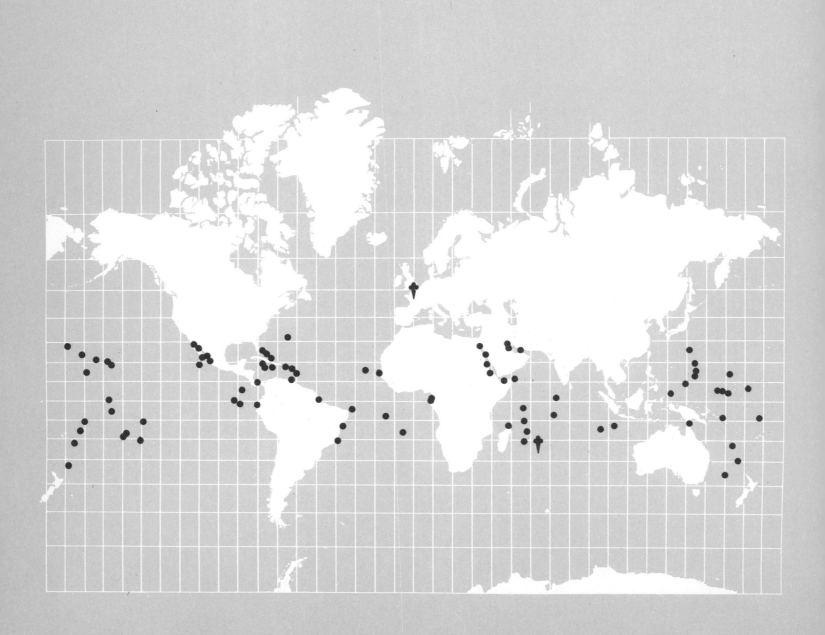

26 Pelicans

Family Pelecanidae, Lower Miocene→
Genera: 1 living, 1 fossil
Species: 16 known; 6 living, 15 fossil
Origin: probably tropical; earliest fossil,
Pelecanus gracilis, France

p. 30

27 Cyphornis and Palaeochenoïdes

Family † Cyphornithidae, Lower Miocene
Genera: 2 fossil
Species: 2 fossil
Have been also placed in suborder Cladornithes,
before family 34

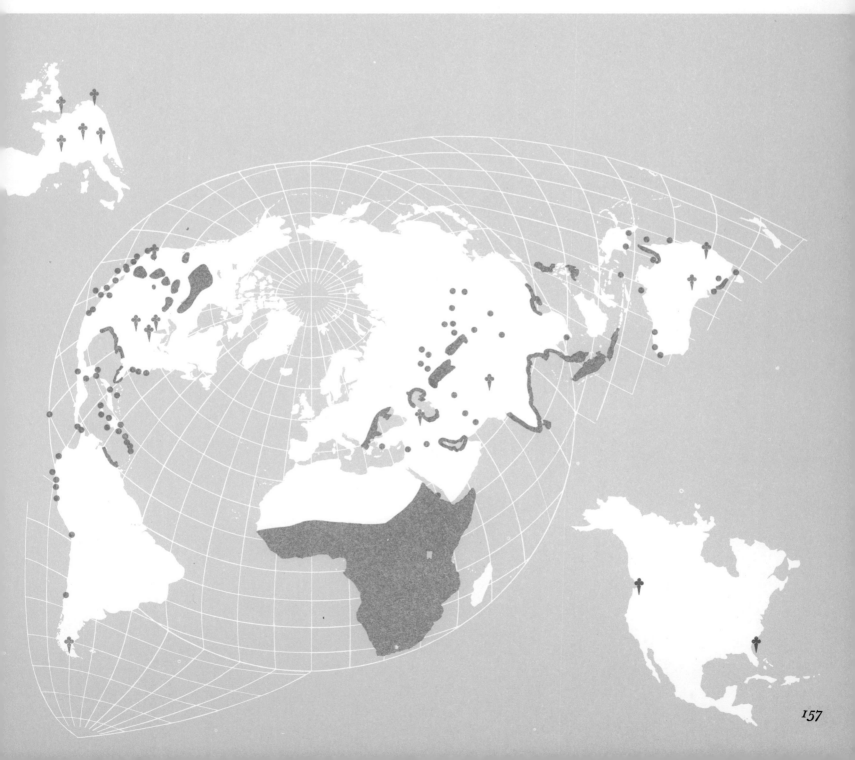

28 Pelagornis
Family † Pelagornithidae, Middle Miocene
Genus and species: 1 fossil
Has been also placed in order
Odontopterygiformes, after family 36

29 Gannets and boobies
Family Sulidae, Lower Oligocene→
Genera: 2 living, 2 fossil
Species: 26 known; 9 living, 21 fossil
Origin: probably tropical; earliest fossil,
Sula ronzoni, France

30 Elopteryx and allies
Family † Elopterygidae, Upper Cretaceous –
Middle Eocene
Genera: 3 fossil
Species: 3 fossil
Earliest fossil, *Elopteryx*, Rumania

p. 30

31 Cormorants

Family Phalacrocoracidae, Upper Paleocene→
Genera: 2 living, 3 fossil
Species: 50 known; 26 living, 1 lately extinct, 31 fossil
Origin: probably tropical, possibly Indian Ocean; earliest fossils, *Graculavus*, New Jersey

32 Snake birds

Family Anhingidae, Middle (?) Eocene→
Genera: 1 living, 1 fossil
Species: 6 known; 1 living, 6 fossil
Origin: probably tropical; earliest fossil *Protoplotus*, Sumatra

p. 30

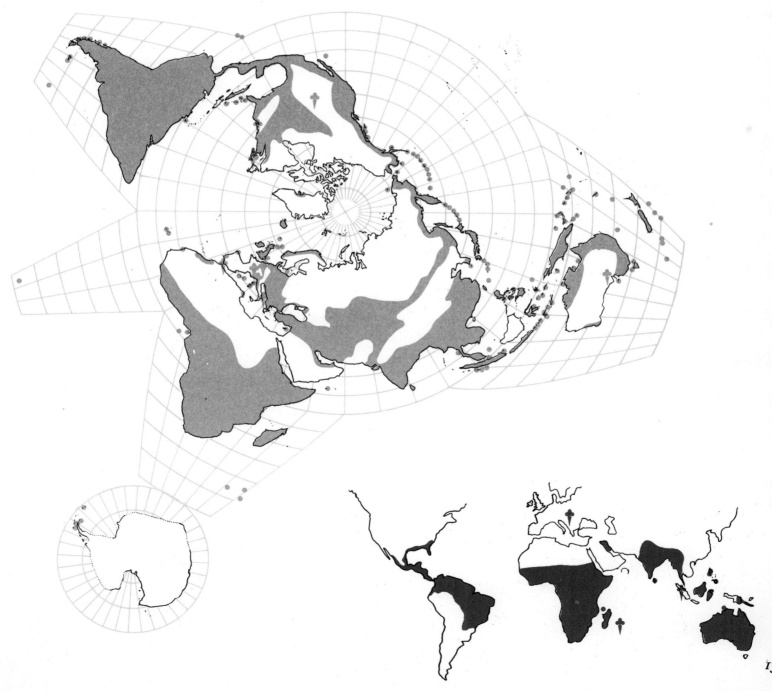

159

33 Frigate birds
Family Fregatidae, Recent→
Genus: 1 living
Species: 5 known; 5 living, 2 fossil
Origin: doubtless tropical

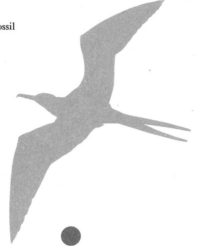

p. 30

34 Cladornis and Cruschedula
Family † Cladornithidae, Lower Oligocene
Genera: 2 fossil
Species: 2 fossil
Based on poorly preserved metatarsi; have been
placed by several authorities in penguin order,
near family 7

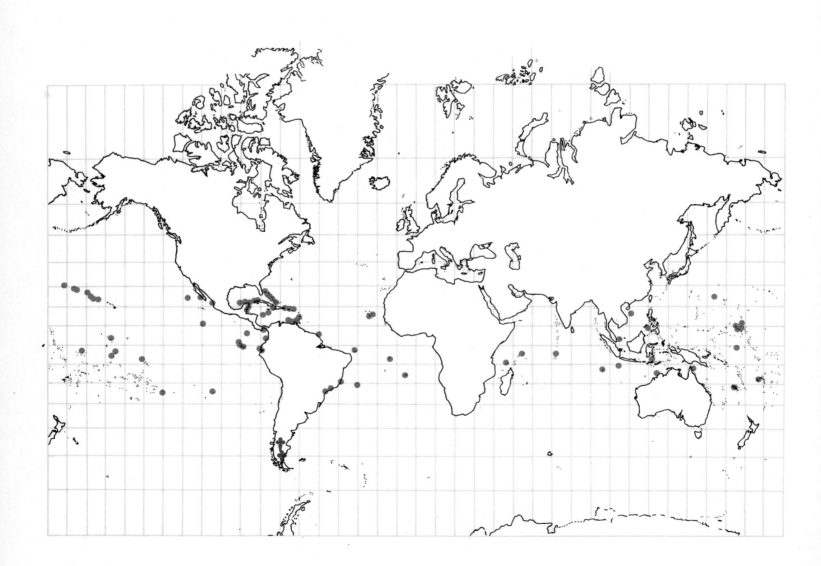

35 Odontopteryx
Family † Odontopterygidae, Lower Eocene
Genus and species: 1 fossil

36 Osteodontornis and Pseudodontornis

Family † Pseudodontornithidae, Miocene
Genera: 2 fossil
Species: 2 fossil
Osteodontornis from Upper Miocene, California;
Pseudodontornis of uncertain age and locality,
? Brazil or Germany; not plotted on map

37 Herons
Family Ardeidae, Lower Eocene→
Genera: 15 living, 7 fossil
Species: 78 known; 63 living, 1 lately extinct,
34 fossil
Origin: probably tropical or subtropical;
earliest fossil, *Proherodius*, England

p. 76

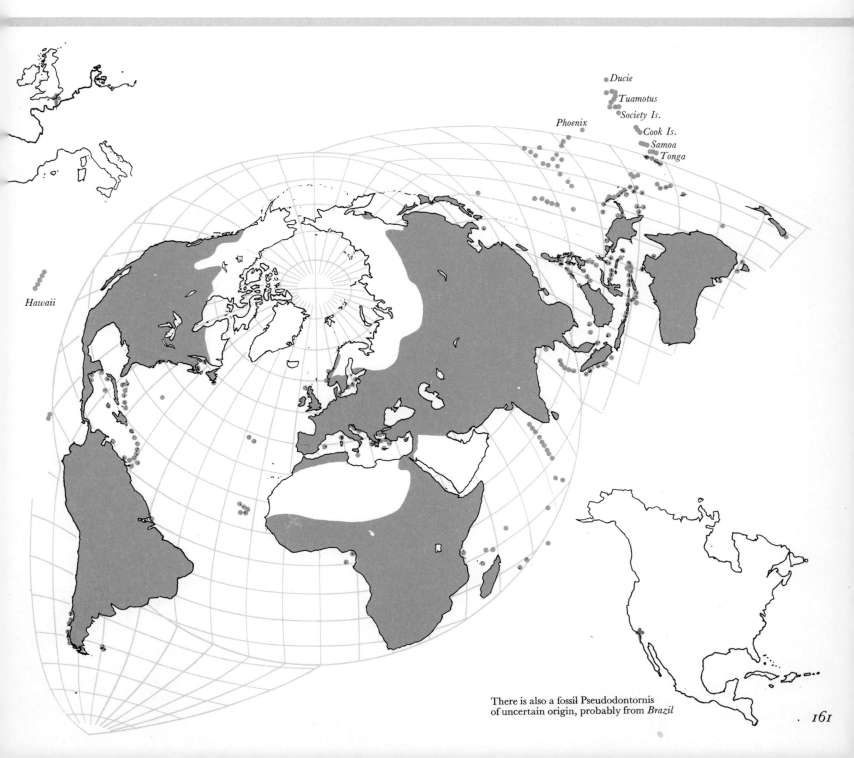

There is also a fossil Pseudodontornis
of uncertain origin, probably from *Brazil*

38 Hammerhead

Family Scopidae, no fossil known
Genus and species: 1 living
Origin: doubtless Ethiopian

39 Storks

Family Ciconiidae, Lower Oligocene→
Genera: 10 living, 9 fossil
Species: 37 known; 17 living, 27 fossil
Origin: probably tropical or subtropical;
earliest fossils France and Patagonia

p. 60

p. 28

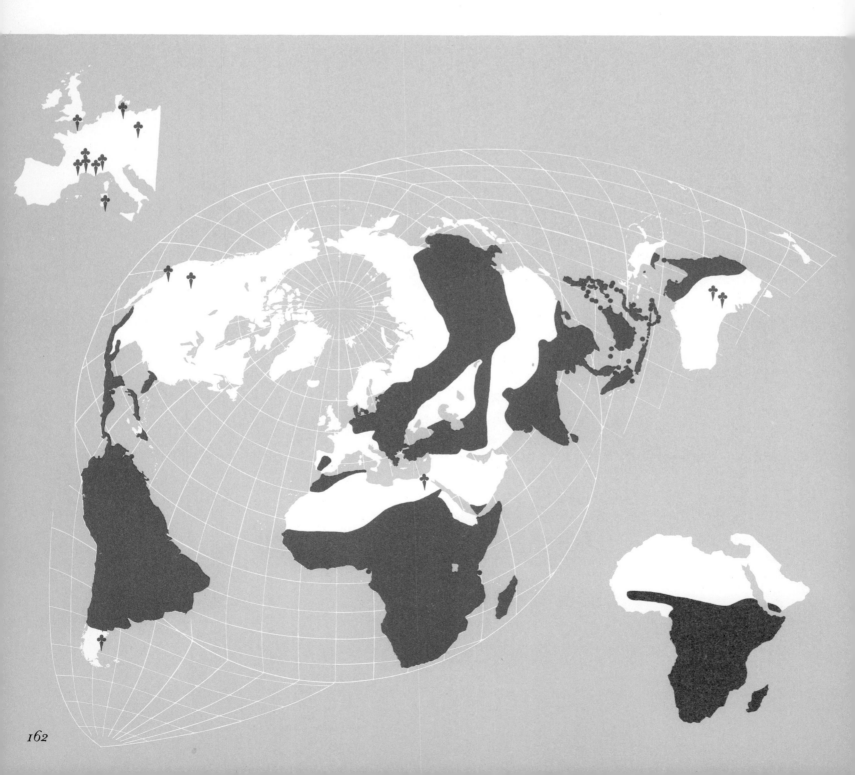

40 Shoebill

Family Balaenicipitidae, no fossil known
Genus and species: 1 living
Origin: doubtless African

p. 60

41 Ibises and spoonbills

Family Plataleidae, Upper Eocene→
Genera: 20 living, 3 fossil
Species: 37 known; 30 living, 15 fossil
Origin: probably tropical or subtropical;
earliest fossil, *Ibidopsis*, England. In 1962
Wetmore proposed a new family (40A), the
† Plegadornithidae, to precede this, with
Plegadornis antecessor, Upper Cretaceous, Alabama

p. 28

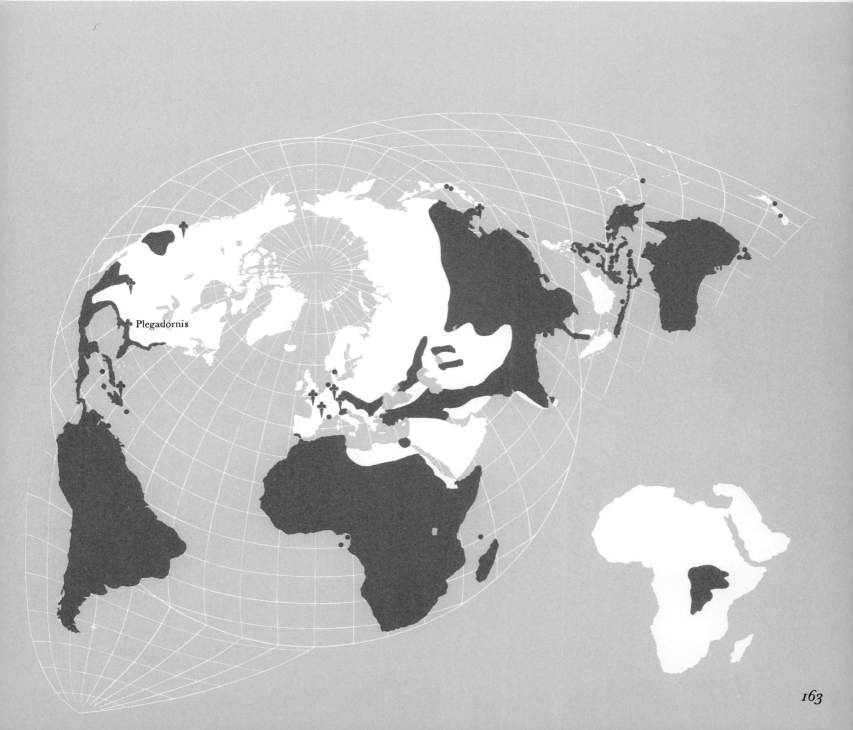

42 Scaniornis and Parascaniornis

Family † Scaniornithidae, Upper Cretaceous –
Lower Paleocene
Genera: 2 fossil
Species: 2 fossil
In 1963 Brodkorb proposed a new family (41A),
the † Torotigidae, to precede this, containing 3
species, *Gallornis* from family 49, *Parascaniornis*,
and the new *Torotix clemensi* from the Upper
Cretaceous of Wyoming. If *Scaniornis* alone
remains, family is Lower Paleocene

43 Telmabates

Family † Telmabatidae, Lower Eocene
Genus and species: 1 fossil

44 Agnopterus

Family † Agnopteridae, Upper Eocene –
Upper Oligocene
Genus: 1 fossil
Species: 3 fossil
Earliest fossil, *Agnopterus hantoniensis*, England

45 Palaelodus and Megapaloelodus

Family † Palaelodidae, Lower Miocene – Lower
Pliocene
Genera: 2 fossil
Species: 8 fossil
Earliest fossils, France and Germany

These families are all believed to have
been primitive flamingo-like birds.

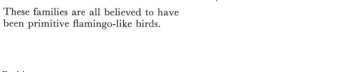

p. 44

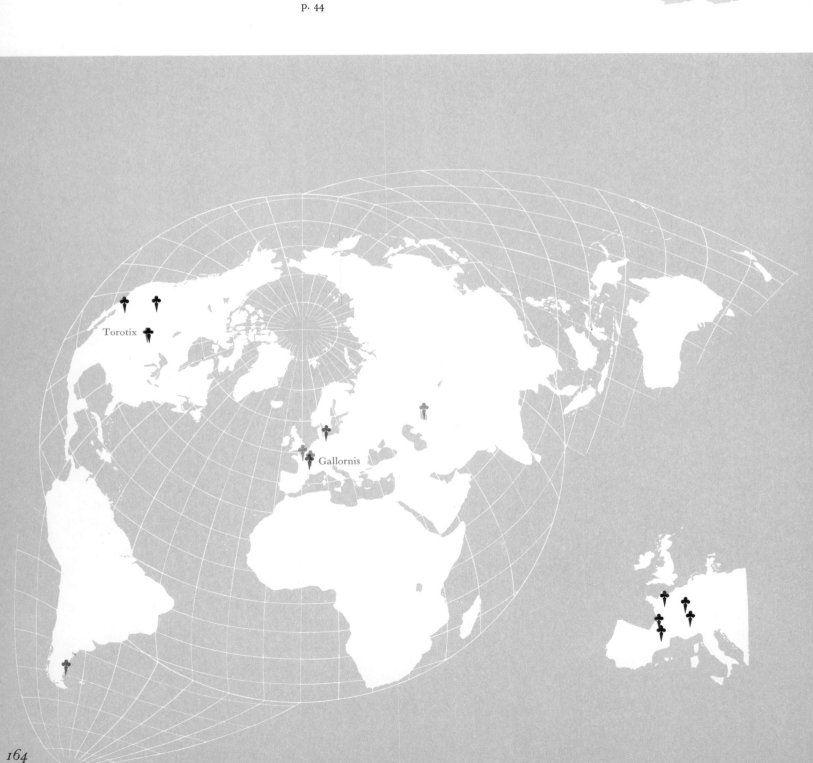

46 Flamingos

Family Phoenicopteridae, Upper Eocene→
Genera: 3 living, 2 fossil
Species: 14 known; 5 living, 11 fossil
Origin: possibly subtropical; earliest fossil,
Elornis, England

p. 28

47 Screamers

Family Anhimidae, Pleistocene→
Genera: 2 living
Species: 3 known; 3 living, 1 fossil
Origin: doubtless South American; only fossil,
crested screamer *Chauna torquata*, Argentina

48 Paranyroca

Family † Paranyrocidae, Lower Miocene
Genus and species: 1 fossil
Family status has been questioned; may be
tribe in family 49, between pochards etc. (tribe
Aythyini) and eiders, sawbills etc. (Mergini)

p. 59

49 Waterfowl

Family Anatidae, Lower Cretaceous→
Genera: 41 living, 2 lately extinct, 21 fossil
Species: 239 known; 146 living, 4 lately
extinct, 1 extinct before dodo, 160 fossil
Origin: ancient and geographically uncertain;
earliest fossil, *Gallornis*, France (oldest known
save *Archaeopteryx*), may be in flamingo order,
family 41A; if so, earliest fossil is *Eonessa*,
Upper Eocene, Utah

p. 29

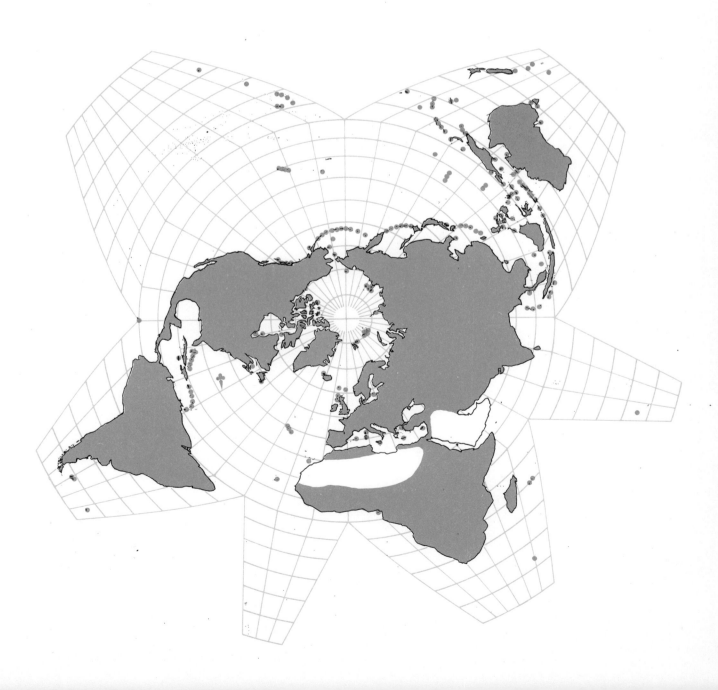

167

50 Neocathartes
Family † Neocathartidae, Upper Eocene
Genus and species: 1 fossil

p. 43

51 New World vultures
Family Cathartidae, Middle Eocene→
Genera: 5 living, 7 fossil
Species: 19 known; 6 living, 17 fossil
Origin: held to be North American; though
earliest fossil, *Eocarthartes*, France; earliest
New World fossils Lower Oligocene, Colorado

p. 9

52 Teratorns
Family † Teratornithidae, Upper Pleistocene
Genera: 2 fossil
Species: 3 fossil

p. 46

introduced

53 Secretary birds
Family Sagittariidae, Upper Eocene or Lower
Oligocene→
Genera: 1 living, 1 fossil
Species: 3 known; 1 living, 2 fossil
Origin: probably Ethiopian; earliest fossil,
Amphiserpentarius schlosseri, France. May be close
to the S. American seriemas, family 80

p. 60

54 Hawks and eagles
Family Accipitridae, Lower Eocene→
Genera: 58 living, 24 fossil
Species: 265 known; 208 living, 97 fossil
Origin: possibly Old World; earliest fossil,
Lithornis, England

p. 31

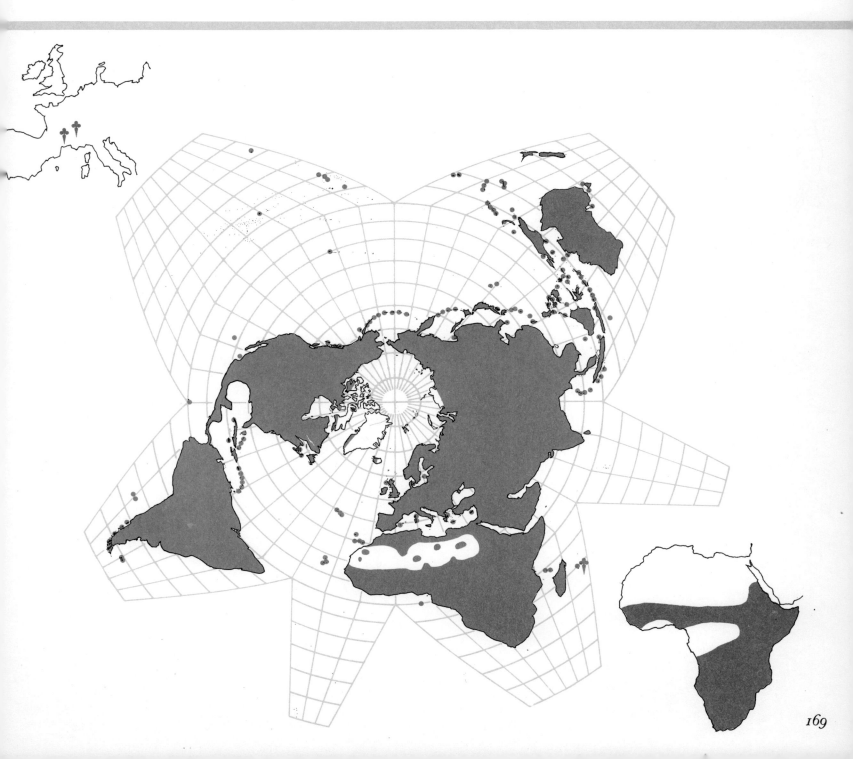

55 Osprey
Family Pandionidae, Pleistocene→
Genus and species: 1 living and fossil
Origin: uncertain; is cosmopolitan

p. 31

56 Falcons
Family Falconidae, Lower Oligocene→
Genera: 12 living, 3 fossil
Species: 71 known; 58 living, 1 lately extinct,
27 fossil
Origin: uncertain; earliest fossil,
Climacarthrus, Patagonia

p. 31

57 Hoatzins
Family Opisthocomidae, Upper Eocene or
Lower Oligocene→
Genera: 1 living, 2 fossil
Species: 5 known; 1 living, 5 fossil
Origin: earliest fossils, *Filholornis*, France,
have been but provisionally assigned to this
family; if they do not belong, earliest is
Hoazinoides, Upper Miocene, Colombia, and
family is doubtless South American

p. 59

58 Gallinuloides
Family † Gallinuloididae, Middle Eocene
Genus and species: 1 fossil
A precursor of family 59

p. 43

59 Guans and curassows
Family Cracidae, Lower Oligocene→
Genera: 11 living, 4 fossil
Species: 47 known; 39 living, 9 fossil
Origin: probably North or Central American;
earliest fossils, *Procrax*, South Dakota and
another, Colorado

p. 58

introduced

introduced

60 Megapodes

Family Megapodiidae, Pleistocene→
Genera: 7 living, 1 fossil
Species: 11 known; 10 living, 2 fossil
Origin: doubtless Australasian; earliest fossil,
Chosornis, Queensland

61 Grouse

Family Tetraonidae, Lower Eocene→
Genera: 11 living, 3 fossil
Species: 26 known; 17 living, 18 fossil
Origin: highly probably Nearctic; earliest
fossil, *Palaeophasianus*, Wyoming

p. 61

p. 75

62 Quails, pheasants, etc.

Family Phasianidae, Upper Eocene→
Genera: 48 living, 1 lately extinct, 10 fossil
Species: 221 known; 174 living, 1 lately
extinct, 65 fossil
Origin: highly probably Palearctic; earliest
fossils, *Palaeortyx*, France. Map omits domestic
fowl

p. 27

63 Guineafowl

Family Numididae, Upper Pleistocene→
Genera: 5 living
Species: 7 known; 7 living, 1 fossil
Origin: doubtless Ethiopian; earliest fossil,
helmeted guineafowl, *Numida meleagris*,
Czechoslovakia; reintroduced into Europe
c. 6th century B.C.

p. 27

64 Turkeys

Family Meleagrididae, Lower Pleistocene→
Genera: 2 living, 1 fossil
Species: 9 known; 2 living, 8 fossil
Origin: doubtless North American; earliest
fossil, *Meleagris leopoldi*, Texas

p. 45

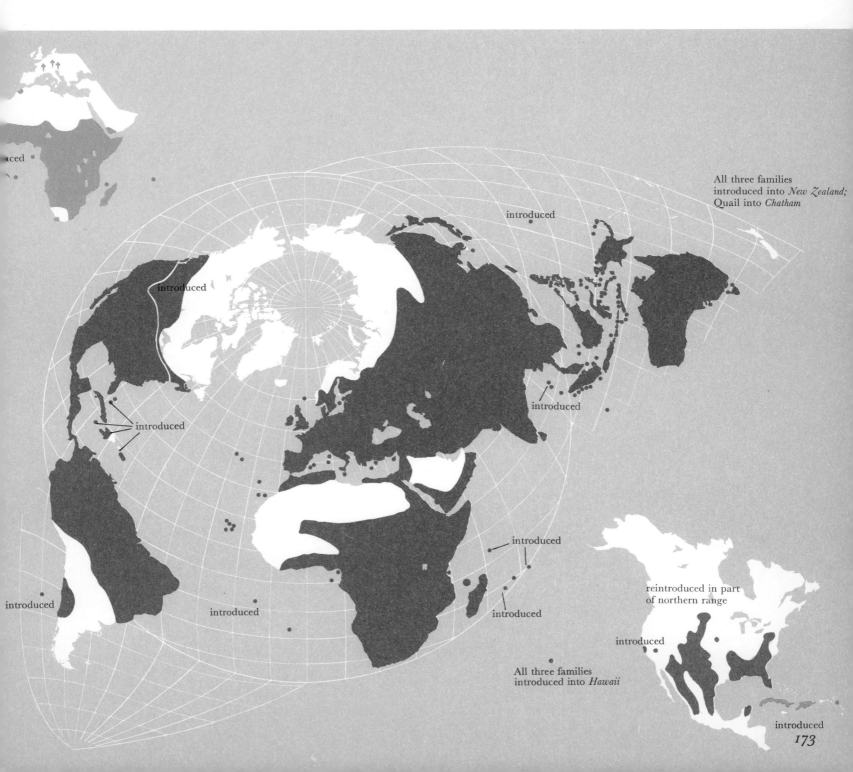

ced

introduced

introduced

introduced

introduced

introduced

introduced

introduced

introduced

introduced

introduced

All three families
introduced into *New Zealand;*
Quail into *Chatham*

reintroduced in part
of northern range

introduced

All three families
introduced into *Hawaii*

introduced

Order Gruiformes
Suborder Mesoenatides

Suborder Turnices

65 Roatelos or mesites
Family Mesoenatidae, no fossils known
Genera: 2 living
Species: 3 living
Origin: doubtless Madagascan

66 Bustard quails
Family Turnicidae, Pleistocene→
Genera: 2 living
Species: 15 known; 15 living, 1 fossil
Origin: tropical Old World; only fossil, Asia

67 Plains wanderer
Family Pedionomidae, no fossil known
Genus and species: 1 living
Origin: doubtless Australian; could perhaps
be relegated to subfamily of 66

p. 60

p. 61

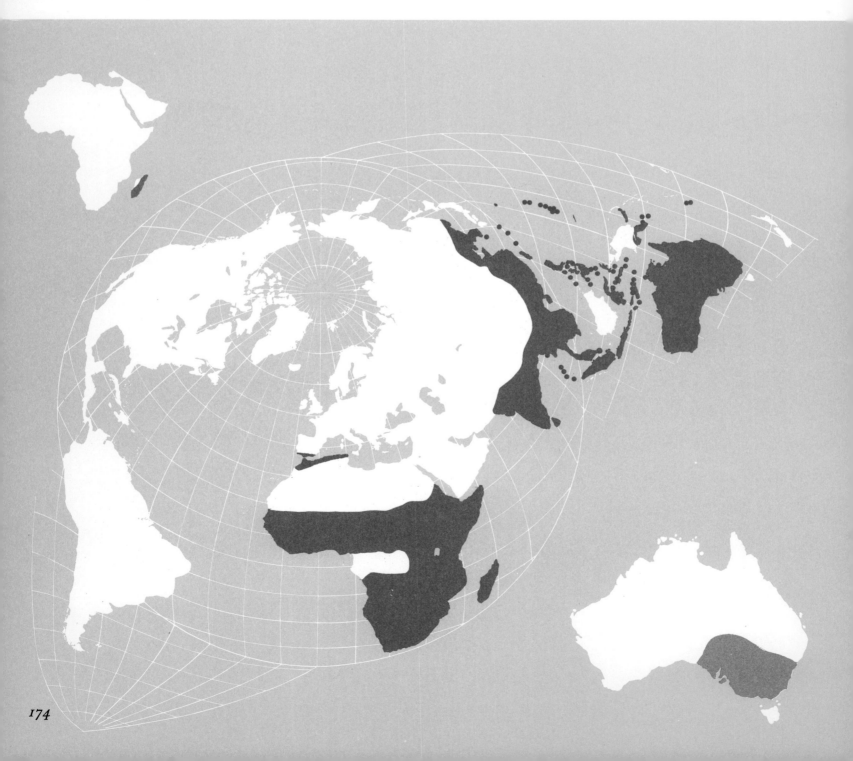

174

68 Geranoides
Family † Geranoididae, Lower Eocene
Genus and species: 1 fossil

69 Eogrus
Family † Eogruidae, Upper Eocene – Upper Miocene
Genus and species: 1 fossil (so far named)

70 Cranes
Family Gruidae, Lower Eocene→
Genera: 4 living, 11 fossil
Species: 38 known; 14 living, 31 fossil
Origin: probably Palearctic, though earliest fossil, *Paragrus*, Wyoming

p. 57

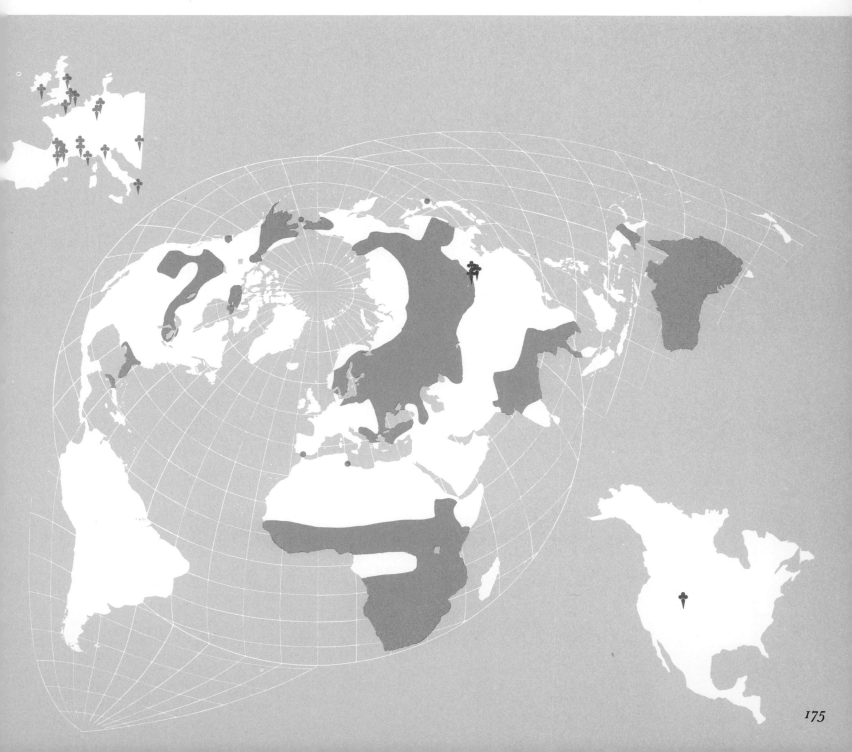

71 Limpkins

Family Aramidae, Lower Oligocene→
Genera: 1 living, 5 fossil
Species: 7 known; 1 living, 7 fossil
Origin: possibly North American, though
earliest fossil, *Aminornis*, Patagonia

72 Trumpeters

Family Psophiidae, no fossils known
Genus: 1 living
Species: 3 living
Origin: doubtless South American

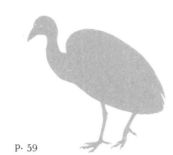

p. 59

p. 59

73 Ergilornis and Proergilornis
Family † Ergilornithidae, Oligocene
Genera: 2 fossil
Species: 2 fossil

74 Orthocnemus and ally
Family † Orthocnemidae, Upper Eocene
or Lower Oligocene
Genera: 2 fossil
Species: 7 fossil

75 Rails
Family Rallidae, Upper Paleocene→
Genera: 46 living, 5 lately extinct, 24 fossil
Species: 177 known; 119 living, 11 lately
extinct, 1 extinct before dodo, 67 fossil
Origin: uncertain; earliest fossils, *Telmatornis*,
New Jersey

p. 26

Rails introduced *Macquarie* ●

76 Finfoots

Family Heliornithidae, no fossils known
Genera: 3 living
Species: 3 living
Origin: doubtless tropical

p. 29

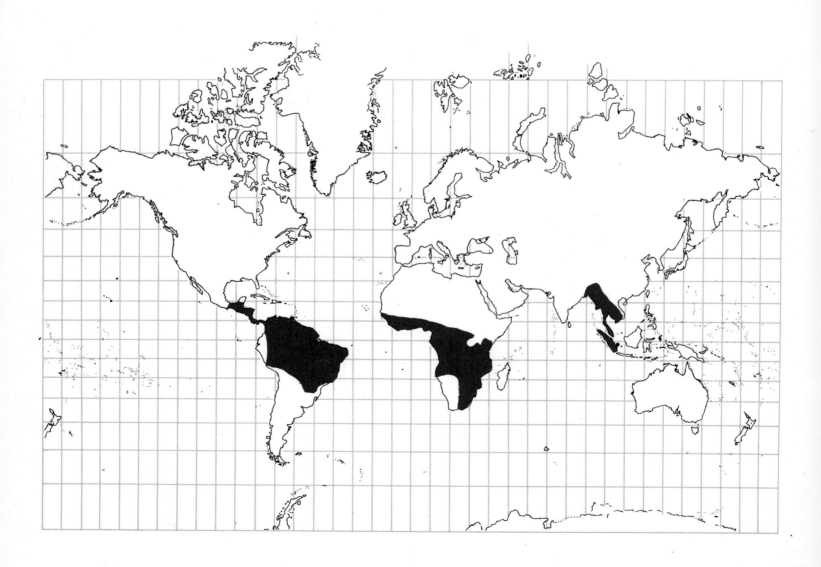

77 Kagu
Family Rhynochetidae, no fossil known
Genus and species: 1 living
Confined to New Caledonia

p. 60

78 Sun bittern
Family Eurypygidae, no fossil known
Genus and species: 1 living
Origin: doubtless South American

p. 59

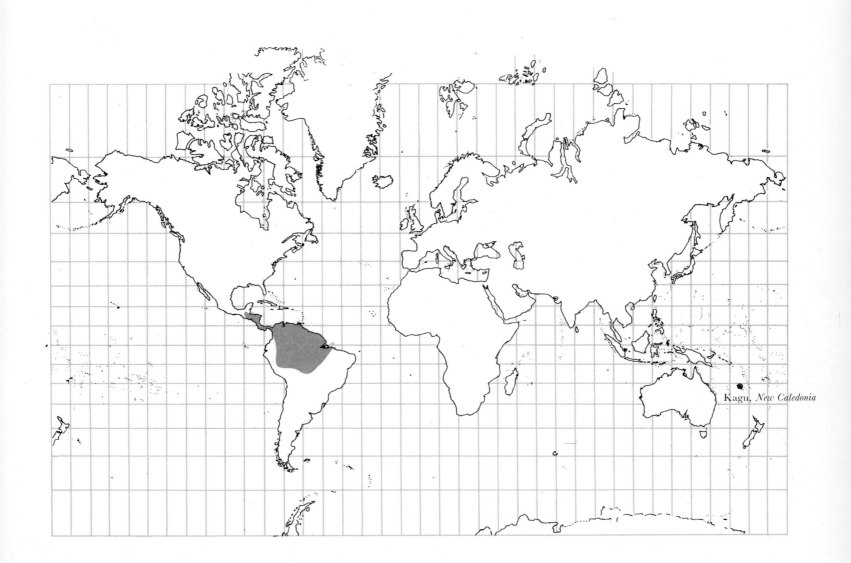

Kagu, *New Caledonia*

79 Bathornis
Family † Bathornithidae, Lower Oligocene –
Upper Oligocene
Genus: 1 fossil
Species: 4 fossil
Earliest fossil, *Bathornis veredus*, Colorado,
Nebraska and South Dakota

80 Seriemas
Family Cariamidae, Lower Oligocene→
Genera: 2 living, 1 fossil
Species: 3 known; 2 living, 2 fossil
Origin: unless directly descended from
Bathornithids, probably South American;
earliest fossil, *Riacama*, Patagonia

81 Psilopterus and allies
Family † Psilopteridae, Lower Miocene –
Lower Pleistocene
Genera: 5 fossil
Species: 12 fossil
Earliest fossil, *Psilopterus*, Patagonia

p. 59

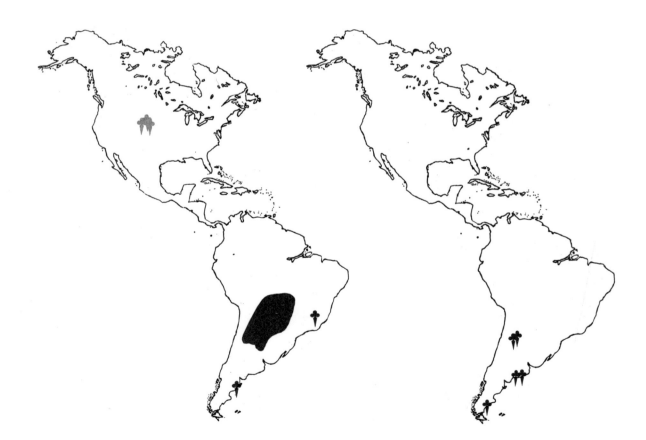

82 Phororhacos and allies

Family † Phororhacidae, Lower Oligocene –
Upper Pleistocene
Genera: 6 fossil
Species: 13 fossil
Earliest fossil, *Andrewsornis*, Patagonia

P. 45

83 Brontornis and allies

Family † Brontornithidae, Lower Oligocene –
Miocene
Genera: 8 fossil
Species: 12 fossil
Earliest fossils, *Aucornis* and *Pseudolarus*,
Patagonia

84 Cunampaia

Family † Cunampaiidae, Oligocene
Genus and species: 1 fossil

85 Bustards

Family Otididae, Middle Eocene→
Genera: 11 living, 1 fossil
Species: 25 known; 22 living, 6 fossil
Origin: probably Ethiopian, though earliest
fossil, *Palaeotis*, Germany

p. 22

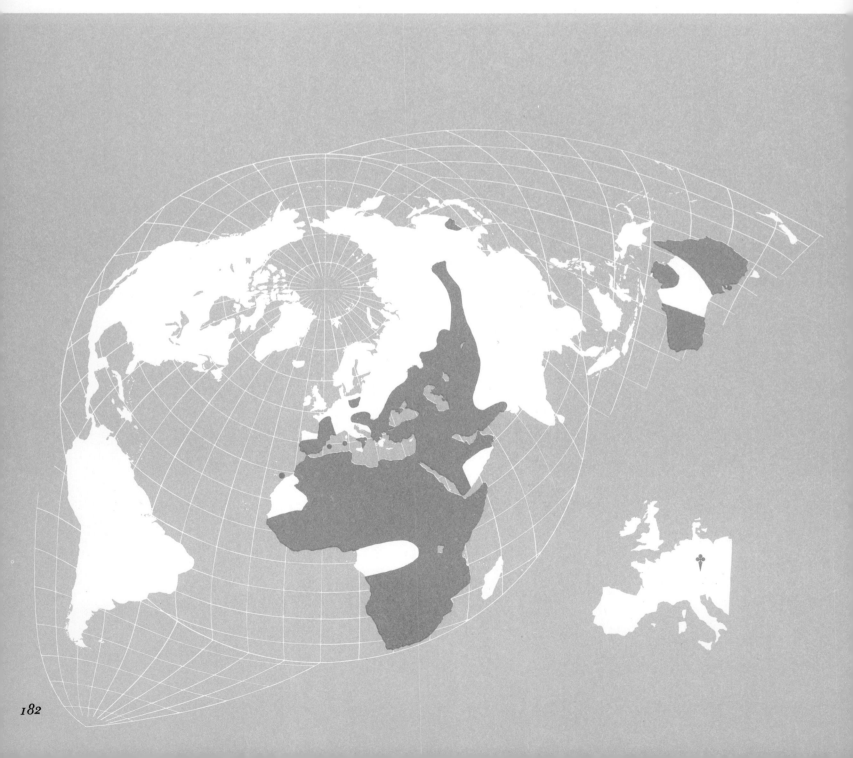

86 Gastornis and allies
Family † Gastornithidae, Upper Paleocene –
Upper Eocene
Genera: 4 fossil
Species: 6 fossil
Earliest fossils, *Gastornis* and *Remiornis*,
France and England

87 Diatryma and allies
Family † Diatrymidae, Eocene
Genera: 3 fossil
Species: 7 fossil
Origin: uncertain; earliest fossils (Lower Eocene),
Diatryma and *Omorhampus*, France, Wyoming and
New Mexico

p. 25

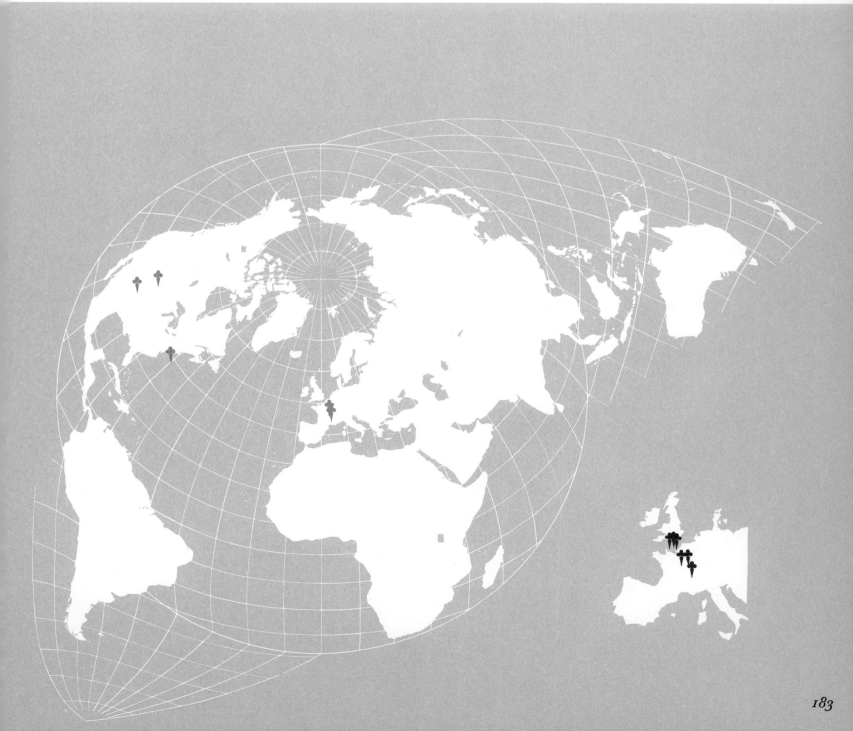

88 Jaçanas

Family Jacanidae, Upper Pleistocene→
Genera: 6 living
Species: 7 known; 7 living, 1 fossil
Origin: tropical, possibly Old World; only
fossil, wattled jaçana *Jacana spinosa*,
Brazil

p. 28

89 Rhegminornis

Family † Rhegminornithidae, Lower Miocene
Genus and species: 1 fossil

90 Painted snipe

Family Rostratulidae, Middle Eocene→
Genera: 2 living, 1 fossil
Species: 3 known; 2 living, 1 fossil
Origin: probably Old World; only fossil,
Rhynchaeites, Germany

p. 28

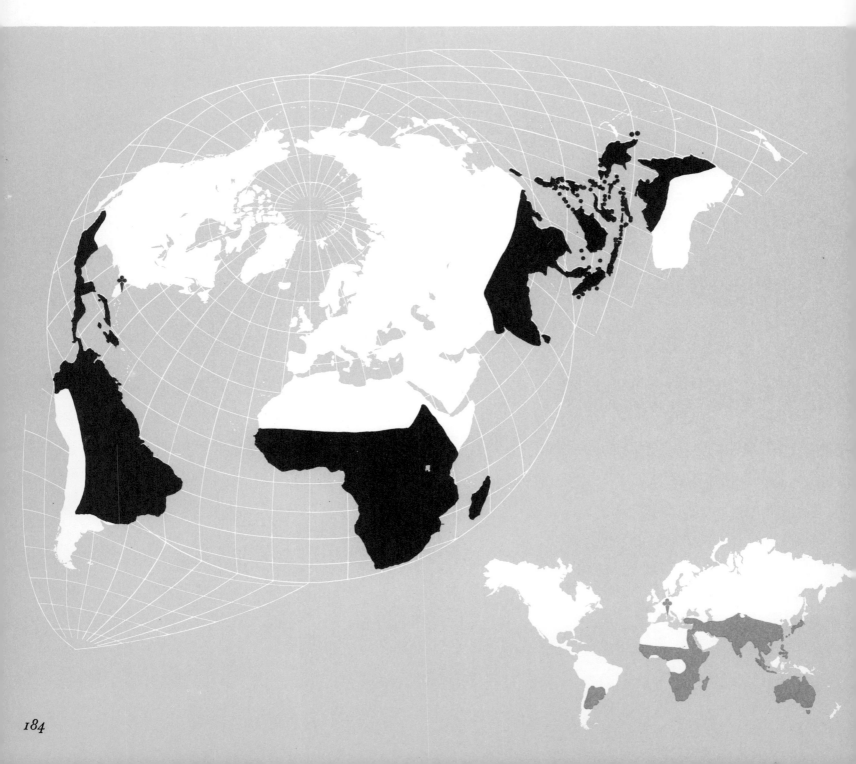

91 Oystercatchers

Family Haematopodidae, Lower Miocene→
Genera: 1 living, 2 fossil
Species: 6 known; 4 living, 3 fossil
Origin: possibly New World; earliest fossil,
Paractiornis, Nebraska

p. 29

92 Plovers and turnstones

Family Charadriidae, Lower Oligocene→
Genera: 9 living, 2 fossil
Species: 65 known; 60 living, 17 fossil
Origin: uncertain; earliest fossil,
Dolichopterus, France

p. 28

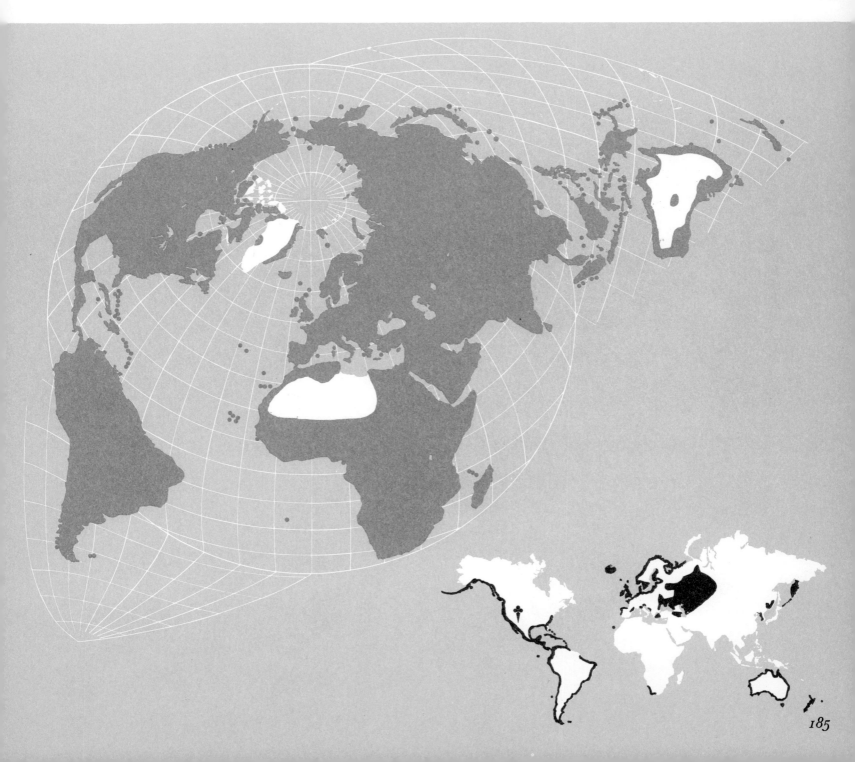

93 Snipe, sandpipers and allies
Family Scolopacidae, Upper Paleocene→
Genera: 21 living, 1 lately extinct, 3 fossil
Species: 100 known; 75 living, 1 lately extinct,
55 fossil
Probably of Holarctic origin; earliest fossils,
Palaeotringa, New Jersey

94 Avocets and allies
Family Recurvirostridae, Lower Eocene→
Genera: 4 living, 1 fossil
Species: 8 known; 7 living, 3 fossil
Geographical origin uncertain; earliest fossil,
Coltonia, Utah

p. 28

p. 26

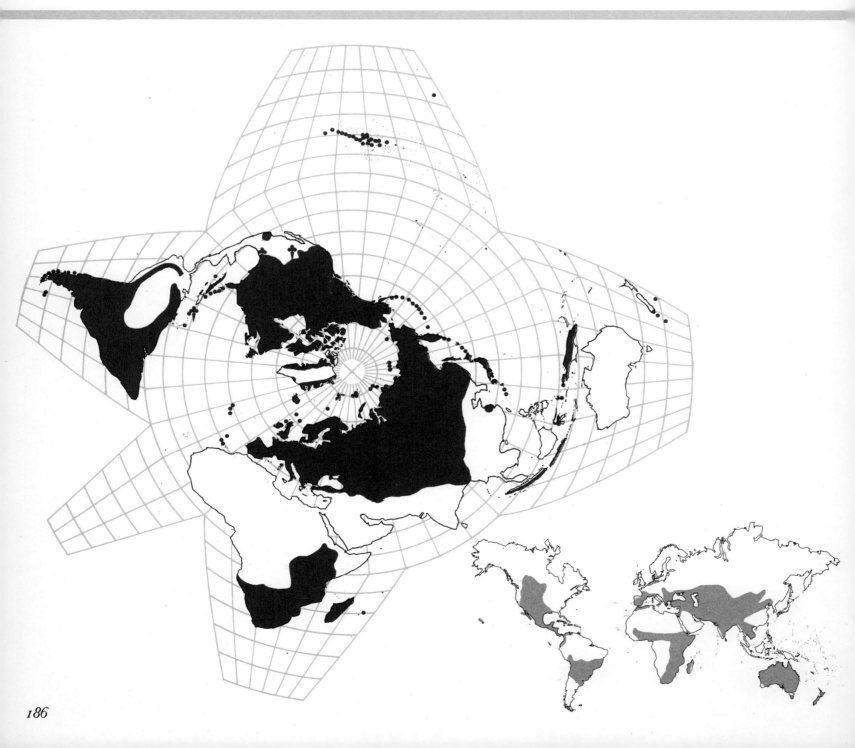

95 Presbyornis
Family † Presbyornithidae, Lower Eocene
Genus and species: 1 fossil

96 Phalaropes
Family Phalaropodidae, Upper Pleistocene→
Genus: 1 living
Species: 3 known; 3 living, 1 fossil
Origin: North American; only fossil, northern or red-necked phalarope *Phalaropus lobatus*, Oregon

97 Crab plover
Family Dromadidae, no fossil known
Genus and species: 1 living
Origin: probably Indian Ocean

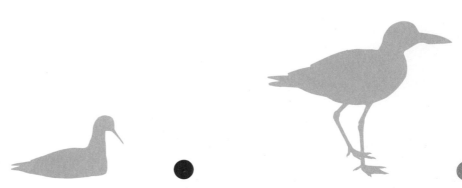

p. 61

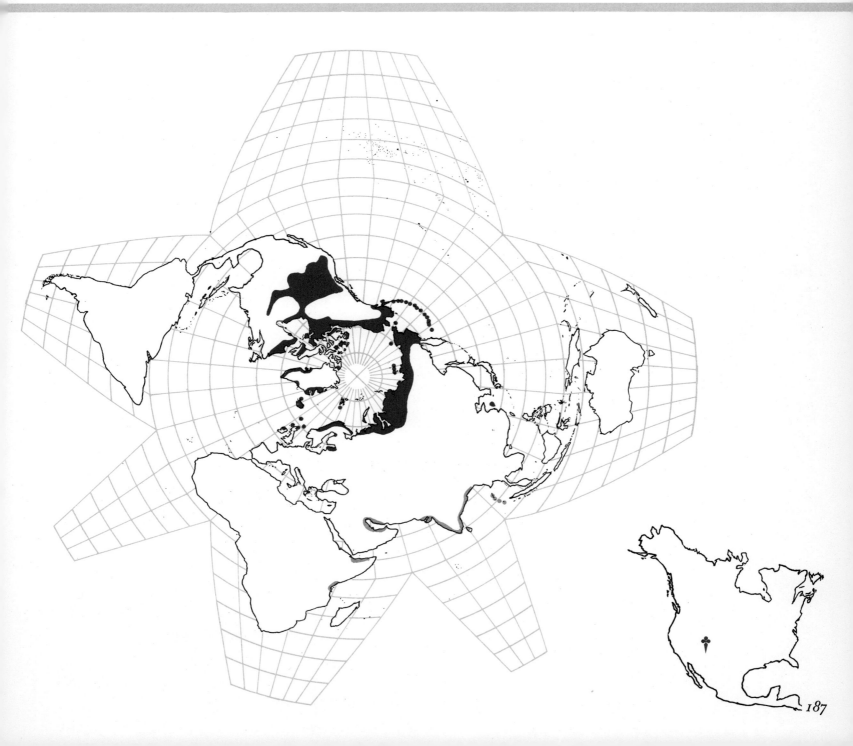

98 Thick-knees

Family Burhinidae, Lower Miocene→
Genera: 3 living, 1 fossil
Species: 11 known; 9 living, 3 fossil
Origin: probably Old World; earliest fossil, *Milnea*, France

99 Coursers and pratincoles

Family Glareolidae, no fossils known
Genera: 5 living
Species: 16 known; 15 living, 1 lately extinct
Origin: probably Ethiopian

100 Seed snipe

Family Thinocoridae, no fossils known
Genera: 2 living
Species: 4 living
Origin: doubtless South American

P. 59

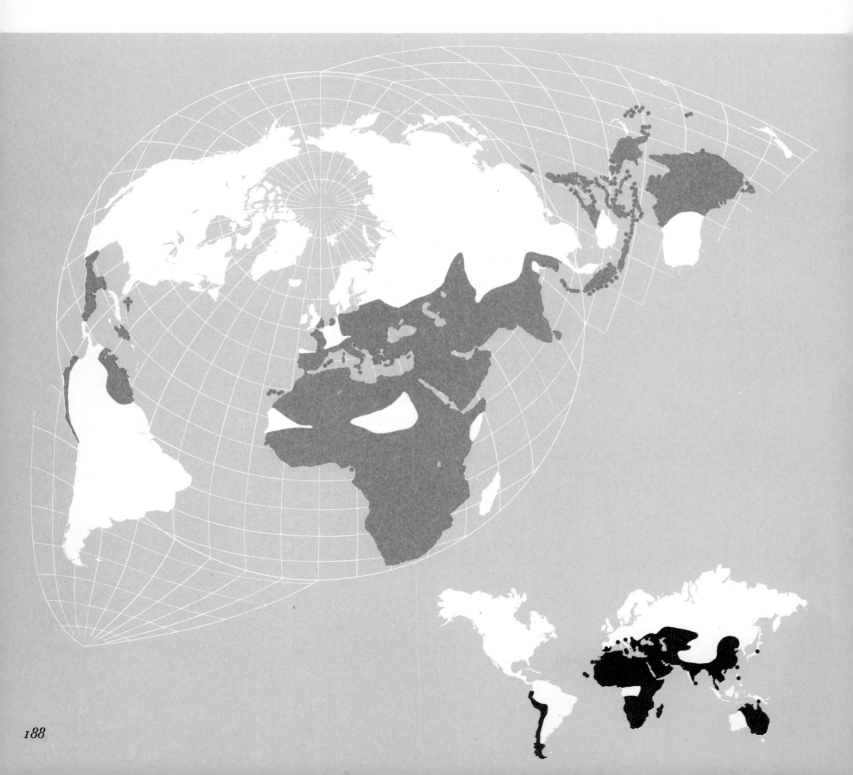

101 Sheathbills

Family Chionididae, no fossils known
Genus: 1 living
Species: 2 living
Origin: probably subantarctic

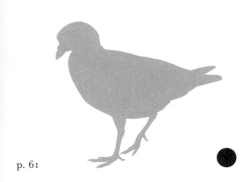

p. 61

102 Skuas

Family Stercorariidae, Upper Pleistocene→
Genera: 2 living
Species: 5 known; 4 living, 1 fossil
Origin: doubtless Holarctic; earliest fossil,
Stercorarius shufeldti, Oregon

p. 67

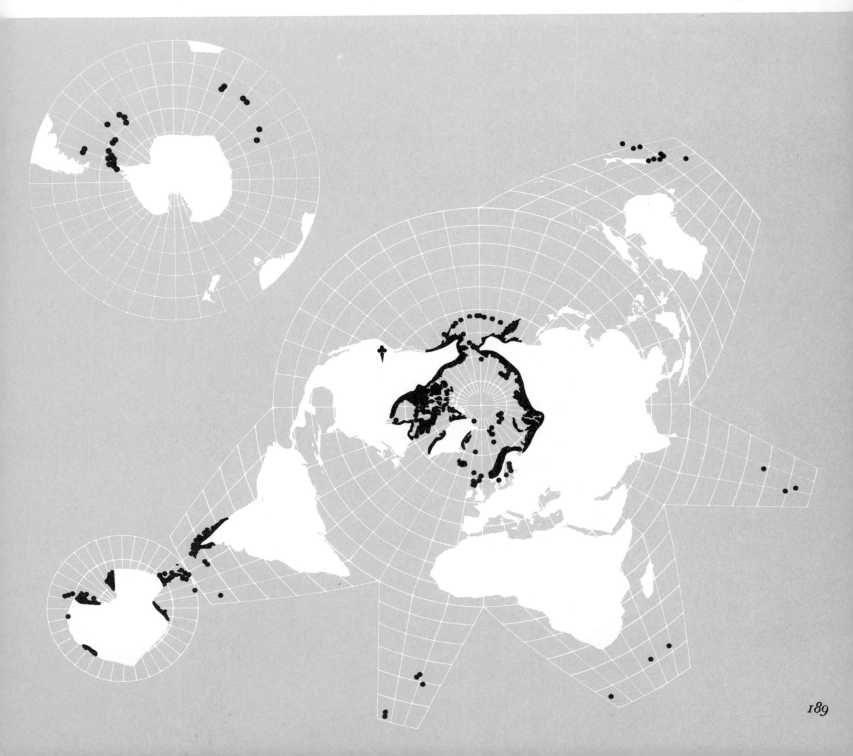

103 Gulls and terns

Family Laridae, Lower Eocene→
Genera: 4 living, 5 fossil
Species: 92 known; 78 living, 31 fossil
Origin: doubtless Holarctic; earliest fossil,
Halcyornis, England

p. 52

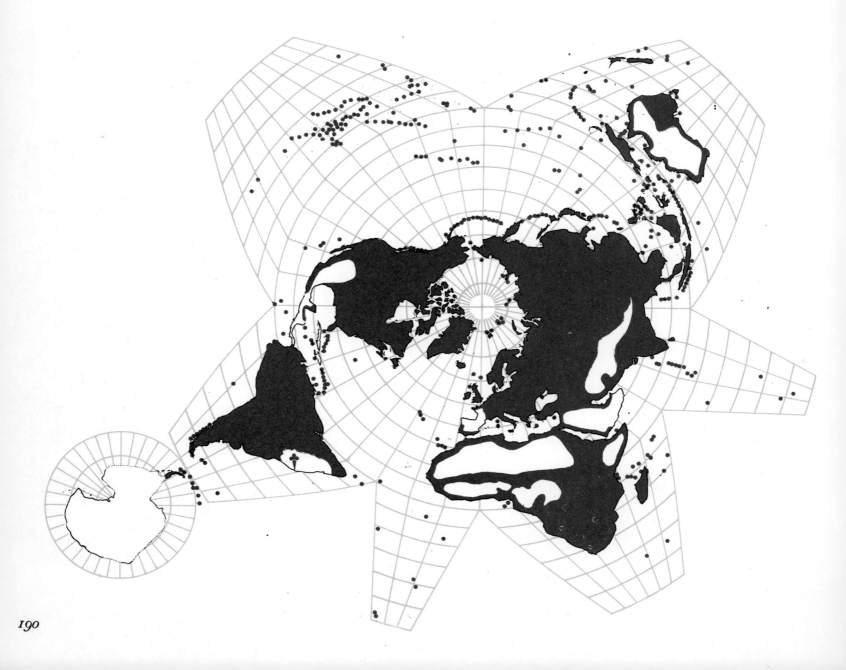

104 Skimmers
Family Rynchopidae, no fossils known
Genus: 1 living
Species: 3 living
Geographical origin uncertain, probably
tropical

p. 21

105 Auks
Family Alcidae, Lower Eocene→
Genera: 11 living, 1 lately extinct, 4 fossil
Species: 31 known; 19 living, 1 lately extinct,
20 fossil
Probably of North Pacific (? Bering Sea)
origin; earliest fossil, *Nautilornis*, Utah

p. 30

106 Lucas auks
Family † Mancallidae, Pliocene
Genus: 1 fossil
Species: 2 fossil
Known only from California; could perhaps be
relegated to subfamily of 105

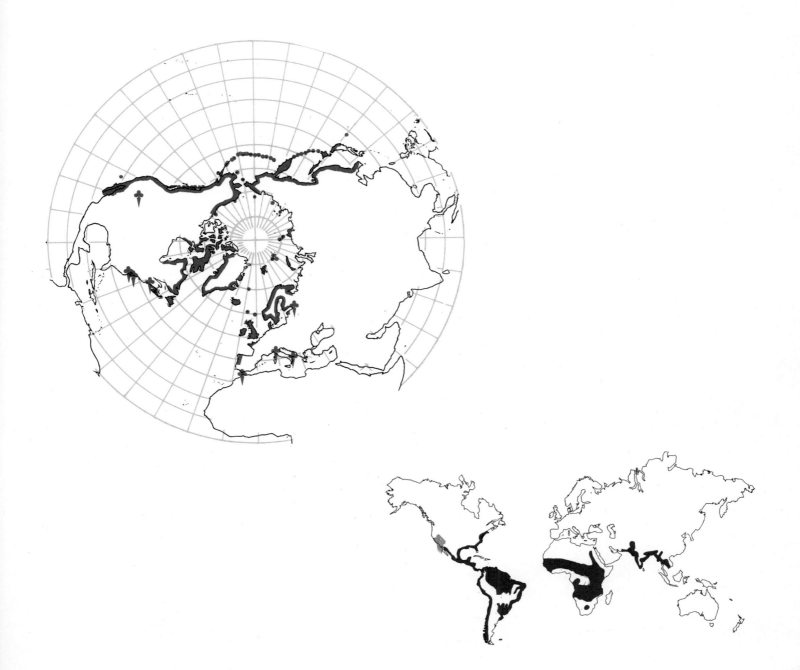

191

107 Sand grouse
Family Pteroclidae, Upper Eocene or Lower
Oligocene→
Genera: 2 living
Species: 19 known; 16 living, 4 fossil
Origin: doubtless Ethiopian; earliest fossils,
Pterocles validus and *P. larvatus*, France

p. 91

108 Pigeons
Family Columbidae, Lower Miocene→
Genera: 48 living, 2 lately extinct, 4 fossil
Species: 298 known; 285 living, 5 lately
extinct, 1 extinct before dodo, 35 fossil
Origin: possibly Australasian; earliest fossil,
Gerandia, France

p. 56

109 Dodo and solitaires
Family Raphidae, Recent
Genera: 2 lately extinct
Species: 3 lately extinct and fossil
Origin: doubtless Mascarene; probably
descended from pigeons (108), possibly
from rails (75)

p. 56

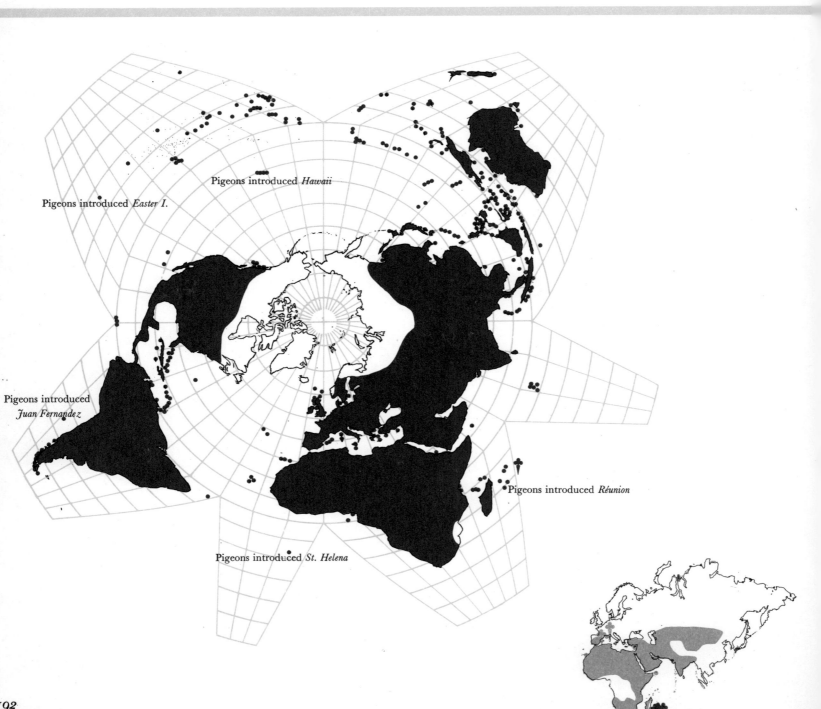

Pigeons introduced *Hawaii*

Pigeons introduced *Easter I.*

Pigeons introduced
Juan Fernandez

Pigeons introduced *Réunion*

Pigeons introduced *St. Helena*

110 Parrots

Family Psittacidae, Lower Miocene→
Genera: 69 living, 3 lately extinct, 3 fossil
Species: 340 known; 317 living, 15 lately
extinct, 4 extinct before dodo, 19 fossil
Origin: probably Australasian, though earliest
fossil, *Archaeopsittacus*, France

p. 56

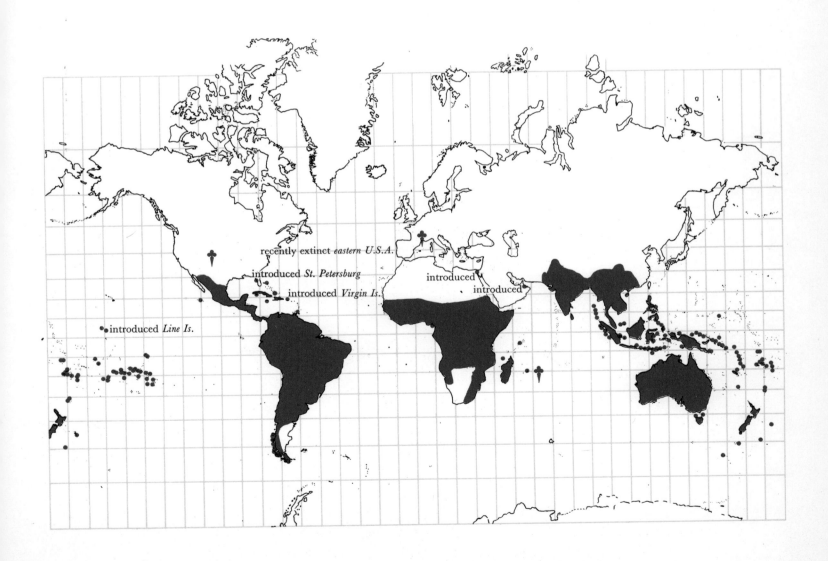

recently extinct *eastern U.S.A.*

introduced *St. Petersburg*

introduced

introduced

introduced *Virgin Is.*

introduced *Line Is.*

111 Touracos

Family Musophagidae, no fossils known
Genera: 5 living
Species: 18 living
Origin: doubtless Ethiopian

p. 33

112 Cuckoos

Family Cuculidae, Upper Eocene or Lower
Oligocene→
Genera: 34 living, 2 fossil
Species: 130 known; 125 living, 1 lately
extinct, 11 fossil
Origin: probably Old World; earliest fossil,
Dynamopterus, France

p. 96

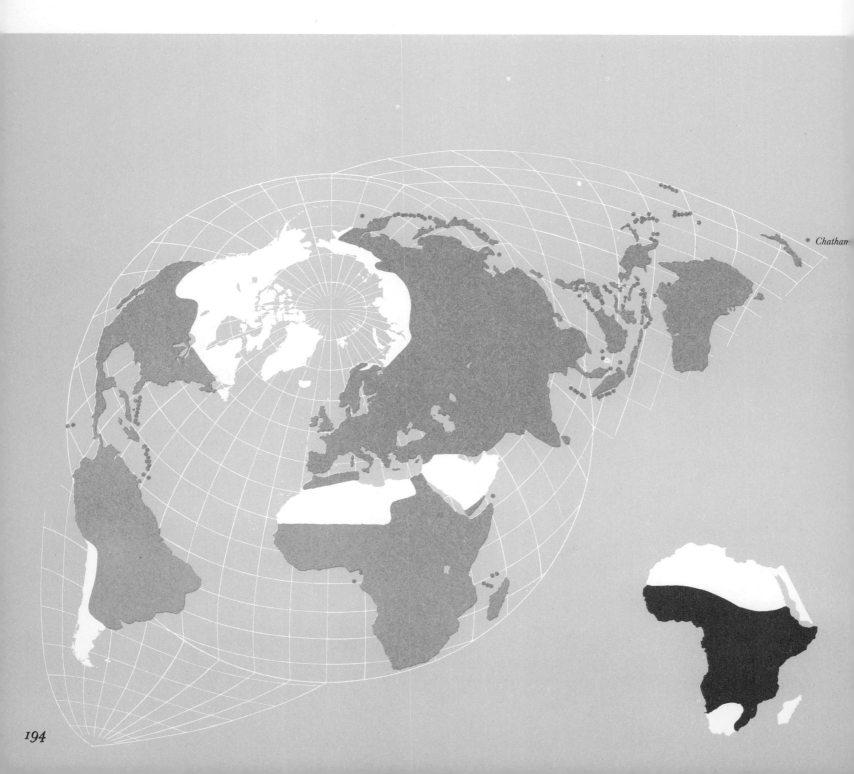

Chatham

194

113 Barn owls

Family Tytonidae, Lower Miocene→
Genera: 2 living, 1 fossil
Species: 17 known; 11 living, 7 fossil
Origin: probably Palearctic; earliest
fossils, 2 species of modern genus *Tyto*,
France

p. 60

114 Protostrix

Family † Protostrigidae, Lower Eocene –
Middle Eocene
Genus: 1 fossil
Species: 4 fossil
Origin: probably North American; earliest
fossil, *Protostrix mimica*, Wyoming

p. 43

115 Typical owls

Family Strigidae, Upper Eocene or Lower
Oligocene→
Genera: 22 living, 3 fossil
Species: 144 known; 121 living, 2 lately
extinct, 47 fossil
Origin: probably Palearctic; earliest fossils,
4 genera (including modern *Bubo* and *Asio*),
France

p. 31

Hawaii

Barn owls
introduced
Hawaii

Barn owls
introduced
Seychelles

Order Caprimulgiformes
Suborder Steatornithes

Suborder Caprimulgi

116 Oilbird
Family Steatornithidae, no fossil known
Genus and species: 1 living
Origin: doubtless South American

117 Owlet frogmouths
Family Aegothelidae, no fossils known
Genus: 1 living
Species: 5 living
Origin: probably Australasian

118 Frogmouths
Family Podargidae, no fossils known
Genera: 2 living
Species: 12 living
Origin: probably Oriental

p. 58

p. 61

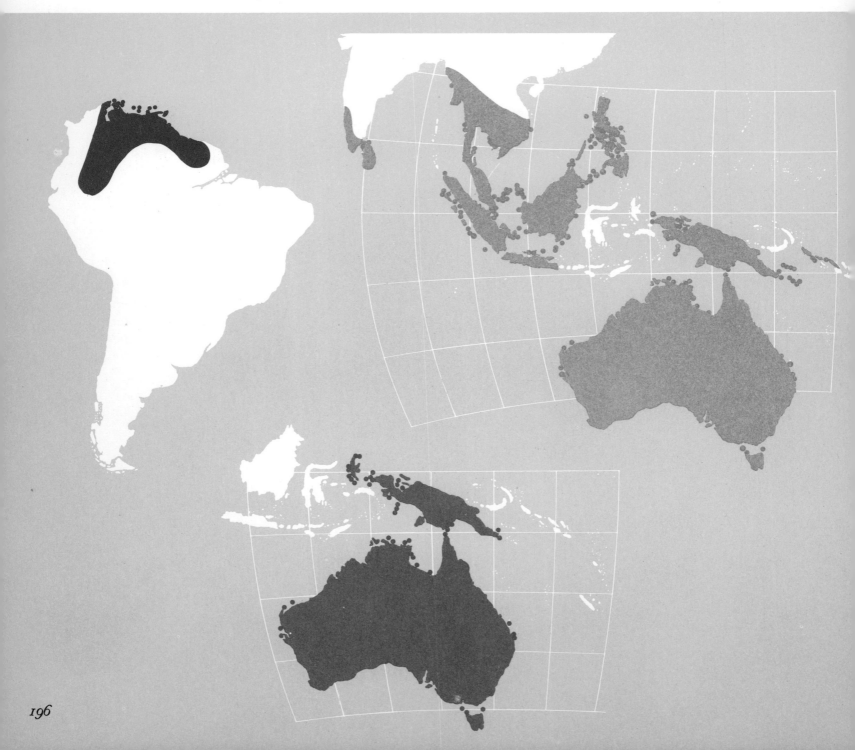

119 Nightjars

Family Caprimulgidae, Lower Pleistocene→
Genera: 18 living
Species: 69 known; 69 living, 7 fossil
Origin: probably New World, though earliest
fossil, living nightjar *Caprimulgus europaeus*,
Rumania

p. 96

120 Potoos

Family Nyctibiidae, Upper Pleistocene→
Genus: 1 living
Species: 5 known; 5 living, 1 fossil
Origin: doubtless South American; only fossil,
Brazil

p. 58

121 Aegialornis
Family † Aegialornithidae, Upper Eocene or
Lower Oligocene
Genus: 1 fossil
Species: 2 fossil
Origin: probably Old World; only fossils,
France

122 Swifts
Family Apodidae, Upper Eocene or Lower
Oligocene→
Genera: 8 living, 1 fossil
Species: 69 known; 65 living, 9 fossil
Origin: possibly Old World; earliest fossil,
Cypselavus gallicus, France

123 Crested swifts
Family Hemiprocnidae, no fossils known
Genus: 1 living
Species: 3 living
Origin: probably Oriental

p. 36

p. 85

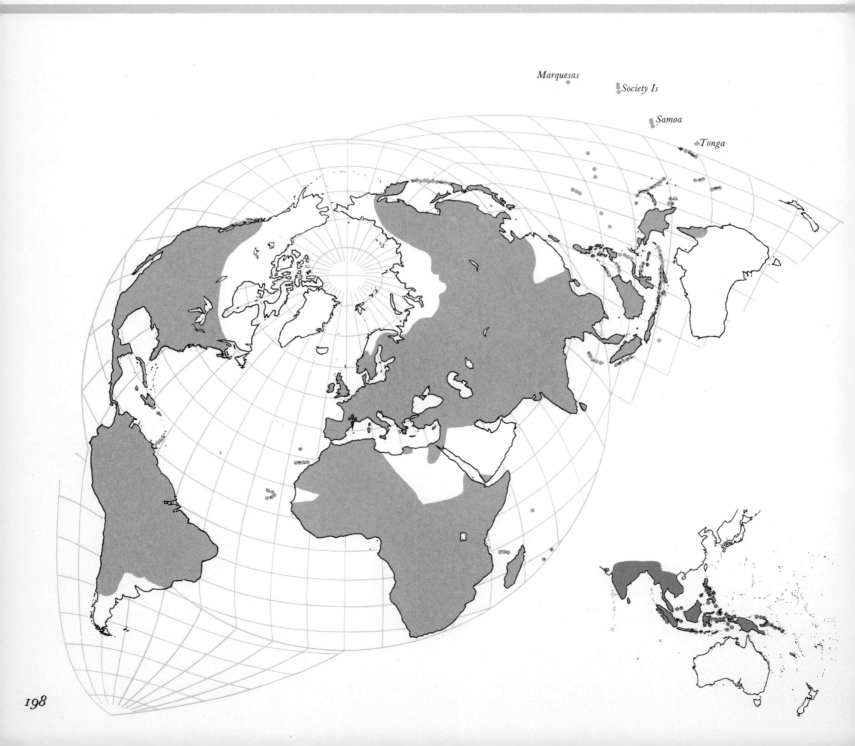

124 Hummingbirds

Family Trochilidae, Upper Pleistocene→
Genera: 123 living
Species: 320 known; 320 living, 1 fossil
Origin: probably South American; only fossil,
Brazil

p. 96

125 Colies

Family Coliidae, no fossils known
Genus: 1 living
Species: 6 living
Origin: doubtless Ethiopian

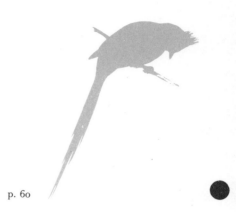

p. 60

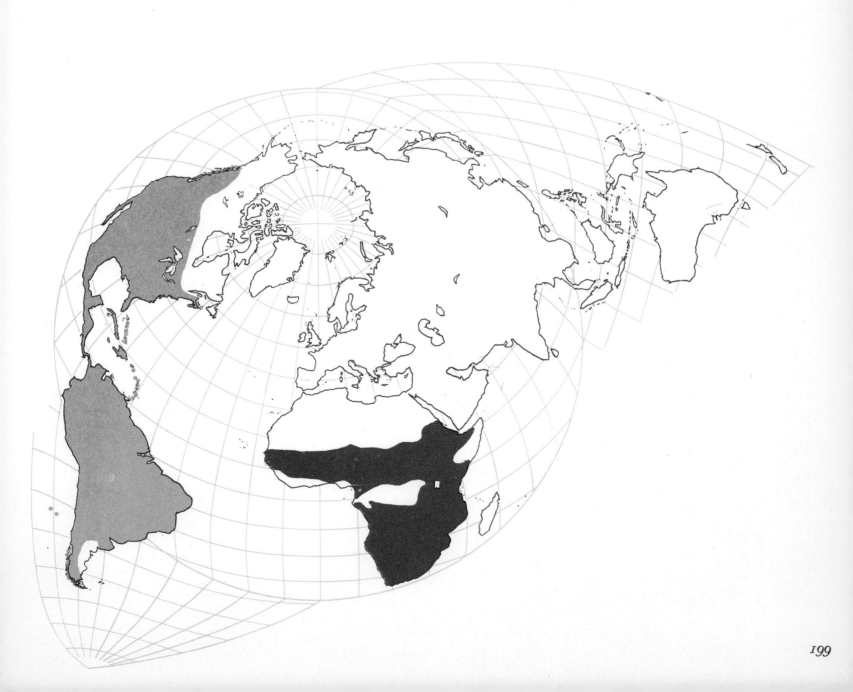

126 Trogons

Family Trogonidae, Upper Eocene or Lower
Oligocene→
Genera: 8 living, 2 fossil
Species: 39 known; 35 living, 6 fossil
Origin: possibly New World, though earliest
fossils, *Archaeotrogon*, France

p. 23

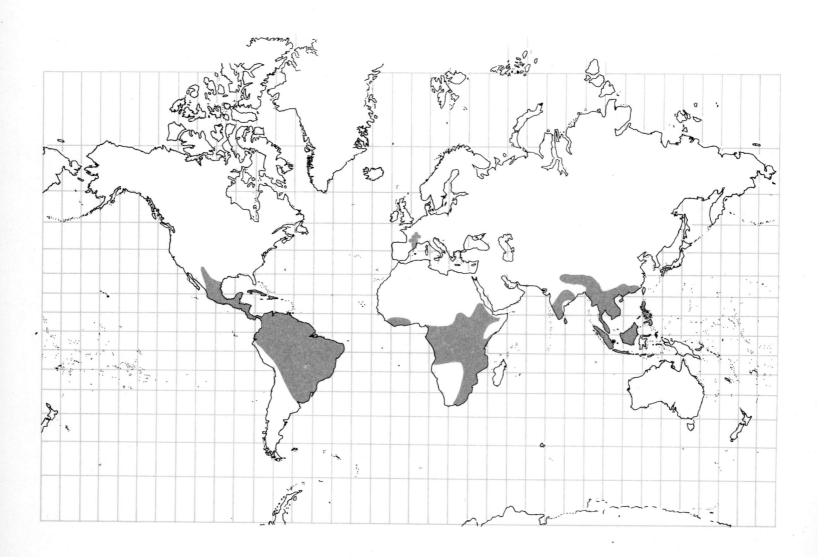

127 Kingfishers

Family Alcedinidae, Upper Eocene→
Genera: 12 living, 1 fossil
Species: 89 known; 86 living, 1 lately extinct,
7 fossil
Origin: doubtless Old World; earliest fossils,
Protornis, Switzerland

128 Todies

Family Todidae, no fossils known
Genus: 1 living
Species: 5 living
Origin: probably North American

p. 38

p. 36

Cuba

Isle of Pines

WEST INDIES

Hispaniola

Jamaica

Puerto Rico

129 Motmots

Family Momotidae, Middle Eocene→
Genera: 6 living, 1 fossil
Species: 9 known; 8 living, 2 fossil
Origin: probably North American; earliest
fossil, *Uintornis*, Wyoming

p. 58

130 Bee eaters

Family Meropidae, Pleistocene→
Genera: 6 living
Species: 25 known; 25 living, 1 fossil
Origin: doubtless Ethiopian; only fossil,
living common bee eater *Merops apiaster*,
Don Valley, U.S.S.R.

p. 84

131 Rollers

Family Coraciidae, Upper Eocene or Lower
Oligocene→
Genera: 2 living, 1 fossil
Species: 12 known; 11 living, 3 fossil
Origin: doubtless Old World; earliest fossil,
Geranopterus, France

p. 96

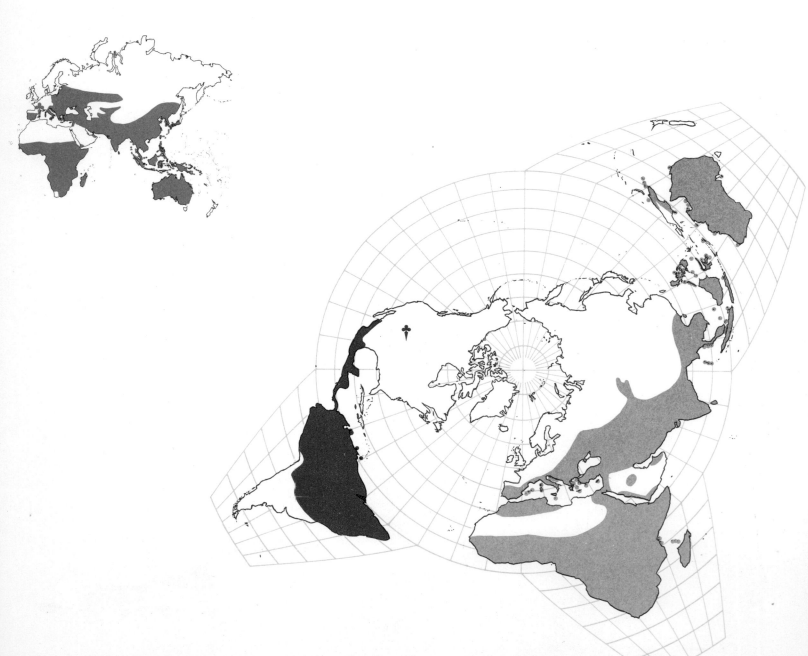

132 Ground rollers
Family Brachypteraciidae, no fossils known
Genera: 3 living
Species: 5 living
Origin: doubtless Madagascan

133 Cuckoo roller
Family Leptosomatidae, no fossil known
Genus and species: 1 living
Origin: doubtless Madagascan

134 Hoopoe
Family Upupidae, Middle Pleistocene→
Genus and species: 1 living and fossil
Origin: doubtless Ethiopian; earliest fossil
Palestine

p. 60

p. 60

p. 96

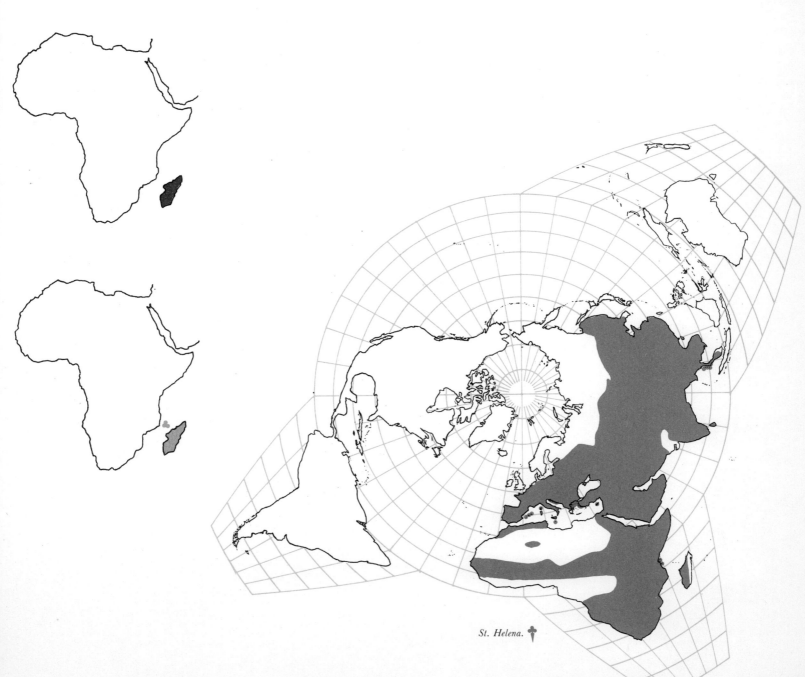

St. Helena.

203

135 Wood hoopoes

Family Phoeniculidae, Lower Miocene→
Genera: 2 living, 1 fossil
Species: 7 known; 6 living, 1 fossil
Origin: probably Ethiopian; only fossil,
Limnatornis, France

p. 60

136 Hornbills

Family Bucerotidae, Middle Eocene→
Genera: 12 living, 2 fossil
Species: 46 known; 44 living, 2 fossil
Origin: probably Ethiopian; earliest fossil,
Geisleroceros, Germany

p. 84

137 Jacamars
Family Galbulidae, no fossils known
Genera: 5 living
Species: 15 living
Origin: doubtless South American

138 Puffbirds
Family Bucconidae, Upper Pleistocene→
Genera: 10 living
Species: 30 known; 30 living, 2 fossil
Origin: doubtless South American; only fossils
Brazil

p. 58

p. 59

139 Barbets

Family Capitonidae, Upper Pleistocene→
Genera: 13 living
Species: 72 known; 72 living, 1 fossil
Origin: probably Old World, though only
fossil Brazil

140 Honeyguides

Family Indicatoridae, no fossils known
Genera: 4 living
Species: 14 living
Origin: doubtless Ethiopian

p. 34

p. 89

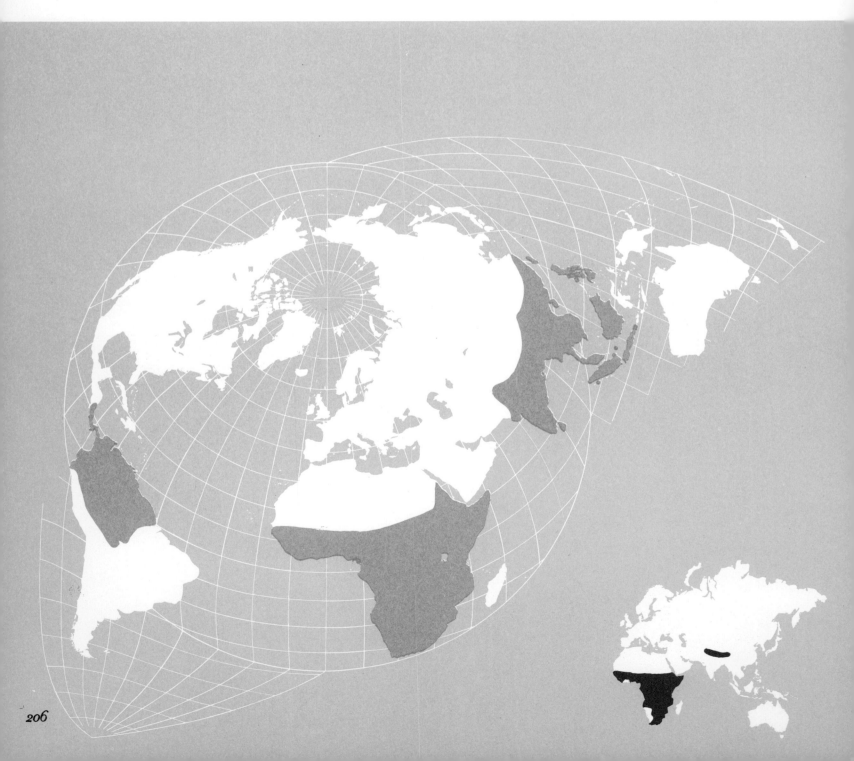

141 Toucans

Family Ramphastidae, Upper Pleistocene→
Genera: 5 living
Species: 37 known; 37 living, 2 fossil
Origin: doubtless South American; only fossils
Brazil

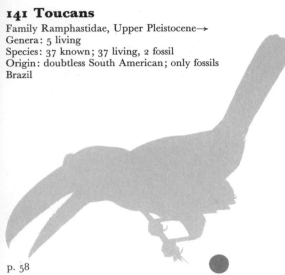

p. 58

142 Woodpeckers

Family Picidae, Lower Miocene→
Genera: 36 living, 2 fossil
Species: 213 known; 209 living, 24 fossil
Origin: possibly New World, though earliest
fossil, *Palaeopicus*, France

p. 54

143 Broadbills
Family Eurylaimidae, no fossils known
Genera: 8 living
Species: 14 living
Origin: probably Oriental

144 Furnariids Family Furnariidae, 2 subfamilies raised by some authorities to family rank

144a Woodhewers
Subfamily Dendrocolaptinae; Upper
Pleistocene→
Genera: 13 living
Species: 47 known; 47 living, 2 fossil
Origin: doubtless South American; only fossils
Brazil

144b Ovenbirds
Subfamily Furnariinae, Upper Pleistocene→
Genera: 58 living
Species: 215 known; 215 living, 2 fossil
Origin: doubtless South American; only
fossils Brazil

p. 11

p. 59

p. 59

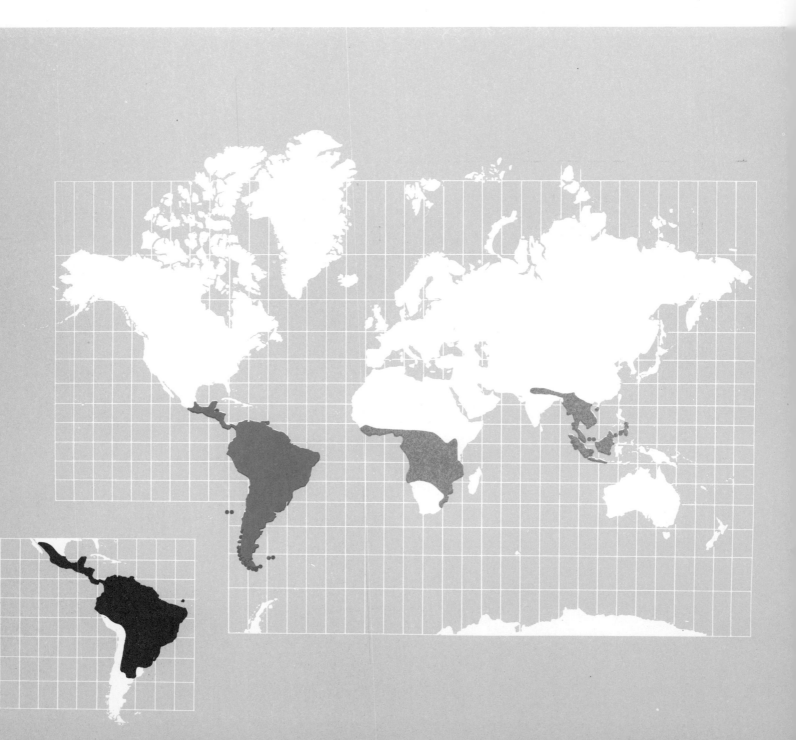

145 Ant thrushes

Family Formicariidae, Upper Pleistocene→
Genera: 53 living
Species: 224 known; 224 living, 1 fossil
Origin: doubtless South American; only fossil
Brazil

P. 37

146 Ant pipits

Family Conopophagidae, no fossils known
Genera: 2 living
Species: 11 living
Origin: doubtless South American

P. 37

147 Tapaculos

Family Rhinocryptidae, Lower or Middle
Eocene→
Genera: 12 living, 1 fossil
Species: 30 known; 29 living, 1 fossil
Origin: probably South American; only fossil,
'*Hebe*' (an invalid generic name), Wyoming,
is but provisionally assigned to this family

P. 59

148 Pittas
Family Pittidae, no fossils known
Genus: 1 living
Species: 25 living
Origin: probably Oriental

149 Asities
Family Philepittidae, no fossils known
Genera: 2 living
Species: 4 living
Origin: doubtless Madagascan

150 New Zealand wrens
Family Acanthisittidae, no fossils known
Genera: 2 living
Species: 4 known; 3 living, 1 lately extinct
Origin: doubtless New Zealand

p. 37

p. 60.

p. 61

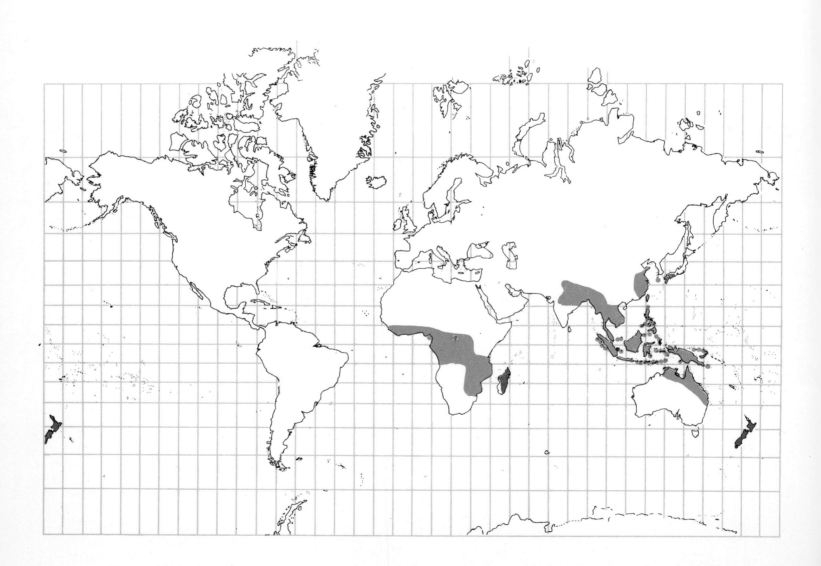

151 Tyrant flycatchers

Family Tyrannidae, Upper Pleistocene→
Genera: 116 living
Species: 364 known; 364 living, 7 fossil
Origin: probably South American; only
fossils Brazil, California and W. Indies

p. 63

152 Manakins

Family Pipridae, no fossils known
Genera: 21 living
Species: 61 living
Origin: doubtless South American

p. 58

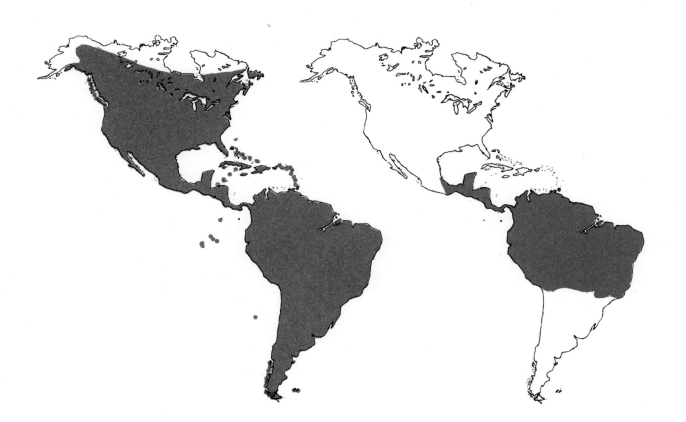

153 Cotingas

Family Cotingidae, no fossils known
Genera: 33 living
Species: 91 living
Origin: doubtless South American

p. 23

154 Plantcutters

Family Phytotomidae, no fossils known
Genus: 1 living
Species: 3 living
Origin: doubtless South American

p. 58

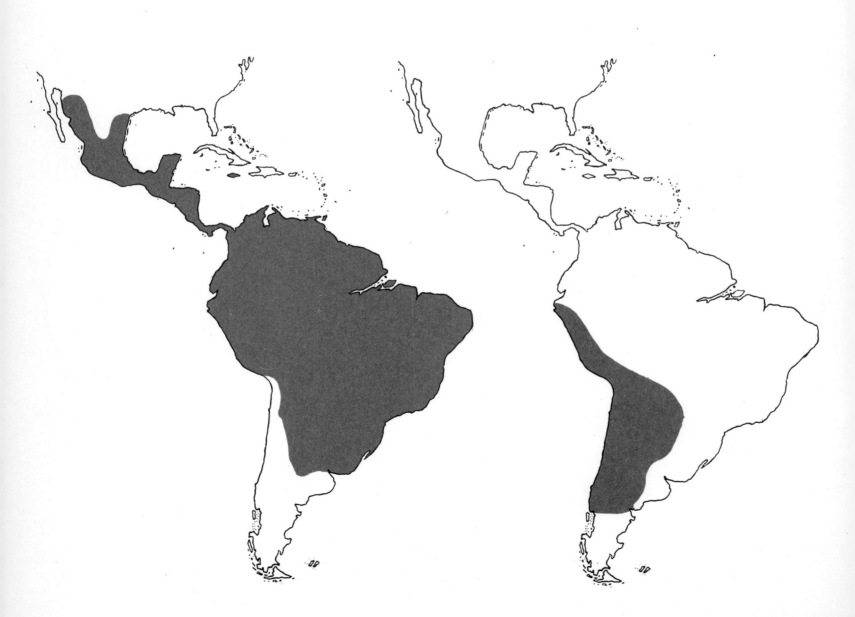

155 Lyrebirds

Family Menuridae, no fossils known
Genus: 1 living
Species: 2 living
Origin: doubtless Australian

p. 60

156 Scrub birds

Family Atrichornithidae, no fossils known
Genus: 1 living
Species: 2 living
Origin: doubtless Australian

p. 57

Lyrebirds introduced *Tasmania*

157 Larks

Family Alaudidae, Lower Pliocene→
Genera: 15 living
Species: 78 known; 75 living, 11 fossil
Origin: possibly Ethiopian; earliest fossils,
Alauda gypsorum and *A. major*, Italy

158 Palaeospiza

Family † Palaeospizidae, Middle or Upper
Oligocene
Genus and species: 1 fossil
Colorado only

p. 34

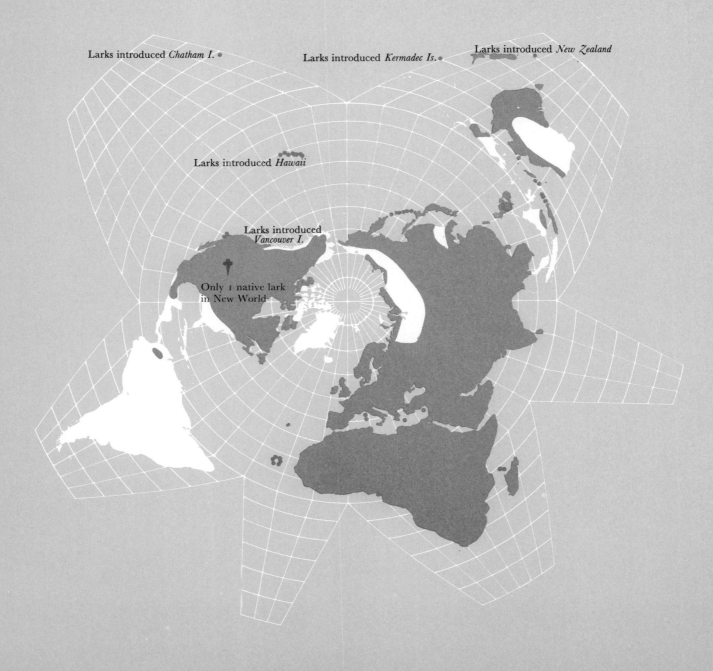

Larks introduced *Chatham I.*

Larks introduced *Kermadec Is.*

Larks introduced *New Zealand*

Larks introduced *Hawaii*

Larks introduced
Vancouver I.

Only 1 native lark
in New World

159 Swallows

Family Hirundinidae, Lower Pleistocene→
Genera: 20 living
Species: 80 known; 79 living, 9 fossil
Origin: probably Oriental; earliest fossil,
living barn swallow *Hirundo rustica*, Rumania

p. 70

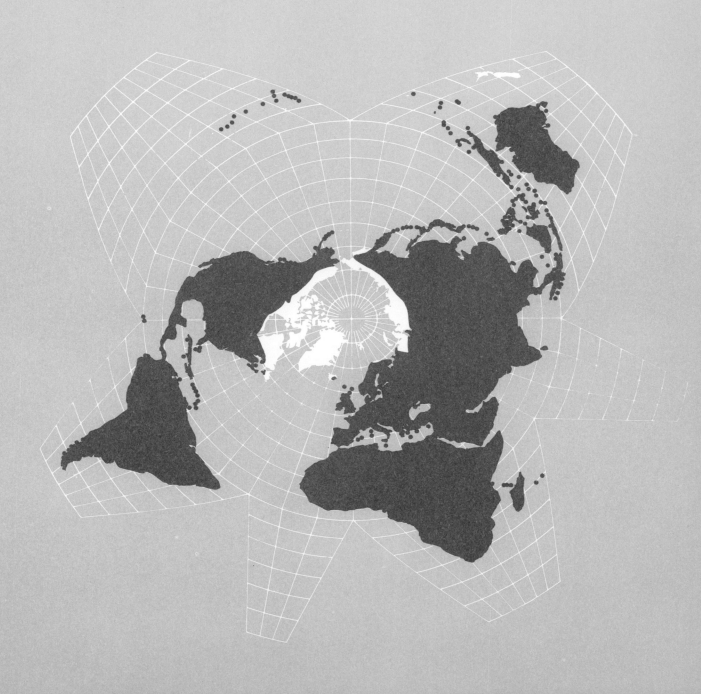

160 Wagtails and pipits

Family Motacillidae, Lower Miocene→
Genera: 5 living
Species: 56 known; 53 living, 9 fossil
Origin: probably Ethiopian, though earliest
fossils, *Motacilla humata* and *M. major*, France

161 Cuckoo shrikes

Family Campephagidac, no fossils known
Genera: 9 living
Species: 70 living
Origin: probably Australasian, possibly
Oriental

p. 36

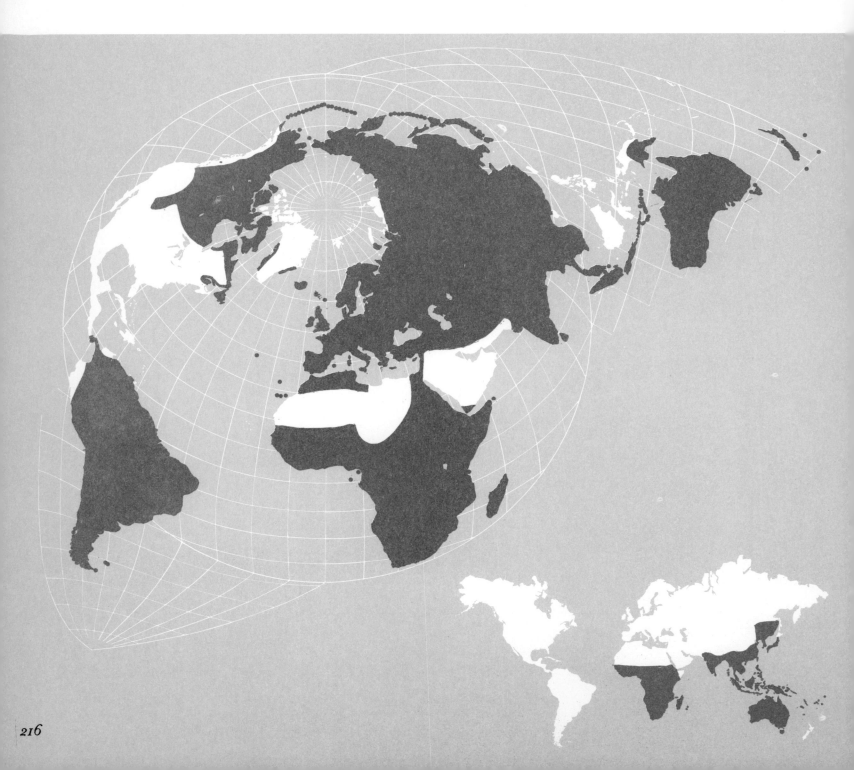

162 Bulbuls

Family Pycnonotidae, Middle Pleistocene→
Genera: 15 living
Species: 119 known; 119 living, 1 fossil
Origin: probably Ethiopian; only fossil,
common bulbul *Pycnonotus barbatus*,
Palestine

p. 64

163 Leaf birds

Family Irenidae, no fossils known
Genera: 3 living
Species: 14 living,
Origin: doubtless Oriental

p. 61

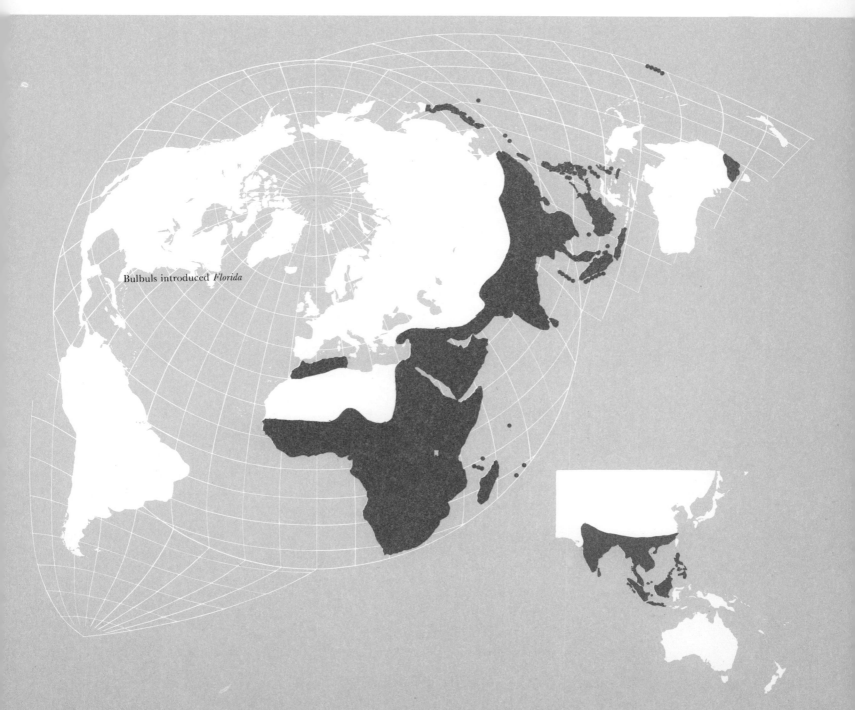

Bulbuls introduced *Florida*

164 Shrikes

Family Laniidae, Lower Miocene→
Genera: 12 living
Species: 75 known; 74 living, 7 fossil
Origin: probably Palearctic; earliest fossil,
modern genus *Lanius*, France

165 Vanga shrikes

Family Vangidae, no fossils known
Genera: 9 living
Species: 13 living
Origin: doubtless Madagascan

p. 60

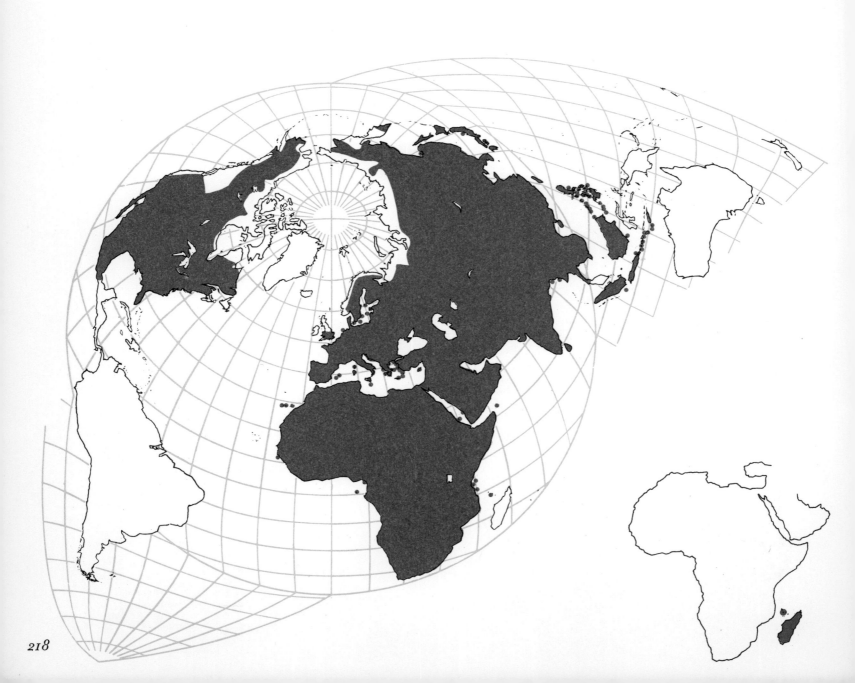

166 Waxwings and allies

Family Bombycillidae, Upper Pleistocene→
Genera: 5 living
Species: 8 known; 8 living, 2 fossil
Origin: probably North American; earliest
fossil, waxwing *Bombycilla garrulus*, Monaco

167 Palm chat

Family Dulidae, no fossil known
Genus and species: 1 living
Origin: doubtless West Indian

p. 75

p. 58

WEST INDIES

Hispaniola

219

168 Dippers

Family Cinclidae, Upper Pleistocene→
Genus: 1 living
Species: 4 known; 4 living, 1 fossil
Origin: probably North American; earliest
fossil, dipper *Cinclus cinclus*, Austria

169 Palaeoscinis

Family † Palaeoscinidae, Middle Miocene
Genus and species: 1 fossil
California only; some would place not here,
but near families 162 and 163

170 Wrens

Family Troglodytidae, Middle Pleistocene→
Genera: 14 living
Species: 60 known; 59 living, 2 fossil
Origin: probably North American; earliest
fossil, *Cistothorus brevis*, Florida

p. 38

p. 37

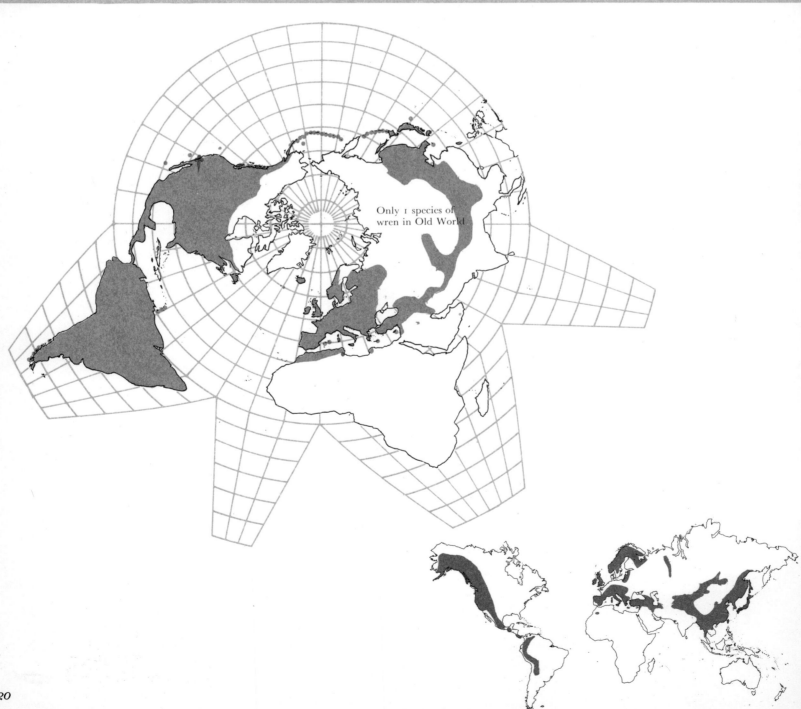

Only 1 species of
wren in Old World

171 Thrashers and mockers
Family Mimidae, Upper Pleistocene→
Genera: 13 living
Species: 31 known; 31 living, 6 fossil
Origin: probably North American; fossils
Brazil, California and Puerto Rico

172 Accentors
Family Prunellidae, Pleistocene→
Genus: 1 living
Species: 12 known; 12 living, 2 fossil
Origin: doubtless Palearctic, fossils Italy,
Monaco, England, Wales

p. 57

p. 61

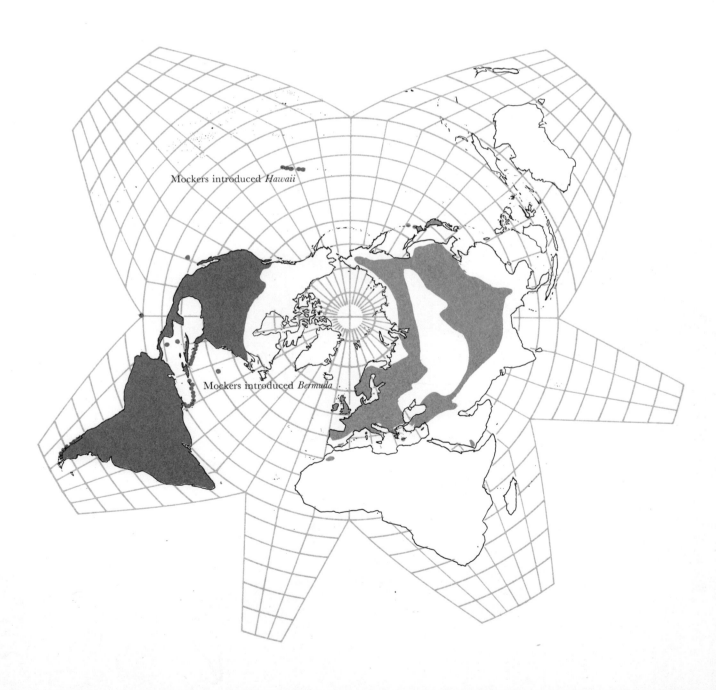

Mockers introduced *Hawaii*

Mockers introduced *Bermuda*

173 Muscicapids   Family Muscicapidae; this is so large that we break it down into subfamilies (which some authorities rate as full families) as follows:

173a Thrushes

Subfamily Turdinae, Upper Pliocene→
Genera: 41 living
Species: 303 known; 301 living, 2 lately
extinct, 23 fossil
Origin: probably Old World; earliest fossil,
blue rock thrush *Monticola solitarius*, France

p. 50

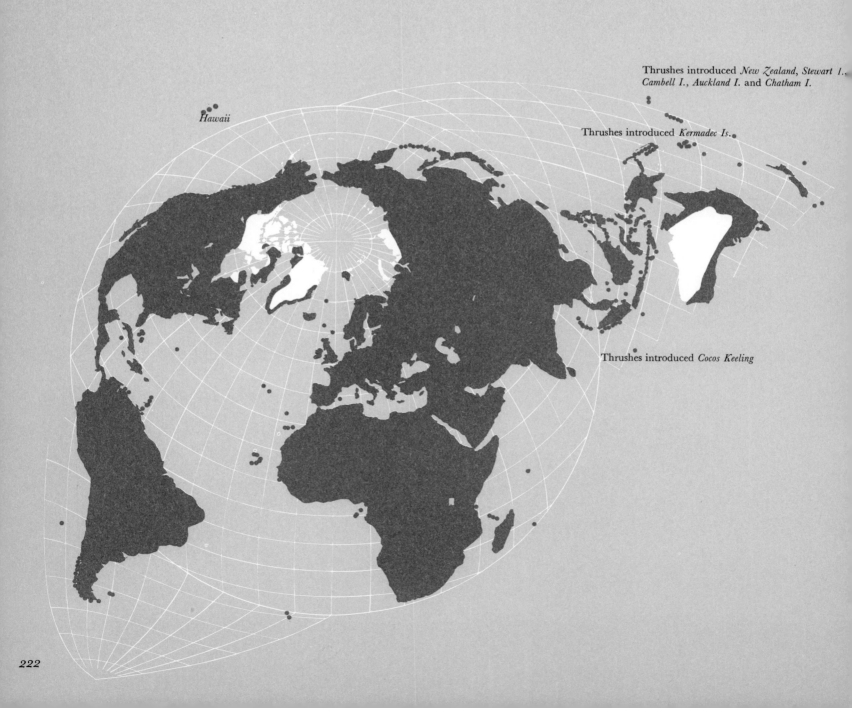

Thrushes introduced *New Zealand, Stewart I.,
Cambell I., Auckland I.* and *Chatham I.*

Thrushes introduced *Kermadec Is.*

Hawaii

Thrushes introduced *Cocos Keeling*

173b Babblers

Subfamily Timaliinae, Middle Pleistocene→
Genera: 57 living
Species: 258 known; 258 living, 2 fossil
Origin: Old World, possibly Palearctic; earliest fossil, brown babbler *Turdoides squamiceps*, Palestine

173c Bearded tit and parrotbills

Subfamily Panurinae, no fossils known
Genera: 3 living
Species: 19 living
Origin: probably Palearctic

p. 96

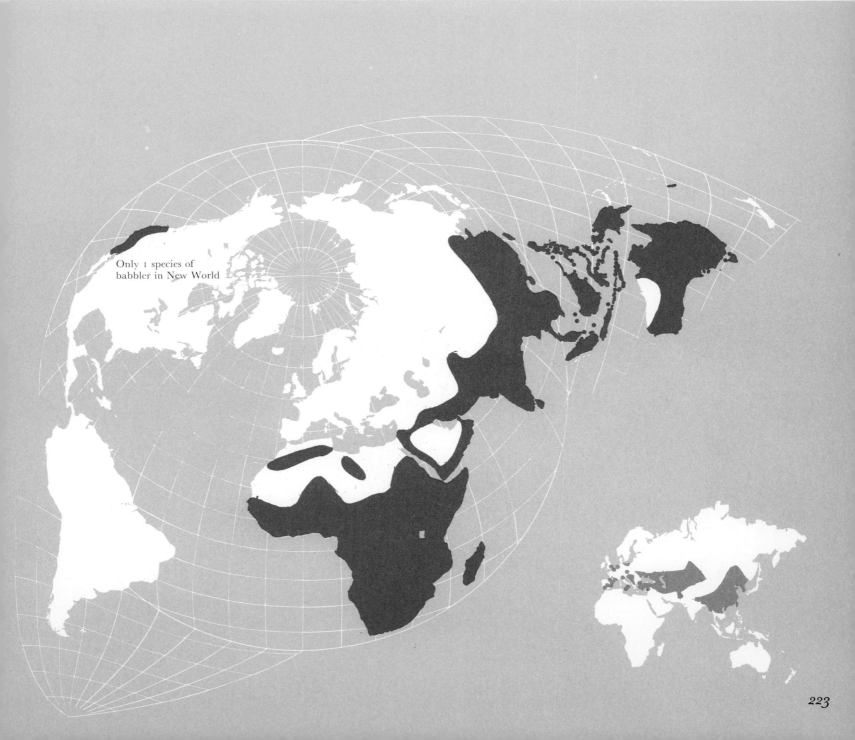

Only 1 species of babbler in New World

173 Muscicapids (continued)

173d Gnatcatchers
Subfamily Polioptilinae, no fossils known
Genus: 1 living
Species: 11 living
Origin: doubtless North American

173e Old World warblers and gnatwrens
Subfamily Sylviinae, Lower Miocene→
Genera: 61 living
Species: 322 known; 321 living, 10 fossil
Origin: Old World (only 7 species in New);
earliest fossil, *Sylvia* species, France

p. 36

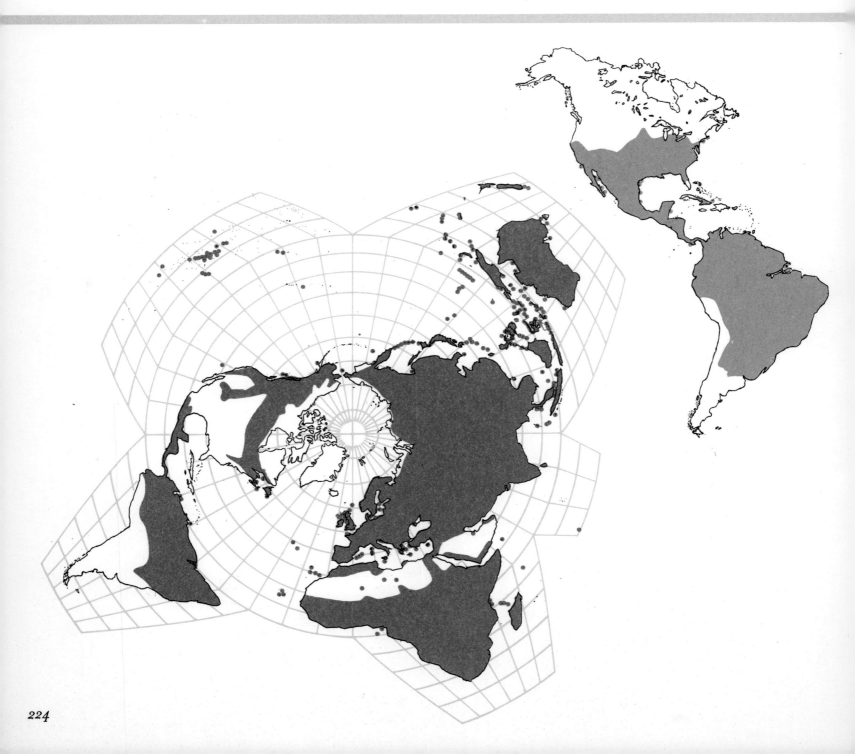

173f Australian warblers

Subfamily Malurinae, no fossils known
Genera: 25 living
Species: 83 living
Origin: doubtless Australasian

173g Old World flycatchers and fantails

Subfamily Muscicapinae, Middle Pleistocene→
Genera: 35 living
Species: 286 known; 286 living, 2 fossil
Origin: Old World, but zone uncertain; earliest fossil, spotted flycatcher *Muscicapa striata*, Palestine

p. 36

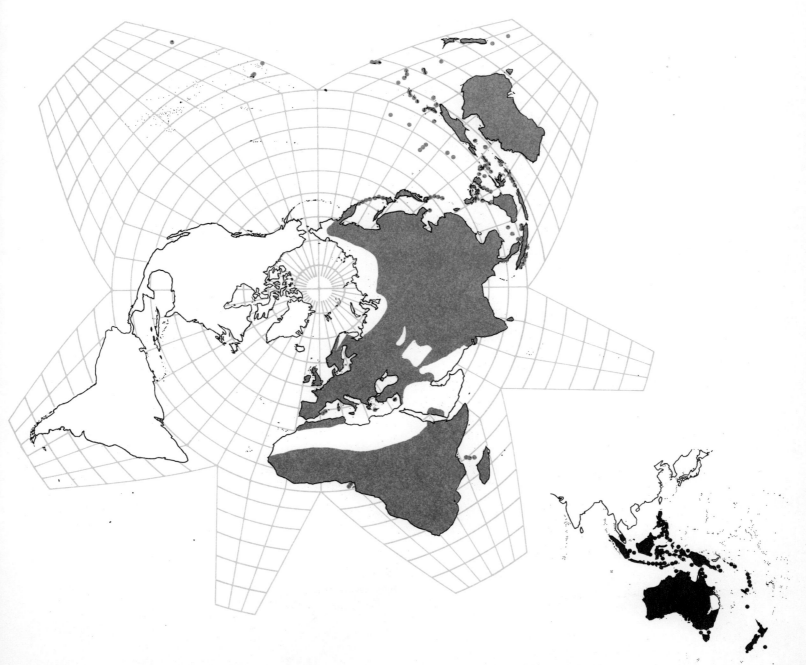

173 Muscicapids (continued)

173h Monarchs
Subfamily Monarchinae, no fossils known
Genera: 9 living
Species: 63 living
Origin: doubtless Australasian

173i Whistlers and piopio
Subfamily Pachycephalinae, Pleistocene→
Genera: 13 living
Species: 49 known; 49 living, 1 fossil
Origin: doubtless Australasian; only fossil,
piopio *Turnagra capensis*, New Zealand

173j Bald crows
Subfamily Picathartinae, no fossils known
Genus: 1 living
Species: 2 living
Origin: doubtless Ethiopian

p. 64

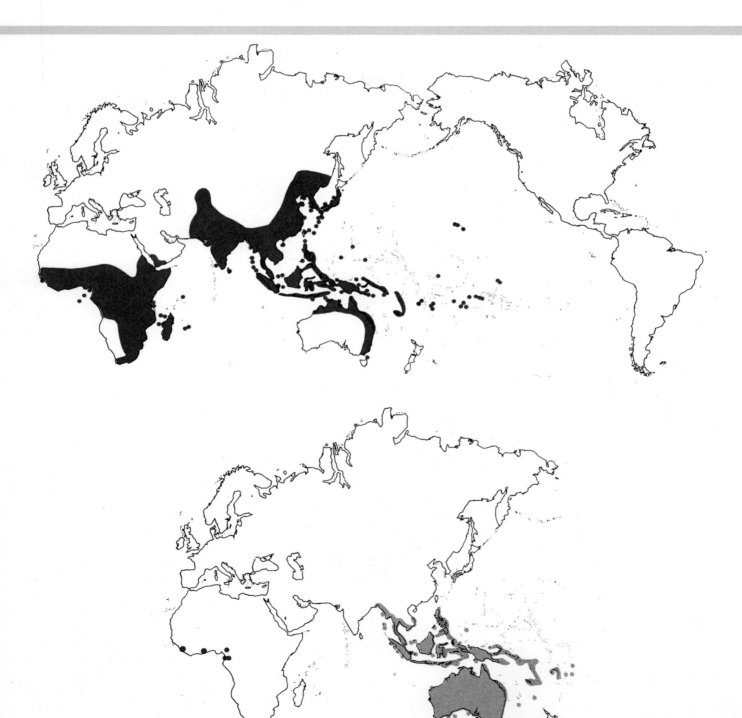

174 Titmice

Family Paridae, Upper Eocene→
Genera: 9 living, 1 fossil
Species: 63 known; 62 living, 9 fossil
Origin: probably Palearctic; earliest fossil,
Paiaegithalus, France

p. 96

175 Nuthatches

Family Sittidae, Lower Pliocene→
Genera: 6 living
Species: 32 known; 31 living, 5 fossil
Origin: probably Palearctic; earliest fossil,
Sitta senogalliensis, Italy. 6 species of *Climacteris*,
Australian tree creepers, no fossils known,
have been separated by one authority as
family Climacteridae

p. 75

176 Creepers

Family Certhiidae, Lower Pleistocene→
Genera: 2 living
Species: 6 known; 6 living, 1 fossil
Origin: doubtless Old World, possibly
Palearctic; only fossil, tree creeper *Certhia
familiaris*, earliest Rumania

p. 37

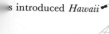

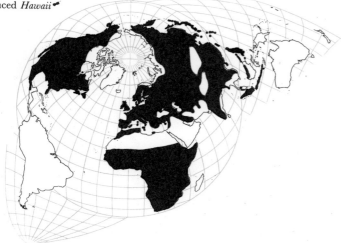

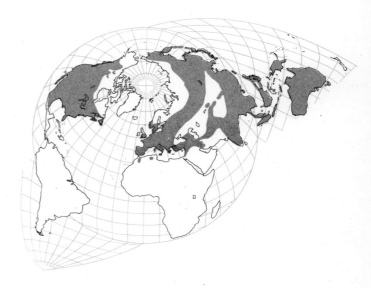

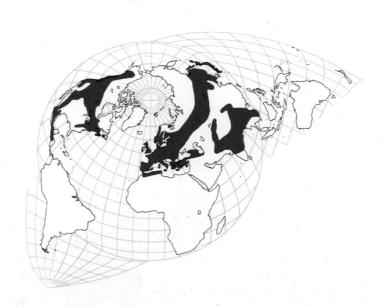

227

177 Flowerpeckers

Family Dicaeidae, no fossils known
Genera: 7 living
Species: 54 living
Origin: probably Oriental

p. 24

178 Sunbirds

Family Nectariniidae, no fossils known
Genera: 4 living
Species: 105 living
Origin: probably Ethiopian

p. 39

179 **Whiteyes**

Family Zosteropidae, no fossils known
Genera: 10 living
Species: 79 known; 78 living, 1 lately extinct
Origin: probably Oriental

p. 55

180 **Honeyeaters**

Family Meliphagidae, Pleistocene→
Genera: 65 living, 1 lately extinct
Species: 162 known; 158 living, 4 lately
extinct, 1 fossil
Origin: doubtless Australasian; only fossil,
tui *Prosthemadera novaeseelandiae*, New
Zealand

p. 56

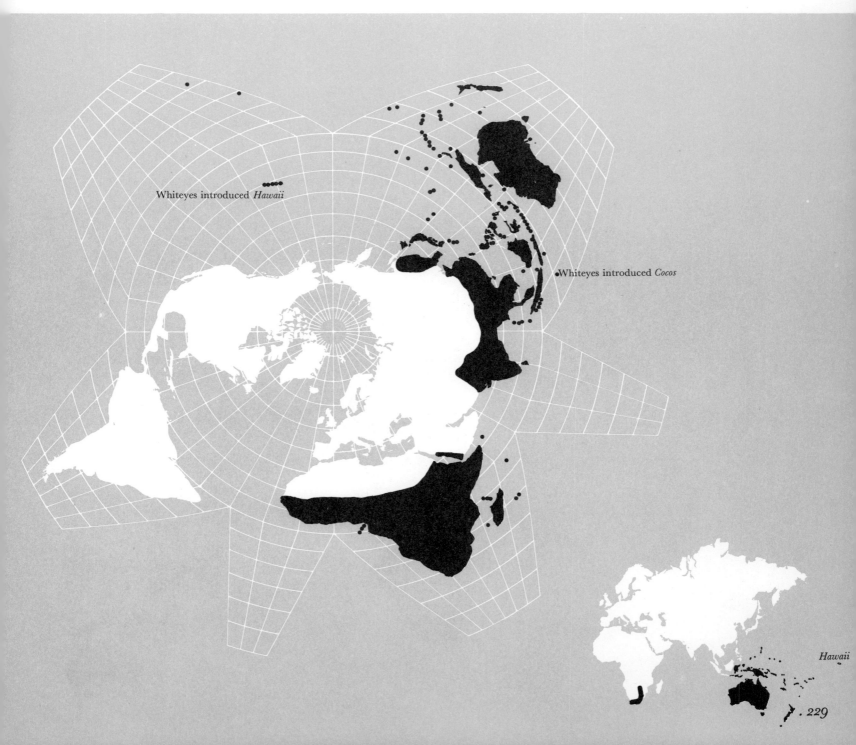

Whiteyes introduced *Hawaii*

Whiteyes introduced *Cocos*

Hawaii

229

181 Emberizids

Family Emberizidae; this is so large that we break it down into subfamilies and tribes as follows

181a Emberizinae

(i) Buntings and American sparrows
Tribe Emberizini, Lower Pliocene→
Genera: 56 living, 1 fossil
Species: 199 known; 197 living, 19 fossil
Origin: probably North American, earliest
fossils, *Palaeostruthus*, Kansas and Florida

(ii) Darwin's finches
Tribe Geospizini, no fossils known
Genera: 4 living
Species: 14 living
Origin: doubtless Galápagos Is., probably from
C. or S. American Emberizine ancestor

p. 13

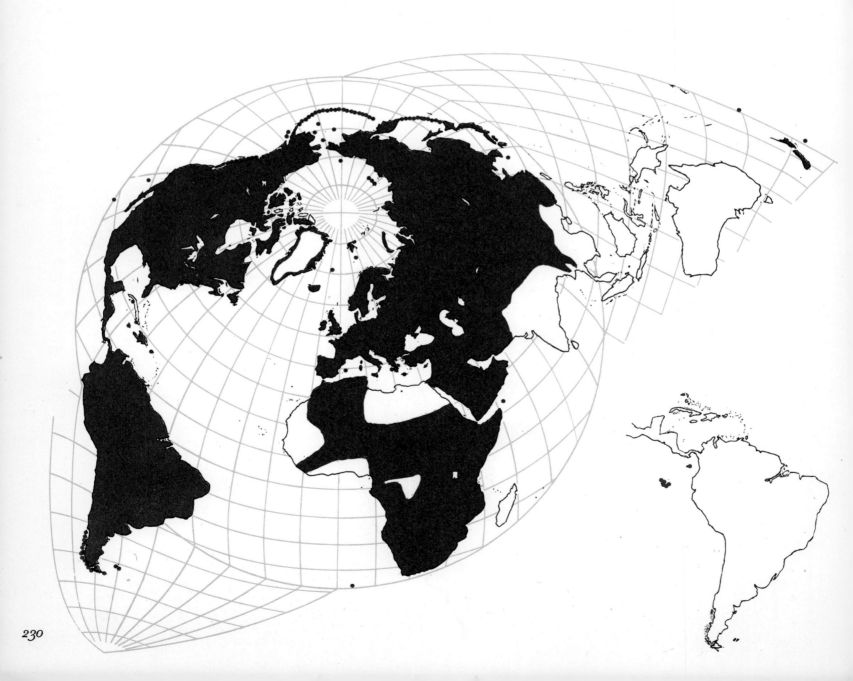

181b Cardinals and allies

Subfamily Cardinalinae, Upper Pleistocene→
Genera: 31 living
Species: 110 known; 110 living, 5 fossil
Origin: doubtless American, possibly South
American; fossils Brazil, Florida, California
and Puerto Rico

p. 13

181c Plush-capped finch

Subfamily Catamblyrhynchinae, no fossil known
Genus and species: 1 living
Origin: doubtless South American

181d Tanagers

Subfamily Tanagrinae, Upper Pleistocene→
Genera: 61 living
Species: 191 known; 191 living, 2 fossil
Origin: doubtless American, possibly South
American, only fossils Puerto Rico

p. 36

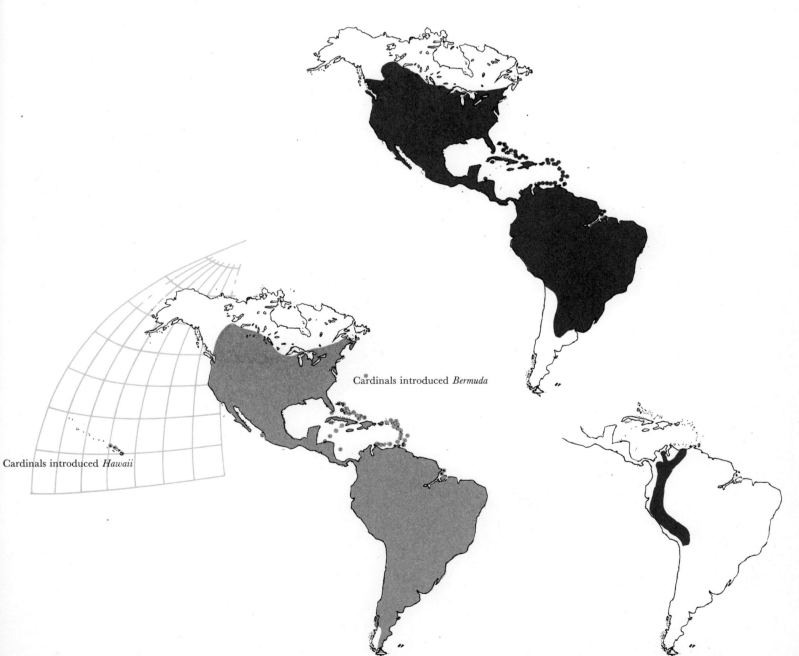

Cardinals introduced *Bermuda*

Cardinals introduced *Hawaii*

181 Emberizids (continued)

181e Swallow tanager

Subfamily Tersininae, Upper Pleistocene→
Genus and species: 1 living and fossil
Origin: doubtless South American; only fossil
Brazil

p. 13

181f Honeycreepers

Subfamily Coerebinae
(i) Tanager-like honeycreepers
Tribe Dacnini, no fossils known
Genera: 9 living
Species: 26 living
Origin: doubtless South American; may be in
subfamily 181d

(ii) Wood warbler-like honeycreepers
Tribe Coerebini, Recent→
Genera: 3 living
Species: 10 known; 10 living, 1 subfossil
Origin: doubtless South American, fossil
Puerto Rico, may be in family 182

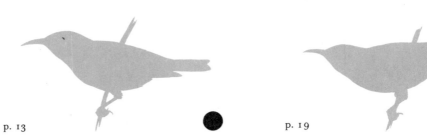

p. 19

182 Wood warblers

Family Parulidae, Middle Pleistocene→
Genera: 18 living
Species: 113 known; 113 living, 4 fossil or
subfossil
Origin: probably North American; earliest fossil,
yellowthroat *Geothlypis trichas*, Florida

p. 62

183 Hawaiian honeycreepers

Family Drepaniidae, no fossils known
Genera: 7 living, 2 lately extinct
Species: 22 known; 14 living, 8 lately extinct
Origin: doubtless Hawaiian, from Emberizid
or Fringillid ancestor from the Americas

p. 55

184 Vireos and allies

Family Vireonidae, Upper Pleistocene→
Genera: 8 living
Species: 42 known; 42 living, 2 fossil
Origin: probably North American, though only
fossils Brazil and Puerto Rico

p. 71

Hawaiian
honeycreepers

185 Icterids

Family Icteridae, Middle Pleistocene→
Genera: 35 living, 3 fossil
Species: 94 known; 88 living, 19 fossil
Origin: doubtless New World, possibly South
American; earliest fossil, Florida

p. 88

186 Finches

Family Fringillidae, Lower Pleistocene→
Genera: 29 living, 1 lately extinct
Species: 124 known; 123 living, 1 lately
extinct, 19 fossil
Origin: probably Old World, possibly
Palearctic; earliest fossils, chaffinch
Fringilla coelebs and hawfinch *Coccothraustes
coccothraustes*, Rumania

p. 63

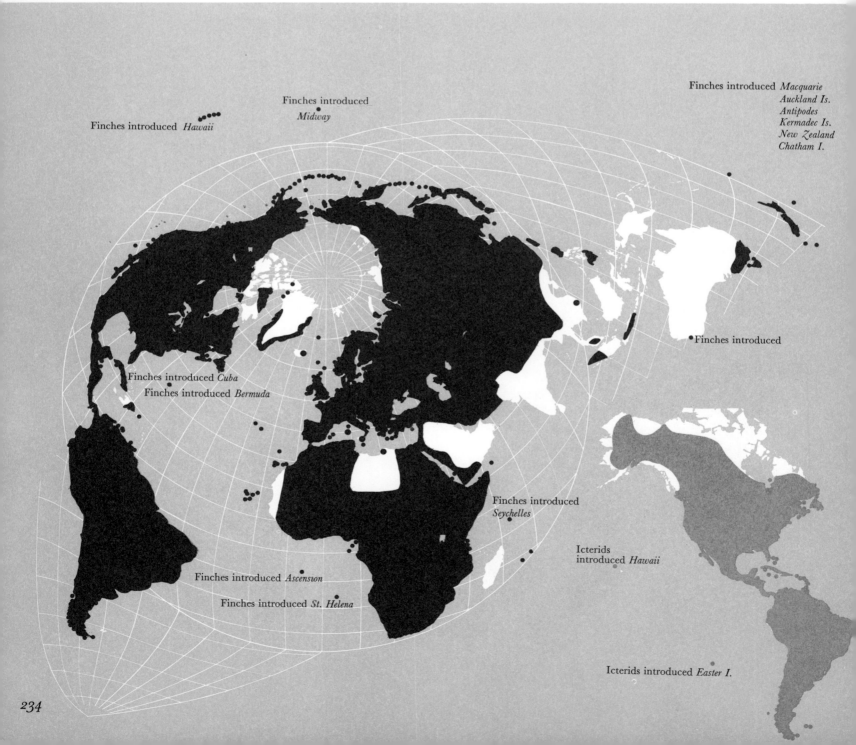

Finches introduced *Macquarie
Auckland Is.
Antipodes
Kermadec Is.
New Zealand
Chatham I.*

Finches introduced
Midway

Finches introduced *Hawaii*

Finches introduced

Finches introduced *Cuba*

Finches introduced *Bermuda*

Finches introduced
Seychelles

Icterids
introduced *Hawaii*

Finches introduced *Ascension*

Finches introduced *St. Helena*

Icterids introduced *Easter I.*

187 Waxbills and allies

Family Estrildidae, no fossils known
Genera: 17 living
Species: 107 living
Origin: doubtless Old World, possibly
Ethiopian

p. 65

188 Widow birds

Family Viduidae, no fossils known
Genera: 2 living
Species: 8 living
Origin: doubtless Ethiopian

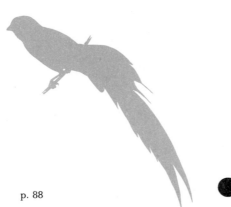

p. 88

189 Weavers and true sparrows

Family Ploceidae, Lower Miocene→
Genera: 17 living, 1 lately extinct
Species: 136 known; 132 living, 2 lately
extinct, 8 fossil
Origin: doubtless Old World, probably
Ethiopian; earliest fossil, sparrow, *Passer*
species, France

p. 51

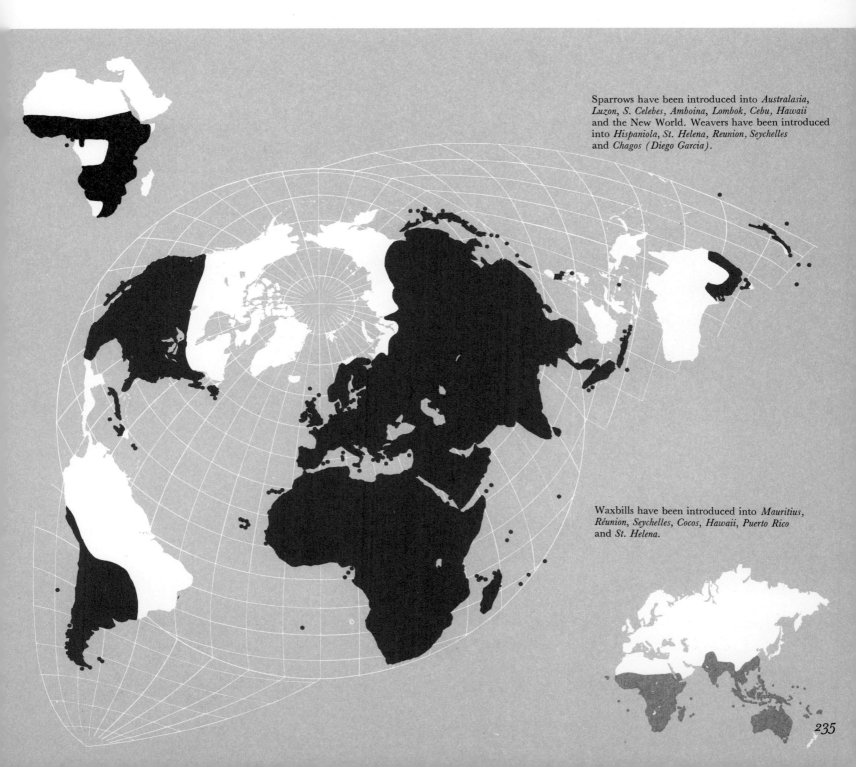

Sparrows have been introduced into *Australasia,
Luzon, S. Celebes, Amboina, Lombok, Cebu, Hawaii*
and the New World. Weavers have been introduced
into *Hispaniola, St. Helena, Réunion, Seychelles*
and *Chagos (Diego Garcia)*.

Waxbills have been introduced into *Mauritius,
Réunion, Seychelles, Cocos, Hawaii, Puerto Rico*
and *St. Helena*.

235

190 Starlings

Family Sturnidae, Upper Eocene→
Genera: 24 living, 1 lately extinct, 1 fossil
Species: 114 known; 107 living, 4 lately
extinct, 9 fossil
Origin: doubtless Old World, possibly
Ethiopian; earliest fossils, *Laurillardia*,
France

191 Old World orioles

Family Oriolidae, Pleistocene→
Genera: 2 living
Species: 28 known; 28 living, 2 fossil
Origin: doubtless Old World, possibly
Australasian; earliest fossils, golden oriole
Oriolus oriolus, Europe and Palestine

p. 76

p. 35

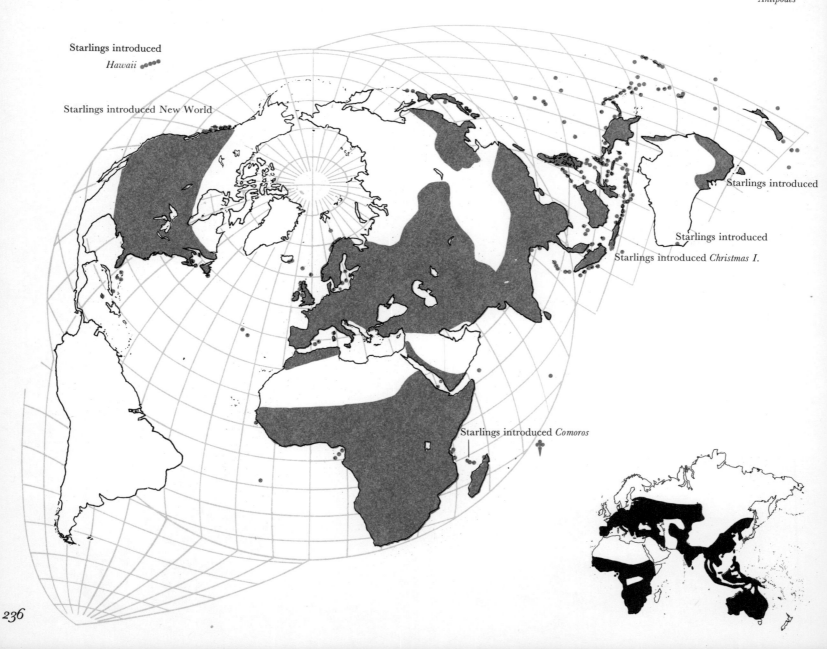

Starlings introduced *Kermadec Is.*
Chatham I.
Macquarie
Auckland Is.
Antipodes

Starlings introduced
Hawaii

Starlings introduced New World

Starlings introduced

Starlings introduced

Starlings introduced *Christmas I.*

Starlings introduced *Comoros*

192 Drongos

Family Dicruridae, Pleistocene→
Genera: 2 living
Species: 19 known; 19 living, 1 fossil
Origin: doubtless Old World, possibly Oriental;
may be close to Old World flycatchers, family
173; only fossil, *Dicrurus* species, China

p. 36

193 Wattled crows

Family Callaeidae, Pleistocene→
Genera: 2 living, 1 lately extinct
Species: 3 known; 2 living, 1 lately extinct,
3 fossil
Origin: doubtless New Zealand; where all found

p. 61

194 Magpie larks

Family Grallinidae, no fossils known
Genera: 3 living
Species: 4 living
Origin: doubtless Australian

p. 60

Drongos introduced *Saipan*

237

195 Wood swallows
Family Artamidae, no fossils known
Genus: 1 living
Species: 10 living
Origin: probably Australasian, possibly
Oriental

196 Bell magpies
Family Cracticidae, no fossils known
Genera: 3 living
Species: 10 living
Origin: doubtless Australian

p. 61

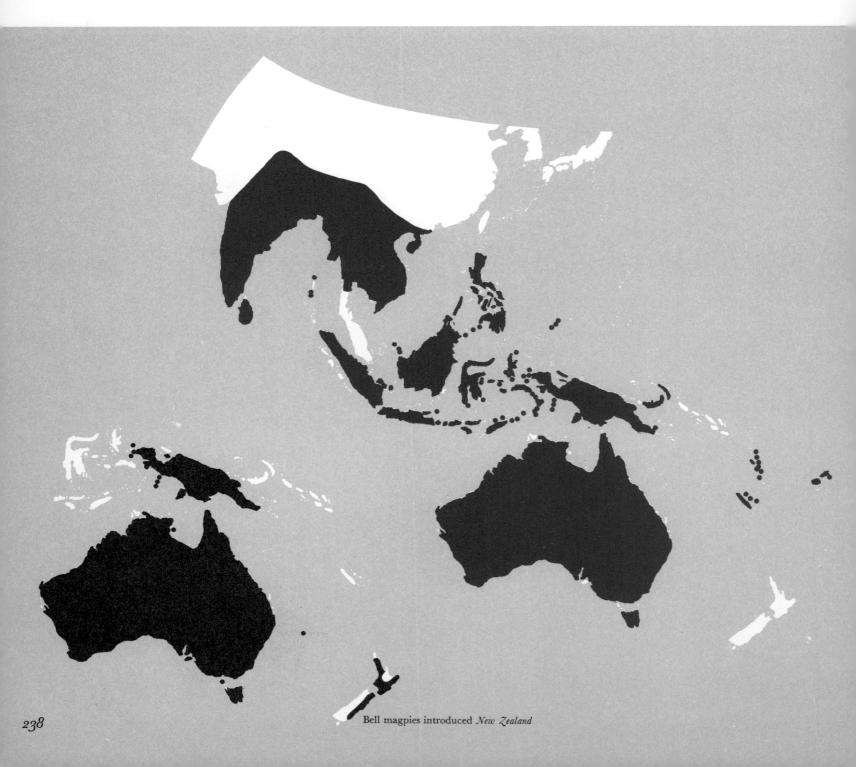

Bell magpies introduced *New Zealand*

197 Bower birds
Family Ptilonorhynchidae, no fossils known
Genera: 8 living
Species: 17 living
Origin: doubtless New Guinea or tropical
Australia

198 Birds of paradise
Family Paradisaeidae, no fossils known
Genera: 20 living
Species: 40 living
Origin: doubtless New Guinea

p. 61

p. 61

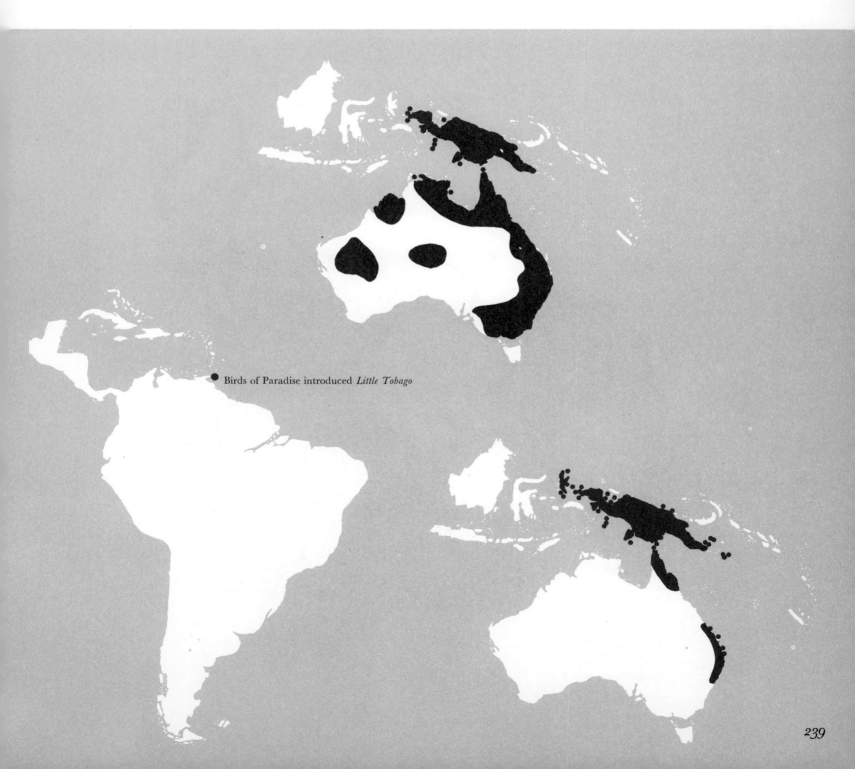

● Birds of Paradise introduced *Little Tobago*

199 Crows

Family Corvidae, Middle Miocene→
Genera: 20 living, 4 fossil
Species: 112 known; 102 living, 31 fossil
Origin: probably Palearctic; earliest fossil,
Miocorax, France

p. 94

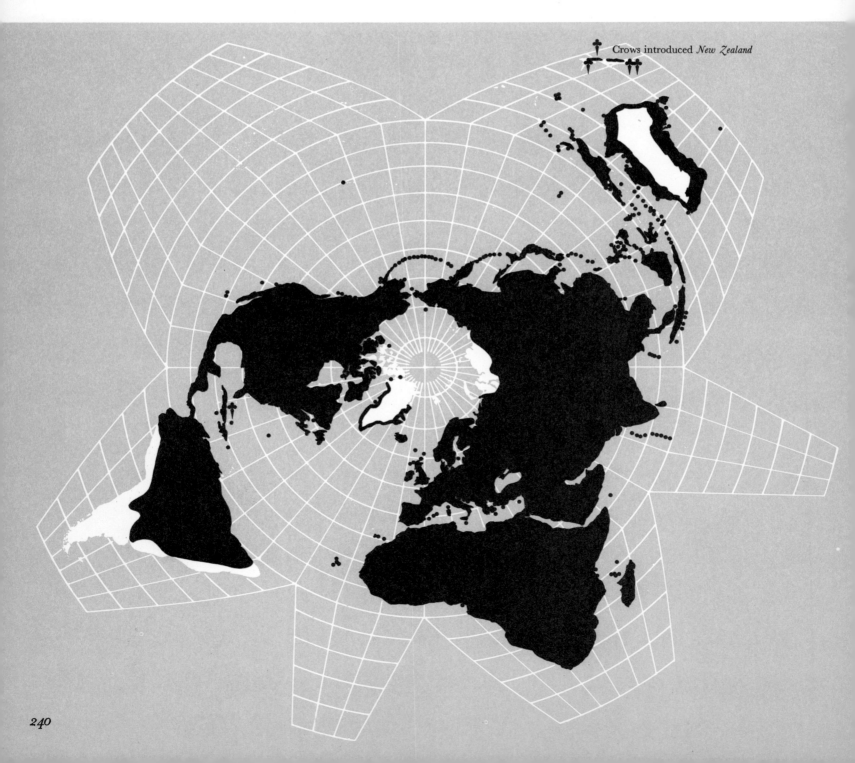

Crows introduced *New Zealand*

The regimental tally

The systematic regimentation of the birds has been done to the best of our knowledge and judgment with minimal departure from the universally respected Wetmore system.

As far as we know it is the first attempt at a complete system of the class of birds down to families (and in some cases beyond), including all fossils and with a census of genera and species formally described by 1962 and in our judgment good. The census is summarized in table 2, below; and in table 1 our figures for the number of birds alive since 1600 are compared with the counts of living and recently extinct genera and species made by predecessors to whose careful work and judgment we owe much.

Previous counts of paleospecies by Pierce Brodkorb were published in 1957 (794) and 1960 (834). In February 1962 he kindly gave us a new, unpublished figure of 841. Our own count of 854 differs very little indeed from his. It includes some more novelties published in 1962 but *excludes* about 10 in his total which we regard as neospecies since they became extinct after 1600. Brodkorb's paleospecies were birds extinct by 1758, the year of Linnaeus's tenth edition of *Systema Naturae*. Our figure of 331 for the paleogenera gives 2.58 paleospecies to the genus and compares fairly closely with Brodkorb's 2.96 (1957).

Since Ernst Mayr's very thorough count at the end of 1945, 52 good new species have been described in the 17 years to the end of 1962, of which 38 were passerines. All were found in the tropics. Two were sea birds; the rest belonged to the Oriental (10), Ethiopian (16), Neotropical (20) and Australasian (4) faunas. Most novelties (7) were found in the Philippines including Palawan; but Perú had 6, Venezuela 5, Colombia and Brazil each 4. The total number, at about three a year, was unexpectedly high and due largely to the harvest of big, well-planned expeditions in regions where least prewar collecting had been done. This hunt seems to have ended by 1960, when no less than 7 novelties were described; and we do not believe that more than another 50 existing species remain to be discovered; though new ones will of course evolve and can be proved to be in the process of doing so at the moment.

Taking the novelties into account, the agreement between the different recent assessors is amazingly close, within one per cent or much less, and reflects the present stability of the concept of species. The accepted genera are clearly decreasing, though their number has not been so often measured. This reflects very well the broadening of genera that is the present trend in most vertebrate systematics.

At present an average genus has just over four species according to our count (2,128). This is probably still a little too small for both the jobs of a genus, the adequate celebration of biological relationship, and practical convenience. Mayr's estimate published in 1963 (1,700–1,800) reflects the judgments of a supreme working systematist whereas ours is but a judgment of published judgments; his figure doubtless involves a highly educated guess of the extent of lumping in future published revisions.

We have made no census ourselves of the lowest systematic category, the subspecies or geographical races. As new areas are worked, this number has lately tended to increase faster than the rejection of old races through reassessment, though here as everywhere new rules are being applied to racial validity and acceptable races are broader than they used to be. By the end of 1945 Mayr estimated that about 28,500 'good' races had been described. A new count by Wynne (1949) cut this down to 25,897, of which 9,779 were non-passerines. The non-passerine races accepted in the first six volumes of the Peters *Check-list of Birds of the World* (1931–48) were 9,389. Since then the number has certainly advanced again and it is likely that Mayr's total of 28,500 in 1945, possibly then an overestimate, may now probably be about right.

TABLE 1. Living and recently extinct birds (neogenera and neospecies): counts by recent authorities.

	Non-passerines		Passerines		Total	
	Genera	Species	Genera	Species	Genera	Species
Sharpe (1909)						c. 19,000
Mayr (1963) several authors around 1920					6–7000	
Mayr (1935)					c. 2600	8500
Mayr (1946) to end 1945		3523		5093		8616
Peters (1931–48) end 1930 to end 1946	1094	3730				
Wynne (1949)	1065	3702	1325	5424	2390	9126
Mayr & Amadon (1951)		3522		5073		8595
Brodkorb (1957)	1117	3729	1246	5080	2363	8809
van Tyne & Berger (1959) to March 1958		3534		5040		8574
Storer (1960)	1063	3668		4982		8650
Austin (1961)						8635
Mayr (1963)					17–1800	
Present census to 1962	941	3529	1187	5134	2128	8663

TABLE 1

We guess that our total of 8,663 neospecies includes extinct species (especially those extinct before the dodo) not counted by others; in most cases at least 8, in some perhaps considerably more.

TABLE 2

Our total of 200 families here includes no. 40A †Plegadornithidae Wetmore 1962.

Of the 83 extinct neospecies in the census 8 became so between 1600 and 1681, when the dodo was last seen, and the other 75 since 1680. On pp. 272–73 the 'black list' cites 85 birds extinct since 1600. The other two birds were unnamed as this book went to press: a blue dove last seen on the island of St. Helena in 1775; and a flightless crake closely resembling the African crake and probably of the same genus, *Crecopsis*, last seen on Ascension Island in 1656.

TABLE 2. Census of accepted bird orders, families, genera and species described by 1962.

ORDERS

Extinct by 1600, fossil only		6			
Extinct since 1600		1			
Living		29	30	36	

FAMILIES

Non-passerine;	extinct by 1600, fossil only		41			
	extinct since 1600	3				
	living	99	102	143		
Passerine; suboscinine (nos. 143–56);	living	14				
oscinine;	extinct by 1600, fossil only	2				
	living	41	43	57	200	
ALL;	extinct by 1600, fossil only		43			
	extinct since 1600	3				
	living	154	157		200	

GENERA

Non-passerine;	paleogenera		318			
	neogenera; extinct	19				
	living	922	941		1259	
Passerine; suboscinine;	paleogenera		1			
	neogenera; extinct	0				
	living	324	324	325		
oscinine;	paleogenera		12			
	neogenera; extinct	7				
	living	856	863	875	1200	2459
ALL;	paleogenera		331			
	neogenera; extinct	26				
	living	2102	2128			2459

SPECIES

Non-passerine;	paleospecies		816			
	neospecies; extinct	59				
	living	3470	3529		4345	
Passerine; suboscinine;	paleospecies		1			
	neospecies; extinct	1				
	living	1095	1096	1097		
oscinine;	paleospecies		37			
	neospecies; extinct	23				
	living	4015	4038	4075	5172	9517
ALL; known as fossil;	paleospecies		854			
	neospecies; extinct	20				
	living	709	729	1583		
not known as fossil;	neospecies; extinct	63				
	living	7871		7934		9517
	paleospecies		854			
	neospecies; extinct	83				
	living	8580	8663			9517

Above: Australian aboriginals, still partly at the food-gathering stage of culture, no longer use Stone Age hunting tools exclusively. Firearms have made life easier for indigenous hunters, have brought new pressures to bear on stocks of many birds, as Australian pelican here.

Left: Hausa bowmen in northern Nigeria still hunt prey under disguise of stuffed ground hornbill headdress, a stalking horse technique known, from cave paintings, to be thousands of years old

Right: a sample of the capacity for separate invention of bird catchers. Center: Maori snare; parrots decoyed or baited to perch are caught by feet when hunter pulls string; l. and r.: Egyptian gin and Chinese noose traps, for larks

CHAPTER IX

Birds and Men

The fowlers

If the total mass of wild birds living today were divided equally among the human population, it is unlikely that each of us would receive more than a day's rations.

Ancient hunters lived and fared in a different world entirely. Only ten thousand years ago, when civilization and history were but a sunrise in Mesopotamia, late Stone Age men were confined to the Old World, though just on the point of their first invasion of the New across the Bering Sea. Their population was limited by the supporting capacity of the land, and is thought to have been no more than from 7 to 10 million. Today, man numbers about 300 times as many.

With their crude instruments, ancient hunters were in an ecological relationship with their prey scarcely different from that of any other animal predator. Their main meat was mammals: but they were formidable fowlers, with plenty of birds to exploit. Among the favorite animals of the chase, the European and Mediterranean hunters figured (p. 108) the largest and most edible members of their local bird fauna.

We may be sure that after perhaps a hundred thousand years of the dart and throwing stick, and 70 or 80 thousand years' use of the bow and arrow, not to mention snare, deadfall and bird-lime, the Stone Age hunters were well aware that some birds were good to eat, others not.

They found that herons, most big flightless birds, ducks and geese, and nearly all members of the game bird families, were palatable, as were many rails, bustards, cranes and waders, some parrots, pigeons and nightjars, all larks, most weavers, some buntings, finches and flycatchers, most thrushes and even owls and wry-necks.

On the other hand some contrastingly colored, warningly conspicuous birds were doubtful prey, suitable only for hard times and special cookery – among them loons, some ducks (shelduck, smew, scoter), certain coursers, plovers and auks, touracos, cuckoos, hoopoes, kingfishers, hornbills, crows, starlings, tits, shrikes, swallows, drongos, flycatchers, wheatears and finches.

As eggers, too, ancient hunters must have been well aware of another hierarchy of palatability. Modern experiments have shown that the domestic fowl's egg is most palatable of all: close to it, the eggs of other game birds, most big flightless birds, rails, gulls, waders, penguins, albatrosses, bustards, petrels, herons, ducks, cranes, auks and sand grouse.

At the other – practically uneatable – end of the scale are the eggs of several hole-nesting families, notably hoopoes, tits, nuthatches, woodpeckers, wrens, hornbills and honeyguides. Some open-nesting birds like storks and specially mousebirds also have highly unpalatable eggs: the conspicuous white eggs of the speckled mousebird are probably the most foul-tasting of all.

The vast majority of the human population of the wealthier countries now eats chicken eggs and meat (p. 251) and no longer relies on what is a relatively tiny supply of wild birds and their eggs. Yet a few special human communities, mostly isolated and some highly civilized, still exploit wild birds on a major scale with traditional, almost Stone Age, methods.

Sticky bird-lime is a typical invention, now generally prohibited in law in Europe and North America. Just how many times, and in how many places it has been separately discovered, is uncertain; but nearly all cultures and races of mankind have smeared it on foliage or sticks to which birds are baited. The ancient Romans used mistletoe juice, the Greeks fig juice, as do many Asians, and South Africans. Modern Italians use thistle juice, the Japanese evergreen oak, trochodendron gum, wheat. In Britain bird-lime was made of linseed or holly bark. In Egypt it is laced with treacle. Central Africans catch big hornbills with euphorbia gum; Amerindians entangle hummingbirds with slug-slime. On many remote islands, from Réunion in the Indian Ocean to widely separated groups in the Pacific it has been separately invented. Indonesians and Polynesians use it much to this day.

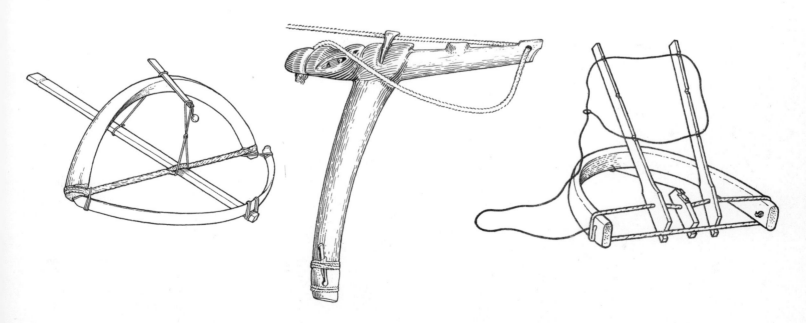

Other inventions have independently evolved several times in different places. The stalking horse technique – hunter disguised as large mammal, as ostrich, as bush – goes back to Old Stone Age cave paintings, and is known from Europe, India, Africa, North America and Australia. The blowpipe and poisoned dart must have been separately evolved, at least in South-east Asia and the Americas. Nightingale traps of western Europe, Russia, China, India and North Africa may all have had separate origins.

Techniques of driving molting ducks, geese and swans, flightless adults running with their well-grown young, into corrals were worked out by men of nine different regional cultures. The Heligoland trap (p. 121), most efficient tool of the modern bird observatory, had prototypes in eleven cultures. A butterfly-net-like puffin net used in the Faeroes and Iceland had an almost exact counterpart among the Aleuts of the Commander (Komandorski) Island in the Bering Sea.

The continuance of traditional, and often cruel methods of catching land birds in highly civilized countries brought about a marked, if somewhat belated, revolution in public conscience and legislation. In Europe and North America, in the last century, the bird catcher has almost inevitably become the overcropper, the public menace. The days are not long past when half a million larks were offered for sale in Leipzig, Germany, one October; when a third of a million thrushes were taken in 25 fall days at the mouth of the Rhône in France; when 26,000 molting ducks were killed in three days by half a dozen hunters near Tomsk in Siberia; when one dealer could sell 5,000 lapwing eggs in a season in Yarmouth, England. As late as 1950 one man took over 14,000 moorhen eggs in Spain.

Latter-day traditional sea bird fowlers

Top left: part of the murre egg harvest in the Westmann Islands, Iceland, in 1949

Left: G. W. Whyte's classic photograph of the St. Kildan climbers sharing out fulmars on the village beach in August 1884

Below: the staple St. Kildan food bird. Each islander used to eat about 115 young fulmars, dried or pickled in brine, each year

Many (not all) of the unreasonable exploitations of wild birds have ceased or run down, at least in those countries with a high standard of living. Many of their engines and inventions have found their way into museums. However, modern hunters, struggling toward a new harmony with their bird prey (p. 258) can learn a lot from one sphere in which men (some men, at least) *have* been harmonious predators for a millennium or more. This is the cropping of sea birds, their young and their eggs.

Much of the story of sea bird exploitation in civilized times is a history of greed, bloodshed, overcropping and cruelty that has been arrested only by a tardy public conscience followed by legislation and enforcement. The plume-hunters of Florida, the Carolinas and Virginia, the Asian raiders of some Pacific Islands, the murre eggers of California and Canada, the exploiters of the murre 'bazaars' of Novaya Zemlya, the mutton birders of Australia and New Zealand, the penguin eggers of the Cape of Good Hope – all these have, in the course of history, had to be controlled by governments and regulations because they would not control themselves.

Yet in the more ancient sea-fowling communities, notably those of Greenland, Iceland, the Faeroes, and St. Kilda, the fowlers arrived long ago at an harmonious relationship with their prey. All but the St. Kildans survive and all may boast a millennium of the practice and thus a formidable tradition.

By trial and error all seem to have arrived at the same practical rules. They take a crop of eggs, young or adults large in proportion to the breeding stock. Large though this crop has been, though, the stock has remained stable, subject to fluctuations which appear natural. In some cases, such as that of the fulmar in the last two centuries and the gannet in the present century, it has increased.

The egg rule that has emerged is that from large colonies such as those of murres which readily lay replacements, more (but not much more) than half the first laying can be safely cropped. Birds like fulmars, which do *not* normally lay replacements, should be egged mildly – better not at all.

From fulmars (and other tube-nosed birds like 'mutton birds') a crop of fat young can be taken just before they fledge, amounting in most big colonies to half, but not more than half of the lot. Birds like gannets, which lay replacement eggs, can be egg-cropped *and* young-cropped, provided the total represents not much more than half the annual reproductive output. Adults can be cropped if eggs and young are not taken: the puffin population of all these communities has been harvested for centuries.

By accepting these rules the real traditional fowlers have made themselves the only important predators of their prey, but, through centuries of trial, error and adjustment, *natural* predators. They long ago reached, paradoxically, the position that only now, in the present century, has presented itself to ecologists, game technicians and conservationists: that of *rational* exploiters of wildlife. They have enjoyed cheap and good food without killing the geese that laid their golden eggs. The gallant and marvelously skillful rock-climbers of Iceland's Westmann Islands, St. Kilda's stacks and Faeroe's incredible basalt cliffs had, in their lore, long before biological scholars saw the point, the secret of the preservation of Africa's diminishing big game, of the great whales of the oceans, of the fishes of the continental shelves – a tender culture of the breeding grounds, and a traditional discretion toward the size of the crop.

Below: from about 1700 until recently Yorkshire 'climmers' took a big harvest of murre (guillemot) eggs on the cliffs of Bempton

Some of the largest sea bird harvests known since 1829:

Scotland	St. Kilda: average young fulmar crop 10,000, 1829–1929; 89,600 puffins 1876.
England	Leadenhall market: 300,000 black-headed gull eggs 1935.
	Bempton Cliffs: 130,000 common murre eggs 1884.
Iceland	112,234 murres 1912; 250,000 puffins 1950.
Faeroe	common murre: *c.* 500,000 eggs early 1940s, *c.* 100,000 birds 1950s; puffin: 4–500,000 1950s.
South Africa	Cape penguin islands: 630,000 jackass penguin eggs 1901.
Seychelles	1,996,400 tern (mostly sooty tern) eggs 1946.
California	Farallones: 650,000 common murre eggs 1850–56.
New Zealand	30,000 young sooty shearwaters (New Zealand mutton birds) 1940s.
Australia	Islands in Bass Strait: slender-billed shearwater (Tasmanian mutton bird); *c.* 100,000 eggs early 1920s, 500,000 young early 1960s.
	Norfolk I.: *c.* 200,000 sooty tern eggs early 1900s.
S. Atlantic	Ascension I.: over 160,000 sooty tern eggs 1920s.
Greenland	Gronne I.: 100,000 arctic tern eggs 1940s.
	South-west area: 200,000 murres (nearly all arctic murres) 1940s.
Novaya Zemlya	Bezymyannaya Bay: 342,500 arctic murre eggs 1933.

World headquarters of the guano industry is today off the coast of Perú, where teeming anchovetas, small fishes of cool Humboldt current, support millions of sea birds

Left: excavating the phosphorus-rich deposits. Still dug mostly by hand, guano resource is now scientifically husbanded

Above: richest islands of all, the Chinchas; guano deposit extends to highest peaks

Right: on solid guano breed the great guano birds, the abundant guanay (a species of cormorant), and the big alcatráz (a pelican), in foreground

Guano

The word 'guano' comes from *huanu*, which means dung in the language of the Quechua Indians of South America: and here is restricted to mean such excretions and regurgitations of sea birds as have accumulated at their breeding places. This smelly, powdery substance is very valuable as fertilizer in agriculture. Only at places with a rainfall consistently below 100 centimeters (about 40 inches) a year can guano normally build up.

The distribution of such places has varied over the face of the earth during the ages of birds. There were, for instance, guano islands off Florida in early Pliocene times (p. 45). By far the greatest amount of guano which has been quarried during the last 120 years was formed not recently but during the million years or more of the Pleistocene period. Some of it has been found on islands which now have no sea birds. The important factor in its accumulation has been dry climates with a rainfall not great enough to wash it all away.

About 200 million tons of Pleistocene guano were available at the beginning of the guano rush of the mid-nineteenth century. This contained over 32 million tons of valuable phosphorus. Some of this remains, but most of it was quarried, shipped and plowed into the world's fields in less than a century. It is true that the greatest deposits of all these are still yielding: most important is that of Nauru in the Pacific, whose original 'fossil' guano reserve was about $87\frac{1}{2}$ million tons.

Compared with the Pleistocene guano, the resources of recent guano (less than 10,000 years old) were relatively small, though accumulating, when first discovered by Western man (in South America in 1589). These deposits were swiftly reduced in the last century. Nearly 1,000 places (nearly all islands, a few headlands) have been discovered to bear valuable guano.

Of these less than 200, probably, are now worked – three-quarters of them in Perú. Nearly 3 million tons of phosphorus, representing nearly 20 million tons of recent guano, have already gone. No less than a fifth has been contributed by the 'guaneras' of the Mejillones Peninsula of Chile. These ceased to be sea bird colonies a few thousand years ago and subsequently became elevated by local earth movements some hundreds of feet: they are still being worked.

Perhaps two or three thousand years ago the dry conditions in which guano could quickly accumulate shifted

north to the coast of Perú. On the greatest 'living' guano islands of all, the Chinchas off Pisco Bay, guano has been worked by Indians since 1628 (at least), commercially since 1841. About one sixth of all the world's recent guano has been taken there.

Each year, at least during the last century, the resident population of guanays (cormorants) and the relatively less important brown pelicans and piqueros (boobies) has produced an average of about three inches of guano. Each guanay contributes about 35 pounds (15.9 kg.) of guano or nearly 2 pounds of valuable phosphorus and over 5 pounds of useful nitrogen in a season: all this from a daily take of about 11 ounces (just over 300 gm.) of its staple fish-food in the Humboldt current, the anchoveta.

Apart from Perú, the most important commercial sources of recent guano since the middle of the nineteenth century have been in the Pacific islands, where the approximate yield since they were first exploited has been 400,000 tons of guano, produced mainly by the brown booby, the sooty and noddy terns and the Laysan albatross. Areas each with a yield around 100,000 tons have been Australia and its neighbors (Australasian gannet, sooty and noddy); the west Indian Ocean and

Red Sea; and the east coasts of the Americas and the Caribbean (in the two last, blue-faced booby, sooty and noddy). The west coast of México (Brandt's cormorant, brown and blue-faced boobies) has produced about 50,000 tons, and the south-west coast of Africa (Cape gannet, jackass penguin, Cape cormorant) about 18,000.

Today the remaining guano deposits are, for the most part, being jealously husbanded on scientific lines by government agencies and corporations. A profitable industry is now based on, and is balanced with, the quite substantial yearly land excretion of some of our sea bird populations. It can be managed with not the slightest interference with the lives of the birds as in Perú, where a fully-planned economy has developed in which removal now keeps pace with deposition.

In Perú it is realized that heavier direct fishing exploitation of the teeming anchovetas of the Humboldt current might be immediately profitable, but in the long run could damage the whole basis of the guano industry. The steady guano profit has so far been chosen; a deal has been made with nature which disturbs no ecological process, and regains for man, at the expense of no animal, a little over 8,000 tons of natural phosphorus every year.

A 'sport of kings'

Such antique terms as austringer, bewit, bowse, cadge, creance, eyass, eyrie, feak, hack, haggard, imp, jesses, mews, pounces, rufter, stoop, tiercel, varvels, yarak express in private language the medieval mystery that pervades an old, now dying sport of kings and nobles. Falconry still inspires fighting men and challenge-men – soldiers, airmen, climbers, explorers. The training, for killing, of killer birds, fascinates certain gentlemen of power who dream of yesterday, and love the drama of the aerial chase.

Grant the falconers this: that for more than 1,000 years – perhaps 4,000 – they have made a psychological deal with rival predators. They have admitted their beloved avian slaves to fellow-membership in the order of the chase. It has been their way of dominating nature while showing their respect for it.

Upon the funeral stele of the Serpent King of the first dynasty of Egypt (around 3000 B.C.) is the unmistakable relief of a medium-sized falcon, the hobby. It may be deduced from this, comments F. E. Zeuner, that in ancient Egypt falcons played an important part in the cult of the dead. But, he adds, whether they were ever used for hunting is another matter and very little evidence exists.

There is some evidence, however, that trained falcons were flown at prey in China, if not in Egypt, around 2000 B.C., in Persia about 1700 B.C. Zeuner thinks true falconry probably reached the Nile around 800 B.C. or a little after. By about 600 B.C. it had spread into Arabia and Syria and – probably from China *via* Korea – into

Japan. In a crude form it was known to the ancient Greeks at the time of Aristotle (384–322 B.C.).

The penetration of true falconry into Europe was slow; it was mentioned in Rome by the naturalist Pliny (A.D. 23–79) and reached western Europe in the fourth century A.D. By the seventh century the game was popular enough in France to have its own scale of values: a hawk capable of flying at cranes was worth twice as much, a trained yearling four times as much as an untrained bird.

From the eighth century until the seventeenth falconry was the rage and fashion of every kingly court of Europe. Among its keen aficionados were Ethelbert II, the King of Kent; Alfred the Great; Athelstan, King of Mercia; Howel the Good, King of Wales; King Edward the Confessor; Harold and William the Conqueror; King Stephen; King Henry II; Thomas à Becket, who often carried a hawk as a status symbol; King Sancho VI of Navarre; King John of England; and King Henry III.

The Emperor Frederick II of Germany, a fine naturalist, wrote a great treatise, *De Arte Venandi cum Avibus* – 'concerning the art of hunting with birds'. From the fourteenth century on the hawking of the English monarchs became proverbial. Edward I, Edward II, Richard II, Henry VIII, Elizabeth I, Mary Queen of Scots, James I, were all passionate devotees. The royal mews in London employed more than half as many trainers as there were birds. A class structure of falconry even developed: gyrfalcons for royalty only; peregrines for high noblemen; merlins for noblewomen; the short-winged hawks

(goshawks and sparrowhawks) for the landed gentry and clergy.

The last great royal gesture to the sport was made in 1686 when James II created his nephew, Charles Beauclerk (the illegitimate son of his brother Charles II and Nell Gwyn), Hereditary Grand Falconer of England at a salary of £1,000 a year. The office still stands and his heirs continued to receive the money until the present century when, as Phillip Glasier presumes, 'someone rumbled the fact that they were being paid for nothing'.

With its special links with the courtly past, its private language, its complex training discipline, and the vicarious thrill of the avian chase, falconry still appeals to a proud coterie of amateurs.

It must be pointed out that seldom if ever have they put undue pressure on the quarry. Rather, the menace of falconry is to some of the falcons themselves. Although some experienced practitioners have arrived at a gentlemen's agreement to fly only passage hawks (birds caught in migration) others, less responsible, have endangered local stocks of their beloved raptors by an excessive search for eyasses (young birds taken from the nest). Canadian conservationists report that Peale's falcon (the dark western race of the peregrine) and the ferruginous hawk have been seriously depleted by tyro falcophiles who run through many birds in their fumbling attempts to train them.

A rigid licensing system permits a very few experienced men to pursue the hobby in Britain, where the smallish British Falconers' Club, founded in 1927, comprises the only active falconers. The Deutscher Falkenorden, founded in 1923, is also active but small; and there are small practicing groups also in Canada, the U.S.A., France, Italy, Egypt, Japan, Hungary and Jugoslavia. In North Africa and the East, particularly Iran, Arabia, India, China and Russia, it is still followed on traditional lines.

At least 28 diurnal birds of prey have been broken to the lure (an imitation prey attached to a line) and entered (induced to take quarry). These include six short-winged hawks (*Accipiter*): goshawk (northern world), shikra (Africa and Asia), Old World sparrowhawk, rufous sparrowhawk (Africa), besra (Asia) and Cooper's and sharp-shinned hawks (North America). Five American species of *Buteo* have been trained: ferruginous, red-tailed, red-shouldered, broad-winged and rough-legged hawks (or buzzards). Of the world's eagles we list seven: the crowned hawk eagle and martial eagle (Africa), Bonelli's eagle (Old World), bald eagle (North America), golden eagle (northern world), Verreaux's eagle (Africa), and (experimentally) imperial eagle (Old World). Ten species of the genus *Falco* have been worked: the lanner or Barbary falcon (Europe and Africa), saker (Eurasia), prairie falcon (North America), laggar or jugger (Asia), gyrfalcon, peregrine and merlin (northern world), hobby (Eurasia), common kestrel (Old World) and American kestrel.

Apart from these birds, a few owls have been successfully trained for falconry of a kind, and two shrikes have been taught to hawk little birds.

In Tien Shan range of Central Asia hawking remains an economic pursuit of Kirghiz and Tadzhik peoples of the U.S.S.R.

Left: young golden eagles are trained to the lure for at least a month before being entered to hare, wild goat, gazelle, corsac fox, even wolf

Right: eagle hooded on master's right fist (not left as in West). A good bird may take 30 to 50 valuable foxes a year; one veteran eagle, Alagym, once took 14 wolves in a day

Below: bronze falcon head from 7th c. B.C. Egypt may represent falconer's hood

Domestication

What was the first bird to be domesticated – fowl or pigeon? F. E. Zeuner's *History of Domesticated Animals* (1963) contains many profound and scholarly observations on early domestic birds, and establishes pretty conclusively that the rock pigeon was the first. All the stock of common domestic pigeons derives from this cliff- and cave-nesting species.

Zeuner thinks it likely, though unproved, that New Stone Age people bred pigeons: but the earliest proof of the rock pigeon (or dove) as a dooryard bird consists of terra-cotta figurines from the Halafian period at Arpachiyah in Iraq, which have been dated around 4500 B.C. Pigeons feature in all later cultures of the Near East – Assyrian, Minoan, Egyptian, Greek, Roman. In Greece by the fourth century B.C. several breeds were known.

In Roman times the pigeon seems to have been used as a message carrier, a custom which may have started around the time of the Pharaoh Rameses III (1204 B.C.); the Arabs had perfected a pigeon post in Baghdad by the twelfth century A.D., in Egypt by the thirteenth. The pigeon post was used effectively in warfare until World War I, and was not by any means entirely superseded by electronic devices in World War II, when French patriots sent information in plastic tubes on the legs of pigeons which promptly homed to the top story of a big department store in London's Oxford Street.

Pigeon-racing now involves millions of enthusiasts and tens of millions of birds. Homing pigeons now race courses of up to 500 miles at speeds about twice that of their wild ancestors, thanks to generations of effective breeding, loving care, training and management.

Other pigeons, or rather doves (such as turtle, Barbary and spotted dove), have been kept and trained for show and food since early times. But the next oldest domestic bird to the rock pigeon is probably the domestic fowl. Some authorities give it a multiple origin, but there is strong evidence that it may be descended only from the red jungle fowl and not partly from any of the other three species of jungle fowl in South-east Asia.

There is a difference of opinion among archaeologists as to what are the first undoubted images of domestic

Top: cormorants, now wild caught but in old days hatched out under fowls, are still used for night fishing by light of braziers. In estuary of Nagara River in Gifu, Japan, big Japanese cormorant, fished since fifth century, still dives on long necklines as tourist attraction. Similar fishery was operated in France and England with common cormorant in 17th century

Mid: mobile British army carrier pigeon cote of World War I

Below (l. to r.): figures from Mohenjo-Daro c. 2500–2800 B.C.; fowl; fowl with food dish; probable fighting cock; fowl; and dove from Arpachiyah, c. 4500 B.C.

fowls found in the digs of the ancient cities. The earliest known cities of India, Mohenjo-Daro and Harappa, are believed to have flourished between 3300 and 2500 B.C. In both cities clay figurines have been found which indicate that fowls were captive birds, and in Mohenjo-Daro bones which show that they were bred for size. Zeuner conservatively puts full domestication before 2000 B.C.

The culture of the fowl in old Egypt is rather mysterious. It seems likely that it was known to the earliest dynasties, but full domestication and use cannot be proved until the Ptolemaic times around 60 B.C.

The Biblical evidence shows that the fowl was possibly domesticated in Jerusalem, if not in Egypt, at the time of Solomon (tenth century B.C.). By the eighth century B.C. it was also a poultry bird in Assyria, Mesopotamia and the first Corinthian civilization on the Mediterranean shore. Much earlier – probably around 1500 B.C. – it had reached China, and by the seventh century B.C. had reached Japan in the east and perhaps even Greece, Sicily and Sardinia in the west. In the sixth century B.C. it was a farmyard bird of Turkey; in the fifth in Italy and Crete; in the fourth in Cyprus; in the first in France and Switzerland. Shortly after the birth of Christ, and before the Roman invasion, it was domesticated in England; by the third century A.D. in Central Europe; by the tenth on the Volga; by the thirteenth throughout Europe as far as Viking Scandinavia.

In early Greece and Rome particular breeds (Hadrian bantam, Italian, Tanagran, Chalcidian, Median, Delian, Rhodian, Alexandrian) were cultivated for both sport and table; but the best hens laid only 60 eggs a year (compared with the modern 200). At any rate, a foreshadowing existed of the present intensive poultry industry with over 200 breeds and a trade that has recently involved high diplomatic activity between the U.S., the world's greatest producer of bird protein, and Europe.

Several other game birds have been domesticated. In Japan a race of the common quail has been kept, with some skill, as a source of small but tasty eggs, and as cage birds some hen quail have attained an egg-output worthy of a domestic fowl – up to 200 a year.

Also cultivated in old classical times, though never truly domesticated, were rock partridge, common partridge, francolin and pheasant. The pheasant was a treasure in the aviaries of Greece, Rome and Ptolemaic Egypt, and may in Rome have started its long history as a half-wild game bird. Today the pheasant is quite capable of breeding and maintaining itself wild in habitats varying from those of England to the Dakotas (where it is a great biological success). It responds well to rearing by bantams and silkies and in much of its introduced range is supported by such propagation. The Romans almost certainly brought it to Britain: and its success in North America dates from as recently as the 1880s.

The Romans, too, probably brought the Indian peafowl to Britain. It had reached the Mediterranean by the days of Solomon, and Athens by about 450 B.C., where it fetched the equivalent of a thousand dollars a pair. It began to be bred in Italy in flocks from the time of Varro (116–27 B.C.), its eggs being often set under hens.

Today in many parts of the world this fantastic bird is kept and reared in semi-captivity in parks and gardens, no longer to be ceremonially eaten, as it was in royal feasts in England and Scotland until the 16th century, but ceremonially exhibited among borders of flowering plants imported and cultivated from lands as far.

Fossil evidence shows that one member of the Ethiopian family of the guineafowl extended into southern Europe in the late Pleistocene (p. 173). However, by civilized times this species, the helmeted guineafowl, was extinct outside Africa; but it seems to have been reintroduced to Greece around the 5th century B.C. and to lower Italy around the 4th. First bred in the early first century B.C. (Varro), it spread with the Roman empire to Germany and Britain, where a leg bone encircled by a metal ring was found at Silchester (p. 118).

From mosaics and other works of art we know it survived as a domestic bird in Turkey and Palestine until at least the 6th century A.D., and it appears on a Mesopotamian mural dated between 836 and 839. Although the bird was still known to English scholars of the 16th century, it seems to have become extinct as domestic poultry

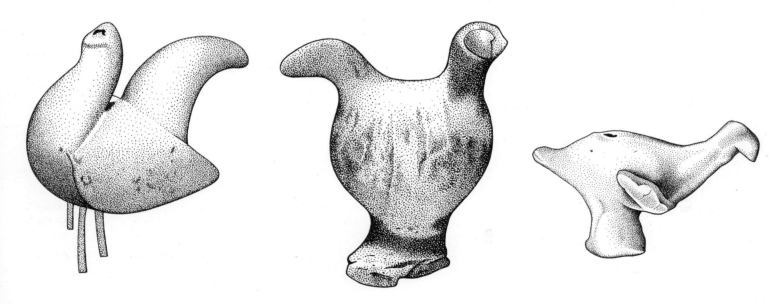

in Europe in the Middle Ages, only to be reintroduced by the Portuguese who discovered it south of the Sahara on the Guinea coast in 1455 and imported it into Europe a few decades later. Around 1550 it was re-domesticated in many places in France, but not before the first half of the 18th century in Germany, England and Italy.

The only domestic bird to have originated in the Americas, apart from the Muscovy duck, is the turkey. The Pueblo people of New Mexico and Arizona kept it at least fourteen hundred years ago. It was domesticated enough by Columbian times for early explorers to have noted white hens; though the conquistadores thought that they were peacocks. Early travelers, returning from México, brought the turkey with them and it was established in Europe in or before 1524: in England positively by 1541, probably before, in Germany by 1560. The name 'turkey' is a consequence of confusion with the guinea-fowl: several early importations of American birds were wrongly assigned to Old World sources in vernacular speech – no Muscovy duck ever originated in Moscow, nor macaw in Macao!

The mute swan has been a semi-domestic bird in Britain and other parts of Europe since the tenth century. But other members of its family are of greater importance as domestic birds. The gray lag goose of Europe may have been farmed almost as early as the pigeon and the fowl.

Stock was certainly reared from wild eggs or goslings on farms in eastern England until the gray lag became extinct there in the early 19th century: but for many centuries – back to Greek and Roman times – domestic strains larger than the wild ancestor have been maintained in Europe.

Homer's immortal account of the Trojan wars (c. 1200 B.C.) tells of Odysseus's wife Penelope keeping 20 geese, and records that some tame yard geese were white. Goose farming was a big business in Thessaly in 414 B.C. In the first century B.C. in Italy there was a large white farm breed and a *foie-gras* industry; geese were crammed on figs. In Pliny's time, a century later, geese were driven on foot to Roman markets all the way from Picardy, and there was a good trade in German goose down.

The theater of domestication of the gray lag was doubtless Europe, even though this goose, and the white-front too, seem to have been well known and probably at least fattened, if not truly domesticated, in the farm-yards of ancient Egypt.

It is also likely that the ancient Egyptians truly domesticated their own native breeding Egyptian goose, recognizably figured on their monuments back to around 2000 B.C., and that this bird also had a period of domestication in Greece from the fifth century B.C. In Aristotle's time its eggs were held second only in palatability to those of the much-prized peafowls.

The only New World duck ever to have been domesticated is the Muscovy of tropical America. The beginnings of its culture among the Amerindians are lost in uncertainty; but domestic stocks were already variable in early post-Columbian days and it was already well-known in Europe in the late 16th century.

By far the most successful of the anatids, with a modern industry depending on it second only to the fowl industry, is the common domestic duck, a descendant of the mallard. As with the gray lag, the mallard's origins as a true domestic bird are uncertain. It features as very small figures in the same early Mesopotamian culture as does the domestic pigeon. Possibly the theaters of its development as a farm bird were Germany in the West and China in the East.

One bird may fairly be said to be the only new domestic bird of the 20th century. The budgerigar of Australia was imported into England by the naturalist John Gould in 1840. Soon established in the aviaries of Europe, it proved a prolific breeder in captivity. From 1864 on its stock began to produce color variations differing from the natural parrot green. Today, with hundreds of color forms (whose genetics are well known) ranging from white to yellow or almost pink, from cobalt to moss green and gray, the 'budgie' is the world's most popular cage bird. It breeds more freely, and (learning, as it can, to talk) proves more entertaining than the canary, which is the only passerine bird ever truly domesticated.

The canary *does* come from the Canary Islands, where it is the local replacement of a fairly widespread finch, the serin. It was mentioned for the first time in a treatise of 1558, not much more than 70 years after the first conquest of the islands. In that same century it reached England and Germany, where the most popular breeds (Norwich, Yorkshire, Hartz Mountain, Roller) evolved. Canaries have, throughout their domestic existence, been bred for show and song, and for nothing more, but have reached a considerable variety.

A bounty of broiler and battery bargains, bred in boxes for breakfast and banquet. We neither condemn nor praise the industrialization of poultry. We report it. Here we show scenes from European poultry factories; in Britain alone, from a fowl stock around 90 million, 11 billion eggs and nearly 200 million chickens are produced each year. The U.S. laying flock of 300 million produces 64 billion eggs and 2 billion broilers

Left: Norfolk turkey farm; Britain produces 6 million table birds yearly

Above: an English egg battery; layers see no sun or earth; on far right, its daily harvest

Near right: Belgian goose-stuffing machine; end product, the profitable pâté de foie gras

Aviculture

In this short history of bird domestication we can also trace the rise of aviculture, as we know it today: the keeping of birds for pleasure and show. Often, as in the royal courts of Egypt, Greece and Rome, ornamental birds were status symbols. Birds became fancied as birds: the zoo and the aviary evolved.

The 'fancy' of captive wild birds, as opposed to domestication, probably started in earnest in the fourth millennium B.C. in Egypt, where there seem to have been zoos in the earliest dynasties, importing exotic animals down the Nile. Queen Hatshepsut, in about 1500 B.C., sent an expedition to collect live animals from Somaliland, or the land of Punt as it was then called. Around 1200 B.C. there were zoos of a sort in ancient China. In Babylonia, Assyria and ancient Palestine kings like Solomon (about 950 B.C.) did a big trade in mammals and birds with friendly monarchs; and we learn that both Assur-bani-pal (*c.* 650 B.C.) and Nebuchadnezzar (*c.* 580 B.C.) were royal zoo proprietors.

In the sixth century B.C. there is evidence that showy birds like purple gallinules were exhibited in Samos; and in the Greek realm a century later sparrows, nightingales, blackbirds, magpies, and starlings were favorite cage birds. In 414 B.C., when *The Birds* was first produced in Athens, the flamingo was known, perhaps even in captivity; Aristophanes makes it say 'torotix, torotix' (which last year gave our colleague Pierce Brodkorb inspiration

for the name for a genus of fossil, flamingo-like birds, *Torotix*). Hoopoes were well known, and probably kept as cage birds: live jackdaws, crows and coots could be bought in the market, though perhaps the last were bought to eat.

The zoo birds and cage birds which have had perhaps the greatest appeal are the members of the parrot family. Colorful, and most versatile of all the avian talkers, they were doubtless first caged by the ancient kings of India. However, they penetrated west less fast than the domestic fowl. No Greek seems to have written about them until 401 B.C., when Ctesias visited the court of Persia, and made so excellent a description of a talking bird that it can be confidently identified as the blossom-headed parakeet, which nowadays ranges naturally no further west than northern India.

Alexander the Great encountered the parrot family on his invasion of India, and in about 323 B.C. his officer Nearchus appears to have made the first importation into Greece of what were either Alexandrine or ring-necked parakeets.

There were plenty of parrots (or parakeets) in the great procession of Ptolemy II at Alexandria in about 280 B.C., no doubt borrowed for the day from the first almost scientific zoo established in that city – a zoo which lasted for at least a century and a half. A century later the birds were so popular in Rome that Cato the elder (who disapproved of most things new) protested at 'our men carrying parrots in their hands'. Trained talkers were valuable in the time of the emperor Augustus; when, as Octavian, he returned to Rome after the defeat of Mark Antony in 29 B.C., he bought a parrot that had been taught to greet him.

Probably the talking parrots of his time were still only the ring-necked parakeets found in Asia and Africa, possibly also the Alexandrine and blossom-headed species which belong to the same genus. These are not 'sophisticated talkers'; and the triumphal general appears to have spent much more – about the equivalent of 450 dollars – on a raven which had been made to say '*Ave, Caesar Victor Imperator*'. (The trainer had taught another bird to say '*Ave, Victor Imperator Antoni*', just in case the campaign in Egypt had gone the other way!) In A.D. 77 Pliny gave so accurate a description of the most popular parrot of the day in Italy that we can be sure it was the ring-necked parakeet, figured (pp. 109, 142) on the walls of a house at Pompeii where he must have dined. The half-crazed emperor Elagabalus, who ruled from 218 to 222, fed parrots to his lions, and ate their brains himself. (He was a great bird-brain eater; he even ate flamingo brains.) By the time of the Crusades parrots of various kinds had spread west to the houses of the nobles of Europe and the withdrawing rooms of their ladies, and even to ecclesiastical cloisters. By the Columbian voyages (which brought the first macaws) and the Renaissance, wealthy merchants all over the civilized world had become parrot-fanciers.

To retrace our steps: early Greek and Roman aviculture, essentially husbandry, nevertheless experimented widely with birds for birds' sake. We hear of caged owls in Athens in the early fourth century B.C.; of many songbirds in Varro's aviary at Casinum in Italy a century later. His friend Lucullus's aviary at Tusculum seems to have been the first known 'walk-through aviary', for the great gourmet had a dining-room in which many birds flew free, while the diners regaled themselves on fattened thrushes and ortolans.

Roman aviculture was an abiding hobby of the rich until the fall of the Empire, and the copious poetry and prose of this realm is full of birds, not all easy to identify. Lesbia's sparrow, of which Catullus wrote toward the middle of the first century, was probably a bullfinch; others kept goldfinches. Not only parakeets and ravens were taught to talk, but also crows, magpies, starlings and even, apparently, at least one thrush. The capercaillie, found 'difficult' even by the zoo keepers of today, was kept in the days of Caligula, but was inclined, Pliny says, to mope to death. A 'phoenix' shown in Rome in A.D. 47 or 48 may have been a golden pheasant from the Far East. A white nightingale fetched the equivalent of over 100 dollars.

Some of the Roman animal collections were vast. That of Augustus in 29 B.C. had more individual mammals in

it (and on the average much larger ones) than the largest collection of mammals in captivity today (West Berlin's 1,093), as well as numbers of birds and reptiles.

It is possible that the ancient Romans performed at least one avicultural feat that has been repeated only in recent decades: the breeding of flamingos. George Jennison, the zoologist-historian, believes that this was done in the Augustan age.

After Roman times we hear of many regal zoo proprietors and aviary builders all over the world; among them Harun al Raschid, a famous sultan of Baghdad (A.D. 797), the great Khan Kublai at Xanadu in the 13th century, the Aztec kings of México. In England the first zoo was established in the early 12th century by Henry I at Woodstock, near Oxford. It was stocked with various mammals from Europe and Africa, and included ostriches. The royal collection was moved to the Tower of London in the middle of the 13th century, at the time of Henry III; and if we regard its few traditional ravens as constituting a 'zoo', the Tower is the oldest surviving zoological garden in the world.

Collections of living animals burgeoned during the age of exploration that began at the end of the 15th century. By the end of the next century the wealthy of western Europe often had garden aviaries full of exotics from five continents. Famous zoos of that period were those of Pope Leo X at the Vatican and of Augustus I, king of Poland and elector of Saxony, at Dresden.

The oldest zoo (excluding the aviary at the Tower) and still in its ancient glory (with some fine modern improvements) is the menagerie at Schönnbrunn in Vienna, built in 1752 by the Holy Roman Emperor Franz Josef of Austria for his wife Maria Theresa. There are now close on 450 zoos (including aquaria) in the world; but only 22 are over 100 years old. Collections of living exotic birds can be seen by the public in at least 73 countries.

In 1961, the last year for which we have statistics, the greatest living bird collection in the world was London's, with 689 species, closely followed by the Bronx, in New York, with 640; the rest of the top ten were San Diego, Copenhagen, Antwerp, Rome, West Berlin, Wassenaar (Holland), Washington D.C., and Amsterdam, in that order. The top ten in size, rather than rarity, of collection were Wellington (New Zealand), with 3,104 individual specimens, followed by Cairo, Askania-Nova (U.S.S.R.), Sydney, Lisbon, Pretoria, San Diego, Alexandria, Hamburg and Nishinomaya (Japan).

Several of the great bird zoos have followed the example of Rome, where nearly thirty years ago a hundred-foot, many-sided stainless steel flight cage was built for long-legged marsh birds (ibises, storks, herons) in which they could freely wheel in flocks. They have built huge new aviaries of considerable architectural imagination, often with indoor and outdoor spaces into which the public can walk among the birds, as they did in the days of Lucullus. In some aviaries the birds are lit, the public space is dark, and the 'cages' have neither bars nor glass. The stock keeps to its own enclosures partly by its natural territorial disposition, partly because it has no urge to fly into the dark. Fine new 'flights', in which the public can walk and birds of many species sing and even breed, can be seen in Perth (Australia), Antwerp, West Berlin, Frankfurt, Hamburg, London, Chester, Wassenaar, Zürich, San Diego, St. Louis, and several other zoos.

The remarkable collection founded by Peter Scott and the Wildfowl Trust at Slimbridge in Gloucestershire had no less than 122 of the 146 living species of swans, geese and ducks at our last visit; and many of the birds were free-winged, tied to their ponds by food and territory alone.

In 1954 it was calculated that the world population of the Hawaiian goose or néné was only 68. Early in 1962 it was 432, over six times as many. (See p. 141.) This is largely due to the Wildfowl Trust, which acquired a male and two females in 1950–51. From the progeny of these, and from their progeny's progeny, they have been distributed over European and American zoos and even lately restored to the Hawaiian island of Maui on which they had become extinct.

Zoos and aviaries can, indeed, do their share to restore the fallen fortunes of wild birds. The breeding of pheasants in captivity is now as well organized as the breeding of wildfowl – and we can be comforted by the fact that such rare Asian species as the imperial, Edwards's, Swinhoe's and mikado pheasants, disappearing in the wild, have sound captive populations in Western collections.

Left: modern Rome, where nearly 30 years ago this hundred-foot many-sided stainless steel flight cage was built for long-legged marsh birds (ibises, storks, herons) in which they can freely wheel in flocks

Right and below: cock fighting, as a sport, may go back 4½ millennia to early India. In Bali today cocking remains extremely popular; in upper photo owners set birds to test aggressiveness, on left attach blades to feet. Right photo shows a (probably illegal) contest, or 'mains', in Austria

Coins are 1. Silver drachm, Sicily, 5th century B.C., with cock; 2. Bronze, Campania, Italy, 3rd c. B.C., with cock; 3. Silver, Asia Minor, 5th c. B.C., cocks with spurs; 4. Reverse of 1., with hen

1.
2.

3.
4.

Probably more than half the world's birds have already been bred by aviculturists, well-organized with fine journals and societies to spread the knowhow among their fellows. Modern zoos and big aviaries are no longer slums where birds of prey linger for years in cages too small for them, or hummingbirds are ordered by the dozen every season to replace the dead; nor are they dedicated to spectacles or to the satisfaction of collectors' instincts. They are, for the most part, places where the public can learn ornithology and where the proprietors and staff are dedicated to that end. Over 4 million visit the zoos of México City and Pekin every year; over 3 million those of Barcelona, Tokyo, Buenos Aires and Cairo.

The study of the captive bird is essential to our science, and to the preservation of its wonderful material. People who think – as some still do – that birds and other animals are bound to pine for a lost 'freedom' cannot understand much about the animal mind, or want to know about the techniques that curators are working out to secure a healthy and congenial life for every bird. Such people just cannot have visited a modern zoo.

Cock fighting

Our two oldest domestic birds have been long involved in special sports. Pigeon-racing we know (p. 250). Cock fighting, which dates back to the fifth century B.C., has, with the evolution of human ethics, been prohibited in the British Isles since 1849, and in some parts of North America since 1836. However, sporting gentlemen in both western Europe and the Americas still attend the 'mains', legally or illegally, and wager money in the grand style of ancient Rome. The sport still flourishes in Asia.

About a dozen strains of fighting cocks are still bred in this twentieth century with close attention to pedigrees. At secret mains in northern England or in the south-eastern U.S., gamecocks still fight, to death or rare submission, with metal spurs, in traditional cockpits, for the entertainment of gamblers bent on re-creating the brutal sporting atmosphere of the early nineteenth century. In so far as few of these cocking aficionados remain, ornithologists can celebrate the passing of one of the most callous exploitations of the drives and natural behavior of male game birds.

Hunting and management

Around 1850 refined, efficient breech-loading shotguns with percussion-fired cartridges came into fairly wide use. We have had modern hunting since then over the world.

For rather over a century man's potential as a predator has been fantastic, and his own increase in numbers, skill, wealth and leisure, has put him in a new relationship with the larger or more edible wild birds. Of these he is now *the* predator, the great cropper. In England alone one small party, in one day, has shot 3,937 pheasants, another 2,929 red grouse, another 2,119 partridges.

Like the older seafowlers, the modern hunter has evolved rules and laws to govern his own impact and power. But to say that man's self-denying ordinances of sporting custom, game laws and conservation have been ever perfect is far from the truth.

The fate of the two maincrop wild pigeons of North America is a case in point. The last and most intensive years of the exploitation of the now extinct passenger pigeon were between 1866 and 1896. It was estimated that 1,200,000 were slaughtered on an average in each of these years. The estimated peak total population of the species rather earlier in the century was between 3 and 5 billion (p. 112). In proportion to this the crop was not high: yet the stock collapsed.

On the other hand, the mourning dove, which has never swarmed, has a fairly stable population far, far lower than that of the passenger pigeon in its heyday; yet lately the annual hunter's crop has been estimated at 4 million! At the opening of the season in California in September 1963 no less than 25,000 dove hunters fanned out in the 900-square-mile Imperial Valley alone, each with a daily bag limit of 10. There is no evidence (yet) that the mourning dove is on the way out: the demise of the passenger pigeon may well have been due to the destruction by hunting not simply of its populations but of its own, close, overspecialized social system.

All this shows that shooting pressures have unpredictable results. The mourning dove *may* be able to stand as great a cropping as the passenger pigeon, and survive.

Educated and wealthy though Western man has been through the century of the sophisticated shotgun and the record bag, he has lacked the ancient experience and lore of the finest seafowlers. He has been stupid, greedy and unforeseeing; egocentric, proud and masterful; has banged his way around marsh, moor, hedgerow and woodland as if he owned the earth.

Man does not own the earth, or any part of it, save his home and tools: of nature he is but the inheritor, the central node of a transient web, alone capable of knowing what he is doing. There would be few problems if so many did not *want* to know, and cared not for the consequences.

The problems are in fact complex and legion. Even though devoted students of animal ecology are now of a

third generation in the wildlife services, the necessity for management – which goes far beyond laws and their enforcement into the sphere of applied morality – is only beginning to dawn on (for example) the nation that nurtured Audubon, the kingdom that kindled Gilbert White, the republic that raised Rousseau, the Germany that gave us Goethe.

Game managers control the environment mainly by planting or supplying the birds' favored food and by judiciously manipulating the cover and (if necessary) the drainage. Most modern wildlife technicians eschew the attitude of the traditional Scottish gamekeeper who eliminated all predators. And most biologists are cautious about introducing birds to places which lie outside their present range, unless it seems biologically desirable – for instance, in an area that presents a vacant ecological niche.

Game management of a sort was practiced in Mongolia in the time of the Khans, and was known in fifteenth-century Europe in the time of Frederick II. But as a science it is young. Its operations may sound simple: in practice they need deep research, sensible relations between ecologists and hunters, and quite a lot of tough political maneuvering.

Refuges, especially necessary for migratory wildfowl, date in the U.S.A. from 1870; in Britain, on an official

Of all gun hunters, modern wildfowlers have perhaps best inherited ancient sporting lore and a code of chivalry toward their prey. A few hunt bag-mad, but most rate the atmosphere of their hardy sport as high as achievement, despite the evolution of their weapons' lethal powers. Western wildfowlers, now mostly organized in disciplined associations and clubs, pay great attention to safety and humanity in their shooting, drill novices with benign severity, and cooperate wholeheartedly with government law enforcement officers and conservation programs. In England no record duck bag has been scored since 1913, or record goose bag in the present century. In North America long cooperation between Canada (where many wildfowl breed) and the U.S. (where many winter and are shot) can secure, and has under the present licensing system largely secured, a stable human predation on a fairly stable stock; but the pressure of increasing hunters has to be very carefully watched

Left: masked English wildfowler in typical lakeside duck-hide (in U.S., 'blind')

Right: punt gives scope for shooting from natural reed cover; guns are using 5-shell (cartridge) pump-action repeating 12-gauge (bore) scatterguns (shotguns) probably loaded with BB or other heavy pellets

scale, only from after World War II. The British grouse survey published in 1911, and forever associated with the work of Edward Wilson, who died with Scott in the Antarctic, paid early attention to disease. In the U.S. Herbert Stoddard, who published his famous book on the bobwhite in 1931, finally began to convince hunters that game stock depended on habitat management.

It was in the 'thirties, too, that the late Paul Errington made what was then a most revolutionary observation. 'Too often', he commented, 'the persecution of predators – however futile – is the one thing that is stressed in the name of conservation, whereas measures of the utmost merit are barely toyed with, if not disregarded altogether'. Errington's point was that natural predation was not, in most cases, any sort of threat to the prey 'which, barring drastic change in environment, will continue to occupy all livable quarters and produce the usual annual surplus. . . . Whether taken by predators or otherwise lost, the surplus must disappear; population sooner or later coincides with carrying capacity'.

The population of every bird basically depends on the amount and accessibility of feed. It is the numbers of predators that depend on the numbers of their prey – not *vice versa*. Indeed, predators are necessary to the well-being of wildlife, because of their tendency to cull the

weaker stock; though this idea of natural pruning was once regarded, as the late P. A. Taverner put it, 'as one of those highly speculative theories in which detached scientists like to indulge but which common sense rejects'.

The birds of prey are on top of the pyramid of life, dependent only on their prey for survival; in a vulnerable position. Despite the fact that Britain has accepted the Erringtonian position and, as of 1933, totally protected every last buzzard, hawk, eagle, falcon or owl that could cast a shadow over its islands, and that in the same year 19 of the United States protected all raptors, 26 at least some and only 3 none, the birds of prey are declining almost everywhere, not so much for lack of food as for a more unnatural and sinister reason that we will presently (p. 266) discuss.

But at least the vast majority of the English-speaking world, and of the sporting and game-loving countries of Europe, is now no longer a prey to the medieval superstition that man cannot tolerate a rival predator, and recognizes that, to quote the late Aldo Leopold, 'the fight over predator control is no mere conflict of interest between field-glass hunters and gun hunters. It is a fight between those who seek utility and beauty in the biota as a whole, and those who see utility and beauty only in pheasants or trout'.

Above: in North America more people now go bird watching than shoot ducks. This has inevitably resulted in governmental projects such as this one where a non-game bird is the target species. In Michigan three 4,000-acre tracts are now managed for the rare Kirtland's warbler by state and federal agencies.

Left: punt gunners have now almost given up the vast, destructive fixed cannon that have killed up to 90 wigeon or 443 knot with one shot. Clad suitably for a winter estuary, this wildfowler is using a heavy 4-gauge shoulder gun which packs punch but not wholesale slaughter.

Right: gibbet on keeper's hut in Devon, with remains of 8 buzzards, 2 sparrowhawks, a magpie and (parts of) a crow: mute evidence of some men's continued intolerance of rival predators and ignorance of their true place in nature. Gibbets still desecrate British estates, despite the total protection of hawks

The aficionados of biota are now beginning to out-number those of the chase. Bird watching is becoming more popular than hunting. The nature lobby has become as powerful as, or a little more powerful than (though not particularly anxious to quarrel with) the game lobby.

At last we can recognize a climate of public opinion that is no longer utilitarian about nature: that demands all nature; that is more concerned about the fate of Britain's only colony of avocets than whether protection should be removed from the brent goose; would rather know that rare Kirtland's warbler flourished happily in the jack-pine barrens of Michigan than get a better duck quota for their license season. Many wildfowl hunters share this view.

After years of preaching by Audubonites and their equivalent in other lands, the cult of the useless is coming to power – useless flowers, useless butterflies, useless war-blers and singing birds, useless hawks, useless fossils, useless wilderness: all the useless things that by their very useless-ness are useful, indeed redeeming and refreshing and needful to the human spirit. In the forefront stride the ornithologists, acolytes of gloriously useless animals whose going would leave the world a colorless and silent place.

What the world is beginning to demand, and with its burgeoning human population (which will double before half its readers of this book are dead) must for its own safety demand, is a general ecological management of its living sheath, in which the tending of game and other natural resources will be an essential part of the activity; but in its planned place in a new scale of values.

There is heartening evidence of this trend. Foresters, particularly in Germany, are switching from lifeless (but profitable) spruce biota back to the old mixed woodland with its dawn chorus. In the U.S. the Fish and Wildlife Service is engaging researchers not only for game but for general wildlife programs. In Britain exploitable sporting birds have no special niche in the affairs of the Nature Conservancy, apart from wildfowl refuges; funds are pro-vided for the long-term study of bird migration and the stocks of interesting, useless birds. Led, if not driven, by private national and international groups, governments are at last moving, as Leopold (a quarter of a century ago) believed they might, 'to preserve samples of original biota as standards against which to measure the effects of violence'.

Some recent violence needs no yard-stick. The dust bowls produced in our northern hemisphere by only a few generations of bad land management will be visible to the naked eye of the first man to land on the moon; and if he knows his ecological geography he will be able to identify, too, the latest slashes and clearings in the world's great forests. Each such area represents the total des-truction of many living communities, each with its own complex pyramid of life (birds included) and the substi-tution of others, more simple and usually less stable.

It is because the community matters, and not some unimportantly edible member of it, that our energies must go to save the present biota from further erosion. Erosion need not be by agricultural violence; it can be subtle.

When civilization of the Western kind first came to the Hawaiian Isles they had a most interesting natural community of about 64 species of breeding birds. Today the list is about 86. A gain? No less than 36 of the 86 are introduced aliens, and no less than 14 of the indigenous native birds of the islands have become extinct – more than on any other archipelago in the world. That human agriculture and forest cutting accounted for some of them seems certain. That the competition of the introduced aliens extinguished others is less easy to prove, but seems very likely (p. 56). Man, especially colonizing man, has for long had an urge to populate his new homes with exotics. For once, these really *are* useless birds. New Zealand suffered similarly, though not quite so badly: before the colonization, about 148 breeding species: now, about 177; successfully introduced, 35; extinct, at least 6. At a conservative estimate about 125 species of *all* the world's birds have been introduced somewhere quite out of their range. Starlings and house sparrows have by this means subsequently colonized whole continents. Some carefully thought out introductions have been useful, and we judge that about half the introducing human agents may have had a bit of sense, or at least did no harm. But the mistaken and harmful rest were ecological trouble-makers and had no idea at all of the balance of nature or – to use a better expression – the precarious pyramid of life in an old and fairly stable community.

Locust birds

Certain land birds are capable of almost locust-like behavior – swarming in hundreds of thousands or even millions. The famous Swiss brambling flocks of 1950, though probably much overestimated at 72 million, fit this category, but the top locust bird of the world must be the red-billed quelea of Africa. This weaver is widely distributed throughout the open veldt and acacia scrub of most of that continent south of the Sahara. The nesting colonies may occupy every thorn tree (up to 5,000 nests per tree) in areas up to 3,000 acres; the larger ones have been estimated at 10 million nests. After fledging, such a colony may number 40 million. They are undoubtedly the biggest social groups of birds since the days of the passenger pigeon.

Land birds whose flocks may exceed a hundred thousand are known among the sand grouse, pigeons, parrots, thrushes, weavers, waxbills, icterids, starlings and crows. A few species in these families are often rated as pest birds.

'Pest' like 'vermin' is a pejorative word. It has often been unfairly attached. But there is no doubt that in the present state of agriculture, a few birds are serious problems: the greatest, beyond doubt, is the quelea. It did not really become a widespread problem in Africa until modern large-block cultivation of grains began to supplant small-scale crops. In parts of East Africa the queleas have sometimes taken two-thirds of the local wheat crop; in Senegal and South Africa they damage rice and sorghum. Control is far from easy. Nesting colonies have been destroyed by flame-throwers; roosts have been bombed and napalmed. Researchers have tried biological control by disease, chemical control by toxic sprays, poisoned gas and water; and physical control by recorded alarm calls and ultrasonics, designed to keep adults from their nests.

Also astronomical are the numbers of icterids and starlings in the winter 'blackbird' roosts in the south-eastern United States. Roosts estimated to contain 15 or 16 million birds have been recently studied at Slovac in Arkansas, at Dismal Swamp in Virginia and at Rome in Georgia. Predominant is the red-winged blackbird, found to number about 10 million at Dismal Swamp during the Christmas count of 1960. At the roost in Rome in 1962 Brewer's blackbird numbered nearly 4 million, the grackle about 2.3 million, the cowbird about 1.6 million and the rusty blackbird about 675,000 – record flocks for these

four. The European starling numbered about 2 million at a mixed roost at Nashville, Tennessee (English roosts may occasionally number around 3 million).

No rice was grown in Arkansas state until 1902: but lately around half a million acres have been cultivated. Old style farms have evolved into modern food factories. Ten years ago a team of researchers agreed that in Arkansas alone the vast flocks of icterids took a yearly toll of nearly a quarter of a million bushels of rice worth from half a million to a million dollars or more.

All over the south-eastern United States the swarms of redwings, grackles, cowbirds and starlings now give concern to farmers, state and federal authorities and conservationists alike. But if it had been available instead to humans the grain they have already eaten in the whole of the present century cannot be worth a billion dollars. Relatively, this is chicken feed, or rather blackbird feed; though no sensible economic conservationist can deny Arkansas ricemen the right to use any humane methods to reduce the depredations.

One of us spent four years measuring the effect of increased food-factory farming in Britain in World War II on the rook population, and *vice versa*. The new grain-growing produced an increase in the population of Britain's commonest large passerine of the order of a quarter; and about half the grain the rooks ate would otherwise have been eaten by man.

Few bird pest problems are at present clearly soluble: they are largely political – political in the sense that big steals by birds tend to be from *individual* farmers who may really suffer, but that steals by birds evened out over the total food-raising industry are almost negligible in comparison to the total crop.

If half the American icterids were exterminated, the food loss would be halved: but the political problem would not. It is probably something we must live with until farming *methods* themselves change further – and specially if they show a return to the older diversity from the newer, one-crop production pitches (big enough to be sprayed from the air) that have swept away so many woods, spinneys, hedges, marshes, thickets, ponds and prairie corners.

Modern farming techniques nakedly invite locust birds. Yet the farmers who complain the most are usually first to plant the crop again. If they want their profit they must pay the bird tax. If we want cheaper bread and cereal food (in a Western world which can scarce store its surplus) we must pay the bird tax, too. If we do not want to pay it, we have only to return to a more joyous, lovely, natural and – in the long run – biologically sounder and more balanced landscape. At present big farm business, private or collective, does not like the idea very much. But it would be good business. Locust birds are no more than the indicators of agriculture's overreachment.

Perils and poisons

Man now numbers more than 3 billion on this planet. As his burgeoning populations soar on toward 4 billion, there will be more and more direct conflicts with birds.

Man-made structures – lighthouses, high buildings, radio towers – stand as hazards to migrating birds at night or in fog and take a serious toll of their numbers as we have already shown (p. 126). Birds die in thousands by hitting television towers; 20,000 were killed in one night in September 1957. Ornithologists, regretting this toll, nevertheless find the birds so killed useful for analysis. Those whose scientific duty it has been to study the kills at airport ceilometers, whose powerful reflecting beams measure the height of clouds at night, and which can result in the death of up to 50,000 birds a night, will be the first to applaud any device that can reduce these casualties. Some lighthouses in Britain have been floodlit by arrangement with protection societies, and this has provedly saved lives; but floodlighting may actually lure birds to death at other kinds of towers.

Birds and aircraft have found themselves in collision ever since the early days of aviation. The unwitting enemies of flying men have brought several airliners with their human freight to tragic doom and killed ornithologists in light aircraft. From World War II on, airfields have been cleared of birds by all sorts of devices from trained peregrines to amplified alarm calls. Plane killers like starlings and gulls have been the subjects of research programs, notably at Boston Airport, situated disadvantageously between a garbage dump and the Fish-picks.

The albatrosses of Midway Island were under sentence of death as menaces to the runways until public protest inspired research. By bulldozing the big sand-dunes off the end of the main runway (where the birds soared on the updraughts) aircraft damage was reduced by four-fifths. But birds and flocks of birds continue to hit aircraft and sometimes to be sucked into jets. The more crowded our air channels become and the more this hazard increases, the more we realize that the most sensible answer may well be the redesign of aircraft, or of their engine intakes. This thought is neither crazy nor is it, in the long run, necessarily uneconomic.

One aspect of human filthiness has brought millions of sea birds to an untimely end – the dumping of waste oil. Oil-burning and oil-carrying ships (tankers) still are tempted to dump waste residue into the sea. But international agreement to install separators and stop dumping at sea has recently been arrived at, after many decades of procrastination. At least a hundred thousand sea birds were found oiled around Britain's coasts in the bad winter of 1951–52; and there were big kills off Sweden, Denmark, Holland and Belgium. Some east Atlantic auk colonies were reduced to a small fraction of their normal population at that time and have been recovering rather slowly since. Similar tragedies have been known on the coasts of North America.

By far the greatest threat to birds in all the years of man's history is the recent and still undisciplined use of pesticides.

In Germany in 1874, an organic chemical called dichloro-diphenyl-trichloro-ethane was first synthesized in a routine series of explorations of the properties of carbon-containing molecules. It was a chlorinated hydrocarbon of no great complexity or molecule size. Its preparation techniques lay buried in scientific journals, but not until 1939 did Paul Müller of Switzerland discover that DDT (for short) was one of the most powerful insecticides known. With it, one of the minor horrors of war, the swarming of the insect parasites of man, was effectively removed. Müller got a Nobel Prize.

First used in powder form on humans, DDT had then no ill effects. It can in this state hardly be absorbed through the skin. But it was soon found that dissolved in oils and fats it was a marvelous insecticide for agricultural spraying. Even more effective were some of the swarm of related hydrocarbons that were quickly synthesized. It is possible that as many as 50,000 pesticides may now be in use: more than twenty times as many as were known before World War II. To quote Rachel Carson, 'the production of synthetic pesticides in the United States soared from 124,259,000 pounds in 1947 to 637,666,000 pounds in 1960 – more than a five-fold increase. The wholesale value of these products was well over a quarter of a billion dollars'.

Nearly all of these poisons dissolve in the body fat of the animals that eat them. Twenty years ago, when the rain of chemicals was a spray and not a deluge, the U.S. Public Health Service went on record with its concern that DDT and other chlorinated hydrocarbons might have an effect on the animals that preyed on insects. As long ago as 1945 it was proved that five pounds of DDT to the acre kills nesting bird life, that one pound does not, and that two pounds will do so if continued for five consecutive years.

The chemical fall-out, the monstrous bath emptied over civilized and backward countries alike from Europe to North America, from Africa to the Solomon Islands, is the creature of the chemical industry. It is Frankensteinian; the industry knew not what it was making, or at least not the consequences. Its effort, we hasten to say, was dedicated as much to service as to profit, backed by every agricultural department of every government, and demanded by farmers. In her famous book *Silent Spring* Rachel Carson has argued, emotionally (why not?) and overwhelmingly, that the poison deluge may have created more problems than it has solved. That spray poisons *can* work without danger to wildlife is true. That they

have been so applied is generally false. The *biological* control of pests, known to be effective when properly contrived, has been gravely neglected during the poison syndrome.

Some of the more spectacular mistakes have now become classic skull-and-crossbone warnings. We could mention the DDT spruce budworm campaign in Canada which ruined the salmon population of the Miramichi River for years; or the notorious fire ant campaign in the southern states in the late 'fifties. The latter campaign, for the chemical industry, was, by the admission of their own trade journals, a 'sales bonanza'. It was directed at an alleged pest, introduced after World War I at Mobile, Alabama. Its pest status, however, is doubtful. Yet at the start of the notorious fire ant campaign, heptachlor and dieldrin, hydrocarbons respectively 10 and 60 times stronger than DDT in their toxicity, were broadcast at two pounds to the acre. Fortunately the campaign never soaked the 27 million acres it aimed at; but it started in 1958 with a million, and killed almost every sort of domestic poultry and mammal, many wild mammals, in places at least half the birds, including nearly all the ground birds, meadowlarks, quail and turkeys. The U.S. Department of Agriculture (responsible for the campaign) gave an imitation of an ostrich, burying its head in the sand. It took the birds a full three years to recover. The fire ants survived. So did the pesticide companies.

A fungus, borne by bark beetles, has fatally attacked elms in North America. DDT seemed the cheap solution to the decline of this favorite tree in the Middle West with seventeen, twenty-four, even once a hundred pounds to the acre. Result: elm disease continues; and in places there was a ninety per cent mortality of breeding passerines (they have since recovered). Meanwhile a lot of robins were watched dying with pesticide tremors on university campuses (at least a million died in the Midwest); and it was discovered that methoxychlor could have been used instead. This does not kill birds: but DDT is cheaper, and DDT is still used widely.

Hydrocarbon pesticides murder differentially, because they mostly have a long life without chemical breakdown, and *accumulate* in soil and water, and in the bodies of all members of the animal pyramid based upon the earthworms, plankton, insects and other invertebrates of the soil and water. In Clear Lake in California DDT was applied, with several treatments within eight years at 20 parts a million, to kill gnats. It did. It was also eaten and concentrated 250 times by the water plankton, the tiny invertebrate animals. It was found in 500 times concentration in the small fishes that ate the plankton. It killed most of the western grebes that ate the fishes, and they died with an 80,000 times concentration.

Those birds at the top of the pyramid are particularly vulnerable, for they take poison biologically concentrated by their prey and their prey's prey. In Britain the hydrocarbon syndrome seems to be the only factor that can account for the terrible decline of the peregrine's breeding success to a tenth of what it was a decade ago. The same catastrophe has overtaken the North American peregrine population.

In the last few years one of the greatest concentrations of breeding ospreys in the world – near the mouth of the Connecticut River (p. 99) – has failed to raise more than a few young. In the addled eggs, three lethal hydrocarbons. In Scotland, to which the osprey has returned only recently, the first second-generation pair had infertile eggs in 1963. In the eggs: again three kinds of toxic hydrocarbons.

Peregrines and ospreys have long life spans and are slow breeders. They are not like the small songbirds that quickly recover from a crash. The decline of the birds of prey is not safely reversible, and bald eagles, golden eagles, ospreys, peregrines, short-winged hawks too, are putative dodos, if we do not alter our ways.

There are tiny signs now that ways *can* alter. New Zealand, whose export meat has been held up at ports through pesticide contamination, has totally banned at least six of the most powerful hydrocarbons from all its farms. Will Europe and the U.S. have to learn the same hard way? We fear they may, but ask why. Is the fate of wild animals not reason enough?

Survival

Man has become the most dangerous, the most lethal animal upon the face of the earth. Poisonous, he can, through his endless proliferation of toxic chemicals, change his venom, a thing no snake can do. But he may not be immune to his own venom. He is also the filthiest animal that ever evolved and lived, polluting the streams, the sea and the air.

We believe that now man has the power to destroy nature and himself almost totally, he has been compelled to make a searing reassessment of himself; of his own aggressiveness, greed, power and impact. Those who now face each other with machines of almost cosmic destruction and talk seriously of peaceful co-existence are pre-occupied with political systems. But it is significant that healthy doubt is beginning to replace old, sick doctrine, in all the major political faiths. A new reasonableness – and we mean this literally – is being admitted at the summits and at most levels below; and the breath of fresh sense that is wafting (albeit rather gently still) over the councils of the world, is beginning to produce results. Many international conferences in the last few years have been concerned not so much with the world's appalling political confusion, but with its equally appalling ecological muddle.

The rise in strength in the last decade of the International Union for the Conservation of Nature and Natural Resources, and the emergence of the World Wildlife Fund, are not fortuitous processes, brought about by a coterie of idealistic do-gooders and doomed to breed more words than deeds. They are part of a philosophical revolution. Inherent in this new philosophy: the assumption that the planet will *not* involve itself in an atomic holocaust. As consequence of this assumption: the target of the re-naturalization of the world. A world at peace is still a world grossly disturbed ecologically, sadly and expensively damaged agriculturally; a world of insufficient and polluted water, vanished wetlands, slashed forests, lost and poisoned soil, pests and weeds (that is to say, with animals and plants in the wrong communities), extractive farming, over-fishing: and semistarvation for half its humans.

This is rather a bad world; but it is not sick to death. It is a world in which the great old philosophical concept of nature as a whole has been for a century strengthened and promoted by Darwin's discovery of organic evolution, Haeckel's discovery of ecology and Mendel's discovery of genetics. Now we are beginning to learn what nature is, and discovering its rules and laws. We can dissect it to a certain extent, analyze its mechanisms and measure its parts. As nature is not an edifice, but a process, we can seldom put a piece of it into repair by simple action. The biologists' answers to the problems of conservation are complex, and none of them is final.

Some issues, however, are simpler than others, and with one such we end our book on birds: the issue of survival. It embraces philosophical problems of conservation in perhaps as simple a form as they can assume. Yet highly civilized people find serious intellectual difficulties, and even blocks, in coming to terms with the fact that man has more than doubled the extinction rate of birds (p. 56) in less than three centuries. 'Why bother', we have been asked, 'with birds that might become extinct anyway? Why get hot under the collar about the prospect of the disappearance of the whooping crane, or the ivory-billed woodpecker? Who minds whether the Chatham Island robin still survives or not'.

It may be rationalized that in the natural course of evolution and without the help of man, between two species (RTP) and ten (according to JF) are likely to become extinct every century; and perhaps as many are likely to emerge. In the last three centuries the extinction figure has been between 25 and 30 per century. It would be philosophically unsound, perhaps, to say that the majority of these dodos, whose going was hastened by man, had 'rights'. What are rights?

It is not so much a question of nature's rights as of man's duty. On the following pages are listed the seventy-six full bird species that have become extinct since the dodo, and about twice as many which are very rare, with world populations around or under 2,000. The list of rarities – some of which have not been seen for many years – does not include over 80 species (p. 57) based on one or a few specimens whose status is quite mysterious. It corresponds closely to the official Survival Service List of the World Wildlife Fund.

Within each of these lists is a majority of species whose extinction or rarity is the responsibility of man, not nature. They are the products of many thousands of years of evolution and as such are a reproach to human civilization; an indicator of the grave extent to which man's central role in nature's network is uneasy and mal-adjusted.

Milton wrote this, in *Paradise Lost*:

> *Accuse not Nature, she hath done her part;*
> *Do thou but thine, and be not diffident*
> *Of wisdom, she deserts thee not, if thou*
> *Dismiss not her.*

Let us, on our way (we hope) to paradise regained (in other words, peaceful co-existence with nature), pause to learn lessons from the fate of birds. Birds are the most beautiful of all the animals, the flower garden of animal evolution. Evolution is a process, and in time each species must pass from the earth, and others (doubtless as beautiful) come. To hasten this process by ignorance or foolishness is an outrage to nature, and an affront to human dignity.

Most of the rare birds in this list are in some kind of danger. Some are in grave straits or may even be extinct.

This red list numbers 143; and we considered at least as many others very seriously before discarding them, because we had no *reasonable* certainty that their world population was less than 2,000. It is pretty clear that many of them are also in danger.

Without circulating every museum and important private collector it is impossible to find out just how many living species are known from under ten specimens; but we are rather sure the number is around a hundred. A considerable number are known only from the type, that is from one specimen. The status of at least 80 birds, many of which have been lately discovered, is uncertain simply because the collectors and the field watchers have scarcely explored their habitat, usually in the least accessible tropical forests. We know practically nothing about the distribution and numbers (for instance) of Kleinschmidt's falcon, or the diabolical nightjar, or the small-billed false sunbird, or the New Britain thicket warbler, or Rueck's blue flycatcher, or what (as we write) is the latest bird to be described – the pigmy tit babbler. This bird has been encountered so far only once: on 11 August 1961 Manuel Celestino and Godofredo Alcasid met a flock of more than ten at the forest-edge on Mount Lobi on Leyte in the Philippines, and collected four. Dean Amadon erected not only a new species for it, but a new genus; it is the smallest babbler known, and one of the world's smallest birds. But whether *Micromacronus leytensis* should be on the red list of the Survival Service Commission history alone will show. It may turn out to be fairly common in the remote hill forests of the big island of Leyte; or it may not.

Quite a number of birds that have been well enough collected still have a quite mysterious status, because there are not (yet) enough ornithologists to work their range over: we could mention the great Indian bustard, the ground parrot (much of whose range is in impenetrable Tasmanian forest), the fearful owl, the earthworm-eating kingfisher.

Others are now over the 2,000 mark, or probably so; but fluctuate in numbers and could be by no means safe.

The Red List

A collection of full species believed to be still living, and of which it is likely that the world population may be, or may have recently been, 2,000 or fewer.

Family 20. Grebes, Podicipitidae

Lake Junin grebe, *Podiceps taczanowskii*
Confined to Lake Junin, Perú, where scarce.

Alaotra grebe, *Podiceps rufolavatus*
Confined to Lake Alaotra, Madagascar.

Titicaca grebe, *Podiceps micropterus*
Confined to Lake Titicaca, Bolivia.

Pied-billed grebe, *Podilymbus podiceps*
Giant race *P.p. gigas* (by some regarded as full species) confined to Lake Atitlan, Guatemala, where now probably under 200 breeding birds.

Family 21. Albatrosses, Diomedeidae

Short-tailed albatross, *Diomedea albatrus*
Confined as breeder now to Torishima, s. of Japan, where 47 birds in 1962.

Family 22. Petrels and **shearwaters,** Procellariidae

Capped petrel or **diablotin,** *Pterodroma hasitata*
Dark Jamaican race *P.h. caribbaea* extinct since *c.* 1880; typical race *P.h. hasitata* now restricted as breeder probably to Hispaniola only, where colonies on Massif de la Selle, Haiti, at least 4,000 birds 1963.

Cahow, *Pterodroma cahow*
Restricted as breeder to Bermuda, where population small and restricted, estimated *c.* 100 1951; under 20 breeding holes located lately.

Family 29. Gannets and **boobies,** Sulidae

Abbott's booby, *Sula abbotti*
Now breeds only on Christmas Island, Indian Ocean, where 1,000–1,500 birds estimated 1941.

Family 33. Frigate birds, Fregatidae

Ascension frigate bird, *Fregata aquila*
About two thousand birds in 1957–59.

Family 41. Ibises and **spoonbills,** Plataleidae

Giant ibis, *Thaumatibis gigantea*
Formerly Cochin China, Cambodia and peninsular Siam; by 1963 extremely rare and possibly confined to one locality.

Nippon ibis, *Nipponia nippon*
Much restricted in range in e. Asia; doubtful if more than 10 survived in Japan 1963, when 1 young fledged.

Family 49. Waterfowl, Anatidae

Trumpeter swan, *Cygnus buccinator*
World population *c.* 1,700 1963.

Néné, *Branta sandvicensis*
World population *c.* 432 early 1962 (*c.* 151 wild).

Laysan teal, *Anas laysanensis*
Reduced to *c.* 200 after gale in 1963.

Brown teal, *Anas aucklandica*
New Zealand. Of 3 races, New Zealand race *A.a. chlorotis* now found only in few places, though some hundreds; Auckland Is. flightless race *A.a. aucklandica* now restricted to 6 outlying is.; Campbell I. *A.a. nesiotis* may be extinct.

Family 51. New World vultures, Cathartidae

California condor, *Gymnogyps californianus*
60–65 wild, 1960.

Family 54. Hawks and **eagles,** Accipitridae

Cuban hook-billed kite, *Chondrohierax wilsonii*
Confined Oriente Province; very small numbers.

Gundlach's hawk, *Accipiter gundlachi*
Confined to Cuban lowlands; very rare.

Gápagos hawk, *Buteo galapagoensis*
World population certainly under 200 1962.

Hawaiian hawk, *Buteo solitarius*
Hawaii only; a few hundred at most.

Monkey-eating eagle, *Pithecophaga jefferyi*
Eastern Philippines, getting rare; *c.* 100 lately.

Isidori's crested hawk eagle, *Oroaëtus isidori*
Andes from Colombia to Bolivia, where getting very rare and possibly no more than 200.

Family 56. Falcons, Falconidae

Teita falcon, *Falco fasciinucha*
Known from Abyssinia, Kenya and Rhodesia, but very rare.

Mauritian kestrel, *Falco punctatus*
On verge of extinction; late estimate 10–15.

Seychelles kestrel, *Falco araea*
Becoming very rare indeed in the archipelago.

Family 60. Megapodes, Megapodiidae

La Pérouse's megapode, *Megapodius lapérouse*
Palau Is. race *M.l. senex* now restricted to three islands; Marianas race *M.l. lapérouse* to five. Has become extinct on six already.

Pritchard's megapode, *Megapodius pritchardii*
Found only on Niua Fo'ou Island between Horne Is. and Fiji; small population.

Maleo, *Macrocephalon maleo*
Celebes; now very rare.

Family 62. **Quails, pheasants,** etc., Phasianidae

Tadjoura francolin, *Francolinus ochropectus*
Known only from about 9 square miles of forest on Plateau du Day, French Somaliland.

Swierstra's francolin, *Francolinus swierstrai*
Known only from a few square miles of patchy forest in 3 places in Angola.

Imperial pheasant, *Lophura imperialis*
Known only from very restricted areas of Annam and Laos; good stock in captivity.

Edwards's pheasant, *Lophura edwardsi*
Known only from restricted area Annam; good stock in captivity.

Swinhoe's pheasant, *Lophura swinhoei*
Formosa, where very rare; good captive stock.

Mikado pheasant, *Syrmaticus mikado*
Formosa, restricted area of high mountains, where rare; fair captive stock.

Family 70. **Cranes,** Gruidae

Hooded crane, *Grus monacha*
Japan, a few hundred; headwaters R. Amur, a small breeding group.

Manchurian crane, *Grus japonensis*
Up to 200 Hokkaido, Japan, 1962; small groups also breed L. Khanka, Manchuria and R. Amur.

Whooping crane, *Grus americana*
World population winter Aransas, Texas, where 33 (7 young of the year) 1963, also 6 in captivity.

Siberian white crane, *Grus leucogeranus*
Breeding stock in Siberia now very low, judging by winter range population; only about 60 wintered India lately.

Family 75. **Rails,** Rallidae

Lord Howe Island wood rail, *Tricholimnas sylvestris*
A small population in 1936; may also live or have lived on Apiang I., Gilberts.

Zapata rail, *Cyanolimnas cerverai*
Confined to within a mile of the high ground in the wooded part of the Zapata swamp, Cuba.

Platen's Celebes rail, *Aramidopsis plateni*
Only 10 specimens known; rare and localized.

Henderson Island rail, *Nesophylax ater*
Good population 1956, though world population possibly under 2,000.

Takahé, *Notornis mantelli*
Now known only from Murchison and Kepler Mts., Fjordland, South Island, New Zealand, where at most 300 1963.

Horned coot, *Fulica cornuta*
Rare scattered population in small areas of High Andes of Bolivia, Chile and n.w. Argentina.

Family 77. **Kagu,** Rhynochetidae

Kagu, *Rhynochetos jubatus*
Small population occupies less than 40 sq. km. of forests in New Caledonia.

Family 92. **Plovers** and **turnstones,** Charadriidae

New Zealand shore plover, *Thinornis novaeseelandiae*
Now restricted Chatham Islands where about 140 breeding birds 1937; holding its own 1961.

Family 93. **Snipe, sandpipers,** etc., Scolopacidae

New Zealand snipe, *Coenocorypha aucklandica*
Six races, all confined to New Zealand islands excepting North and South Islands; Little Barrier I. race *C.a. barrierensis* extinct 1870; some of others have become restricted and in danger, especially those on South Cape Islands (*C.a. iredalei*) and Chathams (*C.a. pusilla*).

Little whimbrel and **Eskimo curlew,** *Numenius borealis*
Eskimo curlew race, *N.b. borealis* (by some regarded as full species), one or two still sighted almost annually on passage Texas coast; breeding place unknown.

Hudsonian godwit, *Limosa haemastica*
Judging by winter and passage population in North America may be in no immediate danger; but world population may not long ago have been under 2,000.

Family 103. **Gulls** and **terns,** Laridae

Audouin's gull, *Larus audouinii*
Mediterranean and one spot west of Gibraltar; very rare and local; about 160 breeding birds main colony (Corsica) 1963.

Family 108. **Pigeons,** Columbidae

Cloven-feathered dove, *Drepanoptila holosericea*
Forests of New Caledonia; very little known and rare.

Giant imperial pigeon, *Ducula goliath*
Mountain forests of New Caledonia; increasingly restricted range.

Mindoro imperial pigeon, *Ducula mindorensis*
Confined to island, over 4,500 ft., rare.

Riu Kiu wood pigeon, *Columba jouyi*
Now extinct Okinawa; only small numbers on other islets.

Abyssinian white-winged dove, *Streptopelia reichenowi*
Very local and rare, only in s. Abyssinia and Juba R. valley.

Grenada dove, *Leptotila wellsi*
Very rare; small population in lower part Grenada and perhaps Glover's Island.

Palau ground dove, *Gallicolumba canifrons*
Thought nearing extinction 1931; but less rare 1945, though perhaps under 2,000.

Marquesan ground dove, *Gallicolumba rubescens*
Confined to Fatuhuku and Hatuta, where rare enough to have escaped notice between 1813 and 1922.

Tooth-billed pigeon, *Didunculus strigirostris*
Confined to Upolu and Savaii, Samoa, where has recently recovered from a low population.

Family 110. **Parrots,** Psittacidae

Night parrot, *Geopsittacus occidentalis*
Formerly w. and s. Australia and n.w. Victoria. Was probably not seen between 1935 and 1962, when rediscovered.

Kakapo, *Strigops habroptilus*
New Zealand; extinct North Island 1930; probably extinct Stewart I. since 1951; now very small numbers scattered parts western South Island; believed under 100 1961, c. 30 one area.

Orange-fronted parakeet, *Cyanoramphus malherbi*
South Island, New Zealand, whence only five reports in last 80 years, most of them unconfirmed.

Turquoise parakeet, *Neophema pulchella*
Extreme s.e. Australia; thought once to be extinct but has recovered; a few pairs breeding near Sydney 1945.

Splendid parakeet, *Neophema splendida*
Small population s. Australia has lately been found to have recovered; fair breeding stock in captivity.

Beautiful parakeet, *Psephotus pulcherrimus*
Very rare in scattered localities n.e. Australia.

Paradise parakeet, *Psephotus chrysopterygius*
Tropical Australia; both races now very rare.

Puerto Rican parrot, *Amazona vittata*
Puerto Rico race *A.v. vittata* confined to Luquillo National Forest, where c. 200 1958, status seems sound; Culebra Island race *A.v. gracilipes* now extinct, though common 1899.

St. Vincent parrot, *Amazona guildingii*
Confined to St. Vincent; rather rare.

St. Lucia parrot, *Amazona versicolor*
Now rather rare and restricted to central part of island.

Imperial parrot, *Amazona imperialis*
Confined to high mountain forest of Dominica, where rare.

Family 111. **Touracos,** *Musophagidae*

Prince Ruspoli's touraco, *Tauraco ruspolii*
Known so far to occupy not more than about 10 sq. mi. of juniper woods at Arero, s. Abyssinia.

Family 115. **Typical owls,** Strigidae

Seychelles Island owl, *Otus insularis*
Mahé only, where recently rediscovered, not having been heard since 1906. Very rare.

Palau owl, *Otus podargina*
Confined to Koror, Peliliu and Babelthuap; in 1945 *c.* 122 breeding birds K., 8 P. Rare.

Giant scops owl, *Otus gurneyi*
Known only from a few specimens from Mindanao and Marinduque, Philippines; doubtless under 2,000.

New Zealand laughing owl, *Sceloglaux albifacies*
North Island race *S.a. rufifacies* last seen 1890; South Island race *S.a. albifacies* has been once or twice reported but not confirmed in last 25 years. Very rare if not extinct.

Forest spotted owlet, *Athene blewitti*
Forests of central India; no report since 1872.

Family 119. **Nightjars,** Caprimulgidae

Least pauraque, *Siphonornis americanus*
Last known specimen of Jamaican race *S.a. americanus* collected 1859. Hispaniolan race *S.a. brewsteri* survives with very restricted range in Magasin Caries and Gonave I.

Puerto Rican whip-poor-will, *Caprimulgus noctitherus*
Thought extinct; but rediscovered 1961 when small population studied and sound-recorded.

Family 124. **Hummingbirds,** Trochilidae

Racket-tailed hummingbird, *Loddigesia mirabilis*
Known from one skin until 1880 when rediscovered in small valley of R. Utcubamba, Perú; has never been found elsewhere, though leaves for season (or ? hibernates).

Family 132. **Ground rollers,** Brachypteraciidae

Long-tailed ground roller, *Uratelornis chimaera*
Confined to a small area near Tulear in s.w. Madagascar, where rare.

Family 139. **Barbets,** Capitonidae

Kinabalu barbet, *Megalaima pulcherrima*
Confined to Kinabalu mountains, Borneo, where rare.

Family 142. **Woodpeckers,** Picidae

Fernandina's flicker, *Nesoceleus fernandinae*
Confined to palm groves of Las Villas and Camagüey provinces of Cuba; rare.

Ivory-billed woodpecker, *Campephilus principalis*
U.S. mainland race *C.p. principalis* unconfirmed reports of survival 1961; Cuban race *C.p. bairdii* confined to Oriente Province, Cuba, where 12 or 13 1956.

Family 143. **Broadbills,** Eurylaimidae

Grauer's green broadbill, *Pseudocalyptomena graueri*
Known only from 3 places in mountain forest about 6,500 ft., n. of L. Tanganyika, c. Africa.

Family 144. **Woodhewers** and **ovenbirds,** Furnariidae

Sclater's spinetail, *Asthenes sclateri*
Known only from Sierra de Cordoba, Argentina, where has been thought extinct.

Family 145. **Ant thrushes,** Formicariidae

Red-rumped ant thrush, *Myrmotherula erythronotos*
Only known from Nova Friburgo, s.e. Brazil, where recent collectors have not found it.

Family 148. **Pittas,** Pittidae

Koch's pitta, *Pitta kochi*
Confined to a few oak forest ravines in high mountains of n. Luzon, Philippines, where rare.

Family 150. **New Zealand wrens,** Acanthisittidae

Bush wren, *Xenicus longipes*
All three races very rare; North Island race *X.l. stokesi* may still exist L. Waikaremoana area; South I. race *X.l. longipes* very sporadic high forests; Stewart I. race *X.l. variabilis* now seldom reported main island, survives South Cape Is.

Family 156. **Scrub birds,** Atrichornithidae

Rufous scrub bird, *Atrichornis rufescens*
Both New South Wales (*A.r. rufescens*) and Queensland races (*A.r. jacksoni*) are very rare and restricted, particularly the latter.

Noisy scrub bird, *Atrichornis clamosus*
S.w. Australia. Thought to be extinct between 1920 and 1961, when small population rediscovered at Two People Bay near Albany.

Family 157. **Larks,** Alaudidae

Raza Island lark, *Calandrella razae*
Confined to this Cape Verde I., only 3 sq. mi.

Family 161. **Cuckoo shrikes,** Campephagidae

Grauer's cuckoo shrike, *Coracina graueri*
Confined to forests on w. side Albertine Rift, Congo; fewer than 12 specimens known.

Family 162. **Bulbuls,** Pycnonotidae

Olivaceous bulbul, *Hypsipetes borbonicus*
Réunion race *H.b. borbonicus* rare and local but not in extreme danger; Mauritius race *H.b. olivaceus* 'dangerously small'.

Family 164. **Shrikes,** Laniidae

Kupé Mountain bush shrike, *Telephorus kupeensis*
Confined to this mountain in British Cameroons; known from 4 specimens (discovered 1951), may have range of less than 8 sq. mi.

Family 170. **Wrens,** Troglodytidae

Zapata wren, *Ferminia cerverai*
Restricted to 5 sq. mi. of Zapata swamp, Cuba; where not uncommon but probably under 2,000.

Family 171. **Thrashers** and **mockers,** Mimidae

White-breasted thrasher, *Ramphocinclus brachyurus*
Two races: Martinique race *R.b. brachyurus* confined to Presqu'île de la Caravelle, may be extinct; St. Lucia race *R.b. sanctae-luciae* confined n.e. part island, very rare and localized.

Family 173. Muscicapidae

Subfamily 173a, **Thrushes,** Turdinae

Seychelles magpie robin, *Copsychus seychellarum*
Formerly five islands; now only Frégate, where *c.* 20 birds present 1959.

Puaiohi, *Phaeornis palmeri*
Kauai, Hawaiian Is., thought to be extinct but rediscovered 1960. Perhaps 30 birds.

Ashy ground thrush, *Zoothera cinerea*
Peculiar to mountains of Mindoro, Philippines, where rare.

Teita olive thrush, *Turdus helleri*
Confined to four forest patches totaling not more than 1,000 acres of Teita Hills, s. Kenya.

Gray-headed blackbird, *Turdus poliocephalus*
Lord Howe I. race *T.p. vinitinctus* extinct soon after 1918; Norfolk I. race *T.p. poliocephala* survives, but population doubtless under 2,000.

Grand Cayman thrush, *Turdus ravidus*
Rare and apparently restricted to e. and n.e. of island; perhaps not seen since 1938.

Subfamily 173b. **Babblers,** Timaliinae

Spiny babbler, *Turdoides nipalensis*
None collected or seen between 1844 and 1948, very rare in w. Nepal and neighboring Indian Himalayas.

Mallee whipbird, *Psophodes nigrogularis*
Two races, both very rare and local in southwestern and southern Australia; either or both together may number under 2,000.

Subfamily 173e. **Old World warblers** and **gnatwrens,** Sylviinae

Miller bird, *Acrocephalus familiaris*
Race on Laysan *A.f. familiaris* extinct by 1923, probably by 1912; Nihoa race *A.f. kingi* survives, doubtless under 2,000.

Seychelles warbler, *Bebrornis sechellensis*
Confined to Cousin I. (60 acres); 30 birds in 1959.

Long-legged warbler, *Trichocichla rufa*
Viti Levu, Fiji; has not been seen in the present century and may be extinct.

Silktail, *Lamprolia victoriae*
Two races, Taviuni *L.v. victoriae* and Vanua Levu, Fiji, *L.v. kleinschmidti*: both in mountain forest, poorly known, may number under 2,000.

Subfamily 173f. **Australian warblers,** Malurinae

Eyrean grass wren, *Amytornis goyderi*
Rediscovered in small numbers 25 mi. north of L. Eyre in 1961, having not been seen since first collected same area S. Australia in 1875.

Subfamily 173g. **Old World flycatchers** and **fantails,** Muscicapinae

Chatham Island robin, *Petroica traversi*
Confined to Little Mangare Island (1 acre) where 40 to 70 birds in 1937–38.

Subfamily 173h. **Monarchs,** Monarchinae

Tahitian flycatcher, *Pomarea nigra*
Three races: Tahitian race *P.n. nigra* certainly very rare; Maupiti Island race *P.n. pomarea* of uncertain status; Tongatabu race *P.n. tabuensis* described on spot (no specimen) in 1773, not seen in 1777 or since.

Truk monarch, *Metabolus rugensis*
Confined to this island, where rare or extinct.

Tinian monarch, *Monarcha takatsukasae*
Confined to this island, where population in 1945 possibly no more than 50.

Seychelles black paradise flycatcher, *Terpsiphone corvina*
Survives only on la Digue, where plenty (though probably under 2,000) in 1959.

Subfamily 173i. **Whistlers** and **piopio,** Pachycephalinae

Piopio, *Turnagra capensis*
New Zealand; two races; North Island race *T.c. tanagra* half a dozen reports in last 40 years, unconfirmed, may be extinct; South Island race *T.c. capensis* neither recent report (1947, 1948) confirmed, may possibly be extinct.

Family 179. **Whiteyes,** Zosteropidae

Truk great whiteye, *Rukia ruki*
Confined to Truk Island, where very rare.

Ponapé great whiteye, *Rukia sanfordi*
Confined to this island over 1,800 ft.; very rare.

Family 180. **Honeyeaters,** Meliphagidae

Kauai oo, *Moho braccatus*
Confined to this island (Hawaiian Is.) where just survives.

Stitchbird, *Notiomystis cincta*
Confined to Little Barrier I., off North Island, New Zealand; small stable population.

Helmeted honeyeater, *Meliphaga cassidix*
Australia; now probably confined to a few square miles near Melbourne.

Family 181. Emberizidae

Subfamily 181a. **Buntings, American sparrows** and **Darwin's finches,** Emberizinae

Cape Sable sparrow, *Ammospiza mirabilis*
Confined to a small area of s.w. Florida where doubtless under 2,000.

Subfamily 181b. **Cardinals** and allies, Cardinalinae

Puerto Rican bullfinch, *Loxigilla portoricensis*
Two races: mainland *L.p. portoricensis* now very rare and local: St. Christopher race *L.p. grandis* collected 1880; apparently extinct since.

Family 182. **Wood warblers,** Parulidae

Bachman's warbler, *Vermivora bachmanii*
South-eastern U.S. distribution very patchy; so rare that population must be under 2,000.

Kirtland's warbler, *Vermivora kirtlandii*
Breeds central Michigan only, where 502 singing males, representing a breeding population around 1,000, in 1961.

Semper's warbler, *Leucopeza semperi*
Confined to mountain forest of St. Lucia, West Indies, where extremely rare, seen 1947, one heard singing 1962.

Family 183. **Hawaiian honeycreepers,** Drepanididae

Kauai akialoa, *Hemignathus procerus*
Apparently survives, though very rare; one collected 1960.

Nukupuu, *Hemignathus lucidus*
Three races: Maui *H.l. affinis* last seen 1896; Oahu *H.l. lucidus* last seen 1860; Kauai *H.l. hanapepe* seen as lately as 1960, though very rare.

Akiapolauu, *Hemignathus wilsoni*
Hawaii; uncommon, but survives.

Maui parrotbill, *Pseudonestor xanthophrys*
Maui; extremely rare; small population 1950.

Ou, *Psittirostra psittacea*
Very rare on Hawaii, Maui and Kauai; now extinct Lanai (*c.* 1932), Oahu (*c.* 1900) and probably Molokai.

Laysan finch, *Psittirostra cantans*
Two races: Nihoa *P.c. ultima* 500–1,000 birds *c.* 1941, but possibly 10,000 recently; Laysan *P.c. cantans* at least 1,000 1938; introduced Midway where now extinct.

Palila, *Psittirostra bailleui*
Reduced (1961) to a few scattered flocks of 5 to 15 birds, Mauna Kea Mountain, Hawaii; but may be increasing.

Crested honeycreeper, *Palmeria dolei*
Maui, where still survives, extinct Molokai since 1907.

Family 184. **Vireos** and allies, Vireonidae

Slender-billed vireo, *Vireo gracilirostris*
Confined to Fernando Noronha (Atlantic), just over 3 sq. mi.

Family 185. **Icterids,** Icteridae

Arment's cowbird, *Tangavius armenti*
Colombia; restricted and patchy distribution, very few specimens known.

Slender-billed grackle, *Cassidix palustris*
Confined to marshes near México City, where may possibly be extinct.

Nicaraguan grackle, *Cassidix nicaraguensis*
Confined to shores of Ls. Managua and Nicaragua, Nicaragua.

Family 187. **Waxbills** and allies, Estrildidae

Pink-billed parrot finch, *Erythrura kleinschmidti*
Confined to Viti Levu, Fiji, where very rare.

Family 189. **Weavers** and **true sparrows,** Ploceidae

Seychelles fody, *Foudia sechellarum*
World population in 1959 *c.* 460 birds (250–300 Frégate, *c.* 105 Cousin, *c.* 80 Cousine).

Family 190. **Starlings,** Sturnidae

Norfolk Island starling, *Aplonis fuscus*
Norfolk I. race *A.f. fuscus* survives, population possibly may be under 2,000; Lord Howe I. race *A.f. bullianus* extinct soon after 1918.

Ponapé mountain starling, *Aplonis pelzelni*
Confined to forested uplands of this island in Carolines, where very rare in 1947–48.

Family 193. **Wattled crows,** Callaeidae

Saddleback, *Creadion carunculatus*
New Zealand; two races; North Island race *C.c. rufusater* now confined to 1,000-acre Taranga (Hen and Chicken Is.); South Island race *C.c. carunculatus* now apparently confined to three of the South Cape Islands, off Stewart Island.

Family 199. **Crows,** Corvidae

Hawaiian crow, *Corvus tropicus*
Restricted to slopes of Haleakala Mountain, Hawaii, where possibly only 25 to 50 in 1961.

The Black List

All the full species of birds believed to have become extinct since 1600.

Main list: those extinct since 1680, the year before the dodo was last seen.

Family 14. **Lesser moás,** Emeidae

Megalapteryx äidina
Survived in Takahé Valley, South Island, New Zealand until 17th century, possibly after 1773.

Family 23. **Storm petrels,** Oceanitidae

Guadalupe storm petrel, *Oceanodroma macrodactyla*
Probably extinct; not seen since 1912.

Family 31. **Cormorants,** Phalacrocoracidae

Spectacled cormorant, *Phalacrocorax perspicillatus*
Extinct (Bering I.) by *c.* 1852.

Family 37. **Herons,** Ardeidae

Flightless night heron, *Nycticorax megacephalus*
Extinct on Rodriguez I. in or shortly after 1730.

Family 49. **Waterfowl,** Anatidae

Crested shelduck, *Tadorna cristata*
Very probably extinct, last alleged sight record 1943.

Pink-headed duck, *Rhodonessa caryophyllacea*
India, last reliable wild record 1935; probably became extinct in captivity in England, 1944.

Labrador duck, *Camptorhynchus labradorius*
Last specimen shot Long Island, N.Y., 1875.

Auckland Island merganser, *Mergus australis*
Not seen since 1905.

Family 56. **Falcons,** Falconidae

Guadalupe Island caracara, *Caracara lutosa*
Last seen alive 1900.

Family 62. **Quails, pheasants,** etc., Phasianidae

Himalayan mountain quail, *Ophrysia superciliosa*
Known only from Mussorie and Naini Tal in n.w. Himalayas, where not seen since 1868. Believed extinct despite rumors one shot in period 1948–52.

Family 75. **Rails,** Rallidae

Tahiti red-billed rail, *Rallus ecaudata*
Discovered in 1773 or 1774; doubtfully survived until about 1925.

Wake Island rail, *Rallus wakensis*
Became extinct in 1945.

Chatham Island banded rail, *Rallus dieffenbachii*
One collected 1840; not seen before or since.

Chatham Island rail, *Rallus modestus*
Last specimen collected between 1895 and 1900; not seen since.

New Caledonian wood rail, *Tricholimnas lafresnayanus*
Not found since *c.* 1904; very probably extinct.

Fiji bar-winged rail, *Nesoclopeus poeciloptera*
Extinct; last collected not later than 1890.

Flightless blue rail, *Aphanapteryx leguati*
Rodriguez, extinct; last seen *c.* 1730.

Laysan Island rail, *Porzanula palmeri*
Finally became extinct on Midway I. (where introduced) 1944.

Hawaiian rail, *Pennula sandwichensis*
Last certainly seen 1884, possibly seen 1893, not seen since.

Kusaie Island crake, *Aphanolimnas monasa*
Two collected 1828; not seen before or since.

Samoan wood rail, *Pareudiastes pacificus*
Savaii Island: no record since 1873.

Family 93. **Snipe, sandpipers,** etc., Scolopacidae

Tahitian sandpiper, *Prosobonia leucoptera*
Collected in Tahiti in 1773 and 1777; never seen alive before or since.

Family 99. **Coursers** and **pratincoles,** Glareolidae

Jerdon's courser, *Cursorius bitorquatus*
Formerly central India; no specimen since 1871; none seen since 1900.

Family 105. **Auks,** Alcidae

Great auk, *Pinguinus impennis*
Finally exterminated Eldey, Iceland, 3 or 4 June 1844.

Family 108. **Pigeons,** Columbidae

Mauritius blue pigeon, *Alectroenas nitidissima*
Extinct since 1830.

Bonin wood pigeon, *Columba versicolor*
Last specimen taken on Nakondo Shima in 1889.

Passenger pigeon, *Ectopistes migratorius*
Became extinct in the Cincinnati (Ohio) Zoo, 1 September 1914.

Tanna ground dove, *Gallicolumba ferruginea*
Seen, drawn and collected (specimen lost) in 1774; not seen before or since.

St. Helena blue dove, as yet unnamed. Seen in 1775, but not in 1825, 1836 or since; also known from Pleistocene fossil bones. Not in census p. 192.

Crested Choiseul pigeon, *Microgoura meeki*
Collected in 1904; not seen before or since.

Family 109. **Dodo and solitaires,** Raphidae

Dodo, *Raphus cucullatus*
Mauritius: extinct since about 1681.

Solitaire, *Raphus solitarius*
Réunion; extinct since about 1746.

Rodriguez solitaire, *Pezophaps solitaria*
Rodriguez; extinct since about 1791.

Family 110. **Parrots,** Psittacidae

New Caledonian lorikeet, *Charmosyna diadem*
Last specimen taken before 1860.

Tahiti parakeet, *Cyanoramphus zealandicus*
Last specimen taken 1844.

Raiatea parakeet, *Cyanoramphus ulietanus*
Two specimens collected 1774. Not seen before, in 1777, or since.

Mascarene parrot, *Mascarinus mascarinus*
Réunion. Last known living bird in garden of king of Bavaria, 1834.

Rodriguez parakeet, *Necropsittacus rodricanus*
Rodriguez; last seen *c.* 1730 or after. This, or close species in same genus, may also have inhabited Mauritius in 17th and 18th centuries.

Exiled ring-necked parakeet, *Psittacula exsul*
Rodriguez; no information since 1875.

Guadeloupe parrot, *Amazona violacea*
Based on good description but no specimen. Extinct since early 18th century.

Martinique parrot, *Amazona martinica*
Based on good description but no specimen. May have been close to or even same species as predecessor. Extinct since early 18th century.

Guadeloupe conure, *Aratinga labati*
Based on good description but no specimen. Extinct since early 18th century.

Carolina parakeet, *Conuropsis carolinensis*
Extinct; last living bird may have been pet that died in 1914.

Cuban red macaw, *Ara tricolor*
Extinct about 1885.

Jamaican red macaw, *Ara gossei*
Collected about 1765 (specimen lost); not seen since.

Jamaican green-and-yellow macaw, *Ara erythrocephala*
Extinct early 19th century.

Guadeloupe red macaw, *Ara guadeloupensis*
Based on good description but no specimen. Extinct since early 18th century.

Dominican green-and-yellow macaw, *Ara atwoodi*
Based on good description but no specimen. Extinct since late 18th century.

Family 112. **Cuckoos,** Cuculidae

Delalande's Madagascar coucal, *Coua delalandei*
Was confined to small forest area; none trapped since 1930 and considered extinct.

Family 115. **Typical owls,** Strigidae

Commerson's scops owl, *Otus commersoni*
Mauritius; extinct by 1837.

Rodriguez little owl, *Athene murivora*
Extinct *c.* 1730 or after.

Family 127. **Kingfishers,** Alcedinidae

Riu Kiu Island kingfisher, *Halcyon miyakoensis*
One specimen collected 1887, not found since.

Family 150. **New Zealand wrens,** Acanthisittidae

Stephen Island wren, *Xenicus lyalli*
Extirpated by the lighthouse-keeper's cat in 1894.

Family 173. Muscicapidae

Subfamily 173a. **Thrushes,** Turdinae

Kittlitz's thrush, *Zoothera terrestris*
Four specimens collected Peel Island, Bonins, 1828; never seen since.

Raiatea thrush, *Turdus ulietensis*
Seen (and drawn) on the island in 1774; no specimen; never found since.

Family 179. **Whiteyes,** Zosteropidae

Lord Howe Island whiteye, *Zosterops strenua*
Extinct after 1918, certainly by 1928.

Family 180. **Honeyeaters,** Meliphagidae

Molokai oo, *Moho bishopi*
Extinct perhaps by 1904, certainly by 1915.

Hawaii oo, *Moho nobilis*
Extinct by about 1934.

Oahu oo, *Moho apicalis*
Extinct by 1837.

Kioea, *Chaetoptila angustipluma*
Hawaii Island; extinct by *c.* 1859.

Family 183. **Hawaiian honeycreepers,** Drepanididae

Great amakihi, *Loxops sagittirostris*
Hawaii; last report 1900.

Akialoa, *Hemignathus obscurus*
All three races extinct; Hawaii *H.o. obscurus* after 1895; Oahu *H.o. lichtensteinii c.* 1837; Lanai *H.o. lanaiensis c.* 1894.

Hopue, *Psittirostra palmeri*
Hawaii; last certainly seen 1896.

Lesser koa finch, *Psittirostra flaviceps*
Hawaii; last seen 1891.

Kona finch, *Psittirostra kona*
Hawaii; last seen 1894.

Ula-ai-hawane, *Ciridops anna*
Hawaii; extinct by 1892.

Mamo, *Drepanis pacifica*
Hawaii; extinct by 1898.

Black mamo, *Drepanis funerea*
Molokai; extinct by 1907.

Family 186. **Finches,** Fringillidae

Bonin Islands grosbeak, *Chaunoproctus ferreorostris*
Bonins, first collected on Peel Island 1827; may have lingered in Bailley group until *c.* 1890; now extinct.

Family 189. **Weavers** and **true sparrows,** Ploceidae

São Thomé grosbeak weaver, *Neospiza concolor*
May have become extinct on this African island shortly after description published in 1888.

Réunion fody, *Foudia bruante*
Extinct in or before 1776; no specimens survive.

Family 190. **Starlings,** Sturnidae

Kusaie starling, *Aplonis corvina*
Collected in 1828; never seen since.

Mysterious starling, *Aplonis mavornata*
Collected in 1774 somewhere in the Pacific; one specimen. Never seen since.

Leguat's starling, *Fregilupus rodericanus*
Rodriguez, where known from subfossil bones, and neighboring Met Island, where only known specimen taken *c.* 1832.

Bourbon crested starling, *Fregilupus varius*
Réunion; extinct 1862 or later.

Family 193. **Wattled crows,** Callaeidae

Huia, *Heteralocha acutirostris*
North Island, New Zealand, where probably extinct since *c.* 1907, in spite of rumors.

Addendum: Extinct before dodo (1600–1680)

Family 10. **Elephant birds,** Aepyornithidae

Great elephant bird, *Aepyornis maximus*
Probably survived in s. Madagascar in 1649; 'blown', not sub-fossil, egg handled *c.* 1840.

Family 49. **Waterfowl,** Anatidae

Poua (a swan), *Cygnus sumnerensis*
Probably survived on Chatham Is., New Zealand until between 1590 and 1690.

Family 75. **Rails,** Rallidae

Van den Broecke's red rail, *Aphanapteryx bonasia*
Mauritius; described from bones, but accounts and pictures show may have survived to 1675.

Ascension Island flightless crake, *Crecopsis* sp. ?
An, as yet, unnamed bird, flightless, seen and figured in 1656; not seen since. Bones probably belong to this species. Not in census p. 177.

Family 108. **Pigeons,** Columbidae

Bourbon pink pigeon, *Columba duboisi*
Described well enough on Réunion in 1669, never seen since.

Family 110. **Parrots,** Psittacidae

Broad-billed parrot, *Lophopsittacus mauritanus*
Sketched in Mauritius in 1638; otherwise based on subfossil bones.

Bourbon parakeet, *Necropsittacus borbonicus*
Described well enough on Réunion in 1669 for genus to be probably correct; never seen since.

Mysterious macaw, *Ara erythrura*
From 'one of the West Indian islands', on a description published in 1658; no record since.

Martinique macaw, *Ara martinica*
Martinique, on Bouton's description published in 1640; no record since.

Bibliography

This guide to further reading has been selected with great difficulty, as much fine work has had to be omitted for reasons of space. Publications of fewer than forty pages are only cited when of very special importance. Years of publication marked * are those of the first editions of works of which subsequent editions are or have recently been available, not necessarily from the original publisher.

Fossil birds

LAMBRECHT, Kálmán (1933). Handbuch der Palaeornithologie. Berlin, Bornträger, 1024 pp.

WETMORE, Alexander (1956). A check-list of the fossil and prehistoric birds of North America and the West Indies. *Smithson Misc. Coll. 131:* no. 5; 105 pp.

SWINTON, W. E. (1958). Fossil birds. London, British Museum (Nat. Hist.), 63 pp.

BRODKORB, Pierce (1963). Catalogue of fossil birds. Part 1. *Bull. Fla. State Mus. 7:* 179–293.

General and introductory

PETERS, James Lee and others (1931→). Check-list of birds of the world. Cambridge, Mass., Harvard University Press, 10 (out of 15) vols. to 1964.

FISHER, James (1940*). Watching birds. Harmondsworth, Penguin, 192 pp.

HICKEY, J. J. (1943*). A guide to bird watching. New York etc., Oxford University Press, 262 pp.

FISHER, James (1954). A history of birds. London, Hutchinson, vol. 1, 205 pp.

WALLACE, G. J. (1955). An introduction to ornithology. New York, Macmillan, 443 pp.

PETTINGILL, Olin Sewall Jr. (1956). A laboratory and field manual of ornithology. Minneapolis, Burgess, 379 pp.

PETERSON, R. T. *ed.* (1957). The bird watcher's anthology. New York, Harcourt Brace, 401 pp.

GREENWAY, James C. Jr. (1958). Extinct and vanishing birds of the world. New York, American Committee for International Wild Life Protection, 518 pp.

GILLIARD, E. Thomas (1958). Living birds of the world. New York, Doubleday, 400 pp.

van TYNE, Josselyn and BERGER, Andrew J. (1959). Fundamentals of ornithology. New York, Wiley, 624 pp.

MARSHALL, A. J. *ed.* (1960–61). Biology and comparative physiology of birds. New York etc., Academic Press, 2 vols., 518+468 pp.

AUSTIN, Oliver L. Jr. and SINGER, Arthur (1961). Birds of the world. New York, Golden Pleasure Books, 317 pp.

BERGER, Andrew J. (1961). Bird study. New York, Wiley, 389 pp.

DARLING, Lois and DARLING, Louis (1962). Bird. Boston, Houghton Mifflin, 261 pp.

WELTY, Joel Carl (1962). The life of birds. Philadelphia etc., Saunders, 546 pp.

PETERSON, Roger Tory and others (1963). The birds. New York, Time, 192 pp.

LANYON, Wesley E. (1963). Biology of birds. Garden City, N.Y., Natural History Press.

General bibliography

ZOOLOGICAL SOCIETY OF LONDON (1864→). The Zoological Record. Aves. London, Z.S.L., annually.

ZIMMER, J. T. (1926). Catalogue of the Edward E. Ayer ornithological library. *Field Mus. Publ.* (Zool.) *16:* 706 pp.

ANKER, Jean (1938). Bird books and bird art. . . . Copenhagen, Munksgaard, 251 pp.

STRONG, Reuben Myron (1939–59). A bibliography of birds. *Field Mus. Publ.* (Zool.) *25:* 937+528+186 pp.

SITWELL, Sacheverell, BUCHANAN, Handasyde and FISHER, James (1953). Fine bird books 1700–1900. London, Collins, 120 pp.

RIPLEY, S. Dillon and SCRIBNER, L. L. (1961). Ornithological books in the Yale University Library. New Haven, Yale University Press, 338 pp.

Special aspects of natural history

ARMSTRONG, Edward A. (1958). The folklore of birds. London, Collins *New Naturalist,* 272 pp.

HUTCHINSON, George Evelyn (1950) . . . The biogeochemistry of vertebrate excretion. *Bull. Amer. Mus. Nat. Hist. 96:* 554 pp.

HORTON SMITH, C. (1938). The flight of birds. London, Witherby, 182 pp.

STORER, J. H. (1948). The flight of birds. . . . *Cranbrook Inst. Sci. Bull.,* no. 28; 94 pp.

ROMANOFF, A. L. (1960). The avian embryo. . . . New York etc., Macmillan, 1305 pp.

—— and ROMANOFF, A. J. (1949). The avian egg. London, Chapman and Hall, 918 pp.

HOWARD, H. Eliot (1935). The nature of a bird's world. Cambridge, University Press, 102 pp.

LORENZ, Konrad (1935*). Der Kumpan in der Umwelt des Vogels. *J. Orn. 83:* 137–213, 289–413; English transl. (1937). *Auk 54:* 245–73.

GOODWIN, Derek (1961). Instructions to young ornithologists. No. 2. Bird behaviour. London, Museum Press, 123 pp.

ARMSTRONG, Edward A. (1942*). Bird display [and behaviour]. London, Lindsay Drummond, 381 pp.

MEINERTZHAGEN, Richard (1959). Pirates and predators. Edinburgh etc., Oliver & Boyd, 230 pp.

ROWAN, William (1931). The riddle of migration. Baltimore, Williams & Wilkins, 151 pp.

THOMSON, A. Landsborough (1936*). Bird migration. London, Witherby, 192 pp.

LOCKLEY, R. M. and RUSSELL, Rosemary (1953). Bird-ringing. London, Crosby Lockwood, 119 pp.

DORST, Jean (1956*). Les migrations des oiseaux. Paris, Payot, 422 pp.; English transl. (1962).

MATTHEWS, G. V. T. (1955). Bird navigation. Cambridge, University Press, 141 pp.

HOWARD, H. Eliot (1920*). Territory in bird life. London, John Murray, 308 pp.

DARLING, Frank Fraser (1938). Bird flocks and the breeding cycle. Cambridge, University Press, 124 pp.

THORPE, W. H. (1960). Bird song. Cambridge, University Press, 143 pp.

Recent published bird voice discs (some with booklets or books):—Number × diameter in inches (RPM)

London, E.M.I. (or H.M.V.)
Peter DUDDRIDGE (1962) one × 7(45)
Ludwig KOCH (1958) 7EG 8315/6 × 7(45)
London, Odhams Press
John KIRBY (1962) two × 7(45)
London, Talking Book Co.
Ludwig KOCH (1960) 2/1351/26 (one) × 7(33)
London, Witherby
Myles E. W. NORTH and Eric A. SIMMS (1958) HFGI/13 × 10(78)
Paris, Chantes
Jean-Claude ROCHÉ (1960) CLA 1002 × 7(45); (1961) CLA 1009 × 7(45)
Paris, Pacific
Jean-Claude ROCHÉ (1959) LDP-B 250 × 10(33); (1960) LDP-B 260 × 10(33); (1961) LDP 2304 × 10(33); (1962) LDP 2305 × 10(33)
Paris, La Vie des Bêtes
Jean-Claude ROCHÉ (1961) three × 7(45)
Moscow, All-Union Studio of Disc Recording
Boris VEPRINTSEV (1960) 6227–8 one × 10(33); (1961) 7751–2 one × 10(33)
Stockholm, Sveriges Radio
Sture PALMER (1958–62) RFEP 201/30 × 7(45)
Copenhagen, Rhodos
Carl WEISMANN (1960) one × 10(33)
Lyngby (Denmark) C. Weismann
Carl WEISMANN (1955) one × 10(78)
Amsterdam, European Phono Club
Ko ZWEERES (1960) EFC 8/9 × 7(33)
John KIRBY (1962) three × 7(33)
Zürich, Swiss Soc. for Bird Protection
Hans TRABER (1954–55) eleven × 10(78); (1959) five × 7(33); (1961) one × 7(33); material reissued Sandy (Beds., England), RSPB
Yokohama, Victor
Kasuke HOSHINO and T. KABAYA (1959) LV 519/20 × 10(33)
Toronto, Federation of Ontario Naturalists
D. J. BORROR and W. W. H. GUNN (1958) one × 12(33); (1960) one × 12(33)
W. W. H. GUNN (1959) four × 12(33); (1962) one × 12(33)
Boston, Houghton Mifflin
Peter Paul KELLOGG and Arthur A. ALLEN (1959) two × 12(33); (1962) three × 12(33): to go with RTP's *Field Guides*
Ithaca, Cornell University Press
Arthur A. ALLEN and Peter Paul KELLOGG (1957) one × 10(33); (1961) one × 10(33)
L. Irby DAVIS (1958) one × 12(33)
P. P. KELLOGG and A. A. ALLEN (1958) one × 10(33); (1960) one × 10(33)
Myles E. W. NORTH (1958) one × 12(33)
São Paulo, Brazil, S.O.M.
Johann Dalgas FRISCH (1961) SCLP 10502 × 12(33)
Wellington, New Zealand, A. H. and A. W. Reed
K. and J. BIGWOOD (1959) EC 14/16 × 7(45); (1961) EC 25 × 7(45)
Melbourne, Score Recordings
Peter BRUCE (1961) POLO 25 × 7(33)
Sydney, E.M.I.
Peter BRUCE (1956) SE GO 70006 × 7(45); (1957) SE GO 70010 × 7(45);

Geographical section: selected books, journals and societies

Marine

ALEXANDER, W. B. (1928*). Birds of the ocean. New York etc., Putnams, 428 pp.

WYNNE-EDWARDS, V. C. (1935). On the habits and distribution of birds on the North Atlantic. *Proc. Boston Soc. Nat. Hist. 40:* 233–346

MURPHY, R. C. (1936). Oceanic birds of South America. New York, Macmillan, 2 vols., 1245 pp.

FISHER, James and LOCKLEY, R. M. (1954). Sea-birds. . . . London, Collins *New Naturalist*, 320 pp.

HARRISON, P. P. O. (1962). Sea birds of the South Pacific Ocean. Narberth, Wales, Royal Naval Bird Watching Society, 144 pp.

STOKES, T. (1963). A sailor's guide to ocean birds, Atlantic and Mediterranean. London, Adlard Coles, 64 pp.

JOURNAL: *Sea Swallow*

SOCIETIES: Royal Naval Bird Watching Society. Netherlands Seafarers' Bird Watching Society

Ancient World

EVANS, A. H. ed. (1903). Turner on birds. Cambridge, University Press, 223 pp.

GURNEY, J. H. (1921). Early annals of ornithology. London, Witherby, 240 pp.

THOMPSON, d'Arcy Wentworth (1936). A glossary of Greek birds. London, Oxford University Press, 342 pp.

Palearctic and Oriental fauna

WYNNE, Owen E. (1953–55). Key-list of the Palaearctic and Oriental passerine birds. *Northw. Nat.* (n. ser.) *1:* 580–97; *2:* 123–37, 297–319, 436–59, 619–47 (revision 1956)

VAURIE, Charles (1959). The birds of the Palearctic fauna. Vol. 1. Passeriformes. London, Witherby, 762 pp.

Europe

GÉROUDET, Paul (1946–57*). La vie des oiseaux. Neuchâtel and Paris, Delachaux and Niestlé, 6 vols.

PETERSON, Roger [Tory], MOUNTFORT, Guy and HOLLOM, P. A. D. (1954*). A field guide to the birds of Britain and Europe. London, Collins, 318 pp.

VOOUS, K. H. (1960*). Atlas van de Europese Vogels. Amsterdam, Elsevier, 284 pp. English transl. London, Nelson.

Great Britain and Ireland

COWARD, T. A. (1920*). The birds of the British Isles and their eggs. London, Warne, 3 vols.

WITHERBY, H. F. and others (1938–41*). The handbook of British birds. London, Witherby, 5 vols.

FISHER, James (1947*–64). Bird recognition. Harmondsworth, Penguin, 4 vols.

NICHOLSON, E. M. (1951). Birds and men. London, Collins *New Naturalist*, 256 pp.

DOBSON, R. (1952). Birds of the Channel Islands, London, Staples, 264 pp.

FITTER, R. S. R. and RICHARDSON, R. A. (1952*). The pocket guide to British birds. London, Collins, 240 pp.

HOLLOM, P. A. D. ed. (1952*). The popular handbook of British birds. London, Witherby, 424 pp.

BRITISH ORNITHOLOGISTS' UNION (1952). Checklist of the birds of Great Britain and Ireland. London, B.O.U., 106 pp.

BAXTER, E. V. and RINTOUL, L. J. (1953). The birds of Scotland. Edinburgh etc., Oliver & Boyd, 2 vols., 816 pp.

BANNERMAN, D. A. and LODGE, G. E. (1953–63). The birds of the British Isles. Edinburgh etc., Oliver & Boyd, 12 vols.

KENNEDY, P. G. and others (1954). The birds of Ireland. Edinburgh etc., Oliver & Boyd, 437 pp.

DEANE, C. D. (1954). Handbook of the birds of Northern Ireland. *Bull. Belfast Mus. 1:* 120–90.

FITTER, R. S. R. and others (1955). The pocket guide to nests and eggs. London, Collins, 172 pp.

HOLLOM, P. A. D. (1960). The popular handbook of rarer British birds. London, Witherby, 133 pp.

FITTER, R. S. R. (1963). Collins guide to bird watching. London, Collins, 254 pp.

JOURNALS: *Avicultural Magazine, Bird Migration, Bird Notes, Bird Study, British Birds, Bulletin of the British Ornithologists' Club, The Ibis, Irish Bird Report, Scottish Birds, Zoological Record (Aves)*

SOCIETIES: Avicultural Society, British Ornithologists' Club, British Ornithologists' Union, British Trust for Ornithology, Irish Ornithologists' Club, Jourdain Society, Royal Society for the Protection of Birds, Scottish Ornithologists' Club, Wildfowl Trust

Germany

NIETHAMMER, Günther (1937–42). Handbuch der Deutschen Vogelkunde. Leipzig, Akademische Verlagsgesellschaft, 3 vols.

JOURNALS: *Anzeiger für Ornithologie, Journal für Ornithologie, Mitteilungen Thüringer Ornithologie, Mitteilungen uber der Vogelwelt, Ornithologische Abhandlungen, Ornithologische Mitteilungen, Vogelwarte, Vogelwelt*

SOCIETIES: Deutsche Ornithologische Gesellschaft, Ornithologische Gesellschaft in Bayern

Austria

JOURNAL: *Vogelkundliche Nachrichten aus Österreich*

Czechoslovakia

JOURNAL: *Sylvia*

Hungary

SZEKESSY, V. ed. (1958). Fauna Hungariae, vol. 21, Aves. Budapest.

KEVE, A. (1960). Nomenclator Avium Hungariae. Budapest, Hungarian Ornithological Institute, 89 pp.

JOURNALS: *Aquila, Kóczag*

SOCIETIES: Madartani Intézet, Magyar Ornithologiai Központ

France

MAYAUD, N. (1953). Liste des oiseaux de France. *Alauda, 21:* 1–63.

JOURNALS: *Alauda, l'Oiseau*

SOCIETIES: Ligue pour la Protection des Oiseaux, Société ornithologique de France et de l'Union française

Italy

JOURNALS: *Avocetta, Rivista Italiana di Ornitologia*

SOCIETY: Associazione Ornitologica Italiana

Malta

ROBERTS, E. L. (1954). The birds of Malta. Malta, Progress Press, 168 pp.

Spain and Portugal

TAIT, William C. (1924). The birds of Portugal. London, Witherby, 260 pp.

de CHAVIGNY, J. and MAYAUD, N. (1932). Sur l'avifaune des Açores. *Alauda* (2) *4:* 133–55, 304–48, 416–41.

LLETGET, A. G. (1945). Sinopsis de las aves de España y Portugal. *Trab. Inst. Cienc. nat. Madrid* (Biol.) *2:* 346 pp.

THEMIDO, A. A. (1952). Aves de Portugal. *Mem. Mus. Zool. Univ. Coimbra 1952:* 242 pp.

BANNERMAN, David A. (1963). Birds of the Atlantic Islands, vol. 1. A history of the birds of the Canary Islands and of the Salvages. Edinburgh etc., Oliver & Boyd, 358 pp.

JOURNAL: *Ardeola*

SOCIETY: Sociedad Española de Ornitologia

U.S.S.R.

DEMENT'EV, Georgi Petrovich and others (1951–54). Ptitsy Sovetskogo Soyuza. Moscow, Sovetskaya Nauka, 6 vols.

IVANOV, Alexander Ivanovich and others (1951–53). Ptitsy SSSR. Moscow etc., Akademii Nauk, 2 vols., 281+344 pp.

TUGARINOV, A. Ya. and PORTENKO, L. A. ed. (1952). Atlas okhotnich'ikh i promyslovikh ptits i zverey SSSR. Tom pervyy ptitsy. Moscow, Akademii Nauk, 371 pp.

JOURNAL: *Ornitologiya*

Finland

MERIKALLIO, Einari (1958). Finnish birds, their distribution and numbers. Helsinki, *Fauna Fennica 5:* 181 pp.

JOURNAL: *Ornis Fennica*

SOCIETY: Ornitologiska Föreningen i Finland

Norway

LØVENSKIÖLD, H. L. (1947–50). Håndbok over Norges fugler. Oslo, Gyldendal, 887 pp.

JOURNAL: *Sterna*

Sweden

CURRY-LINDAHL, Kai and others (1947*). Våra Fåglar i Norden. Stockholm, Natur och Kultur, 1988 pp.

JOURNAL: *Vår Fågelvärld*

SOCIETY: Sveriges Ornitologiska Förening

Denmark

SALOMONSEN, Finn (1963). Oversigt over Danmarks fugle. Copenhagen, Munksgaard, 156 pp.

JOURNALS: *Dansk Ornithologisk Forenings Tidsskrift, Feltornithologen*

SOCIETY: Dansk Ornithologisk Forening

Iceland and Faeroe

SALOMONSEN, Finn (1935). Aves *in* Zoology of the Faroes. Copenhagen, Carlsberg Fund.

TIMMERMANN, Günter (1938–49). Die Vögel Islands. *Vísindafélag Íslendinga* nos. 21, 24 & 28; 524 pp.

Netherlands
van IJZENDOORN, A. L. J. (1950). The breeding birds of the Netherlands. Leiden, Brill, 73 pp.

JOURNALS: *Ardea, Limosa*

SOCIETY: Nederlandse Ornithologische Vereniging

Belgium
VERHEYEN, R. (1943–52*). Les oiseaux de Belgique. Brussels, Institut royal des Sciences naturelles de Belgique, 8 parts.

JOURNALS: *Gerfaut, Wielewaal*

Switzerland
GLUTZ von BLOTZHEIM, U. *ed.* (1961). Die Brutvögel der Schweiz. Aarau, Schweizerische Vogelwarte Sempach, 648 pp.

JOURNALS: *Nos Oiseaux, Ornithologische Beobachter, Vögel der Heimat*

SOCIETIES: Schweizerische Gesellschaft für Vogelkunde und Vogelschutz, Société romande pour l'Étude et la Protection des Oiseaux

Greece
LAMBERT, A. (1957). A specific check list of the birds of Greece. *Ibis 99*: 43–68.

Jugoslavia
MATVEJEV, S. D. (1950). La distribution et la vie des oiseaux en Serbie. *Acad. Serb. Sci. Monogr. 161*: no. 3; 363 pp.

JOURNAL: *Larus*

Bulgaria
PATEFF, P. (1950). The birds of Bulgaria. Sofia, Bulgarian Academy of Sciences, 364 pp. (English summary).

China
CHENG, Tso-Hsin (1947). Check-list of Chinese birds. *Trans. Chin. Assoc. Adv. Sci. 9*: 40–84.

HACHISUKA, Masauji (1952). Bibliography of Chinese birds. *Q.J. Taiwan Mus. 5*: 71–209.

CHENG, Tso-Hsin (1955). A distributional list of Chinese birds. Part 1. Non-Passeriformes. Peking, Academica Sinica, 329 pp. (Chinese).

MacFARLANE, A. M. and MacDONALD, A. D. (1960). An annotated check-list of the birds of Hong Kong. Hong Kong, South China Morning Post, 91 pp.

Korea
AUSTIN, Oliver L. Jr. (1948). The birds of Korea. *Bull. Mus. Comp. Zool. 101*: 1–301.

Japan
AUSTIN, Oliver L. Jr. and KURODA, Nagahisa (1953). The birds of Japan. . . . *Bull. Mus. Comp. Zool. 109*: 280–637.

YAMASHINA, Yoshimaro (1961). Birds in Japan, a field guide. Tokyo, Tokyo News Service, 233 pp.

JOURNALS: *Hyoshikicho, Tori, Yacho*

SOCIETIES: Ornithological Society of Japan, Yacho Society of Japan

Arabia
MEINERTZHAGEN, Richard (1954). Birds of Arabia. Edinburgh, etc., Oliver & Boyd, 624 pp.

India, Ceylon and Pakistan, etc.
WHISTLER, H. (1923*). Popular handbook of Indian birds. London, Gurney & Jackson, 560 pp.

ALI, Sálim (1941*). The book of Indian birds. Bombay, Bombay NHS, 158 pp.

——— (1949*). Indian hill birds. Oxford, University Press, 188 pp.

HENRY, G. M. (1955). Guide to the birds of Ceylon. Oxford, University Press, 432 pp.

RIPLEY, Sidney Dillon II (1961). A synopsis of the birds of India and Pakistan . . . Bombay, Bombay NHS, 703 pp.

ALI, Sálim (1962). The birds of Sikkim. Madras, Oxford University Press, 414 pp.

Asia Minor
von JORDANS, Adolf and STEINBACHER, Joachim (1949). Zur Avifauna Kleinasiens. *Senckenbergiana 28*: 159–86.

BANNERMAN, David A. and BANNERMAN, W. Mary (1958). Birds of Cyprus. Edinburgh, etc., Oliver & Boyd, 384 pp.

ALLOUSE, Bashir E. (1960). Birds of Iraq. Baghdad, Ar-Rabitta Press, vol. 1: 276 pp.

SOCIETY: Ornithological Society of Israel

Siberia
JOHANSEN, Hans (1943–61). Die Vogelfauna Westsibiriens. *J. Orn. 91–92, 95–102*: many parts.

Afghanistan
PALUDAN, Knud (1959). On the birds of Afghanistan. *Vidensk. Medd. Dansk Naturh. Foren. no. 122*; 332 pp.

South-east Asia and rest of Oriental fauna
KURODA, N. (1933–36). Birds of the island of Java. Tokyo, author, 2 vols., 794 pp.

STRESEMANN, E. (1939–41). Die Vögel von Celebes . . . *J. Orn. 87*: 299–425; *88*: 1–135, 389–487; *89*: 1–102.

SMYTHIES, Bertram E. (1940*). The birds of Burma. Obtainable new edition (1953). Edinburgh, etc., Oliver & Boyd, 668 pp.

RIPLEY, S. Dillon (1944). The bird fauna of the west Sumatra islands. *Bull. Mus. Comp. Zool. Harvard 94*: 307–430.

DEIGNAN, H. G. (1945). The birds of northern Thailand. Washington, D.C., Smithsonian Institution, 572 pp.

DELACOUR, J. and MAYR, E. (1946). Birds of the Philippines. New York, Macmillan, 309 pp.

DELACOUR, J. (1947). Birds of Malaysia. New York, Macmillan, 382 pp.

GLENISTER, A. G. (1951). The birds of the Malay Peninsula, Singapore and Penang. London, Oxford University Press, 282 pp.

SMYTHIES, Bertram E. (1960). The birds of Borneo. Edinburgh, etc., Oliver & Boyd, 562 pp.

North Africa (Palearctic fauna)
MEINERTZHAGEN, Richard (1930). Nicoll's birds of Egypt. London, Hugh Rees, 2 vols., 700 pp.

BOURNE, W. R. P. (1955). The birds of the Cape Verde Islands. *Ibis 97*: 508–56.

HEIM de BALSAC, H. and MAYAUD, N. (1962). Les oiseaux du nord-ouest de l'Afrique. Paris, Lechevalier, 487 pp.

Ethiopian fauna
General
SCLATER, W. L. (1924–30). Systema avium Aethiopicarum. London, British Ornithologists' Union, 922 pp.

BOUET, Georges (1955–61). Oiseaux de l'Afrique tropical. Paris, Faune de l'Union française, 798 pp.

Western Tropical Africa
BANNERMAN, David A. (1930–51). The birds of tropical West Africa. London, Crown Agents for the Colonies, 8 vols.

CHAPIN, James P. (1932–54). The birds of the Belgian Congo. *Bull. Amer. Mus. Nat. Hist. 65, 75, 75a and 75b.*

BANNERMAN, David A. (1953). The birds of west and equatorial Africa. Edinburgh, Oliver & Boyd, 2 vols., 1526 pp.

TRAYLOR, Melvin A. (1963). Check-list of Angolan birds. *Publ. Culturais Comp. Diamantes de Angola no. 61*; 250 pp.

Eastern Tropical Africa
ARCHER, G. F. and GODMAN, E. M. (1937–61). The birds of British Somaliland and the Gulf of Aden. Edinburgh, etc., Oliver & Boyd, 4 vols., 1570 pp.

JACKSON, F. J. (1938). The birds of Kenya and the Uganda Protectorate. London, Gurney & Jackson, 3 vols., 1592 pp.

MACKWORTH-PRAED, Cyril W. and GRANT, Claude H. B. (1952–55*). Birds of eastern and north eastern Africa. London, etc., Longmans Green, 2 vols., 836+1100 pp.

CAVE, F. O. and MacDONALD, J. D. (1955). Birds of the Sudan. Edinburgh, etc., Oliver & Boyd, 444 pp.

WILLIAMS, John G. (1963). A field guide to the birds of east and central Africa. London, Collins, 288 pp.

SOCIETY: East African Natural History Society

Southern Africa
HOESCH, W. and NIETHAMMER, Günther (1940). Die Vogelwelt Deutsch-Südwestafrikas . . . *J. Orn. 88*: (suppl.) 404 pp.

ROBERTS, Austin (1940*). The birds of South Africa. London, Witherby, 463 pp.

GILL, E. L. (1936*). A first guide to South African birds. Cape Town, Miller, 223 pp.

MACKWORTH-PRAED, Cyril W. and GRANT, Claude H. B. (1962). Birds of the southern third of Africa. London, Longmans Green, vol. 1: 688 pp.

JOURNALS: *Babbler, Bokmakierie, Ostrich*

SOCIETIES: Rhodesian Ornithological Society. South African Ornithological Society, Witwatersrand Bird Club

Madagascar etc.
RAND, A. L. (1936). The distribution and habits of Madagascar birds. *Bull. Amer. Mus. Nat. Hist. 72*: 143–499.

BERLIOZ, J. (1946). Oiseaux de la Réunion. Paris, Larose's Faune de l'Empire français, no. 4; 81 pp.

ROUNTREE, F. R. G., and others (1952). Catalogue of the birds of Mauritius. *Mauritius Inst. Bull. 3*: 155–217.

BENSON, C. W. (1960). The birds of the Comoro Islands. *Ibis 103b*: 5–106.

The Americas
General
CORY, C. B. HELLMAYR, C. E. and CON-OVER, B. (1918–48). Catalogue of the birds of the Americas . . . *Field Mus. Publ. (Zool.) 13:* 11 numbers; 15 parts.
RIDGWAY, R. and FRIEDMANN, H. (1901–50). Birds of North and Middle America. *Bull. U.S. Nat. Mus.,* 11 vols.

North America generally
BENT, Arthur Cleveland and others (1919→). Life histories of North American birds. *Bull. U.S. Nat. Mus.,* 20 vols. to 1958.
PETERSON, Roger Tory (1934*). A field guide to the birds. Boston, Houghton Mifflin, 290 pp.
——— (1941*). A field guide to western birds. Boston, Houghton Mifflin, 366 pp.
POUGH, Richard H. (1946*). Audubon bird guide: small land birds of eastern and central North America . . . Garden City, Doubleday, 312 pp.
——— (1951*). Audubon bird guide: water birds. Garden City, Doubleday, 352 pp.
AMERICAN ORNITHOLOGISTS' UNION (1957). Checklist of North American birds. Baltimore, A.O.U., 691 pp.
POUGH, Richard H. (1957). Audubon western bird guide. Garden City, Doubleday, 316 pp.
BRODKORB, Pierce (1957). Birds, pp. 359–613 of W. F. Blair and others' Vertebrates of the United States. New York, McGraw-Hill, 819 pp.
PALMER, Ralph S. *ed.* (1962). Handbook of North American birds. New Haven and London, Yale University Press, vol. 1: 567 pp.
JOURNALS: *Audubon, Audubon Field Notes, The Auk*
SOCIETIES: American Ornithologists' Union, National Audubon Society

Canada
AUSTIN, Oliver Luther Jr. (1932). The birds of Newfoundland Labrador. *Mem. Nuttall Orn. Cl.* no. 7; 229 pp.
TAVERNER, P. A. (1934*). Birds of Canada. *Canad. Dep. Mines Bull.* no. 72; 445 pp.
RAND, A. L. (1946). List of Yukon birds . . . *National Mus. Canad. Bull.* no. 105; 76 pp.
MUNRO, J. A. and COWAN, I. McT. (1947). A review of the bird fauna of British Columbia. *B.C. Provincial Mus. Special Publ.* no. 2; 285 pp.
SNYDER, L. L. (1950). Ontario birds. Toronto, Clark Irwin, 248 pp.
PETERS, H. S. and BURLEIGH, T. D. (1951). The birds of Newfoundland. St. John's, Department of National Resources, 431 pp.
SQUIRES, W. Austin (1952). The birds of New Brunswick. *Publ. New Brunsw. Mus.* (Monogr. Ser.) no. 4; 163 pp.
GODFREY, W. Earl (1953). Birds of Prince Edward Island. *Bull. Nat. Mus. Canada* no. 132; 155–213.
SALT, W. Ray and WILK, A. L. (1958). The birds of Alberta. Edmonton, Department of Economic Affairs, 511 pp.
TUFTS, Robie W. (1963). The birds of Nova Scotia. Halifax, Nova Scotia Museum, 481 pp.
JOURNALS: *Blue Jay, Canadian Audubon, Canadian Field-Naturalist*
SOCIETIES: Canadian Audubon Society

North-eastern States
(including New England)
ALLEN, Glover M. (1903). A list of the birds of New Hampshire. *Proc. Manchester Inst. Arts Sci. 4:* 21–222.
STONE, Witmer (1909). The birds of New Jersey. *Rep. New Jersey State Mus.* 1908: 11–347, 409–19.
EATON, E. H. (1910–14). The birds of New York. *Mem. N.Y. State Mus. 12:* (2 parts); 501+719 pp.
SAGE, J. H. and BISHOP, L. B. (1913). The birds of Connecticut. *Bull. Conn. Geol. Nat. Hist. Surv.* no. 20; 370 pp.
FORBUSH, E. H. (1925–29). Birds of Massachusetts and other New England States. Massachusetts Board of Agriculture, 3 vols.
TODD, W. E. Clyde (1940). Birds of western Pennsylvania. Pittsburgh, University of Pittsburgh Press, 710 pp.
PALMER, R. S. (1949). Maine birds. *Bull. Mus. Comp. Zool. Harvard 102:* 1–656
GRISCOM, Ludlow and SNYDER, Dorothy E. (1955). The birds of Massachusetts. Salem, Peabody Museum, 295 pp.
JOURNALS: *Bird Banding, Bulletins of the Maine and Massachusetts Audubon Societies, Cassinia*
SOCIETIES: Nuttall Ornithological Club, State Audubon Societies

South-eastern (S. Atlantic) States
BAILEY, H. H. (1913). The birds of Virginia. Lynchburg, J. P. Bell, 362 pp.
PEARSON, T. G. and others (1919*). Birds of North Carolina. *N.C. Geol. Econ. Surv. 4:* 380 pp.
SPRUNT, Alexander Jr. and CHAMBER-LAIN, E. Burnham (1949). South Carolina bird life. Columbia, University of South Carolina Press, 585 pp.
SPRUNT, Alexander Jr. (1954). Florida bird life. New York, Coward-McCann, 527 pp.
BURLEIGH, T. D. (1958). Georgia birds. Norman, University of Oklahoma Press, 746 pp.
STEWART, Robert E. and ROBBINS, Chandler S. (1958). Birds of Maryland and the District of Columbia. *N. Amer. Fauna* no. 62; 401 pp.
JOURNAL: *EBBA* (Eastern Bird Banding Association) *News*
SOCIETIES: State Audubon Societies

Southern Central (Gulf) States
NICE, Margaret Morse (1931). The birds of Oklahoma. *Publ. Univ. Oklahoma* (Biol. Surv.) *3:* 224 pp.
BAERG, W. J. (1931). Birds of Arkansas. *Univ. Arkansas Agric. Exper. Sta. Bull.* no. 258; 197 pp.
WETMORE, Alexander (1939). Notes on the birds of Tennessee. *Proc. U.S. Nat. Mus. 86:* 175–243.
LOWERY, George H. Jr. (1955). Louisiana birds. Bâton Rouge, Louisiana State University Press, 556 pp.
PETERSON, Roger Tory (1960). A field guide to the birds of Texas. Boston, Houghton Mifflin, 304 pp.
IMHOF, T. A. (1962). Alabama birds. University of Alabama Press, 591 pp.
JOURNAL: *The Migrant*
SOCIETIES: Tennessee Ornithological Society, State Audubon Societies

North Central (Lake) States
ROBERTS, T. S. (1932). The birds of Minnesota. Minneapolis, University of Minnesota Press, 2 vols., 691+821 pp.
BENNITT, Rudolf (1932). Check-list of the birds of Missouri. *Univ. Missouri Stud. 7.*
DuMONT, Philip A. (1934). A revised list of the birds of Iowa. *Univ. Iowa Stud. Nat. Hist. 15:* no. 5; 171 pp.
KUMLIEN, Aaron Ludwig and others (1948–49). The birds of Wisconsin. *Passenger Pigeon 10:* 11–24, 59–68, 107–13, 142–48; *11:* 36–40, 74–79.
WOOD, Norman A. (1951). The birds of Michigan. *Misc. Publ. Mus. Zool. Univ. Mich.* no. 75; 559 pp.
JOURNALS: *American Midland Naturalist, Field Museum Publications* (Ornithological and Zoological series), *Inland Bird Banding News, Jack Pine Warbler, Passenger Pigeon, Wilson Bulletin*
SOCIETIES: State Audubon Societies, Wilson Ornithological Club

Western (Mountain) States
SAUNDERS, Aretas A. (1921). A distributional list of the birds of Montana. *Pacif. Coast Avif.* no. 14; 194 pp.
WOOD, Norman A. (1923). A preliminary survey of the bird life of North Dakota. *Univ. Mich. Mus. Zool. Misc. Publ.* no. 10; 96 pp.
BERGTOLD, William H. (1928). A guide to the birds of Colorado. Denver, Smith-Brooks, 207 pp.
McCREARY, Otto (1939). Wyoming bird life. Minneapolis, Burgess, mimeod.
OVER, William H. and THOMS, Craig S. (1946). Birds of South Dakota. Vermillion, University of South Dakota Museum.
GOODRICH, Arthur L. Jr. (1946). Birds in Kansas. *Rep. Kansas State Board Agric. 64:* no. 267; 340 pp.
TORDOFF, Harrison B. (1956). Check-list of the birds of Kansas. *Univ. Kansas Publ. Mus. Nat. Hist. 8:* 307–59.
LIGON, J. Stokley (1961). New Mexico birds and where to find them. Albuquerque, University of New Mexico Press, 360 pp.
JOURNALS: see under *Pacific States*
SOCIETIES: State Audubon Societies

Pacific States (including Western Desert States)
GABRIELSON, Ira N. and JEWETT, Stanley G. (1940). Birds of Oregon. Corvallis, Oregon State College, 650 pp.
GRINNELL, Joseph and MILLER, Alden H. (1944). The distribution of the birds of California. *Pacif. Coast Avif.* no. 27; 608 pp.
ARVEY, M. Dale (1947). A check-list of the birds of Idaho. *Univ. Kansas Publ. Mus. Nat. Hist. 1:* 193–216.
BRANDT, Herbert (1951). Arizona and its bird life. Cleveland (Ohio), Bird Research Foundation, 725 pp.
JEWETT, Stanley G. and others (1953). Birds of Washington State. Seattle, University of Washington Press, 767 pp.
JOURNALS: *The Condor, Gull, The Murrelet, News from the Banders, Pacific Coast Avifauna*
SOCIETIES: Audubon Association of the Pacific, Cooper Ornithological Club of California, Pacific Northwest Bird and Mammal Club, State Audubon Societies

Alaska and Hawaii

MUNRO, George C. (1944*). Birds of Hawaii. Honolulu, Tongg, 189 pp.

BAILEY, A. M. (1956). Birds of Midway and Laysan Islands. *Mus. Pictorial Denver* no. 12; 130 pp.

GABRIELSON, Ira N. and LINCOLN, F. C. (1959). Birds of Alaska. Washington, D.C., Wildlife Management Institute, 922 pp.

JOURNAL: *Elepaio*

SOCIETIES: State Audubon Societies

México and Central America

CARRIKER, M. A. Jr. (1910). An annotated list of the birds of Costa Rica, including Cocos Island. *Ann. Carnegie Mus. 6:* 314–915.

STURGIS, B. B. (1928). Field book of birds of the Panama Canal Zone. New York, Putnams, 466 pp.

STONE, Witmer (1932). The birds of Honduras . . . *Proc. Acad. Nat. Sci. Philad. 84:* 291–342.

GRISCOM, Ludlow (1932). The distribution of bird life in Guatemala. *Bull. Amer. Nat. Hist. 64:* 439 pp.

—— (1935). The ornithology of the republic of Panama. *Bull. Mus. Comp. Zool. Harvard 78:* 261–382.

DICKEY, D. R. and van ROSSEM, A. J. (1938). The birds of El Salvador. *Field Mus. Publ.* (Zool.) *23:* 609 pp.

FRIEDMANN, Herbert and others (1950–57). Distributional check-list of the birds of México. *Pacif. Coast Avif.* no. 29; 202 pp.: no. 33; 436 pp.

DEVAS, R. P. (1953). Birds of British Honduras. Port of Spain.

BLAKE, Emmett Reid (1953). Birds of México, Chicago, University of Chicago Press, 644 pp.

RAND, A. L. and TRAYLOR, Melvin A. (1954). Manual de las aves de El Salvador. Universidad de El Salvador, 308 pp., mimeod.

SKUTCH, A. F. (1954–60). Life histories of Central American birds. *Pacif. Coast Avif.* no. 31; 448 pp., no. 34; 593 pp.

EISENMANN, Eugene (1955). The species of Middle American birds. *Trans. Linn. Soc. N.Y. 7:* 128 pp.

West Indies

BOND, James (1936*). Birds of the West Indies. Philadelphia, Academy of Sciences, 456 pp. (1960 ed. London, Collins).

VOOUS, K. H. (1957). The birds of Aruba, Curaçao and Bonaire. *Natuurwet Stud. Suriname* no. 14; 260 pp.

HERKLOTS, G. A. C. (1961). Birds of Trinidad and Tobago. London, Collins, 270 pp.

ALLEN, Robert Porter (1961). Birds of the Caribbean. New York, Viking Press, 256 pp.

South America
Brazil

PINTO, O. M. de O. (1938). Catálogo das aves do Brazil. Part 1. *Rev. Mus. Paulista 22:* 566 pp.

—— (1944). Part 2. São Paulo, Dep. Zool. Sec. Agric. Industr. Comércio, 700 pp.

NAUMBERG, E. M. B. (1930). The birds of Matto Grosso, Brazil. . . . *Bull. Amer. Mus. Nat. Hist. 60:* 432 pp.

MITCHELL, M. H. (1957). Observations on birds of southeastern Brazil. Toronto, University of Toronto Press, 258 pp.

Argentina and the Falklands

WETMORE, Alexandra (1926). Observations on the birds of Argentina, Paraguay, Uruguay and Chile. *Bull. U.S. Nat. Mus. 133:* 448 pp.

STEULLET, A. B. and DEAUTIER, E. A. (1935–36). Catalógo sistemático de las aves de la Republica Argentina. Buenos Aires, Museum de La Plata, 492 pp.

OLROG, Claes Chr. (1959). Las aves Argentinas una guia de campo. Tucumán, Universidad Nacional de Tucumán, 345 pp.

JOURNAL: *El Hornero*

SOCIETY: Associatión Ornitólogica del Plata

Chile

GOODALL, J. D. and others (1946–51). Las aves de Chile. Buenos Aires, Platt Establecimientos Gráficos, 2 vols., 358+445 pp.

Bolivia

NIETHAMMER, Günther (1953–56). Zur Vogelwelt Boliviens. *Bonn. Zool. Beitr. 4:* 195–303; 7: 84–150

Perú

MURPHY, R. C. (1925). Bird islands of Perú. New York, Putnam, 362 pp.

ZIMMER, John T. (1931–55). Studies of Peruvian birds. *Amer. Mus. Novit.*, 66 numbers

Northern South America

CHAPMAN, F. M. (1926). The distribution of bird life in Ecuador. *Bull. Amer. Mus. Nat. Hist. 55:* 784 pp.

SWARTH, H. S. (1931). The avifauna of the Galápagos Islands. *Occ. Pap. Calif. Acad. Sci.* no. 18; 299 pp.

de SCHAUENSEE, R. M. (1948–52). The birds of the republic of Colombia. *Caldasia 5:* 251–1223.

PHELPS, William H. and PHELPS, William H. Jr. (1950–58). Lista de las aves de Venezuela con su distribucion. Caracas, Grafolit and Sucre, 2 vols., 427+317 pp.

HAVERSCHMIDT, F. (1955). List of the birds of Surinam. *Publ. Foundation Sci. Res. Surinam* no. 13; 153 pp.

Paraguay and Uruguay

APLIN, O. V. (1894). On the birds of Uruguay. *Ibis* (6) *6:* 149–215.

PODTIAGUIN, B. (1941–45). Catalogo sistemático de las aves del Paraguay. *Rev. Soc. Cienc. Paraguay 5:* (5) 3–107; *6:* (3) 7–119; (6) 63–80.

Australasian fauna
General

MATHEWS, Gregory M. (1927–31). Systema Avium Australasianarum. London, British Ornithologists' Union, 1048 pp.

New Zealand

OLIVER, W. R. B. (1930*). New Zealand birds. Wellington, Fine Arts (later Reed), 541 pp.

FLEMING, Charles A. and others (1953). Check-list of New Zealand birds. Wellington, Ornithological Society of New Zealand, 80 pp.

JOURNALS: *Forest and Bird, Notornis*

SOCIETIES: Forest and Bird Protection Society of New Zealand, Ornithological Society of New Zealand

Australia

LEACH, J. A. (1911*). An Australian bird book. Melbourne, Whitcomb & Toombs, 200 pp.

ROYAL AUSTRALASIAN ORNITHOLOGISTS' UNION (1926). The official checklist of the birds of Australia. Melbourne, Green, 212 pp.

CAYLEY, Neville W. (1931*). What bird is that? A guide to the birds of Australia. Sydney, Angus & Robertson, 319 pp.

CHISHOLM, A. H. (1935*). Bird wonders of Australia. Sydney, Angus & Robertson, 299 pp.

SHARLAND, M. S. R. (1945*). Tasmanian birds, how to identify them. Hobart (later Sydney, Angus & Robertson), 122 pp.

BARRETT, Charles (1945*). Australian bird life. Melbourne, Oxford University Press, 239 pp.

SERVENTY, D. L. and WHITTELL, H. M. (1948*). A handbook of the birds of Western Australia. Perth, Patersons Press, 365 pp.

TERRILL, S. E. and RIX, C. E. (1950). The birds of South Australia, . . . *S. Austral. Orn. 19:* 53–100.

WHITTELL, H. M. (1954). The literature of Australian birds . . . Perth, Paterson Brokensha, 2 parts, 116+788 pp.

JOURNALS: *Emu, South Australian Ornithologist*

SOCIETIES: Royal Australasian Ornithologists' Union, South Australian Ornithological Association

Lesser Sunda Is. and Papuasia

MAYR, Ernst (1941). List of New Guinea birds. New York, American Museum of Natural History, 260 pp.

—— (1944). The birds of Timor and Sumba. *Bull. Amer. Mus. Nat. Hist. 83:* 123–94.

IREDALE, Tom (1956). Birds of New Guinea. Melbourne, Georgian House, 2 vols.

Oceania

MAYR, Ernst (1945). Birds of the southwest Pacific. New York, Macmillan, 316 pp.

BAKER, Rollin H. (1951). The avifauna of Micronesia, . . . *Univ. Kansas Publ. Mus. Nat. Hist. 3:* 359 pp.

Isolated island

ELLIOTT, H. F. I. (1957). A contribution to the ornithology of the Tristan da Cunha group. *Ibis 99:* 545–86.

Polar regions

ROBERTS, Brian B. (1941). A bibliography of Antarctic ornithology. *Sci. Rep. Brit. Graham Land Exped. 1934–37 1:* 337–67.

SALOMONSEN, Finn (1950–51). The birds of Greenland. Copenhagen, Munksgaard, 608 pp.

MILON, Ph. and JOUANIN, Chr. (1953). Contribution à l'ornithologie de l'Île Kerguelen. *Oiseau 23:* 4–53.

LØVENSKIÖLD, Herman L. (1954). Studies on the avifauna of Spitsbergen. *Skr. Norsk Polarinst.* no. 103; 131 pp.

JOHANSEN, Hans (1956–58). Revision und Entstehung der arktischen Vogelfauna. *Acta Arct. Kbn.* no. 8; 98 pp., no. 9; 131 pp.

SNYDER, L. L. (1957). Arctic birds of Canada. Toronto, University of Toronto Press, 300 pp.

USPENSKIĬ, S. M. (1958). Ptitsy sovetskoy arktiki. Moscow, Akademii Nauk, 167 pp.

Monographic

General

MAYR, E. and AMADON, D. (1951). A classification of recent birds. *Amer. Mus. Novit.* no. 1496; 42 pp.

WETMORE, Alexander (1960). A classification for the birds of the world. *Smithson. Misc. Coll. 139:* no. 11; 37 pp.

Family 1. Archaeopteryx

de BEER, G. R. (1954). Archaeopteryx lithographica. London, British Museum (Nat. Hist.), 68 pp.

Family 7. Penguins

RICHDALE, L. E. (1949). A study of a group of penguins of known age. *Biol. Monogrs. Dunedin* no. 1; 88 pp.

——— (1951). Sexual behaviour in penguins. Lawrence, University of Kansas Press, 316 pp.

RIVOLIER, Jean (1956). Emperor penguins. London, Elek, 131 pp., transl. from French.

RICHDALE, L. E. (1957). A population study of penguins. Oxford, Clarendon Press, 195 pp.

SLADEN, W. J. L. (1958). The Pygoscelid penguins. *FIDS Rep.* no. 17; 97 pp.

Families 14 and 15. Moas

ARCHEY, G. (1941). The moa. . . . *Bull. Auckland Inst. Mus.* no. 1; 145 pp.

OLIVER, W. R. B. (1949). The moas of New Zealand and Australia. *N. Z. Dominion Mus. Bull.* no. 15; 206 pp.

DUFF, Roger (1956). The moa-hunter period of Maori culture. *Canterbury Mus. Bull.* no. 1; 400 pp. (2nd ed. much revised; first ed. 1950).

Family 19. Loons

OLSON, S. T. and MARSHALL, W. H. (1952). The common loon in Minnesota. *Minn. Mus. Nat. Hist. Occ. Paper* no. 5; 77 pp.

Family 20. Grebes

HUXLEY, Julian S. (1914). The courtship-habits of the great crested grebe . . . *Proc. Zool. Soc. Lond. 1914:* 491–562.

Family 21. Albatrosses

RICHDALE, L. E. (1949). The pre-egg stage in Buller's mollymawk. *Biol. Monogrs. Dunedin* no. 2; 49 pp.

——— (1950). The pre-egg stage in the albatross family. *Biol. Monogrs. Dunedin* no. 3; 92 pp.

——— (1952). Post-egg period in albatrosses. *Biol. Monogrs. Dunedin* no. 4; 166 pp.

BAILEY, Alfred M. (1952). Laysan and black-footed albatrosses. *Mus. Pictorial Denver* no. 6; 80 pp.

JAMESON, William (1958). The wandering albatross. London, Hart-Davis, 99 pp.

BAILEY, Alfred M. and SORENSEN, J. H. (1962). Subantarctic Campbell Island. *Proc. Denver Mus. Nat. Hist.* no. 10; 305 pp. (five species).

Family 22. Petrels and shearwaters

LOCKLEY, Ronald M. (1942*). Shearwaters. London, Dent, 238 pp.

FISHER, James (1952). The fulmar. London, Collins *New Naturalist*, 496 pp.

Family 23. Storm petrels

ROBERTS, Brian B. (1940). The life cycle of Wilson's petrel, . . . *Brit. Graham Land Exped. Sci. Reps. 1:* 141–94.

Family 29. Gannets and boobies

GURNEY, J. H. (1913). The gannet . . . London, Witherby, 567 pp.

FISHER, James and VEVERS, H. Gwynne (1943–44). The breeding distribution, history and population of the North Atlantic gannet . . . *J. Anim. Ecol. 12:* 173–213; *13:* 49–62.

Family 31. Cormorants

LEWIS, Harrison F. (1929). The natural history of the double-crested cormorant . . . Ottawa, Ru-Mi-Lou Books, 94 pp.

Family 37. Herons

LOWE, Frank A. (1954). The heron. London, Collins *New Naturalist*, 177 pp.

MEYERRIECKS, A. J. (1960). Comparative breeding behaviour of four species of North American herons. *Publ. Nuttall Orn. Cl.* no. 2; 158 pp.

Family 39. Storks

HAVERSCHMIDT, Fr. (1949). The life of the white stork. Leiden, Brill, 96 pp.

Family 41. Ibises and spoonbills

ALLEN, Robert Porter (1947). The flame birds. New York, Dodd Mead, 233 pp.

ZAHL, Paul A. (1955). Coro-coro—the world of the scarlet ibis. London, Hammond & Hammond.

Family 46. Flamingos

ALLEN, Robert Porter (1956). The flamingos: their life history and survival. *Nat. Audubon Soc. Research Rep.* no. 5; 285 pp.

BROWN, Leslie (1959). The mystery of the flamingos. London, Country Life, 116 pp.

Family 49. Waterfowl

HOCHBAUM, A. Albert (1944). The canvas-back on a prairie marsh. Washington, D.C., American Wildlife Institute, 201 pp.

HANSON, Harold C. and SMITH, Robert H. (1950). Canada geese of the Mississippi flyway. *Bull. Ill. Nat. Hist. Surv. 25:* 59–210.

SCOTT, Peter (1951). Wild geese and Eskimos. London, Country Life, 254 pp.

SAVAGE, Christopher (1952). The mandarin duck. London, Black, 78 pp.

SCOTT, Peter and FISHER, James (1953). A thousand geese. London, Collins, 240 pp.

DELACOUR, Jean (1954–64). The waterfowl of the world. London, Country Life, ill. Peter Scott, 4 vols.

HOCHBAUM, H. Albert (1955). Travels and traditions of waterfowl. Minneapolis, University of Minnesota Press, 301 pp.

TICEHURST, Norman F. (1957). The mute swan in England. London, Cleaver-Hume, 133 pp.

BANKO, Winston E. (1960). The trumpeter swan. *N. Amer. Fauna* no. 63; 214 pp.

Family 51. New World vultures

KOFORD, Carl B. (1953). The California condor. *Nat. Audubon Soc. Research Rep.* no. 4; 154 pp.

Family 54. Hawks and eagles

BERG, Bengt (1931). Gypaëtus den flygande Draken i Himalaya. Stockholm, Norstedt, 229 pp.

HERRICK, F. H. (1934). The American eagle. New York, Appleton-Century, 267 pp.

BROUN, Maurice (1949*). Hawks aloft. New York, Dodd Mead, 222 pp.

BROLEY, M. J. (1952). Eagle man. New York, Farrar, Straus & Young, 210 pp.

GORDON, Seton (1955). The golden eagle. London, Collins, 246 pp.

BROWN, Leslie (1955). Eagles. London, Joseph, 274 pp.

KRAMER, Volkhard (1955). Habicht und Sperber. Wittenberg Lutherstadt, Ziemsen, 100 pp.

WENZEL, Frank (1959). The buzzard. London, Allen and Unwin, 86 pp., transl. from Danish.

FISCHER, W. (1963). Die Geier. Wittenberg Lutherstadt, Ziemsen, 144 pp.

Family 55. Osprey

MOLL, K.-H. (1962). Der Fischadler. Wittenberg Lutherstadt, Ziemsen, 95 pp.

BROWN, Philip and WATERSTON, George (1962). The return of the osprey. London, Collins, 223 pp.

Family 56. Falcons

LEWIS, Ernest (1938). In search of the gyrfalcon. London, Constable, 235 pp.

PIECHOCKI, Rudolf (1954). Der Turmfalke. Wittenberg Lutherstadt, Ziemsen, 57 pp.

Family 61. Grouse

LESLIE, A. S., WILSON, E. A. and others (1912). The grouse in health and disease. London, Smith Elder, 472 pp.

BUMP, G. and others (1947). The ruffed grouse. Albany, New York State Legislature, 915 pp.

KNIGHT, J. A. (1947). Ruffed grouse. New York, Knopf, 271 pp.

BOBACK, Alfred Willy (1952). Das Auerhuhn. Leipzig, Geest & Portig, 55 pp.

Family 62. Quails, pheasants, etc.

STODDARD, Herbert L. (1931). The bob-white quail. New York, Scribners, 559 pp.

McATEE, W. L. ed. (1945). The ring-necked pheasant and its management in North America. Washington, D.C., American Wildlife Institute.

DELACOUR, Jean (1951). The pheasants of the world. London, Country Life, 347 pp.

TOSCHI, A. (1959). La Quaglia: Vita, Caccia, Allevamento. Bologna, University of Bologna, 267 pp.

Family 63. Guineafowl

von BOETTICHER, Hans (1954). Die Perl-hühner. Wittenberg Lutherstadt, Ziemsen, 55 pp.

Family 64. Turkeys

McILHENNY, E. A. (1914). The wild turkey and its hunting. Garden City, N.Y., Double-day, 254 pp.

MOSBY, H. E. and HANDLEY, C. O. (1943). The wild turkey in Virginia; . . . Richmond, Virginia Commission for Game and Inland Fisheries, 281 pp.

Family 70. Cranes
HOFFMANN, G. (1936). Rund um den Kranich. Oehringen, Hohenlohe, 146 pp.
WALKINSHAW, Lawrence H. (1949). The sandhill cranes. *Cranbrook Inst. Sci. Bull.* no. 29; 202 pp.
ALLEN, Robert Porter (1953). The whooping crane. *Nat. Audubon Soc. Research Rep.* no. 3; 246 pp.

Family 75. Rails
HOWARD, H. Eliot (1940). A waterhen's worlds. Cambridge, University Press, 84 pp.
JONES, J. C. (1940). Food habits of the American coot, with notes on its distribution. *Wildlife Research Bull.* no. 2; 52 pp.

Family 92. Plovers and turnstones
SPENCER, K. G. (1953). The lapwing in Britain. London, etc., Brown, 166 pp.
RITTINGHAUS, H. (1961). Der Seeregenpfeifer.... Wittenberg Lutherstadt, Ziemsen, 126 pp.

Family 93. Snipe, sandpipers and allies
PETTINGILL, Olin Sewall Jr. (1936). The American woodcock... *Mem. Boston Soc. Nat. Hist. 9:* 169–391.
BERGMAN, G. (1946). Der Steinwalzer, *Arenaria i. interpres* (L.) in seiner Beziehung zur Umwelt. *Acta Zool. Fennica 47:* 1–151.
NETHERSOLE-THOMPSON, Desmond (1951). The greenshank. London, Collins *New Naturalist,* 244 pp.
KIRCHNER, H. (1963). Der Bruchwasserläufer. Wittenberg Lutherstadt, Ziemsen, 86 pp.

Family 94. Avocets and allies
MAKKINK, G. F. (1936). An attempt at an ethogram of the European avocet... *Ardea 25:* 1–74.
BROWN, P. E. (1950). Avocets in England. *Roy. Soc. Protect. Birds Occas. Publ.* no. 14; 40 pp.

Family 96. Phalaropes
TINBERGEN, Niko (1935). The behaviour of the red-necked phalarope . . . in spring. *Ardea 24:* 1–42.

Family 103. Gulls and terns
AUSTIN, Oliver Luther Jr. (1932→). Many papers on terns in *Bird Banding 3:* →
KIRKMAN, F. B. (1937). Bird behaviour a contribution based chiefly on a study of the black-headed gull. London and Edinburgh, Nelson & Jack, 232 pp.
PALMER, R. S. (1941). A behaviour study of the common tern . . . *Proc. Boston Soc. Nat. Hist. 42:* 1–119.
TINBERGEN, Niko (1953). The herring gull's world. London, Collins *New Naturalist,* 255 pp.

Family 105. Auks
GRIEVE, Symington (1885). The great auk. London, Jack, 58 pp.
PALUDAN, Knud (1947). Alken. Copenhagen, Munksgaard, 109 pp.
LOCKLEY, Ronald M. (1953). Puffins. London, Dent, 186 pp.
TUCK, Leslie M. (1960). The murres. Ottawa, Department of Northern Affairs and National Resources, 260 pp.

Family 108. Pigeons
LEVI. W. M. (1941). The pigeon. Columbia, S.C., Bryan, 512 pp.
SCHORGER, A. W. (1955). The passenger pigeon. Madison, University of Wisconsin Press, 424 pp.

Family 109. Dodo and solitaires
HACHISUKA, Masauji (1953). The dodo and kindred birds. London, Witherby, 250 pp.
LÜTTSCHWAGER, J. (1961). Die Drontevögel. Wittenberg Lutherstadt, Ziemsen, 60 pp.

Family 110. Parrots
af ENEHJELM, Curt (1957). Das Buch vom Wellensittich. Pfungstadt, Helène, 199 pp.
von BOETTICHER, Hans (1957). Papageien. Wittenberg Lutherstadt, Ziemsen, 116 pp.

Family 112. Cuckoos
CHANCE, Edgar P. (1940). The truth about the cuckoo. London, Country Life, 207 pp.
BAKER, E. C. Stuart (1942). Cuckoo problems. London, Witherby, 207 pp.
FRIEDMANN, H. (1948). The parasitic cuckoos of Africa. *Wash. Acad. Sci. Monogr.* no. 1; 204 pp.
ROTHSCHILD, Miriam and CLAY, Theresa (1952). Fleas, flukes and cuckoos. London, Collins *New Naturalist,* 304 pp.

Family 113. Barn owls
GUÉRIN, G. (1928). Régime et croissance de l'Effraye commune . . . en Vendée. *Lechevaliers Encyclop. Orn.* no. 4; 156 pp.

Family 116. Oilbird
SNOW, D. W. (1961–62). The natural history of the oilbird . . . in Trinidad, W.I. *Zoologica N.Y. 46:* 27–49; *47:* 199–221.

Family 122. Swifts
LACK, David (1956). Swifts in a tower. London, Methuen, 239 pp.

Family 124. Hummingbirds
MARTIN, A. (1959). La vie des Colibris. Neuchâtel, Delachaux and Niestlé, 246 pp.
GREENEWALT, Crawford H. (1960). Hummingbirds. Garden City, N.Y., Doubleday, 250 pp.

Family 136. Hornbills
RANGER, Gordon (1949–52). Life of the crowned hornbill. *Ostrich 20:* 54–65, 152–67; *21:* 2–13; *22:* 77–93; *23:* 26–36.

Family 140. Honeyguides
FRIEDMANN, Herbert (1955). The honeyguides. *U.S. Nat. Mus. Bull.* no. 208; 292 pp.

Family 142. Woodpeckers
RITTER, William Emerson (1938). The California woodpecker and I. Berkeley, University of California Press, 340 pp.
TANNER, James T. (1942). The ivory-billed woodpecker. *Nat. Audubon Soc. Research Rep.* no. 1; 211 pp.
SIELMANN, Heinz (1958). Das Jahr mit den spechten. Berlin, etc., Ullstein, 155 pp., English transl. London, Barrie and Rockcliff (1959), 139 pp.

Family 155. Lyrebirds
CHISHOLM, A. H. (1960). The romance of the lyrebird. Sydney, Angus & Robertson, 156 pp.

Family 157. Larks
PICKWELL, G. B. (1931). The prairie horned lark. *Trans. Acad. Sci. St. Louis 27:* 153 pp.

Family 160. Wagtails and pipits
SMITH, Stuart (1950). The yellow wagtail. London, Collins *New Naturalist,* 178 pp.

Family 170. Wrens
KENDEIGH, S. Charles (1941). Territorial and mating behaviour of the house wren. *Illinois Biol. Monogr. 18:* no. 3; 120 pp.
ARMSTRONG, Edward A. (1955). The wren. London, Collins *New Naturalist,* 312 pp.

Family 173. Muscicapidae
Subfamily 173a. Thrushes
LACK, David (1943*). The life of the robin. London, Witherby, 200 pp.
——— (1950). Robin redbreast. Oxford, Clarendon Press, 224 pp.
BUXTON, E. John M. (1950). The redstart. London, Collins *New Naturalist,* 180 pp.
SNOW, D. W. (1958). A study of blackbirds. London, Allen and Unwin, 192 pp.

Subfamily 173b. Babblers
ERICKSON, M. M. (1938). Territory, annual cycle and numbers in a population of wrentits . . . *Univ. Calif. Publ. Zool. 42:* 247–333.

Subfamily 173c. Bearded tit and parrotbills
KÖNIG, O. (1951). Das Aktionssystem der Bartmeise. *Österr. Zool. Z. 3:* 1–82, 247–325.

Subfamily 173e. Old World warblers and gnatwrens
HOWARD, H. Eliot (1907–15). The British warblers. London, Porter, 2 vols., 203+260 pp.
LYNES, H. (1930). Review of the genus *Cisticola. Ibis* (12) *6* (suppl.): 673 pp.
TICEHURST, Claud B. (1938). A systematic review of the genus *Phylloscopus.* London, British Museum (Nat. Hist.), 193 pp.
BROWN, P. E. and DAVIES, M. G. (1949). Reed-warblers. East Molesey, Foy, 127 pp.
SIEFKE, A. (1962). Dorn- und Zaungrasmücke. Wittenberg Lutherstadt, Ziemsen, 88 pp.

Subfamily 173g. Old World flycatchers and fantails
von HAARTMAN, Lars (1949–54). Der Trauerfliegenschnäpper. *Acta Zool. Fenn. 56:* 104 pp.; *67:* 60 pp.; *83:* 96 pp.
CREUTZ, Gerhard (1955). Der Trauerschnäpper.... *J. Orn. 96:* 241–326.

Family 174. Titmice
ODUM, E. P. (1941–42). Annual cycle of the black-capped chickadee. *Auk 58:* 314–33, 518–35; *59:* 499–531.
HINDE, R. A. (1952–53). Papers on great tit behavior in *Behaviour,* suppl. 2; 210 pp.: *5:* 189–224.
HAFTORN, S. (1954–57). Contribution to the food biology of tits. . . . *K. norske vidensk. Selsk. Skr. 1953:* no. 4; 123 pp.: *1956:* no. 2; 52+80+54 pp.
DIXON, K. L. (1955). An ecological analysis of the interbreeding of crested titmice in Texas. *Univ. Calif. Publ. Zool. 54:* 125–206.

Family 175. Nuthatches
VOOUS, K. H. and van MARLE, J. G. (1953). The distributional history of the nuthatch, *Sitta europaea* L. *Ardea 41*: suppl.; 68 pp.
NORRIS, Robert A. (1958). Comparative bio-systematics and life history of the nuthatches *Sitta pygmaea* and *Sitta pusilla*. *Univ. Calif. Publ. Zool. 56*: 119–300.

Family 179. Whiteyes
MEES, G. F. (1957–61). A systematic review of the Indo-Australian Zosteropidae. *Zool. Verh. Leiden* no. 35; 204 pp.: no. 50; 168 pp.
MOREAU, R. E. (1957). Variation in the western Zosteropidae (Aves). *Bull. Brit. Mus. (Nat. Hist.) Zool. 4*: 309–433.

Family 181. Emberizidae
Subfamily 181a. Buntings, American sparrows and Darwin's finches
NICE, Margaret Morse (1937–43), Studies in the life history of the song sparrow. *Trans. Linn. Soc. N.Y.* no. 4; 247 pp.: no. 6; 328 pp.
TINBERGEN, Niko (1939). The behavior of the snow bunting in spring. *Trans. Linn. Soc. N.Y.* no. 5; 94 pp.
LACK, David (1947). Darwin's finches. Cambridge, University Press, 208 pp.
DIESSELHORST, G. (1949–50) papers on yellowhammer in *Orn. Ber. 2*: 1–13; *3*: 69–112.
BOWMAN, Robert I. (1961). Morphological differentiation and adaptation in the Galápagos finches. *Univ. Calif. Publ. Zool. 58*: 302 pp.

Family 182. Wood warblers
HANN, H. W. (1937). Life history of the oven-bird. *Wilson Bull. 49*: 145–237.
GRISCOM, Ludlow and others (1957). The warblers of America. New York, Devin-Adair, 356 pp.
MAYFIELD, Harold (1960). The Kirtland's warbler. *Cranbrook Inst. Sci. Bull.* no. 40; 242 pp.

Family 183. Hawaiian honeycreepers
AMADON, Dean (1950). The Hawaiian honey-creepers. *Bull. Amer. Mus. Nat. Hist. 95*: 151–262.
BALDWIN, P. H. (1953). Annual cycle, environment and evolution in the Hawaiian honeycreepers. *Univ. Calif. Publ. Zool. 52*: 285–398.

Family 185. Icterids
ALLEN, Arthur A. (1914). The red-winged blackbird . . . *Proc. Linn. Soc. N.Y.* nos. 24–25; 43–128.
CHAPMAN, Frank M. (1928). The nesting habits of Wagler's oropéndola. *Bull. Amer. Mus. Nat. Hist. 58*: 123–66.
FRIEDMANN, Herbert (1929). The cowbirds. Springfield, Ill., Thomas, 421 pp.
WILLIAMS, Laidlaw (1952). Breeding behavior of the Brewer blackbird. *Condor 54*: 3–47.
NERO, R. W. (1956). A behavior study of the red-winged blackbird. *Wilson Bull. 68*: 5–37, 129–50.
LANYON, Wesley E. (1957). The comparative biology of the meadowlarks (*Sturnella*) in Wisconsin. *Nuttall Orn. Cl. Publ.* no. 1; 67 pp.

Family 186. Finches
ECKSTEIN, Gustav (1937). Canary. London, Faber, 296 pp.
FRIEDMANN, Herbert (1946). The symbolic goldfinch. Washington, D.C., Pantheon, 254 pp.
LOCKLEY, R. M. (1948). The cinnamon bird. London, Staples, 79 pp.
BAILEY, A. M. and others (1953). The red crossbills of Colorado. *Mus. Pictorial Denver* no. 9; 64 pp.
HINDE, Robert A. (1953–54). Papers on behavior of chaffinch and greenfinch in *Behaviour 5*: 1–31; *7*: 207–32: *Proc. Roy. Soc.* (B) *142*: 306–58.
MOUNTFORT, Guy (1957). The hawfinch. London, Collins *New Naturalist*, 176 pp.

Family 187. Waxbills and allies
MORRIS, Desmond (1954). The reproductive behavior of the zebra finch. . . . *Behavior 6*: 271–322.
——— (1957). The reproductive behavior of the bronze mannikin . . . *Behavior 11*: 156–201.
——— (1958). The comparative ethology of grassfinches (Erythrurae) and mannikins (Amadinae). *Proc. Zool. Soc. Lond. 131*: 389–439.

Family 188. Widow birds
FRIEDMANN, Herbert (1960). The parasitic weaverbirds. *Bull. U.S. Nat. Mus.* no. 223; 196 pp.

Family 189. Weavers and true sparrows
KIPPS, Clare (1953). Sold for a farthing. London, Muller, 72 pp.
MOREAU, R. E. (1960). Conspectus and classification of the Ploceine weaver-birds. *Ibis 102*: 298–321, 443–71.
KIPPS, Clare (1962). Timmy. London, Barker, 77 pp.
SUMMERS-SMITH, J. D. (1963). The house sparrow. London, Collins *New Naturalist*, 269 pp.

Family 190. Starlings
AMADON, Dean (1956). Remarks on the starlings, family Sturnidae. *Amer. Mus. Novit.* no. 1803; 41 pp.

Family 194. Magpie larks
ROBINSON, Angus (1947). Magpie-larks; a study in behaviour. *Emu 46*: 265–81, 382–91; *47*: 11–28, 147–53.

Family 197. Bower birds
MARSHALL, A. J. (1954). Bower birds. Oxford, Clarendon Press, 208 pp.
CHISHOLM, A. H. and CHAFFER, N. (1956). Observations on the golden bower-bird. *Emu 56*: 1–39.

Family 198. Birds of paradise
MAYR, Ernst (1945). Birds of paradise. *Nat. Hist. N.Y. 54*: 264–76.
IREDALE, Tom (1950). Birds of paradise and bower birds. Melbourne, Georgian House, 239 pp.
RIPLEY, S. Dillon (1950). Strange courtship of birds of paradise. *Nat. Geogr. Mag. 97*: 247–78.

Family 199. Crows
YEATES, George K. (1934). The life of the rook. London, Allan, 95 pp.
LINSDALE, Jean M. (1937). The natural history of magpies. *Pacif. Coast Avif.* no. 25; 234 pp.
ALDOUS, S. E. (1942). The white-necked raven in relation to agriculture. *U.S. Fish Wildl. Serv. Res. Rep.* no. 5; 56 pp.
AMADON, Dean (1944). A preliminary life history study of the Florida jay . . . *Amer. Mus. Novit.* no. 1252; 22 pp.
GOODWIN, Derek (1949–56). Papers on jay behaviour in *Brit. Birds, 42*: 278–87; *Ibis 93*: 414–42, 602–25; *98*: 186–219; *Behaviour 4*: 293–316; *Avic. Mag. 60*: 154–62.
ZIMMERMAN, D. (1950–51). Papers on breeding of jackdaw in *Orn. Beob. 47*: 15–33, 73; *48*: 72–111.
SKUTCH, Alexander F. (1953–60). Life-histories of 3 species of jays in *Wilson Bull. 65*: 68–74; *Pacif. Coast Avif.* no. 34; 593 pp.

Appendix

Identification of the feathers on page 19. Numbers in brackets refer to the birds' families or subfamilies, as listed in Chapter VIII (pp. 144–241).

1. Quetzal (126)
2. Pennant-wing nightjar (119)
3. Sun bittern (78)
4. American kestrel (56)
5. Ostrich (9)
6. Peacock (62)
7. Superb lyrebird (155)
8. Common touraco (111)
9. King of Saxony bird of paradise (198)
10. Golden cock-of-the-rock (153)
11. Quetzal (126)
12. Mallard (49)
13. Scott's oriole (185)
14. Jaçana (88)
15. Vulturine guineafowl (63)
16. Rufous-sided towhee (181a)
17. Turkey (64)
18. Common pheasant (62)
19. Bohemian waxwing (166)
20. Snake bird or darter (32)
21. Blue-and-yellow macaw (110)
22. Dufresne's parrot (110)
23. Turquoise-browed motmot (129)
24. Roseate spoonbill (41)
25. James's flamingo (46)
26 and 27. Harlequin quail (62)
28. Red-shafted flicker (142)
29. Blue jay (199)
30. Emu (11)
31. Ruffed grouse (61)
32. King bird of paradise (198)

Index

Every bird and other important vertebrate animal mentioned or figured in this book (with the exception of its bibliography, pp. 274–81) is indexed here under a common name that we believe to be jointly acceptable to English-speaking ornithologists on both sides of the Atlantic. Names used in practice alone are here often accompanied by a qualifier in brackets, *e.g.* (American) sparrow and (True) sparrow, to make their meaning fully clear.

This index is also a nomenclator: each species is given here (and in most cases here alone) what we believe to be its most acceptable scientific name. It can thus be used as a systematic glossary.

A typical entry consists of the English vernacular name of the bird (or other animal) in Roman type, followed by its Linnean name in the conventional italics. This scientific name is preceded by the conventional sword when it refers to a fossil form (paleogenus or paleo-species, p. 144). When it appears for a second or further time under a heading a generic name is (for reasons of space) contracted as much as is prudent. For instance, under 'Albatross' the black-browed albatross has its generic name *Diomedea* spelled out: all the other albatrosses subsequently listed belong also to *Diomedea*, and so have this name contracted to *D.* The figure in brackets after a bird name is that of the family (or subfamily) to which the bird or group of birds belongs (see list in Chapter VIII, pp. 144–241). The figures that then follow are page references; those in bold type denote the presence of at least one picture.

Acknowledgments

Our two designers; at least fifteen members of the staff of our printers, Purnell and Sons; and about the same number of staff and associates of Rathbone Books earn our particular thanks for patience, precision and professionalism – especially Frame Hastings.

Special also is our gratitude to our wives, Barbara Peterson and Margery Fisher, for their energy, protection and material help; to Professor Pierce Brodkorb of the University of Florida, who has spent very many hours indeed advising us personally and in long letters from his global knowledge of bird fossils; to artists Sidney W. Woods, Crispin Fisher and Maurice Wilson (a master of the reconstruction of fossils who most modestly painted pilot pictures for RTP's inspiration); and to Miss Theresa Clay, Professor and Mrs. Nicholas Collias, Dr. William C. Dilger, Dr. Hildegarde Howard, Dr. R. C. Murphy and Peter Scott, for substantial and friendly co-operation.

Any omission from this list of other helpers is due only to a *lapsus calami* for which we hope we will be forgiven. Dr. A. R. Akester, Dr. John Aldrich, Dr. Sálim Ali, the late Robert Porter Allen, Dr. Dean Amadon, Peter Ames, Prof. Oliver L. Austin Jr., J. V. Beer, Jeffery Boswall, Dr. François Bourlière, Hugh Boyd, Maurice Broun, Leslie Brown, Carl Buchheister, John Bull, Dr. Clifford Carl, Dr. Rachel Carson, Dr. James P. Chapin, Dr. A. J. Charig, Clara Claasen, Roland C. Clement, Dr. William Conway, Stanley Cramp, Dr. Lee S. Crandall, G. R. Crone, Dr. John Hurrell Crook, Lois and Louis Darling, Dr. H. G. Deignan, Prof. Georgi Petrovich Dement'ev, Nicolette Devas, Dr. William H. Drury Jr., Dr. Robin S. Duff, Whitney Eastman, Dr. E. Eastwood, Dr. Eugene Eisenmann, E. Ellis, I. J. Ferguson-Lees, R. S. R. Fitter, Dr. Charles Fleming, Norman L. Ford, Rudi Freund, Dr. Ira N. Gabrielson, Dr. W. Earl Godfrey, Derek Goodwin, Dr. Richard R. Graber, Crawford H. Greenewalt, Shelley Grossman, Dr. Finnur Guðmundsson, Dr. Lars von Haartman, Mrs. B. P. Hall, Mary Anne Heimerdinger, Philip A. D. Hollom, W. G. Harper, Prof. Joseph J. Hickey, Dr. R. A. Hinde, Eric J. Hosking, Dr. K. Hudec, Dr. Philip S. Humphrey, Sir Julian S. Huxley, Stuart Keith, Dr. Andràs Keve, Dr. Ludwig Koch, Dr. E. Kozlova, Dr. R. Kuhk, Prof. Erik Kumari, Dr. David Lack, Dr. Wesley E. Lanyon, John Livingston, R. M. Lockley, Prof. George H. Lowery Jr., James D. MacDonald, Mrs. Hetty R. McKenzie, Sabra Mallett, Henry Mayer-Gross, Prof. Ernst Mayr, Richard Meinertzhagen, Lorimer Moe, R. E. Moreau, E. M. Nicholson, James T. Nicholson Jr., Myles North, Niels Otto Preuss, Dr. and Mrs. John R. Reeder, Dr. S. Dillon Ripley II, Chandler S. Robbins, Dr. Finn Salomonsen, Dr. Alfred Schifferli, Philippa Scott, Prof. Charles Sibley, Dr. William J. L. Sladen, Dr. Neil Smith, Robert Spencer, Alexander Sprunt IV, Mrs. Eleanor Stickney, Herbert L. Stoddard, Dr. Robert W. Storer, G. B. Stratton, Dr. Ernst Sutter, Marion Swildens, Dr. W. E. Swinton, Sir Landsborough Thomson, Dr. W. H. Thorpe, Dr. Niko Tinbergen, Leslie M. Tuck, Dr. Charles Vaurie, Jack Vincent, Eugene A. Walker, George Wallace, Dr. Alexander Wetmore, Dr. G. R. Williams, John G. Williams, Kenneth Williamson, D. R. Wilson, Dr. J. M. Winterbottom, Dr. Telford H. Work, John Yealland, the late Prof. F. E. Zeuner, Rudolph Zollinger.

We have also used the facilities of, or received unpublished information from the American Museum of Natural History, American Ornithologists' Union, British Broadcasting Corporation, British Museum (Natural History), British Ornithologists' Club, Cornell University Laboratory of Ornithology, Dansk Ornithologisk Forening, Edward Grey Institute of Field Ornithology, Hawaii Audubon Society, Hawk Mountain Sanctuary Association, Illinois Natural History Survey, International Union for the Conservation of Nature and Natural Resources, Laboratoř pro vyzkum obratlovců ČSAV (Czechoslovakia), Linnean Society of London, Loodusuurijate Selts (Estonia), Los Angeles County Museum, Marconi's Wireless Telegraph Company Limited, Massachusetts Audubon Society, Moscow University Museum, Museum of Comparative Zoology (Harvard), National Audubon Society, National Trust for Scotland, Náttúrugripasafnið (Iceland), Nature Conservancy (U.K.), Nederlandse Ornithologische Unie, New York Zoological Society, Ornithological Society of New Zealand, Osterreichische Vogelwarte, Percy FitzPatrick Institute of African Ornithology, Royal Australasian Ornithologists' Union, Royal Geographical Society, Royal Naval Bird Watching Society, Royal Ontario Museum, Royal Society for the Protection of Birds, St. Kilda Club, Scottish Ornithologists' Club, South African Ornithological Society, United States Bureau of Sport Fisheries and Wildlife, United States National Museum, University of Michigan Museum of Zoology, Vogelwarte Helgoland, Vogelwarte Radolfzell, Vogelwarte Sempach, Wildfowl Trust, Yale Botanical Library and Peabody Museum, and Zoological Society of London.

Sources of illustrations

Page by page, credits for picture sources. Key to picture position is (T) top, (M) middle, (B) bottom, (L) left, (C) center, (R) right.

Page 6. After Aztec tile eagle devouring sun's disc; Metropolitan Museum of Art

7. (T) after bronze owl, Chou dynasty of China, (ML) after bronze peacock lamp, IV-VIIC AD Egypt, (TR) after black basalt bird, Egypt, (MR) after bronze cock, V-VIIC AD Syria and bronze eagle, II-IIIC AD Rome; Dunbarton Oaks Collection. (BL) after merganser and young, Pacific Coast Indian; Stanford University Press. (BM) after ibis IIIC BC Egypt; American Museum of Natural History. (BR) after pearl button thunderbird, Tlingit Indian; Washington State Museum

15. (BL) after Allan Brooks, courtesy *The Auk*

16–17. (M) after preparation in American Museum of Natural History

17. (TL) after van Tyne and Berger, courtesy John Wiley & Sons Inc.; (ML) after Fisher; (TR) after A. R. Akester, courtesy *Journal of Anatomy*

18. (TL) after van Tyne and Berger; (BL) eye after Stuart Smith, courtesy Wm. Collins Sons & Co., brain after van Tyne and Berger; (BC and BR) after Fisher and others

38. (MR) after R. P. Allen, courtesy National Audubon Society

46. (B) photos Los Angeles County Museum

50. (BL) after William C. Dilger

51. (L) after Dr. and Mrs. N. Collias

55. (T) information derived from D. Amadon

64–65. information derived from J. P. Chapin

70. (BL) after G. Kramer, courtesy International Ornithological Congress

71. (BL) after E. G. F. Sauer, courtesy *Scientific American*; (BR) after D. R. Griffin, courtesy *Proceedings of the National Academy of Sciences*

73. (TL) after E. Merikallio, courtesy *Fauna Fennica*

74. (T) information derived from J. M. D. MacKenzie and G. R. Williams

76. (TR) after F. Salomonsen, courtesy Int. Orn. Congr.

82–83. Robin postures, some information from D. Lack

84. (TL) after preparation in American Museum of Natural History; (TR) information derived from H. J. Frith

85. (TC) after photo by Geoffrey Allen

86. (TR) after preparation in American Museum of Natural History; (BR) information derived from D. Lack

87. photo by Shelley Grossman, in American Museum of Natural History

88. (B) information derived from H. Friedmann; (TR) information derived from A. Skutch

89. (BR) after Stuart Baker, courtesy H. F. and G. Witherby Ltd.

90. (TL) after C. F. M. Swynnerton, courtesy *The Ibis*

91. (ML) information derived from J. Dorst

92. (T) after Bailey and Sorensen, courtesy Denver Museum of Natural History

94. after O. Köhler, courtesy Carl Winter, Heidelberg

95. (ML) after film by T. H. Work

96. (TL) from RTP's *Field guide to western birds*, 2nd ed. (1961); courtesy Houghton Mifflin Co. Rest from editions of his *Field guide to the birds of (Britain and) Europe:* (TR) Swedish (1955); courtesy Wm. Collins, Sons & Co. and Svensk Natur: (BL) Swiss & French (1954); courtesy Collins and Delachaux & Niestlé S.A.: (BR) German (1954); courtesy Collins and Verlag Paul Parey

98. photo Studio 51

100. (L) photo J. Fisher; (R) after Hosking, Skutch and Tinbergen, courtesy Stanley Paul and British Ornithologists' Union

102. photos (TL) courtesy of Pullin Co. Ltd., (TC) kind permission of E. Leitz Ltd., (TR) T. W. Kenyon Inc.

103. photos (TL) Thagee Kamerawerk A.G., (TC) courtesy Highgate Optical Manufacturing Co. Ltd., (TR) Honeywell (Photo Products) Inc.

104. (BL) photo Cinex Limited

104–105. photo R. T. Peterson

106. photos K. Dustan

107. photo Eric Hosking

108. (TL) photo Alan Houghton Brodrick; (TR) after R. E. Moreau, courtesy Hugh Rees Ltd.; (BL) after W. Verner, courtesy *Country Life*

111. photo Studio 51

113. photo J. Fisher

116. photo Vogelwarte Radolfzell; Ernst Schüz

117. (T and M) photos Nature Conservancy (U.K.); (L) photo Maurice Broun

118. (TL) after W. J. L. Sladen, courtesy British Antarctic Survey

118–19 (B) photos Studio 51

120–21. Nos. 1, 4, 5b, 6, 7 after Lockley and Russell, *Bird Ringing* (Crosby Lockwood); nos. 2 and 3 after Fisher; nos. 5a and 5c after Eric Hosking photos; nos. 8a and 8b after P. Scott, courtesy Wildfowl Trust

123. (T) photo J. Fisher; (M) photo Wildfowl Trust

124. photo Eric Hosking

125. after G. H. Lowery Jr., courtesy University of Kansas

126. A, photo E. Sutter; B, photo Illinois Natural History Survey

127. C, photo British Crown copyright, reproduced by permission of Her Britannic Majesty's Stationery Office; D, photo Marconi's Wireless Telegraph Co. Ltd.; E, F, G, from Lack and Eastwood, courtesy *British Birds*

128. photo R. T. Peterson; nest cards from Ornithological Society of New Zealand, University of Michigan Museum of Zoology, British Trust for Ornithology, Vogelwarte Radolfzell, South African Ornithological Society and Laboratoř pro vyzkum obratlovců ČSAV

131. photo Studio 51

132–33. Nos. 1, 3, 7 after Huxley, courtesy Zoological Society of London; no. 2 after Berg; no. 8 after Dilger, courtesy *The Auk*; no. 9 after Goodwin, courtesy *Behaviour*; nos. 11–14 after Simmons, courtesy *Behaviour*; no. 15 after Tinbergen, courtesy Wm. Collins Sons & Co.; no. 16 after K. Lorenz, courtesy *Journal für Ornithologie*

134–35 after N. Tinbergen, courtesy Collins

136–37. nos. 1–3 after Royal Society for the Protection of Birds; no. 4 after Proen Products Co.; no. 5 after National Audubon Society; no. 6 after Dinah Dee; no. 7 after Gates General Corp; no. 8 after Fish and Wildlife Service

138. (BL) based upon Admiralty chart No. 111 with the permission of the Controller of H.M. Stationery Office and of the Hydrographer of the Navy; (BR) from J. Raine

139. (ML) photo R. T. Peterson; (BL) from U.S. Federa map

140. photo Eric Hosking

142. (BL) photo Studio Briggs; (BR) photo National Audubon Society, New York

143. from the Clubs and Societies cited in the caption

242. (T) photo Axel Poignant; (B) photo Mansell Collection

243. after MacPherson

244. (T) photo J. Fisher; (BL) photo G. W. Whyte

245. photo C. W. Mason

246–47. photos Heinz Sielmann

248. photo G. P. Dement'ev

249. (BL) photo British Museum; (BR) photo G. P. Dement'ev

250. (TR) photo Japanese Embassy in U.K.; (MR) photo Imperial War Museum, British Crown copyright

250–51. (B) after Mallowan and Rose; and copyright Government of India

252. Photo by kind permission of 'Farmer's Weekly', London

253. (T and BR) photos by kind permission of 'Farmer's Weekly', London; (BC) photo 'The People', London

254. (TL) after G. Jennison, courtesy Manchester University Press; (R) photo Keystone Press; by courtesy of Mrs. Williams

255. after plans of Lord Snowdon, in association with Cedric Price and Frank Newby; courtesy Zoological Society of London

256. photo Giardino Zoologico, Rome

257. (TR and MC) photos David Attenborough; (ML) from *A History of Domesticated Animals*, by Professor F. E. Zeuner; Hutchinson & Co. Ltd., London; (MR) photo Radio Times Hulton Picture Library

258. photo by courtesy of Cogswell and Harrison

259. photo Harold M. Lambert Studios

260. (T) photo Les D. Line; (B) photo John Tarlton

261 and 262. photos John Tarlton

263. (T) photo John H. Crook; (M and B) photos by Gérard Morel, Station d'Ornithologie, Richard-Toll, Sénégal

264. (L) photo Associated Press; (R) photo Royal Society for the Prevention of Cruelty to Animals

265. photo United States Information Service

266. photo New York Zoological Society

268 and 273. photos by permission of the British Museum (Natural History)

Artists who have contributed illustrations (apart from RTP) are: Sidney W. Woods: pages 14(B), 16, 17, 18 (except ML), 46 (TR), 47 (L), 48, 49, 50 (BR), 70 (B), 71 (BL, BC), 74 (T), 91 (ML), 100 (R), 114, 120, 121, 125, 136, 137, 138 (BL), 243, 250 (B), 251, 254 (TL), 255

Crispin J. Fisher: page 18 (ML) and, with the assistance of Max Hailstone and J. F. Trotter, the maps on pages 145–240

Brian Lee: page 35 (BR)